Economic Analysis of Law in European Legal Scholarship

Volume 5

The purpose of this book series is to publish high quality volumes in the growing field of law and economics research in Europe, from a comprehensive theoretical and practical vantage point. In particular, the series will place great emphasis on foundational and theoretical aspects of economic analysis of law and on interdisciplinary approaches in European Legal Scholarship. Following Nobel laureate Ronald Coase's famous essay "The Problem of Social Cost" (1960) fifty years ago law and economics has become the lingua franca of American jurisprudence. In recent decades, law and economics has also gained widespread popularity in Europe and its influence on Legal Scholarship is growing significantly. Therefore, the economic analysis of law in European Legal Scholarship academic book series illustrates how law and economics is developing in Europe and what opportunities and problems – both in general and in specific legal fields – are associated with this approach within the legal traditions of European countries. Rather than further exploring economic analysis as such, the main focus of this series lies on the implementation of economic methods in legislation and legal adjudication from a European perspective. It takes into account the particular challenges the European legal systems face. Volumes will address law and economics research in Europe from a critical and comparative viewpoint. The studies in this series are strong and bold narratives of the development of economic analysis of law in European Legal Scholarship. Some are suitable for a very broad readership.Contributions in this series primarily come from scholars in Europe. The purpose is to provide the next generation of European lawyers with the models and skills needed to understand and improve the economic analysis of law in their own legal field. The series includes monographs focusing on specific topics as well as collections of essays covering specific themes.

More information about this series at http://www.springer.com/series/11927

Klaus Mathis • Bruce R. Huber
Editors

Energy Law and Economics

Springer

Editors
Klaus Mathis
Faculty of Law
University of Lucerne
Lucerne, Switzerland

Bruce R. Huber
University of Notre Dame Law School
Notre Dame, IN, USA

Economic Analysis of Law in European Legal Scholarship
ISBN 978-3-030-09041-8 ISBN 978-3-319-74636-4 (eBook)
https://doi.org/10.1007/978-3-319-74636-4

Printed on acid-free paper

This Springer imprint is published by the registered company Springer International Publishing AG part of Springer Nature.
The registered company address is: Gewerbestrasse 11, 6330 Cham, Switzerland

Foreword

This volume is the result of the lectures given at the Sixth Law and Economics Conference held at the University of Lucerne's Law Faculty in April 2016. Prof. Dr. Klaus Mathis, director of the Center for Law and Sustainability, has organized this conference. His tenacity in developing Law and Economics at our Faculty of Law has not only resulted in these annual conferences but has placed the University of Lucerne at the focal point of Law and Economics research in Europe.

I would also like to extend a special thank you to Prof. Bruce Huber from the University of Notre Dame Law School, co-editor of this book and co-organizer of the Sixth Law and Economics Conference. The ongoing partnership both in research and education between the University of Lucerne and the University of Notre Dame Law School has been fruitful and inspiring for interdisciplinary approaches such as Law and Economics.

While it is the Sixth Law and Economics Conference held by the University of Lucerne, for me it is the first as the newly appointed President of the University of Lucerne. But it is also the first Law and Economics Conference where the University has both a Faculty of Law *and* a Faculty of Economics and Management, which was opened last September.

Now it is a matter of fact: that it takes two to tango—in our case: Law *and* Economics. Although I am not a dancer but only a simple business economist, specialized in the psychological field of Human Resource Management, you do not have to convince me how important the field of Law and Economics is. Besides my mandate as the President of this University, I am a member of the Board of the International Committee of the Red Cross. In this role, I have been able to witness the dramatic changes in Columbia. By this, I mean the feeling that perhaps, peace is slowly winning over civil unrest fueled by the drug cartels. The farmers in Columbia have two choices: to plant the unlawful cash-crop coca or to plant coffee. With coca, they could potentially earn a fortune, but a risky fortune. Planting coffee however, is much less lucrative. Faced with the choice between a risky way out of poverty or a more secure but lower income, the farmers choose to grow coffee. By doing so, the farmers are facilitating secure and sustainable development not just for themselves, but their whole community. In this little example, we can see the economic value of the law—perceived and implemented by the Columbian farmers of today.

This volume focuses on the Law and Economics issues surrounding Energy Law. It is clear, that the transition in energy sources is on the agenda for most policymakers. Since the signing of the Paris Agreement last year, there has been an increased push towards decarbonization. Coupled with the Fukushima disaster, many are shifting away from nuclear energy too. Three years ago, I edited a case study in my field of Human Resource Management on the closing of the nuclear power plant in Mühleberg, near Berne, Switzerland. From this experience, I can conclude that the challenges presented by the pursued energy transition have a multifaceted impact. It is no longer a simple tango with two dancers! The many contributions in this volume will provide fascinating insights to the delicate balancing act in energy market regulations, which must cater for the needs of all the different market players. It is my hope that this volume will not only further the academic debates in *Energy Law and Economics*, but also serve to guide lawyers and policymakers in their endeavors to achieve the shift towards a sustainable and environmentally friendly economy.

University of Lucerne
Lucerne, Switzerland
October 2017

Bruno Staffelbach

Preface

This volume, *Energy Law and Economics*, is the result of the Sixth Law and Economics Conference held at the University of Lucerne on the 17 to 18 April 2017. The conference was organized in partnership with Notre Dame Law School. The main focus of the conference lay on European legal questions as presented by European legal scholars. They were complimented by insights from distinguished scholars from the United States to foster the dialogue between the two different legal cultures. The thematic scope of this volume spans both the theoretical and practical developments of Energy Law.

We take this opportunity to thank all those who have contributed to the organization of the conference and to the successful completion of this volume. First, we would like to thank Uta Zehnder for her flawless coordination and organization of the conference. Furthermore, we want to thank Dr. Charlotte Sieber-Gasser, Lynn Gummow, MLaw, Alex Sutter, MLaw, and Niels Röthlin, BLaw for their reviewing and diligent proofreading. A special thank goes to the Swiss National Science Foundation (SNSF), the Research Commission (FoKo) of the University of Lucerne, and the Institute lucernaiuris for supporting the conference. Finally, we are grateful to Anja Trautmann and Anke Seyfried at Springer Publishers for overseeing the publishing process.

Lucerne, Switzerland — Klaus Mathis
Notre Dame, IN, USA — Bruce R. Huber
October 2017

Introduction

In response to waning resources and heightened environmental awareness, many countries are seeking to redefine their energy mix. A wide variety of energy sources present themselves: coal and oil, natural gas, along with a variety of renewables. Which of these can serve the core concerns of energy? Reliability, security, affordability, fairness, and sustainability all require due consideration. And when a target mix has been identified, two challenges remain for legal scholars: what role does the law play in achieving a specified energy mix, and how can the law best fulfil that role? The essential concerns of energy are just as important in defining the way we shape our energy mix as they are in defining the mix itself.

In Switzerland and Germany, governments have decided to pursue the so-called "*Energiewende*" (energy transition). These policies should enable the transition from a non-sustainable use of fossil fuels and nuclear energy to a more sustainable energy supply using renewable sources. On the one hand, a decarbonization of the energy economy is intended by reducing the use of fossil fuels such as petroleum, carbon and natural gas. On the other hand, as a reaction to the Fukushima nuclear accident, a phase out should eliminate the dangers of these technologies. This double goal setting is a huge challenge for the energy policies of these countries. The energy transition will not only affect the production, but also the energy consumption.

From a Law and Economics perspective, a range of questions arises: to what extent is it justifiable to rely on markets and continued technological innovation, especially in relation to the present exploitation of scarce resources? To what extent is it necessary for states to intervene in energy markets? There are many regulatory instruments available to create and maintain more sustainable societies such as: command and control regulations, restraints, Pigovian taxes, emission certificates, nudging policies, and many more. Do neoclassical and behavioral economics provide us with a framework capable of predicting the market's complex reactions to energy policy?

This volume discusses these questions and consists of the following four parts: Part I, Energy Transition; Part II, Investment in Infrastructure; Part III, Regulatory Innovation; Part IV, State Aid. Part I consists of six chapters delving into the changes in law and the effects on the markets resulting from the changes in policies targeting a transition away from predominantly non-renewable energy sources to a more sustainable energy supply. Part II highlights the need for investment in infrastructure for a successful change in energy sources. The three chapters delve into investment challenges posed by the current desire to reduce carbon emissions and procure energy from new renewable resources. The four chapters in Part III focus on the various regulatory innovations such as the use of capacity mechanisms, setting stricter guidelines for the mandatory energy labels on consumer goods, the effects of social norms on legal reasoning as well as the regulatory needs for consumer protection. Finally, Part IV comprises of three chapters analysing the various approaches WTO participating parties implement to provide state aid to encourage the use and further the establishment of renewable energy sources.

Part I starts with the chapter "Sustainability Strategies and the Problem of the Rebound Effect" by Klaus Mathis. He outlines the three main strategies currently discussed in literature for achieving sustainability: efficiency, consistency and sufficiency strategies. While the first two strategies primarily rely on technical innovations, the latter strategy requires a change in consumer habits. Pursuing an efficiency strategy would allow the current continued economic growth. However, the effectiveness of this strategy could be undermined by the so-called rebound effect. This effect describes how financial savings in one area encourages consumers to use their "gained" resources for new activities, which in turn leads to additional energy consumption. The consistency strategy endeavors to achieve closed-loop material cycles to decouple the economic production and consumption cycles from the natural sources and sinks. The sufficiency strategy demands a reduction of resource consumption by changing consumption habits. However, the rebound effect can also occur with this strategy. This is due to the lowering of the price, which results from the reduced consumption by the sufficient consumers, which in turn leads to higher consumption of the relevant good by less frugal consumers.

The next chapter "Energy Transition Law and Economics" by Sebastian Heselhaus describes the many energy transitions that have occurred historically before delving into the current transitions pursued by the European Union, Germany and Switzerland. For each of the three examples he describes the various changes in legislation governing the energy market, giving the background and development. Subsequently the author analyses how these changes in regulation as well as the relevant jurisprudence has influenced the energy markets.

Julia Hänni's chapter "Energy Transition in Switzerland" focuses on the current energy transition law changes occurring in Switzerland. She presents an in-depth analysis of the two-stage approach adopted by Switzerland, not only targeting decarbonization but also a shift away from nuclear energy. The author details the market challenges this transition strategy poses and discusses the various government incentives put in place by the Swiss Federal Government.

In the chapter "The Interplay Between Liberalization and Decarbonization in the European Internal Energy Market for Electricity" Anna-Alexandra Marhold analysis how liberalization of the EU energy market effects the goal of reducing the use of fossil fuels. She begins her chapter by laying out the background of the economic rational behind the European energy market. She draws attention to the difficulty the lack of a clear-cut, legally binding definition of the term "security of energy supply" poses. Subsequently she discusses the steps, which led to a liberalization of the European Energy Market. She focuses on the Commissions' Third Energy Package as a key corner stone in the liberalization movement because of its very stringent unbundling known as Ownership Unbundling coupled with the concept of Third Party Access. Against this background, the author then analysis whether this liberalization movement has provided positive externalities encouraging the use of more clean energy. She argues that the Third Energy Package has opened the market to more clean electricity producers and thereby has increased the share of clean electricity in the energy mix. However, liberalization of the market alone is insufficient in correcting the market failure to curb CO_2 emissions. To remedy this the author shows how Member States which have also implemented more environmental policies show a greater increase in clean energy innovation. This in turn leads to less CO_2 emissions and thereby supports the goal of decarbonization. She concludes that there is a clear link between liberalization and decarbonization and suggests that the targets set forth in the Renewable Energy Directive along with the EU law for State Aid for Environmental Protection and Energy will provide a sufficient legal framework to truly decarbonize the European electricity grid.

The chapter, "The Temperature Target of the Paris Agreement and the Forgotten Aspects of a Meaningful Energy Transition", illuminates the targets set forth in the Paris Agreement. Felix Ekardt and Jutta Wieding draw attention to the failings of the plurality of approaches adopted by the signing parties to achieve the target of limiting global warming to below 2 °C. They then discuss the drawbacks of relying on technical innovations to achieve these targets and argue that a sufficiency strategy requiring a complete change in public opinion and behavior is the best approach. In closing, the authors view the current EU Emissions Trading Schemes as an insufficient approach as the emissions generated by agriculture are largely ignored and outline their suggested governance instruments as a possible solution.

With their provocative title "A Shocking Truth for Law and Economics: Consumer Welfare Explains the Internal Market for Electricity Better than Total Welfare" the authors Fabrizio Esposito and Lucila De Almeida argue that the assumption many economically-informed legal scholars make, that regulation of the electricity market is pursuing total welfare is wrong. By illuminating the debate on the applicability of economic analyses to law they draw our attention to the crux of the difficulties faced by any interdisciplinary approach: language matters. Economic approaches to explaining the law, which are based on the efficiency hypothesis are often faced with the criticism that they are external approaches and do not consider the discursive dimension of the law. It is in the nature of linguistic practice, be that legal reasoning or economic discussion that interdisciplinary approaches can struggle. Both disciplines may mean the same thing, but say something else. Against this background, the authors then analyse the EU electricity market regulations and conclude that the axiological value at their basis is consumer welfare not total welfare.

Part II begins with the chapter "Paying for Energy" by Bruce R. Huber. In this chapter, the author begins by highlighting the need for investment into the energy sector's infrastructure. This of course raises the question of who will pay for this investment and how should such investments be structured. Using historical examples, such as the ingenious approach of Samuel Insull to deliver electricity to the masses in the United States and the investments into hydropower plants, the different investment approaches to spreading the costs are illuminated. Subsequently, the author discusses how proponents of clean energy push for schemes that incentivize consumers to invest in their properties to use renewable energy sources. Schemes such as the of tax-exempt financing schemes known as Property-Assessed Clean Energy or "PACE" programs and on-bill repayment programs. In states with net metering policies, this has meant that building owners are investing in infrastructure such as solar panels, which allows them to sell back any energy they do not use to the grid. As a result, many electricity providers argue that this means that many are not paying their "fair share" for grid resources, which places an extra burden on regular consumers. These are just a few of the issues the current energy transition in Europe and the United States raises that need careful regulation.

In his chapter "Energy Market and Policy Revolutions: Regulatory Process and the Cost of Capital" James W. Coleman delves further into the issues governing bodies face regarding the required investment and its' regulation as a result from the shift towards decarbonization. As a starting point, this chapter describes the tension between the need to maintain economic growth while also meeting global climate goals. The author begins by describing the various areas that require substantial investment to successfully transition to low carbon economy. Not only must capital investment be made into building new renewable energy infrastructure, but also into natural gas power as a back-up source instead of coal. From this backdrop, the author then outlines how the trend towards deregulation and liberalization of the energy markets over the past 30 years has increased uncertainty and the costs of long-term investment in the energy industry. As a key example of this, the author discusses the Keystone XL pipeline project in the United States. In closing, the he presents two principles that policymakers should follow to encourage the necessary investment into the energy market: Principle 1, accommodate wide participation in energy projects while at the same time maintaining the ultimate decision-making authority; Principle 2, rule changes to the way environmental assessments are conducted should only be applied prospectively. By following these principles, the author argues that decarbonization can be achieved while maintaining economic growth.

Stephan Meyer's chapter "Intergenerational Choice Under Uncertainty: The Case of Future Energy Technologies" focuses on sustainability as a policy goal. He begins his chapter by outlining the difficulties current generations face with regards to make policy decision that will impact future generations. But he argues, that because of the longevity nature of the law, it provides an excellent instrument to consider the needs of future generations. Furthermore, he views market-based governance as sharing this future-orientated nature. This thus would mean that an interdisciplinary law and economics approach could potentially be a perfect partnership in achieving intergenerational sustainability. However, issues such as hyperbolic discounting and random preference change add an additional dimension to the challenges policy-makers face. In the author's opinion, the best strategy is to avoid predictions of future utility and instead focus on keeping options open. To illustrate this, the author delves into an in-depth analysis of the electric transportation market in Germany. He begins this by providing an overview of the key instruments implemented by the German Government to encourage the use of electric vehicles. The current policy instruments are aimed at reducing uncertainty in the electric propulsion market while at the same time facilitating the development of innovative technology in this field by means of various subsidies and consumer incentives. Despite these, he argues that the vast investments to provide the necessary charging infrastructure for the many different electric vehicles currently on the market means that the effective indivisibility of products on the market reinforces uncertainty. This in turns acts as a prohibitive measure against investment in the necessary infrastructure. If a consortium of businesses did indeed make the necessary investments, the potential loss when the consumers choose a competing method of charging could be too great to bear. As an example of this he cites the company "Better Place", which had developed a battery swap technology and launched pilot projects in both Israel and Denmark. Unfortunately, consumers did not respond to this method of recharging their electric cars and the company went bankrupt. In short, he summarizes that market risk, indivisibility and the sheer size of the project combined result in market failure. This would imply that state intervention is necessary. But such interventions must always strive to keep the options of future generations open.

The first chapter "Creating Social Norms Through Media, Cascades and Cognitive Anchors: Judicial Activism and the Quality of Energy Law from the Perspective of Behavioural Law and Economics" in Part III, discusses how judges in their decisions are influenced by the media and social norms. Mariusz J. Golecki and Jaraslow Beldowski begin their chapter by showing how the differentiation judge-made law and statutory law is key for the Law and Economics movement as a whole. They begin by outlining the observations made by Ronald Coase in his seminal essay "The Problem of Social Cost" and describe how that led a movement within Law and Economics, which argued for more judge-made law, as it was perceived as a way to maximize efficiency. Much of this was based on the assumption that legislators were more vulnerable to lobbyists and impact groups thereby reducing their quality of law. A judge seeking to maximize allocative efficiency however, would improve the quality of law made. This initial normative postulation gave rise to many subsequent theories elaborating on the criteria and assumptions made to support this approach. However, the authors argue, that this would require the judges to have a deliberative, rational decision-making process, which in their view is not freely possible. When viewed from a behavioral law and economics perspective, it is clear that the decision-making process shows systematic departures from the rational choice model. The attempts by judges to process the vast pieces of information when reaching their decision requires them to rely on rules of thumb, which are largely influenced by the availability bias. The use of rules of thumb or heuristics result from the duality of cognitive processes (or Dual Process Theory). Kahneman's two systems theory, which relies on a fast intuitive and a slower deliberative element in decision-making is then described. This dual process provides the authors with the link to show that emotions are naturally also included into any decision-making process. Therefore, they argue that judge-made law is not as rational as first assumed. Furthermore, this dual nature of decision-making opens judges to be inadvertently influenced by the media, social norms as well as their emotions. To illustrate this, the authors analyse the Love Canal case, which led to the imposition of very strict liability for contaminated land without any rational justification. They argue that this was a direct result of the fears spread by the newspapers and media at the time. To further show how the media influences not only the legislator but also the courts, the authors then discuss the German Federal Constitutional Court ruling regarding the accelerated phase-out of nuclear energy, which resulted after the Fukoshima incident. In this case, the Complainants claimed that this accelerated phase-out was equivalent to expropriation of property rights. While the Court did agree that the right to property had been encroached on, it held that the Phase-Out Amendment Act of 2002 established legitimate expectations, which are worth protecting. This despite there being any new scientific basis verifying the perceived increased risk of nuclear power plants. In conclusion, the authors argue that an in-depth analysis of judicial rationality from the perspective of the dual process theory should take place to better understanding the impacts of heuristics and biases in judge-made law. Furthermore, they argue that through this analysis institutional and procedural changes should be made to consider the complexities of decision-making.

In his chapter "Capacity Mechanisms: An Intervention Needed in Failing Markets?" Markus Schreiber outlines the various capacity mechanisms from a European and Swiss perspective. In particular, the author focuses on the problems posed by the need of a secure electricity supply. He begins his chapter by outlining the potential problems that may arise in the electricity market. Firstly, he turns to the "missing money problem". Because of the inelastic nature of the electricity demands, the current energy transition towards renewable energies could lead to gaps in the generating capacity during peak times. The use of renewable energy sources requires more backup generating capacities, as these sources are intermittent in their energy production characteristics. This combined with the low-marginal cost of energy production, may lead to a price level of zero or close to zero. This means that the current returns may be inadequate to incentivize the necessary investment to provide flexible generating capacity. Subsequently the author discusses how various government actions, such as subsidizing renewable energy sources and price caps have further distorted the market. He also draws a parallel between the "missing money problem" and the "free-rider" problem arguing that the security of supply could be seen as a public good. As a solution to the "missing money" problem, many have suggested the use of capacity mechanisms. Markus Schreiber the various mechanisms currently in play today before focusing on the situation in the European Union and Switzerland. Using these two examples, he illuminates the different legislative approaches to capacity mechanisms and concludes that while there is no consensus on whether there is indeed a failing energy market, the states should receive a margin of discretion to determine whether an energy market failure exists before implementing capacity mechanisms.

Rolf H. Weber shifts our attention to the impact of energy labels in his chapter "Energy Labels: Nudging Policy to Avoid Trade Implications?". While energy labels lend themselves as a good nudging instrument, the author draws attention to the challenges this creates. Energy labels are an ideal medium to provide environmental information to consumers and are viewed as the least restrictive instrument when compared to other trade-related instruments. Despite their relatively unrestrictive nature, energy labels are not completely unproblematic under international trade law. It is these tensions the author illuminates in his chapter. He begins with describing the characteristics of energy labels before describing how they can and are used as part of a nudging policy. He argues that energy labels not only serve to incentivize consumers to make more environmentally friendly choices but also provide an incentive to producers to make more environmentally friendly products. However, because of the variety of competing energy labels, the efficiency of energy labels as a nudge is called into question. Consumers are less willing to invest the time to understand the different energy labels and the information they convey. Energy labels are only efficient when they are government imposed and sufficiently regulated. While the Agreement establishing the World Trade Organization does specifically acknowledge sustainability goals, the WTO Member States still retain their sovereign right to define their own environmental measures. This however, leads to legal insecurity and as a result there has been an increased number of disputes regarding labelling schemes. Especially in view of the ever-growing number of mandatory labelling schemes. These mandatory labels are considered technical regulations and fall under the Agreement on Technical Barriers to Trade as they usually reflect product characteristics. Therefore, labels that result in a less favorable treatment compared to local products are likely to be viewed in violation of the Agreement. Furthermore, the author highlights the challenges the principles of national treatment and most favored nation held in the General Agreement on Tariffs and Trade pose for energy labels. Finally, the author turns his attention to Public Procurement Law, which has gained in importance over recent years. He focuses on the so-called green procurement, which refers to the practice of considering environmental factors when awarding public procurement contracts. Although public procurement is mostly regulated on a domestic level, many states have committed themselves to the WTO's General Procurement Agreement. While this Agreement does support the principle of green procurement, provisions therein preclude the exclusive use of energy labels as the only means of providing technical specifications. The author concludes that while energy labels are a good tool to nudge the market, there are constraints on their use laid out in WTO and international trade law.

The final chapter of Part III discusses how biases and heuristics influence consumer choices in the energy market. Mariusz J. Golecki and Piotr Tereszkiewicz begin their chapter "Consumer Protection in Energy Markets: Selected Insights from Behavioural Law & Economics and Regulatory Practice" by analysing the Dyson Case. At the core of this dispute was the question of what information must be displayed on the energy labels of vacuum cleaners. Dyson Ltd argued that the European Commissions' Regulation 665/2013 mislead consumers regarding the energy consumption of vacuum cleaners. According to Dyson Ltd, the Regulation only required cleaning performance tests to be conducted with empty receptacles which is not a true reflection on their performance with partially or full receptacles. While this was acknowledged by the Court of Justice of the European Union, it held that that alone was insufficient to annul the Regulation. The authors subsequently discuss the influence such labels have on consumers. They begin with an overview of the framing effect and describe how this applies to energy labels before applying it to the arguments raised in the Dyson case directly. While it would be possible to modify the disclosure contained in the energy labels, it is unclear how to design such a disclosure to ensure it is easily understood by consumers. As a next step the authors discuss the decision-making process and describe the use of heuristics and rules of thumb. They describe four methods employed in categorizing or forming groups to serve as a basis for decision-making. According to the authors these four methods are: (1) matching a test object with a rule which defines a given category, (2) determining similarity between the test object and memorized examples of a given category, (3) determining similarities between the test object and a prototype of a given category, and (4) theory based categorization. In conclusion, the authors argue that the framework for disclosures required on energy labels should consider the way we categorize information we receive, as this categorization process is instrumental in our decision-making. In other words, the authors urge for a behavioral law and economics approach to assessing legislation regarding disclosures and labelling.

Part IV begins with the chapter "The Trade and Environment Debate on the Regulation of Energy Subsidies in the WTO: What Kept Fossil Fuel Subsidies Off the Radar Screen?" by Henok Birhanu Asmelash. This chapter begins with a brief overview of the debate surrounding the interaction between trade and the environment. The central issue is the question of whether international trade rules prevent governments from taking effective steps to protect the environment. The author begins with the US-Tuna I and US-Tuna II case in which various European Communities challenged the US import ban on tuna caught using nets that led to a high incident of dolphins also being inadvertently killed. The trade and environment debate has since shifted from such marine conservation issues to competitiveness concerns of states, which strive to limit their emissions in accordance with the Kyoto Protocol. Against this background the author then delves into the issues that renewable energy subsidies and the challenges posed by the Agreement on Subsidies and Countervailing Measures. The provisional category granting "green" subsidies a safe-haven and making them non-actionable subsidies unfortunately expired without a new agreement being reached. This has led to a rise in disputes regarding environmental subsidy schemes. The lacking clarity of how such subsidies should be dealt with has placed a burden on the Appellate Body to resolve the tensions between the need to encourage environmental protection and trade disputes regarding prohibited government subsidies. While some call for a change in the law to provide clarity, others argue that governments should simply structure their environmental support schemes to be compatible under the Agreement. The author then draws attention to the use of support schemes in fossil fuels. While it is clear that these schemes are detrimental to environmental goals, it appears they have received little attention and are therefore rarely mentioned in the trade and environment debate. This lack of attention, the author argues, could be in part because of the lack of any disputes being brought forward. He further lists the lack of definition of sustainable development as a further reason fossil fuel subsidies have received so little attention. While organisations such as the Friends of Fossil Fuels Subsidy Reform has been established to advance intergovernmental efforts to reform fossil fuels subsidies, the author concludes that more critical reflection on whether a multilateral trade system is the appropriate venue to deal with such a reform, or how such a system can contribute to the elimination of fossil fuels, among other questions ought to be conducted first. Only then, will a successful strategy be found.

In his chapter "Promoting Renewable Energies Through State Aid, a Reform Is Required" Régis Lanneau argues that state aid needs to be redefined to effectively incentivize sustainable energy production. In his opinion, controlling state aid or any state support is essential to ensure that the currently emerging support schemes are efficient and thereby successful assist in the transition to a low carbon economy. He begins his chapter by analysing the European Commissions' General Block Exemption Regulations and their development. The GBER is primarily aimed at lowering the administrative costs associated with the requirement for states to notify the Commission of their support schemes. Furthermore, in the case of support schemes for renewable energy sources, the GBER coupled with the Commission's Guidelines provides member states with a clear framework for constructing their support schemes. While the Commission's approach is very detailed, it only focuses on "positive" action by member states. However, the author argues, that if the goal of decarbonization and therefore encourage new renewable energy sources is to be truly achieved then the negative externalities of state aids need to be addressed. While granting below market price pollution permits is as an indirect way to deal with negative externalities, it is only the consequences that are being dealt with rather than tackling the problem at source. The author argues that where transaction costs are too high to ensure an efficient outcome, governments should intervene. This logic should apply regardless of whether there is positive action or abstention. In cases where there is a known negative externality, such as pollution, a government's inactivity should be considered as state aid. While this change in the concept of state aid could greatly serve the environmental goals, its implementation raises questions regarding its lawfulness as well as changes in policy. Subsequently the author outlines the possible challenges such a change would pose. But he concludes that these challenges should not be overestimated. All that is required, is for existing positive law to be re-interpreted. Hence, Lanneau argues that should EU Member States not demand or make the change for themselves, the ECJ could interpret positive law in its rulings accordingly thereby forcing the change.

The final chapter in this section is a case study on the development of policies in various EU Member States to encourage the use of electric vehicles. Ana Trías begins her chapter "State Measures in Support of Sustainable Mobility Infrastructure: The Case of Estonia, the Netherlands and Norway" by outlining the EU legal framework aimed at encouraging electric or clean vehicles. The biggest challenge in changing to electric vehicles is the lack of a unified approach in its infrastructure. She argues the market failure to provide a refueling infrastructure has resulted in the development of a clearer policy framework by EU institutions. Along with this policy framework there are also EU Funds to encourage cohesive development of the necessary infrastructure. Against this background, the author then discusses how Estonia, the Netherlands and Norway have approached the implementation of electric vehicles. While the government funding for the Estonia project did not result in a formal state aid investigation the systems implemented in both Norway and the Netherlands, were assessed. The author subsequently discusses why these two notified state aid systems, were deemed compatible with Article 107(3) TFEU. Subsequently the author discusses the various direct and indirect state support schemes used in Norway and the Netherlands in detail as well as assessing the impact these measures have had on the electricity market. She concludes that the schemes analyzed may not be sustainable as subsidizing charging stations eventually may not be feasible. Furthermore, she calls in to question the supranational bodies' assessment of the schemes in Norway and the Netherlands for not considering the source of the electricity used in the charging stations.

As this volume shows the current energy transition raise a vast range of legal questions. At the root of the problem lies the need for continued economic growth, while recognizing that there are finite resources available. Our energy production and consumption pose environmental challenges coupled with the allocative questions. An economic analysis of law can offer remarkable findings for their solution. The 16 chapters of this volume deliver insights into the multifaceted debates surrounding the changes in energy regulation in Europe and the need to fulfil environmental protection goals.

Lucerne, Switzerland
Notre Dame, IN, USA
October 2017

Klaus Mathis
Bruce R. Huber

Contents

Contributors

Henok Birhanu Asmelash Max Planck Institute Luxembourg for Procedural Law, Luxembourg, Luxembourg

Jarosław Bełdowski International Comparative Studies Department, Warsaw School of Economics, Warsaw, Poland

James W. Coleman Southern Methodist University Dedman School of Law, Dallas, TX, USA

Lucila de Almeida Faculty of Law, University of Helsinki, Helsinki, Finland

Felix Ekardt Forschungsstelle Nachhaltigkeit und Klimapolitik, Leipzig, Germany

Fabrizio Esposito European University Institute, Florence, Italy

Mariusz J. Golecki Department of Legal Theory and Philosophy of Law, Faculty of Law and Administration, University of Łódź, Łódź, Poland

Julia Hänni Faculty of Law, University of Lucerne, Lucerne, Switzerland

Sebastian Heselhaus Faculty of Law, University of Lucerne, Lucerne, Switzerland

Bruce R. Huber Notre Dame Law School, Notre Dame, IN, USA

Régis Lanneau Université de Paris Ouest Nanterre la Défense, Nanterre Cedex, France

Anna-Alexandra Marhold Tilburg Law and Economics Center, Tilburg University, Tilburg, the Netherlands

Klaus Mathis Faculty of Law, University of Lucerne, Lucerne, Switzerland

Stephan Meyer University of Applied Sciences Wildau, Wildau, Germany

University of Erfurt, Erfurt, Germany

Markus Schreiber Faculty of Law, University of Lucerne, Lucerne, Switzerland

Piotr Tereszkiewicz Faculty of Law and Administration, Jagiellonian University of Cracow, Cracow, Poland

Ana Trías Center for European Integration Studies, University of Bonn, Bonn, Germany

Rolf H. Weber Faculty of Law, University of Zurich, Zurich, Switzerland

Jutta Wieding Forschungsstelle Nachhaltigkeit und Klimapolitik, Leipzig, Germany

Part I
Energy Transition

Sustainability Strategies and the Problem of the Rebound Effect

Klaus Mathis

Abstract This essay discusses the efficiency, consistency and sufficiency strategies. In particular, the rebound effect, which can occur with the efficiency, as well as with the sufficiency strategy, is discussed. The rebound effect means that an increase in energy efficiency does not lead to the desired result because the saved financial resources are used for new activities, which are usually associated with additional energy consumption.

1 Introduction

Three prominent strategies for achieving sustainability[1] are presented in literature. Each of these strategies is oriented to the criterion of either efficiency, consistency or sufficiency:[2]

- The *efficiency strategy* is aimed at the reduction of quantitative inputs for production processes without having to abstain from economic growth. This is done by enhancing resource productivity.
- The *consistency strategy* endeavours to achieve closed-loop material cycles and thus to decouple the human-created socio- and technosphere from the natural sources and sinks.
- The *sufficiency strategy* demands a reduction of resource consumption and emissions by changing consumption habits.

The three strategies do not preclude one another, but can also be combined. The question then, however, is what weight should be accorded to the various strategies,

[1]For an in-depth analysis of the issue of sustainable development and intergenerational justice see Mathis (2017).

[2]Freimann (2012), p. 459.

K. Mathis (✉)
Faculty of Law, University of Lucerne, Lucerne, Switzerland
e-mail: klaus.mathis@unilu.ch

K. Mathis, B. R. Huber (eds.), *Energy Law and Economics*, Economic Analysis of Law in European Legal Scholarship 5, https://doi.org/10.1007/978-3-319-74636-4_1

particularly the efficiency and the sufficiency strategy, as is clearly expressed in the study "*Zukunftsfähiges Deutschland*" (Sustainable Germany):

> What if certain environmental goals demand the virtue of forbearance, curtailment or moderation; if technology is definitely not the answer? Whether the diversity of landscapes or animal and plant species can successfully be conserved is not a question of the speed of innovation. The tension between these two modes of argumentation permeates the entire *Sustainable Germany* study. It cannot be resolved, only endured. The question of what ratio of efficiency and sufficiency, technical innovation and proportionality will characterise a sustainable Germany cannot be answered conclusively. Both elements will take on a significant role and the proposition is advanced here that they can complement one another.[3]

Both the efficiency and the consistency strategy principally rely on technical innovations whereas the sufficiency strategy is targeted at the behaviour of consumers.[4] Moreover, because many people in developing countries already live at the existential minimum and therefore cannot reduce their consumption, the sufficiency strategy is addressed primarily to the industrialised countries.

The three strategies and their advantages and disadvantages will be presented and assessed in more detail below.

2 Efficiency Strategy

The efficiency strategy is aimed at increasing resource productivity without having to abstain from growth, which is why it is also referred to as the "efficiency revolution". The idea is to achieve the desired production output whilst keeping inputs of material and energy to the minimum possible levels. This requires an improvement of the input-output ratio, i.e. a gain in material and energy efficiency.[5] In relation to sustainability, the meaning and purpose of the efficiency strategy consists in reducing resource consumption and environmental pollution in both relative and, if possible, absolute terms. This is to be accomplished by means of improved technologies (e.g. more efficient engines), recycling (i.e. the reuse of materials within a circular economy) and prolonging the service life of consumer durables.[6]

If it can be assumed—as is contended in (for example) Ecological Economics—that the world's finiteness, i.e. the finite availability of nature as a source of raw materials and a sink for wastes, is the central sustainability problem, then innovations and an attendant efficiency revolution might represent the solution to that problem. Economic growth without increasing "environmental consumption" would then be possible. In other words, innovations might be a means of decoupling

[3] Bund and Misereor (1997), p. 13 (own translation from the German).

[4] Ecker and Ecker (2014), p. 638.

[5] Huber (1995), p. 40.

[6] Huber (1995), p. 41.

economic growth from "scale", i.e. the quantitative volume of material and energy throughputs.[7]

Aside from this key distinction between economic and scale growth, a further differentiation must be made between relative and absolute decoupling: relative decoupling is when the economy grows faster than environmental consumption. The problem is that when decoupling is merely relative, scale can continue to increase drastically enough to outweigh the efficiency savings in material and energy consumption, given sufficiently high economic growth. If the aim is to ensure that there is absolutely no further growth in scale, absolute decoupling is necessary. Ultimately, absolute rather than relative values are most informative about the ecological impacts of economic processes.[8]

The efficiency strategy enjoys broad approval because it promises resource savings accompanied by greater wealth.[9] For that reason, in the prevailing economic context it is likely to be the easiest to accept. Many economic leaders tend to equate sustainability with efficiency improvements to a greater or lesser extent.[10] But the sustainability discourse itself is strongly dominated by the view that continuing growth of the economy is possible through innovations and efficiency gains. An efficiency revolution stimulated by innovations is then seen as the way to accomplish the necessary decoupling of economic growth and resource consumption.[11]

The classic objection to the efficiency strategy is that in pursuing it one is almost automatically destined to end up in the rebound trap, whereby quantitative growth and the increasing use of material consumer durables combine to cancel out the efficiency gains once again.[12] Often an efficiency gain of 1% leads to a less than 1% reduction in resource consumption, and sometimes an increase in resource consumption can even be observed. The reason for this is that the efficiency gain influences the behaviour of economic actors;[13] for example, energy-saving lightbulbs can result in a more carefree approach to the use of electric power so that, on balance, the energy-saving effect is reduced or even overcompensated in extreme cases (i.e. the strategy backfires).[14]

Various types of rebound effect can be distinguished, the most prominent types being the direct and indirect rebound effects:[15]

- *Direct rebound effect:* Thanks to the efficiency gain, energy can be offered at a lower price, which ceteris paribus leads to demand for a higher quantity.

[7]See Luks (2005), pp. 42 et seqq.

[8]Luks (2005), pp. 48 et seq.

[9]Freimann (2012), p. 459.

[10]Huber (1995), p. 41.

[11]Luks (2013), p. 121.

[12]Freimann (2012), p. 459.

[13]Binswanger (2001), p. 120.

[14]Alcott (2005), p. 9.

[15]Binswanger (2001), p. 122.

- *Indirect rebound effect:* Because of the lower price of energy, households can ceteris paribus spend more money on other goods and services (income effect), which require additional energy to produce or provide.
- *General equilibrium effect:* Lower energy prices lead to a general fall in the cost of all goods and services. Based on substitution and income effects, this leads to a new macroeconomic equilibrium in which more energy is consumed.
- *Transformation effect:* Technical efficiency gains modify consumer behaviour, which in turn has repercussions upon infrastructures or social norms. If transport becomes more efficient, for example, settlement structures change, small shops disappear and shopping centres are built, which ultimately leads to transportation over longer distances.
- *Mental rebound effect:* Occasionally, savings made through more efficient technologies lead to the self-legitimation ("moral licensing") of additional consumption. Car drivers who have converted to a gas-powered vehicle may then be heavier on the gas pedal or make longer journeys with a clear conscience. Thus, a share of the potential energy savings are offset by higher consumption. Likewise, households may leave energy-saving lights on for longer than conventional lightbulbs yet still be doing something positive for the environment.

However great the potential for material and efficiency savings may be on the microeconomic level, the environmental consequences on the macroeconomic level are the ultimate measure of success. Impressive microeconomic efficiency gains may be achieved but if macroeconomic expansion processes can soak up these improvements, then very little has been gained, in sum, from an ecological perspective. At best this approach allows the problem to be postponed for a short while.[16]

An empirical study by John M. Polimeni, who analysed the rebound effect in economically heterogeneous countries in Europe, Asia, North and South America for the period 1980–2004, comes to a devastating conclusion:

> The results strongly suggest that energy-efficient technological improvements as the solution for the world's energy and environmental problems will not work. Rather, energy-efficient technology improvements are counterproductive, promoting energy consumption.[17]

The fact that efficiency gains do not necessarily lead to an absolute reduction in consumption was noted long ago by William Stanley Jevons in his work "The Coal Question" (1865). He pointed out that more efficient use of coal led to increased rather than reduced consumption:[18]

> It is wholly a confusion of ideas to suppose that the economical use of fuel is equivalent to a diminished consumption. The very contrary is the truth.[19]

---

[16]Luks (2005), p. 52.

[17]Polimeni (2008), p. 169.

[18]Luks (2005), Innovation, p. 51.

[19]Jevons (1865/2001), p. 103 (whole passage italicized in the original).

This phenomenon is therefore referred to as the *Jevons paradox*. In his account, Jevons cites C.W. Williams, who impressively drew attention to the described problem even earlier, in the 1840s:[20]

> The economy of fuel is the secret of the economy of the steam-engine; it is the fountain of its power, and the adopted measure of its effects. Whatever, therefore, conduces to increase the efficiency of coal, and to diminish the cost of its use, directly tends to augment the value of the steam-engine, and to enlarge the field of its operations.[21]

Innovations are therefore a double-edged sword from an ecological viewpoint: on the one hand they are the engine of economic development, which—ceteris paribus (i.e. in this case, without "decoupling")—causes environmental problems in a finite world.[22] Added to that, each instance in which scarcity is overcome by means of innovations and growth either contains or creates the potential for new forms of scarcity. The race between problems and innovations therefore resembles a contest between a hare and a tortoise: even when innovation processes contribute to solving a specific problem, there are always new problems ready and waiting.[23] On the other hand, innovations always harbour ecological opportunities, so structural change can at least result in a relative lowering of environmental consumption, i.e. to a certain decoupling of value creation and environmental consumption.[24]

Those who champion the efficiency strategy point out that the rebound effect is not an inexorable law but rather the result of unduly weak environmental policy, which has neglected to internalise external environmental costs and hence failed to put a higher price on environmentally harmful goods and services.[25] However, environmental levies on energy consumption are not conducive to environmental policy when the rebound effect comes into play, because the initial reduction in energy consumption due to the efficiency gain stimulated by the policy measure is offset again in the course of the rebound effect. Moreover, the revenues from the environmental levies are usually redirected to uses which themselves require energy and materials.[26]

This sobering conclusion gives rise to the demand that environmental consumption should be tackled directly instead of focusing on efficiency.[27] The discussion then moves on to rationing and quotas as methods of directly limiting the quantities of resources and energy consumed.[28]

[20]Jevons (1865/2001), p. 107.

[21]Williams (1841), p. 9.

[22]Luks (2005), p. 53.

[23]Luks (2005), pp. 50 et seq.

[24]Luks (2005), p. 53.

[25]Steurer and Trattnigg (2010), p. 19.

[26]Alcott (2005), p. 19.

[27]Luks (2005), p. 56.

[28]Alcott (2005), p. 19.

3 Consistency Strategy

Consistency refers to the quality of substances and, in the metaphorical sense, denotes harmony, compatibility or tolerability. With reference to sustainability issues, consistency refers to environmental compatibility as a quality of material and energy flows.[29] The main aim of the consistency strategy is therefore to achieve closed material cycles, and hence to decouple the human-created socio- and technosphere from the natural sources and sinks.[30] Like the efficiency strategy, it relies on technological solutions, but differs from it in placing the focus on the output side.[31]

The aim is to transform the entire economy into a "circular economy" with closed cycles and as little waste as possible. Products are to be developed in such a way that their materials can be recycled after use as biological or technological raw materials.[32] When wastes are unavoidable, the *resilience* thresholds of ecosystems must not be exceeded. Resilience is a measure of the maximum permissible load that may safely be placed on an ecosystem without disturbing its equilibrium.[33]

The consistency strategy, like the efficiency strategy, promises technical solutions to ecological problems, permitting an expectation that material wealth will be maintained or even enhanced. However, in many cases there are substantial costs attached to the closing of cycles.[34] Moreover, it is not a solution to the problem of "material congestion": what is the use of consistent production processes if the quantity of products and production sites is constantly increasing and competing with the biosphere for scarce space?[35] Added to which, the production-related concentration on technology degrades consumers to passive bit-part players who are not credited with any responsibility of their own.[36]

4 Sufficiency Strategy

In contrast to the efficiency and consistency approach, the sufficiency strategy is not addressed primarily to producers but to consumers. It requires them to turn away from the ever-increasing consumption of goods.[37] Max Weber appears to have

[29] Huber (1995), p. 41.
[30] Freimann (2012), p. 459.
[31] Paech (2012), p. 60.
[32] Stengel (2011), p. 131.
[33] Arrow et al. (1995), p. 93. Hence, the consistency strategy is sometimes also referred to as the "resilience strategy".
[34] Renn (2001), p. 88.
[35] Paech (2012), p. 63.
[36] Paech (2012), p. 63.
[37] Freimann (2012), p. 459.

recognised long ago that economic and technological development also has an influence on people's lifestyles, which ultimately leads to the depletion of natural resources:

> For when asceticism was carried out of monastic cells into everyday life, and began to dominate worldly morality, it did its part in building the tremendous cosmos of the modern economic order. This order is now bound to the technical and economic conditions of machine production which today determine the lives of all the individuals who are born into this mechanism, not only those directly concerned with economic acquisition, with irresistible force. Perhaps it will so determine them until the last ton of fossilized coal is burnt.[38]

With an accent on moderate consumption, the sufficiency strategy directly addresses this cause of growth.[39] By means of a "sufficiency revolution" it sets out to reduce the utilisation of nature and pressure on the environment under the banner of "living well instead of having lots".[40] The transformation in consumption and lifestyle relates primarily to the industrialised countries, whose consumption already exceeds the Earth's carrying capacity even today.[41]

The sufficiency strategy was already mooted by John Stuart Mill in the "Principles of Political Economy" (1848). Unlike the economic classics he does not consider the "stationary state" of the economy to be a nightmare but sees it as a considerable improvement of the situation,[42] as can be seen in this famous passage from his work:

> I confess I am not charmed with the ideal of life held out by those who think that the normal state of human beings is that of struggling to get on; that the trampling, crushing, elbowing, and treading on each other's heels, which form the existing type of social life, are the most desirable lot of human kind, or anything but the disagreeable symptoms of one of the phases of industrial progress.[43]

The stationary state in Mill's work relates only to the population and to capital, but does not oppose social progress in other areas (culture, morality etc.). Even work productivity can be enhanced; not for multiplying wealth, however, but that of shortening working hours.[44]

Another work pointing in the direction of the sufficiency strategy is Warren Johnson's "Muddling Toward Frugality. A Blueprint for Survival in the 1980s" (1979). In the preface he writes:

> If we are to enjoy this planet for a long time, we may as well face the fact that trying to perpetuate the affluent society is going to be an uphill struggle. To maintain the heavy flow of raw materials now being cranked through our economy will become an increasingly

[38]Weber (1958), pp. 180 et seq.

[39]Paech (2012), p. 94.

[40]Bund and Misereor (1997), p. 206.

[41]Freimann (2012), p. 459.

[42]Brodbeck (2006), p. 236.

[43]Mill (1965), Book IV, Chapter VI, § 2, p. 754.

[44]Brodbeck (2006), p. 238.

> laborious and ultimately desperate task. Affluence will grow less comfortable, and there will be less peace and security in it. If the earth is to be a true home for us, a place of refuge and nurture, we may as well start to think about how we can make it such a place. The task will not be as difficult as it may sound, and requires no wishful thinking about technological breakthroughs, effective government, or heightened human consciousness. We can move toward a secure, sustainable way of life easily if we accept the logic of frugality.[45]

Johnson, who sees politics as overtaxed by these problems and unable to solve them, looks instead to changes in private lifestyles for the solution.[46] In 2010 Johnson published an updated version of the book entitled "Muddling Toward Frugality. A New Social Logic for a Sustainable World".

One possibility for realising the sufficiency strategy is in replacing material capital stocks with "non-material forms of capital". In simplified terms, natural and real capital are material forms of capital whereas human and social capital are non-material in nature. In this light, the strategy involves not only the absolute decoupling of economic growth from material capital stocks but also considering the potential for substituting material with non-material forms of capital.[47] In the non-material category, more growth is both possible and desirable. Of prime importance here is the development of social capital, since it sets the societal conditions, which define how the other forms of capital are managed.[48]

Based on the thoughts of Wolfgang Sachs, in concrete terms this might mean:[49]

- *Deceleration* of production and consumption, as for instance with the concept of "slow food";
- *Disentangling of economic production,* i.e. relocalisation of work and production processes to reduce the relevant transport and environmental costs;
- *Decommercialization,* i.e. the revaluation of unpaid work and the return of commercialised work to this sector;
- *Decluttering,* i.e. the systematic elimination of excessive or even harmful products and activities, as well as mindfulness of what is essential and necessary.

One opportunity for dematerialisation consists in the collective use of consumer durables, as in vehicle-sharing, or the use of second-hand marketplaces for redistributing products that are no longer needed.[50]

The concept of the *ecological footprint* developed by Mathis Wackernagel and William Rees in 1994 is a tool, which accounts for a human being's consumption of nature. It aims to measure how much of the Earth people take up, in hectares per person per year.[51] A calculation is made of the land and water area that is necessary

[45]Johnson (1979), p. 9.
[46]Johnson (1979), pp. 26 et seq.
[47]Kunz (2012), p. 68.
[48]Kunz (2012), p. 68.
[49]Sachs (1994), pp. 96 et seqq; Kunz (2012), p. 68.
[50]Renn (2001), p. 93.
[51]Wackernagel and Rees (1997), pp. 23 et seqq.

for a population to continuously manufacture the goods it consumes and to dispose of the resulting wastes.[52] To this end, consumption is broken down into five categories: (1) food, (2) housing, (3) transport, (4) goods and (5) services. For each category of consumption an ecological assessment is carried out, which quantifies the resources and energy consumed by a product over the whole of its life cycle.[53] The ecological footprint can be calculated for entire countries but is normally stated per capita of the population (hectares per person per year).[54] In 2003, Wackernagel founded the Global Footprint Network, which is supported by the Nobel laureate Wangari Maathai, Lester R. Brown, the founder of Worldwatch Institute, and Ernst Ulrich von Weizsäcker, the current President of the Club of Rome. In 2012 the average ecological footprint of Swiss citizens was 5.0, Germans 4.6 and North Americans 6.2.[55]

According to Manfred Max-Neef's *threshold hypothesis*, the quality of life initially increases in step with economic growth but begins to decline again once a certain threshold is reached.[56] In part this happens because the costs of the "rat race" for positional goods only ever escalate.[57] When this threshold is reached, quantitative economic growth needs to be replaced by qualitative development.[58] This calls for "human-scale economics"[59], which is characterised as follows:

> [W]e need new models that, above all else, begin to accept the limits of the carrying capacity of the Earth. We must move from efficiency to sufficiency and well-being. Also necessary is a resolution of the present economic imbalances and inequalities, for without equity peaceful solutions are not possible. We need to replace the dominant values of greed, competition and accumulation with those of solidarity, cooperation and compassion.[60]

In concrete terms, *local production* should be promoted to bring consumption and production closer to one another again. To achieve this, alongside taxes and levies on energy and emissions, protectionist measures like tariffs and quotas are proposed.[61]

Another advocate of *relocalization* is the French economist and philosopher Serge Latouche. In his book "*Petit traité de la décroissance sereine*" (Farewell to Growth [2007]), a critique of growth, he contends that production for the local population should take place predominantly at local level and transportation be restricted to a minimum.[62] However, he does not consider relocalisation a purely economic theme. He thinks it equally important that politics, culture and the

[52]Wackernagel and Rees (1997), pp. 83 et seqq.

[53]Wackernagel and Rees (1997), p. 90.

[54]Wackernagel and Rees (1997), p. 109.

[55]Report of the Global Footprint Network, 7 May 2012.

[56]Max-Neef (1995), p. 117.

[57]Ott (2001), p. 56.

[58]Max-Neef (1995), p. 117.

[59]Smith and Max-Neef (2011), p. 136.

[60]Smith and Max-Neef (2011), pp. 130 et seq.

[61]Smith and Max-Neef (2011), p. 137.

[62]Latouche (2015), p. 63.

meaning of life be brought back to their local roots and the relevant decisions taken at the local level.[63] His overall demand is for "degrowth" (*décroissance*), to bring the economy back into harmony with nature. The concept he lays out for local degrowth consists of two interlocking elements: *political innovation and economic autonomy.*[64]

Latouche is therefore a proponent of *local ecological democracy* combined with *regionalization of the economy.*[65] His approach involves decentralising the energy supply and considering the possibility of "bioregional currencies". Overall, his view of regionalisation means reduced transportation, transparent production processes, incentives for sustainable production and consumption, less dependency on capital flows and multinationals, and more security in every respect.[66] He argues that regionalising the economy and embedding it in local society protects the environment, gives everyone democratic access to the economy, reinforces solidarity, opens new perspectives for developing countries, but also promotes health for the citizens of rich countries thanks to a moderate lifestyle and the reduction of stress.[67]

Under the sufficiency strategy, however, the question of social acceptance arises: are people really prepared to make sweeping changes to their familiar consumer habits?[68] As a strategy of abstinence, the sufficiency strategy must therefore endure the same criticism as the concept of zero growth that preceded it: on the one hand, it is accused of being unrealistic because the masses continue to desire more and more material wealth; on the other hand, it is dismissed as undesirable since it could only be imposed by force, which would destroy the freedoms and rights enjoyed in a state under the rule of law.[69] Occasionally some go so far as to denounce the sufficiency strategy as "back to the Stone Age".[70]

Proponents of the sufficiency strategy point out a fundamental misunderstanding: by considering sufficiency against the backdrop of the growth question and consequently framing it as a pathway of mere abstinence, it is given negative connotations from the outset. Yet what is really called for is not abstinence, they argue, but the capacity for abstinence. Consequently, it is not a matter of restricting freedom but increasing it.[71] Hence the focus is not on abstaining from consumption individually but on making lifestyle changes, aligned with designs for living that place far less emphasis on the satisfaction of material needs. In economic terms, it involves a change in preferences; in philosophical terms, a shift in values.[72] Ultimately it is

[63]Latouche (2015), pp. 63 et seq.
[64]Latouche (2015), p. 72.
[65]Latouche (2015), pp. 73 et seqq.
[66]Latouche (2015), pp. 79 et seqq.
[67]Latouche (2015), pp. 80 et seq.
[68]Freimann (2012), p. 18.
[69]Huber (1995), p. 40.
[70]Kunz (2012), p. 67.
[71]Kunz (2012), p. 67.
[72]Kunz (2012), p. 68.

about defining the idea of the *good life* (in the Aristotelian sense).[73] As part of this, the role of the state and collective actors within the state may be to give people opportunities to engage in self-reflective discourse on their own lifestyles without attempting to determine the conclusions they come to.[74]

The decisive question, though, is whether it might be possible to motivate the mass of consumers to embrace environmentally sound behaviour. Generally, it seems unlikely that more than a minority of people will rein in their material consumption voluntarily.[75] Individual efforts to maintain a sustainable lifestyle may be a good thing for the individual, but it is questionable whether they also culminate in positive impacts, either macroeconomically or globally.[76] Environmental destruction cannot be prevented by a minority of consumers acting ethically. Further reaching political measures are required to induce the majority to change their behaviour.[77]

In this connection, some also urge a "change in mainstream Western culture", without which neither regulatory legal instruments nor incentives for a sufficient lifestyle can be implemented.[78] What they wish to overcome is Western "consumerism", which manifests itself in the phenomenon that identity, status, happiness, meaning and social integration are coupled to the consumption of goods.[79] Changes would have to take place on the cultural level to make a sufficient lifestyle possible on the individual level.[80] A sufficient lifestyle could become established particularly when a benefit accrues to the individual for displaying such behaviour because society, or at least the individual's immediate community and circle of friends, admire and appreciate it.[81]

According to another view, the problem resides less in values and far more in the persistence of the existing consumption patterns. This is when people are "stuck" in entrenched consumption patterns which are the result of habits, on the one hand, and are influenced by structural, technical, socio-economic, political and cultural conditions, on the other.[82] This phenomenon casts doubt on consumer sovereignty and prompts demands for the state to help consumers break out of rigid consumption patterns. Suggested methods of doing so include economic incentives, information, or—where relevant—regulations such as bans on advertising certain products.[83]

---

[73]Ott (2001), p. 55.

[74]Renn (2001), p. 95.

[75]Fuchs (2013), p. 221.

[76]Herring (2009), p. 237.

[77]Herring (2009), pp. 237 et seq.

[78]Ecker and Ecker (2014), p. 644.

[79]Stengel (2011), p. 184.

[80]Ecker and Ecker (2014), p. 644.

[81]Ecker and Ecker (2014), p. 641.

[82]Fuchs (2013), p. 219.

[83]Fuchs (2013), p. 220.

According to Richard Wilkinson and Kate Pickett, the most important driver for ever-increasing growth and resource consumption is unequal distribution of income. In their book "The Spirit Level: Why Greater Equality Makes Societies Stronger" (2009) they argue that social disparities drive people to the conspicuous consumption of positional goods in the attempt to keep up with more affluent people's lifestyles. In their book they also refer to Thorstein Veblen and his famous paper "The Theory of the Leisure Class" (1899).[84] He argues that controlling income disparities would reduce conspicuous consumption and resource use, and ultimately make all people happier.[85] In contrast, other authors suggest that goods from environmentally sound production could assume the role of positional goods, as might be happening with hybrid cars.[86]

The question of how much consumption is necessary has recently also been tackled by Robert and Edward Skidelsky in their book "How Much is Enough? Money and the Good Life" (2013). They do not see money as an end in itself but as a means for realising the good life. For this, the authors argue, the key parameters are the following seven basic goods: health, security, respect, personality, harmony with nature, friendship and leisure. A sufficient quantity of these seven basic goods, they say, makes a good life possible. The state also has an active role to play and must not be neutral towards different conceptions of what is good.[87] Their concrete proposal is that by means of an unconditional basic income and the promotion of part-time work, people can be given free choice between work and leisure, and their frenzied consumption can be combated by means of a progressive consumption tax and a restraint of advertising.[88]

The sufficiency strategy is addressed, as mentioned, to individual consumers, who are expected to critically question their lifestyles. On the one hand it must be asked how people are to be motivated to engage in such behaviour without resorting to coercion. But even if numerous people change their consumer patterns and consume fewer material goods, it is not certain whether this will have a positive overall effect on the environment. Blake Alcott has pointed out that even the sufficiency strategy can fail in the wake of a *consumption rebound effect*: the sufficient consumer's reduction in the consumption of certain goods leads ceteris paribus to a lowering of the price of the relevant goods, which in turn means that other, less frugal consumers, consume more.[89]

It is therefore questionable whether efforts on the demand side are adequate in the end, and whether regulations on the supply side are not also inevitable (e.g. quantity

[84]Wilkinson and Pickett (2009), pp. 217 et seqq.

[85]Wilkinson and Pickett (2009), pp. 235 et seqq.

[86]Fuchs (2013), p. 221.

[87]Skidelsky and Skidelsky (2013), p. xii and pp. 145 et seqq.

[88]Skidelsky and Skidelsky (2013), p. xii and pp. 180 et seqq.

[89]Alcott (2008), p. 770.

restrictions, bans on environmentally harmful products) to bring about an effective change in consumption behaviour.[90]

5 Conclusion

The efficiency and consistency strategies can be implemented without impediment within the modern age's technological approach to problem solving. Since they do not demand abstinence from consumption, their prospects of realisation should be good. However, the efficiency strategy does not work if the rebound effect increases the consumption of energy again. The sufficiency strategy requires a fundamental change of heart in the population, as well as a change in consumption behaviour. Therefore, it is hardly a strategy with mass appeal, even though it could make an important contribution to sustainable development. In addition, a rebound effect can also occur with the sufficiency strategy.

References

Alcott B (2005) Jevons' paradox. Ecol Econ 54:9–21

Alcott B (2008) The sufficiency strategy: would rich-world frugality lower environmental impact? Ecol Econ 64:770–786

Arrow K et al (1995) Economic growth, carrying capacity, and the environment. Science 268:520–521

Binswanger M (2001) Technological progress and sustainable development: what about the rebound effect? Ecol Econ 36:119–132

Brodbeck K-H (2006) John Stuart Mills "stationärer Zustand" als soziales Modell. In: Pechter U, Aßländer MS (eds) John Stuart Mill. Der vergessene politische Ökonom und Philosoph. Haupt, Bern, pp 211–252

Bund and Misereor (eds) (1997) Zukunftsfähiges Deutschland. Ein Beitrag zu einer global nachhaltigen Entwicklung. Studie des Wuppertal Instituts für Klima, Umwelt, Energie GmbH, 4th edn. Springer, Basel

Ecker M, Ecker F (2014) Genügsam leben: Überlegungen zur Suffizienz im rechtlichen Kontext. In: Ewer W, Ramsauer U, Reese M, Hubel R (eds) Methodik – Ordnung – Umwelt: Festschrift für Hans-Joachim Koch aus Anlass seines siebzigsten Geburtstags. Duncker & Humblot, Berlin, pp 637–647

Freimann J (2012) Nachhaltige Unternehmungsführung. Anforderungen – Erklärungsmodelle – Praxis. Wirtschaftswissenschaftliches Studium (WiSt) 41:458–464

Fuchs D (2013) Sustainable consumption. In: Falkner R (ed) The handbook of global climate and environment policy. Wiley-Blackwell, Chichester, pp 215–230

Herring H (2009) Sufficiency and the rebound effect. In: Herring H, Sorrel S (eds) Energy efficiency and sustainable consumption. The rebound effect. Palgrave MacMillan, Basingstoke, pp 224–239

[90] Herring (2009), pp. 237 et seq.

Huber J (1995) Nachhaltige Entwicklung durch Suffizienz, Effizienz und Konsistenz. In: Fritz P, Huber J, Levi HW (eds) Nachhaltigkeit in naturwissenschaftlicher und sozialwissenschaftlicher Perspektive. Universitas, Stuttgart, pp 31–46

Jevons WS (1865) The coal question. An inquiry concerning the progress of the nation, and the probable exhaustion of our coal-mines. MacMillan and Co, London. (facsimile reprint, Houndmills 2001)

Johnson W (1979) Muddling toward frugality. A blueprint for survival in the 1980s. Shambhala

Kunz M (2012) Suffizienz – zurück in die Steinzeit? In: Zukunftsrat S (ed) Haushalten & Wirtschaften. Bausteine für eine zukunftsfähige Wirtschafts- und Geldordnung. Schulthess, Zurich, pp 67–69

Latouche S (2015) Es reicht! Abrechnungen mit dem Wachstumswahn (fr. Original: petit traité de la décroissance sereine). Oekom, Munich

Luks F (2005) Innovation, Wachstum und Nachhaltigkeit. Eine ökologische Betrachtung. In: Beckenbach F et al (eds) Innovationen und Nachhaltigkeit. Jahrbuch Ökologische Ökonomik. Metropolis, Marburg, pp 41–62

Luks F (2013) Theorien der "Nachhaltigkeit" und die Nachhaltigkeit von Theorien. Für Alternativen zum Mainstream- und gegen einfache "Lösungen". In: Endres JC, Remig M (eds) Perspektiven nachhaltiger Entwicklung – Theorien am Scheideweg. Metropolis, Marburg, pp 119–130

Mathis K (2017) Nachhaltige Entwicklung und Generationengerechtigkeit: Eine interdisziplinäre Studie aus rechtlicher, ökonomischer und philosophischer Sicht. Mohr Siebeck, Tübingen

Max-Neef M (1995) Economic growth and quality of life: a threshold hypothesis. Ecol Econ 15:115–118

Mill JS (1965) In: Robson JM (ed) Principles of political economy. With some of their applications to social philosophy. University of Toronto Press, Routledge & Kegan Paul, Toronto and Buffalo

Ott K (2001) Eine Theorie "starker" Nachhaltigkeit. In: Altner G, Michelsen G (eds) Ethik und Nachhaltigkeit. Grundsatzfragen und Handlungsperspektiven im universitären Agendaprozess. VAS, Frankfurt a.M, pp 30–63

Paech N (2012) Nachhaltiges Wirtschaften jenseits von Innovationsorientierung und Wachstum. Eine unternehmensbezogene Transformationstheorie, 2nd edn. Metropolis, Marburg

Polimeni JM (2008) Empirical evidence for the Jevons Paradox. In: Polimeni JM, Mayumi K, Giampietro M, Alcott B (eds) The Jevons Paradox and the myth of resource efficiency improvements. Routledge, London and Sterling, pp 141–172

Renn O (2001) Ethische Anforderungen an eine Nachhaltige Entwicklung. Zwischen globalen Zwängen und individuellen Handlungsspielräumen. In: Altner G, Michelsen G (eds) Ethik und Nachhaltigkeit. Grundsatzfragen und Handlungsperspektiven im universitären Agendaprozess. VAS, Frankfurt a.M, pp 64–99

Sachs W (1994) Die vier E's. Merkposten für einen maß-vollen Wirtschaftsstil. In: Mayer J (ed) Strukturanpassung für den Norden. Modelle und Aktionspläne für eine global verträgliche Lebensweise in Deutschland. Evangelische Akademie Loccum, Rehburg-Loccum, pp 95–100

Skidelsky R, Skidelsky E (2013) How much is enough? Money and the good life. Penguin, London

Smith PB, Max-Neef M (2011) Economics unmasked. From power and greed to compassion and the common good. UIT Cambridge, Totnes

Stengel O (2011) Suffizienz. Die Konsumgesellschaft in der ökologischen Krise. Oekom, Munich

Steurer R, Trattnigg R (2010) Nachhaltigkeit regieren: Eine Einleitung im Wissenschaft-Praxis Dialog. In: Steurer R, Trattnigg R (eds) Nachhaltigkeit regieren. Eine Bilanz zu Governance-Prinzipien und -Praktiken. Oekom, Munich, pp 15–32

Wackernagel M, Reese W (1997) Unser ökologischer Fussabdruck. Wie der Mensch Einfluss auf die Umwelt nimmt. Springer Basel AG, Basel

Weber M (1958) The protestant ethic and the spirit of capitalism. Translated by Talcott Parsons. Scribner, New York

Wilkinson R, Pickett K (2009) The spirit level. Why greater equality makes societies stronger. Bloomsbury Press, London

Williams CW (1841) The combustion of coal and the prevention of smoke: chemically and practically considered, 2nd edn. J. Weale, London

Klaus Mathis Lucerne. Full Professor of Public Law, Law of the Sustainable Economy, and Philosophy of Law at the University of Lucerne. CH-6002 Lucerne, Frohburgstrasse 3, P.O. Box 4466, Tel. + 41 (0)41 229 53 80; Fax + 41 (0)41 229 53 97. klaus.mathis@unilu.ch. Fields of Interest: Public Law (Law of Sustainable Development, Economic Constitutional Law), Economic Analysis of Law, Legal Philosophy and Legal Theory.

Energy Transition Law and Economics

Sebastian Heselhaus

Abstract The author analyses the extent to which the energy sector in Europe is suitable for a law and economics approach, especially regarding a policy of energy transition. To this end, the author provides first a short historic overview of energy transitions in the past and of their framework in Europe. Second, the author analyses the aspects of political sovereignty connected with the supply of energy. Third, the legal and political framework for the regulation of the energy sector pursuing an energy transition in the European Union, its Member State Germany, and in Switzerland with the aim to reduce carbon dioxide emissions are analysed in detail. Besides the European Union, a specific focus is placed on Germany and Switzerland because both countries have chosen to end the use of nuclear energy as well. Thus, they will have to implement an even broader energy transition. The author shows how individual choices by the market participants are often rendered impossible because of government intervention. Furthermore, he depicts how attempts to liberalise the energy market are faced with approaches to utilise the remains of the former monopoly like structure of the market for the regulatory objectives of energy transitions. This leads to the question whether the transaction-based approaches of traditional and modern economics remain beneficial in analysing energy law.

1 Costs of the Energy Transition

The European Union has committed itself to an energy transition to fulfil its obligations under the so-called Paris Agreement on combating climate change.[1] In 2017, US-President Trump declared the withdrawal of the USA from the agreement.

[1]United Nations Framework Convention on Climate Change (UNFCCC), Decision 1/CP.21, accessible at http://unfccc.int/resource/docs/2015/cop21/eng/10a01.pdf [accessed 3 October 2017].

S. Heselhaus (✉)
Faculty of Law, University of Lucerne, Lucerne, Switzerland
e-mail: sebastian.heselhaus@unilu.ch

K. Mathis, B. R. Huber (eds.), *Energy Law and Economics*, Economic Analysis of Law in European Legal Scholarship 5, https://doi.org/10.1007/978-3-319-74636-4_2

The withdrawal will take effect in November 2020, according to the procedural rules of the Paris agreement.[2] The European Union and its Member States are anxiously waiting whether this announcement will attract other states to withdraw as well. However, up to now, this move does not seem to have been followed by other State parties. The Paris Agreement does not expressly call for an energy transition, but obliges State parties to reduce their CO_2-emissions. Since the energy sector is a pivotal sector in achieving this goal, there is a strong incentive to intensify the decarbonisation of energy. Decarbonisation in this sense means the phasing out of fossil fuels emitting carbon dioxide as a main source of energy supply.

Although not called for by strategies for combating climate change, some states are planning or already have in place policies for an exit from nuclear energy as well. This development is closely linked to the incident at the Fukushima Power Plant in Japan in March 2011, which called into question political consensuses on the risk assessment of nuclear energy. In these states, such as Switzerland[3] and Germany,[4] the combination of policies of decarbonisation and of exiting from nuclear energy is severely limiting the governments choices to of other sources of energy. Consequently, they will have to replace considerable parts of their energy resources.[5] Therefore, all State parties to the Paris Agreement—and even some more—will have to considerably increase the supply of energy from renewable resources.

Currently, relying on renewable energy is more expensive than relying on fossil fuels or on nuclear power from plants already in operation.[6] Therefore, from the perspective of the individual homo economicus, as the preferred yardstick of law and economics, such an energy transition seems to be a truly irrational undertaking, which would resist a law and economics analysis at first glance. In the international energy market, in economic terms the individual would be far better off buying energy from fossil fuels than from renewables. Consequently, the law and economics analysis of energy transition seems to be looking for rationality in a rather irrational situation. This situation is well illustrated by the learned colleagues from economic sciences doing research in the Swiss Competence Center for Energy Research named CREST. Basically, they are asked to explain to the public why it should be economically feasible to buy the more expensive energy instead of taking advantage of the cheaper option on the market. Obviously, there is a caveat to this black and white painting: strategies of decarbonisation and exit from nuclear energy follow a clear rationality with reference to climate change and possible risks as well as consequences of nuclear energy. However, these perspectives remain outside the view of the individual market participant in the original setting of law and

[2]Article 28 of the Paris Agreement requires a written withdrawal after a waiting period of 3 years.

[3]Article 12a of the revised Nuclear Energy Act.

[4]§ 7 Atomic Energy Act.

[5]In Switzerland, nuclear energy accounted for 33.5% of the total electricity production in 2015, see Bundesamt für Energie (2016), p. 37. In Germany, that share was 14% in 2015, see Statistisches Bundesamt (2016), p. 22.

[6]Fraunhofer ISE (2013), p. 2.

economics, looking at the allocation of goods and rights by bargaining between private persons.

Nevertheless, at second glance, the issue of energy transition law and economics is very rewarding. First, the field of energy policy is inherently governed by strategic considerations, which go beyond a mere macro-economic analysis and are partly enshrined in the constitutional law framework applicable. Thus, it offers an opportunity to give an example of how sensible it is to include the lawyer's view in an economic analysis of the law. Second, within this given framework, energy transition is about influencing people, their choice of energy and of energy efficiency, while cheaper options might be available on the market. Therefore, the elasticity of prices and the economic availability of energy become a key issue in these policies.

This article will show that the current energy transition is not the first attempt at an economically questionable energy transition. Further, since energy policy is an area in which the perspective of an individual market participant is not prevailing, but is outweighed by a macroeconomic view including political preferences of societies, it seems to be a fruitful area to show that one can explore insights from a legal perspective on (energy) law and economics. Furthermore, we will demonstrate that even in the framework of a forced energy transition together with the public interest in safeguarding energy supply there is room for governance options, which need to be analysed with reference to their economic impacts. In this respect law and economics in its perception as the economic analysis of law is a very helpful tool.

2 A Short History of Energy Transitions

For millenniums the main resource for energy has been wood,[7] which leaves charcoal after the process of burning, a secondary resource not very much appreciated at that time because of its dust. It was not until the eighteenth century that, with the industrial revolution incited by the invention of the steam engine, coal took over as the main energy resource[8]: the first energy transition. Steam power enabled people to pump groundwater from coal occurring in the deep layers of the earth and to exploit this resource with higher energy efficiency than wood.[9] Although restricted to certain regional areas, the new energy resource was available easily enough on the market to create a demand and accelerate further development. In this case, the growth in industries stimulated the growing demand for the new energy resource. At the same time and after years of excessive exploitation of wood, the former main energy resource faced a severe shortage in supply. Not least, in comparison coal is the far more efficient energy resource. Basically, at that time the market was ready to

[7]Bithas and Kalimeris (2015), p. 6.

[8]Bithas and Kalimeris (2015), p. 7 et seq.

[9]Bithas and Kalimeris (2015), p. 7.

accept a transition to a new energy resource without legislation necessary to force people to turn towards the new resource.

However, even in that situation a regulatory intervention was necessary. As coal is a natural resource, many states at that time had laws in action stating the state's property to these resources as states were tempted to get hold of the new resources by subjecting them to state property.[10] Even nowadays, based on the public law setting for the exploitation of coal, German villages are being deconstructed to make way for the excavation of lignite.[11]

Starting in 1910, the second energy transition took place, introducing oil and gas to the market, two energy resources even more efficient than coal. Again, the introduction was accompanied by a new industrial invention, the motorcar powered by a combustion engine. The advantages of oil—after treatment in a refinery—included a higher energy density, easy transportation and a cleaner combustion. Therefore, it was again not necessary to open the markets to the new energy resource by regulation.

Then in 1973, the third energy transition was triggered by the first oil crisis.[12] This was the first energy transition not driven bottom-up by developments in technology or in the market,[13] but by strategic considerations of the Western industrialised states. These states were—with only few exceptions—depending heavily on the import of oil from abroad, especially from countries aligning in the OPEC and influencing the market mechanisms of price building. Western industrialised economies, thus, opted for the introduction of nuclear energy to the energy market. This new energy resource was quite cost-intensive, since it took considerable financial resources to develop the technology for the peaceful use of nuclear resources. Furthermore, the new technology was expensive regarding the installation of nuclear power plants. Finally, the new technology carried with it the burden of the problems posed by the decommissioning of facilities after their lifetime expired. However, once in operation, the production of energy was affordable, since the public heavily financed research and development of nuclear energy, not at least in the legal framework of the former European Atomic Energy Community, without recovering these costs in the consumer prices of that energy.

Today, this situation has not fundamentally changed. With the recent low prices for oil and gas, projects of rebuilding nuclear energy plants such as Hinckley Point C in the United Kingdom rely on subsidies from the government. In that specific case, the subsidies concern not only the construction of the nuclear power plant, but also a guarantee of prices during the time of operation.[14] The granting of the subsidies has

---

[10]For a critical review of state property concerning natural resources, see Lazarus (1986).

[11]For the widely discussed case of the village Horno, see Baer (1997). Such expropriations are governed by federal law, §§ 77 et seqq. Federal Mining Act, and the specific expropriation is stipulated in a separate statute.

[12]See Akins (1973).

[13]It is undisputed that the shortage in supply was affecting the market forces, but that in itself was a regulatory decision by the OPEC-countries.

[14]For a discussion of the subsidies granted to this project, see Cernoch and Zapletalová (2015).

been challenged before the European courts. A first claim issued by NGOs has been declared inadmissible by the European Court of First Instance,[15] but will ultimately be decided by the European Court of Justice.[16] Also, there is still a lawsuit by Austria pending with the European Court of First Instance.[17]

So, the energy transition pursued by Switzerland and Germany is not the first transition that must be implemented against the private market forces. There are certain similarities to the previous transition to nuclear energy, since the policy decision towards the present energy transition is being fuelled by externalities, i.e. climate change and the new assessment of risks of nuclear energy. But, there are differences as well to be considered. The new energy transition calls for a different approach, since the renewable energies pose different challenges. Although the necessary construction of the respective power plants is less expensive than the installation of nuclear power plants, the production costs are considerably higher. With the given low price for oil and gas over the last years, without state interference renewable energies are not competitive in the market. Furthermore, the construction of buildings like tall wind power plants or massive dams for hydropower plants collides with other interests of land use. Not at least, wind, solar and hydro energy are dependent on preconditions in nature limiting their consistency in supply over time, thus, challenging the objective of secured energy supply. Therefore, the energy transition to a low carbon industry resp. society is an unprecedented challenge to policymakers. In the language of economics, it calls for the internalisation of several externalities, i.e. climate change and security of supply.

3 Policy Choices: The Legal/Constitutional Framework

3.1 Energy Supply and Sovereignty

The choices of individual consumers in the energy market are limited by the policy choices reflecting certain objectives of societies. On an abstract level, there is a clear consensus that energy supply is a main interest, indeed a core interest of states. Undoubtedly, securing energy supply is a main task of the modern welfare state. Energy is the pulse of industry. Furthermore, a stable energy supply is a precondition for defending sovereignty, in the ultimate situation by military means. In the 1970s European countries stored oil reserves for at least 3 months with the objective not to lose military and economic options in case of oil embargos by the OPEC countries. In the European Union's constitutional law, this is reflected by Article 192(2) TFEU, which subjects any regulations affecting the choice of Member States on their energy resources to unanimity in the Council of the European Union, thus providing for a

[15]Case no. T-382/15, ECLI: EU:T:2016:589.

[16]Case no. C-640/16 P.

[17]Case no. T-356/15.

veto position for every Member State. However, the approaches to the quest for a new energy supply mix differ considerably between the states.

3.2 Policy Choices in Europe

3.2.1 Market Liberalisation

Not least because of the strategic and normative objective of security of energy supply within their territory, European states have developed monopoly-like structures in the energy market. This is especially true regarding the so-called natural monopoly of the electricity grid or net, respectively.[18] Further, the access to energy from foreign countries has been under constant scrutiny by governments. A recent example is the North Stream Pipeline through the Baltic Sea bypassing Poland and Ukraine on its way from Russia to Germany. In the past, there have been disputes between Russia and Ukraine on the unrestricted transporting of gas through land-based pipelines using the territory of Ukraine.

Furthermore, even inside the territory of a state, quite often the monopoly-like structure has been used to split off markets between competing companies. Regions have been allocated to specific energy supply companies with guaranteed preferential access to their customers.

With a certain time lag, the European Union has undertaken to establish a common, single energy market. Step by step, the European Commission has tackled the issue of establishing a free market in the area of energy. This objective led to four regulatory packages of market liberalisation and was written into the Union's constitution—Article 194 TFEU—in the Lisbon Treaty of 2009. The first "energy package" mainly consisted of Directive 96/92/EC on the internal electricity market[19] and Directive 98/30/EC on the internal natural gas market.[20] It established a framework for third party access to the energy grids, but left the Member States a considerable margin of discretion in how to accomplish this. The second "energy package" replaced those directives with Directive 2003/54/EC on the internal electricity market[21] and Directive 2003/55/EC on the internal natural gas market[22] and called for the unbundling of energy companies, separating the grid operation from the sales business. The third "energy package" featured Directive 2009/72/EC on the internal electricity market[23] and Directive 2009/73/EC on the internal natural

[18]For Switzerland, see BVGer A-7561/2015, E. 4.3.; for Germany BGH KVR 27/04, BeckRS 2005, 08522.

[19]OJ 1997 L 27/20.

[20]OJ 1998 L 204/1.

[21]OJ 2003 L 176/37.

[22]OJ 2003 L 176/57.

[23]OJ 2009 L 211/55.

gas market.[24] It introduced further unbundling requirements, including "ownership unbundling", and provided for the establishment of National Regulatory Agencies. The "Winter Package" of November 2016[25] has been referred to as a "fourth energy package".[26] However, the proposed measures of the "Winter Package" have yet to be implemented. Today, basically all consumers can choose their providers from within the European Union's Member States.

Although European Union law has facilitated trans-boundary supply, the supply by domestic companies is in fact still prevailing. For instance, in Germany, the national electricity production was 648.4 TWh, while only 27 TWh of electricity were imported in 2016.[27]

While under these political restraints, since the 1990s the European Union has promoted deregulation and open markets in the energy sector, a specific political design for the energy sector has been developed in a different policy sector: the fight against climate change under the European Union environmental policy. Climate change policy has not only been a midwife to the birth of a European Union energy policy of its own, but has implemented its genes into the new European Union competence for energy policy of 2009 in Article 194(1) TFEU "with regard for the need to preserve and improve the environment".

In Switzerland, the policy of market liberalisation suffered a major setback because of a people's referendum in 2002. At that time, the electricity market in Switzerland was divided up into natural monopolies, which served their own grid area. This meant that consumers did not have the ability to choose their electricity supplier.[28] The Electricity Market Act (*Elektrizitätsmarkgesetz*) was supposed to fully liberalise the Swiss electricity market to comply with EU market rules as a prerequisite for a future bilateral agreement in this sector.[29] However, the Swiss people rejected it in the referendum of 2002.[30]

Thus, the possibility of choosing the supplier was only introduced in 2009, and was limited to large-scale consumers only, i.e. with an energy consumption of 100 MWh per year or above. This was introduced in the new Electricity Supply Act (*Stromversorgungsgesetz*).[31] Also, the Electricity Supply Act provides for third party access to the electricity grid. A second step in market liberalisation planned for 2014 has recently been postponed. In addition to large consumers, small consumers (including private households) were supposed to be able to choose their supplier as well. To alleviate the fears of private consumers as expressed by the failed referendum on the Electricity Market Act, the second liberalisation step would have left

---

[24]OJ 2009 L 211/94.

[25]See press release IP/16/4009.

[26]Scholtka and Martin (2017).

[27]BMWi (2017), p. 35 et seqq.

[28]Paetsch and Böck (2009), p. 1.

[29]BBl 1999 7370.

[30]BBl 2002 7821.

[31]SR 734.7.

small consumers the option of remaining with their regional supply with regulated tariffs.[32] It is currently unclear when this second step will take place. However, the transmission grids have been transferred to a private company called Swissgrid acting under the supervision of the federal regulatory authority ElCom. Previously, the Swiss transmission grid was divided into eight areas operated by the largest Swiss electricity supply companies. These and other companies are now shareholders of Swissgrid. While Swissgrid had already coordinated the eight areas since 2006, the Swiss transmission grid was only transferred into Swissgrid's property in 2013.

In comparison, both Switzerland and the European Union have undertaken to liberalise their energy markets at least to some extent. From a law and economics perspective this move should be welcomed as a first step to giving more room for private choices instead of a regulatory approach. However, the setbacks and the delay on the way to that target show how resilient the regulatory approach is. Currently, the situation is still far from a free allocation of supply and demand of the traditional law and economics approach would prescribe. While the obstacles in the European Union give an example for the problems of market liberalisation between different countries, the Swiss example shows that even on the national level, restricting market forces is still a popular strategy. However, like in the European Union, in Switzerland the policy target to fight climate change has called for a comprehensive change in energy policy besides the market liberalisation strategies.

3.2.2 Climate Change and Carbon Free Energy

It is interesting to note, that in the European Union like in Switzerland there has been a coexistence of a market liberalisation approach calling for de-regulation or re-regulation, respectively, in a more market-based environment and a strictly regulatory approach pursuing the objective of fighting climate change, i.e. the decarbonization of the energy supply. While the first approach shows a weakening of the influence of sovereignty, the second is based on the sovereign choice of the people in Europe to pursue new objectives in the energy sector, which call for more regulatory approaches.

Under the Kyoto Protocol, which the European Union ratified in 2002 and Switzerland in 2003,[33] and its successor, the Paris Agreement, ratified by the European Union in 2016 and signed by Switzerland in the same year, the European Union like Switzerland adhered to a policy of fighting climate change and pursuing a decarbonisation of energy supply. Shortly before the Paris Agreement, the European Union presented its 2030 climate goals of an at least 40% greenhouse gas emission reduction for 2030 as well as renewable energy and energy

---

[32] BBl 2005 1611, p. 1621.

[33] http://unfccc.int/kyoto_protocol/status_of_ratification/items/2613.php [accessed 3 October 2017].

efficiency targets of at least 27%.[34] Switzerland plans to reduce its greenhouse gas emissions by 50% until 2030.[35]

These objectives call for a major transition in the energy sector in the European Union as well as in Switzerland. Thus, a regulatory approach is designed to interfere with the "free" allocation of energy demand and supply.

This objective is enshrined in the respective constitutions: Article 194(1) TFEU and Article 89(1) Swiss Federal Constitution call for an environment friendly energy supply and consumption. In Germany no such provision is found in the Basic Law. However, likewise para. 1 German Energy Economy Law addresses this issue. These provisions form a normative back up to the policy choice of decarbonisation with regard even to energy supply. For example, the new Swiss Energy Act (*Energiegesetz*),[36] which increases financial aid for renewable energy and calls for ambitious energy consumption reduction targets of 16% until 2020 and 43% until 2035, compared to year 2000 levels, has been based on Article 89(1) Swiss Federal Constitution.[37]

From a traditional Chicago style law and economics perspective, the situation in Europe is far removed from the original ideas of law and economics calling for a free allocation of goods and services, respectively, by private choices without regulatory interferences. However, a modern law and economics approach could focus on the strategies to include the costs of climate change in the energy market sector.[38] This has been labelled the internalisation of external costs. But obviously this has been introduced by regulation, not by individual choice.

3.2.3 Phasing Out Nuclear Energy

Furthermore, Switzerland and Germany have opted for another energy transition. After the incident in Fukushima in 2011 both countries introduced an exit from or a phasing out of nuclear energy, respectively. In Germany, nuclear power plants were successively taken from the grid. According to Article 7(1a) Nuclear Energy Act (*Atomgesetz*), the last nuclear power plant will have to cease operations by the end of 2022 at the latest.

In Switzerland, the phasing out of nuclear energy materialised first in the form of a political decision,[39] which later turned into a prohibition of the granting of new licenses by law.[40] But the remaining nuclear power plants will stay in operation as

---

[34]COM(2016) 110 final.

[35]BBl 2017 317, p. 330.

[36]BBl 2016 7683.

[37]BBl 2013 7561 p. 7578.

[38]For an approach to the internalisation of climate change costs, see Weitzman (2014).

[39]https://www.uvek.admin.ch/uvek/de/home/uvek/medien/medienmitteilungen.msg-id-38101.html [accessed 3 October 2017].

[40]Article 12a of the revised Nuclear Energy Act (Kernenergiegesetz), which has not yet entered into force.

long as that is regarded as being safe enough.[41] This approach has survived a referendum and thereby this has been—positively speaking—directly accepted by the Swiss people. Thus, in both countries, the refusal of nuclear energy has not been incorporated in the constitution, but in the energy laws. However, the new Swiss energy law can additionally rely on the extra legitimation it has obtained by the popular vote. Again, we find a regulatory interference precluding converse private choices.

With the renunciation of nuclear energy, both countries, Switzerland and Germany, follow the much earlier examples of Italy and Austria.[42] From a regional perspective it is interesting to note, that four neighbouring countries in the heart of Europe have thus decided to render the energy transition envisaged by decarbonisation even more complicated: despite the specific environmental challenges posed by nuclear energy with regards to radiation, it is undisputed that it provides carbon free energy.[43] As already pointed out, this objective puts extra pressure on the task of securing the energy supply, since energy from nuclear power plants has accounted for more than a third of the total energy supply in these countries. These additional issues create a strong temptation to restrict the only partly liberalised market or to make use of the non-liberalised parts to implement these policies without risking major negative repercussions on the industry. Consequently, this approach might jeopardise the recent progress made in opening the energy market to allow for more individual choices and thereby creating a more efficient energy market.

4 Examples of Limiting Individual Choices in the Energy Market

There are numerous examples of regulatory interferences with a free energy market in the case of the recent energy transition. The following are selected from the European Union strategy of decarbonisation as well as from specific issues in the Swiss and the German energy market design.

[41] Schmocker and Kalkhof (n.d.), p. 10 et seq.

[42] See Esposto (2008) for the Italian referendum of 1987 following the Tschernobyl disaster. In Austria, the ban of nuclear power was introduced in 1978 in the Federal Law on the Prohibition of the Use of Nuclear Fission for the Energy Supply in Austria, BGBl. Nr. 676/1978, following a popular vote against a specific power plant project.

[43] Buchdahl Roth and Jaramillo (2017). Of cause, there is a caveat regarding CO_2-emissions caused during the establishment of nuclear installations, but that objection equally could be raised against installations of renewable energies.

4.1 The Emissions Trading Scheme

Under the Kyoto Protocol as well as under the Paris Agreement, the European Union and Switzerland have accepted reduction targets for their CO_2-emissions to reduce global warming. However, the overall success of the Protocol has been in doubt from the start, since major high emissions countries, such as the United States, China or India, did not become State Parties to the Protocol. Canada withdrew from the Protocol some years ago. Nevertheless, the Protocol must be regarded as a cornerstone in the world's efforts to fight climate change, because it has established the principle of differentiated responsibility of industrialised countries for global warming.[44] The effort of the states bound by the Protocol paved the way for the newly industrialised countries to join the 2015 Paris Agreement. This agreement includes all industrialised states.[45] However, the United States have announced that they will leave the agreement as soon as this becomes possible under Article 28 of the Paris Agreement, under which the written notice could be submitted on 4 November 2019 at the earliest, and take effect no earlier than 4 November 2020.[46] In contrast, the "BRICS" countries (Brazil, Russia, India, China and South Africa), which have emitted more than 40% of worldwide carbon emissions in 2013, have pledged to reduce their emissions by 10 to 45% compared to the 2000s or, in the case of Russia, the 1990s.[47]

The Kyoto Protocol offered the Emissions Trading Scheme (ETS) as one of the instruments of choice alongside the genuine duty to reduce one's emissions, and other instruments. It will still be the instrument of choice for the European Union under the Paris Agreement.[48] The ETS is a market-based instrument. It sets a cap on the carbon dioxide emissions of a country by only granting a certain amount of emissions allowances equivalent to a certain amount of CO_2-emissions. From year to year, this amount will be reduced by requiring State parties to hand in a certain amount of allowances at the end of a given period. Both the European Union and Switzerland have established their own ETS, which are due to be joined into one in the future, granting the Swiss industry access to a broader market of allowances with lower prices. In doing so, they have passed their ETS duties under the international agreements on to their industries. Thus, allowances are distributed to enterprises, which are under the obligation to hand in a certain amount of allowances at the end of a certain period. To reach that objective, they either must reduce their emissions—by investing in emissions reduction or by improving their efficiency or simply by reducing their production—or they may buy allowances from other enterprises,

[44]"Common but differentiated responsibilities", see UNFCCC (2006), p. 23 et seqq.

[45]See the list of signatories at http://unfccc.int/paris_agreement/items/9444.php [accessed 3 October 2017].

[46]Cf. Plumer (2017).

[47]Liu et al. (2017), p. 490.

[48]European Council, Conclusions on 2030 Climate and Energy Policy Framework, SN 79/14, p. 2; IETA (2016), p. 3.

which do not need them anymore. This is possible because the ETS is based on the ability to buy and sell emissions allowances. This trading can be done not only throughout Europe, but with Kyoto Protocol state parties as well (so-called CDM, i.e. Clean Development Mechanism[49]), if a reduction of emissions is carried out there. Thus, it is possible to gain allowances at the cheapest possible price. From the perspective of law and economics it could be stated, that this mechanism provided for market participants with rights, i.e. the allowances, they were free to allocate between themselves. However, there are certain limits to the implementation of CDM, as the European Union ETS-directive only allows for the acceptance of CDM under the amendments made by the "Linking Directive" 2004/101/EC.[50] Under this Directive, the European Union ETS does not accept CDMs from nuclear power (Article 11a(3)(a) ETS-Directive). Further, CDMs in the sectors of land use, land use change, and forestry activities are not accepted (Article 11a(3)(b) ETS-Directive). Also, regarding large hydropower projects, Member States must ensure the adherence to relevant international criteria and guidelines to prevent negative environmental and social effects (Article 11b(6) ETS-Directive).

In evaluating the Kyoto Protocol and the Paris Agreement, one cannot but accept that the possibility of introducing an ETS has been the central instrument paving the way to a compromise on the common, but differentiated responsibility, because it allows the industrialised states, accepting a heavier burden of reduction targets to take on these duties at the lowest costs possible. This finding clearly departs from the view of many commentators, that the ETS should not be regarded as a genuine duty or option, respectively, under the Kyoto Protocol, because it allows for an externalisation of reduction efforts.[51] This assessment is underlined by the well-known fact, that in the European Union far too many allowances have been allocated to the industry in the first phase by the Member States putting the achievement of a noticeable reduction of emissions at risks.[52] Therefore, in the second phase the European Union has centralised the allocation of allowances with the European Commission.[53] It is a common blueprint of the integration process that a "misuse" of sovereign power in areas with a considerable leeway under the supremacy of European Union law will evidentially lead to a further rollback of national sovereignty and to another step in integration.

Not all sectors of industry have been made subject to the ETS. Right from the start, energy production installations were covered only above the performance of 20 mWh. This has only been changed since 2013 during the third phase, which includes all energy producers. The European General Court has accepted in a decision that the principle of equal treatment must be observed by the European Union legislator, but has given some room for gathering experiences in selected

[49] Article 12 Kyoto Protocol.

[50] OJ 2004 L 338/18.

[51] Cf. the criticism by Winter (2009), p. 296 et seq.

[52] Laing et al. (2013), p. 4.

[53] Article 10(1) EU ETS-Directive as amended by Directive 2009/29/EC.

areas in the starting phase.[54] From the viewpoint of law and economics it may be observed that not all market participants have been allocated the same rights.

Furthermore, there is an exemption for energy intensive industries, which are in strong competition with enterprises from countries not bound by the Kyoto Protocol. According to Article 10a ETS-Directive 2003/87/EC these enterprises will receive allowances for free. Officially, this has been branded as a response to carbon leakage, meaning that these enterprises might opt to shift their production into those non-party countries and thus escaping the emissions reductions targets of the Kyoto Protocol states. However, the likeness of a reallocation of the place of establishment and production has never been scrutinised on an individual basis. There is a list available of the enterprises benefitting from this exemption in Decision 2014/746/EU. Thus, it seems convincing, that the exemption is more because of economic competition than for environmental apprehensions. In the economic analysis it must be added, that this mechanism puts a higher stress on the other enterprises in the ETS, because the occurrence of allowances free of charge puts the overall price for allowances under pressure and thus diminishes the possible gains of companies selling allowances. So, although a market-based mechanism has been introduced, simultaneously a regulatory interference with the market was also introduced.

In comparison, in Switzerland, enterprises with an intense consumption of electricity are included in the Swiss ETS and they do not receive allowances for free. If they do not participate in the ETS, they will be subject to a sanction according to the CO_2-law.[55]

Furthermore, in Switzerland, all fossil fuel power plants primarily producing electricity, as well as plants primarily producing heat with a performance of more than 100 mWh seem to not be included in the Swiss ETS.[56] However, they are subject to a compensation duty, which is set up by individual contracts with the state authorities, requiring these companies to contribute to the reduction of emissions in other countries.[57] In the European Union ETS, electricity generators originally received free allowances. Starting with the third trading period, however, they will have to buy allowances.[58] There is a temporary derogation from this duty for electricity generators from eight Member States[59] under Article 10c ETS-Directive.

---

[54] EGC, case T-16/04, ECLI:EU:T:2010:54; Heselhaus (2014b), pp. 139–141.

[55] Article 21 CO_2-Law, SR 641.71.

[56] See the comment by the FOEN Swiss Federal Office for the Environment), https://www.bafu.admin.ch/bafu/de/home/themen/klima/fachinformationen/klimapolitik/emissionshandel/schweizer-emissionshandelssystem--ehs-/emissionshandelssystem--ehs---schritt-fuer-schritt.html [accessed 3 October 2017].

[57] Article 22 et seqq. CO_2-Law, Article 83 et seq. CO_2-Regulation (SR 641.711.).

[58] https://ec.europa.eu/clima/policies/ets/allowances/electricity_en [accessed 3 October 2017].

[59] These are new Member States that joined since 2004: Bulgaria, Cyprus, Czech Republic, Estonia, Hungary, Lithuania, Poland and Romania. Latvia and Malta would also have been eligible to use the derogation, but decided not waive this option.

4.2 Contributing to the Costs of the Supply Net

In Germany and in Switzerland energy consumers not only have to pay for consuming energy but for using the grids, the supply net, as well. This is established by § 21 Energy Economy Act (*Energiewirtschaftsgesetz*) in Germany and Article 14 Energy Supply Act (*Stromversorgungsgesetz*) in Switzerland. Currently, this results in an energy bill where the cost of the use of the grid equals the price for energy consumption.[60] This has always been a heavy burden on large-scale consumers. But, with rising prices because of the inclusion of more expensive electricity from renewable resources the pressure has risen. So in 2011, Germany set up a regulation (§ 19 para. 2 phrase 2 StromNEV (electricity net fee regulation)) exempting large-scale consumers from 7000 h of utilisation and a consumption of more than 10 GWh from the net fee. But this regulation has been declared void by the German Federal Court of Justice because the exemption was not in line with the corresponding law (§ 24 para. 1 no. 1 and 3 EnWG (Energy Economy Act)) allowing only for a reduction of the fee.[61] The recent version of the regulation offers an individual fee for large-scale consumers. Although a discount for large-scale consumers is common in free markets, in this case it is limited by regulation. Furthermore, the discount places an additional burden on other energy consumers who cannot escape the net fee, which will then be raised to bear the overall costs of the electricity net.

In Switzerland, there is no explicit reduction offered to large-scale consumers. However, in practice they receive their energy from a different net since they are connected to a higher level (maximum voltage) of the grids, which results in being charged lower costs. Furthermore, a large-scale consumer could be assigned to a group of customers with fees at a reduced rate, according to Article 14(3) StromVG (Electricity Supply Act), if that reflects their pattern of consumption. However, it must be noted, that other market participants cannot escape the system by simply turning to another provider. Overall, the regulatory approach seems to be twofold: On one side it tries to copy possible market behaviour and to influence the market by this, while on the other side it is limiting market behaviour.

4.3 Mechanism for Cost Allocation of Renewable Energies

Today, energy from renewable resources is more expensive than from fossil fuels. Therefore, to introduce renewables to the market, states force market participants to accept renewables despite the additional costs. So, in Germany and in Switzerland, electricity from renewable energies by law must be accepted by the providers of the

[60]For Switzerland, see https://www.swissgrid.ch/swissgrid/de/home/company/electricity_price.html. [accessed 3 October 2017]. For Germany, see Bundesnetzagentur (2016), p. 218.

[61]BGH EnVR 32/13, EnWZ 2016, 85.

net and the private energy supply enterprises. They must open their infrastructure for this energy. Furthermore, they must grant these producers a tariff comprising their costs for production, which are higher than electricity from other resources. In Switzerland, this is called the cost covering feed-in tariff.[62] The electricity supply enterprises from different regions must pool the feed-in of renewables and must share the costs across supply regions.[63] Since the costs thereof are higher, this duty leads to a rise in electricity prices. In Germany, although not explicitly ordered by the law, in practice, the energy supply enterprises pass on the extra costs to the end consumer.[64] This is only possible because of the monopoly-like structure of the net. The average end consumer has no choice to escape this so-called EEG-Umlage (the renewable energy law-cost allocation).

Furthermore, in Germany, according to §§ 63–64 Renewable Energy Act (EEG) when reaching a certain threshold of consumption and costs a company may claim a reduction of the allocation fee. Officially this too is explained by reasons of international competition. Only certain large-scale consumers are eligible to receive these advantages. But in practice, not all enterprises receiving this advantage actually face international competition. As an economic consequence, the burden for the average consumer must be raised to reach full compensation for the additional costs of electricity from renewable resources.

As the passing on of the additional costs is not explicitly ordered by law, Germany has argued that this does not amount to a government grant and would not come under the scrutiny of the European Commission in the area of competition law. The Commission has objected and brought the case before the European General Court. The Court upheld the Commission's view[65] and held that both the financial aid for the renewable energy producers as well as the funding mechanism have been mandated by law and can therefore be attributed to the German Government.[66] However, the Commission has approved the grant for reasons of protection of the environment, i.e. fighting climate change with decision (EU) 2015/1585. A judgment by the European Court of Justice acting in second instance is being awaited.[67] While the Commission has approved the measure, Germany seems intent on receiving a fundamental decision on the state aid character of its renewable energy support scheme.

In Switzerland, according to Article 15b^{bis} EnG, Article 3m EnV a similar mechanism is in place. Large-scale consumers, i.e. with costs for electricity of

---

[62]Article 19 et seqq. of the revised Energy Act (Energiegesetz).

[63]For Germany, see Lippert and Kindler (2017), p. 258. In Switzerland, the fee for the funding of renewable energy is governed at the federal level, Article 37 of the revised Energy Act.

[64]German law mandates that the transmission systems operators charge the extra costs to the electricity supply companies that deliver to the end consumers, § 60 Renewable Energy Act (EEG). In practice, these costs are then charged to the end consumers, Lippert and Kindler (2017), p. 258.

[65]EGC, case T-47/15, ECLI:EU:T:2016:281.

[66]EGC, case T-47/15, para. 40.

[67]ECJ, case C-405/16 P.

more than 10% of their gross value added can apply for a refund of the extra net fee amount. The reduction only takes place when the extra net fee is above 20,000 Swiss Francs a year.[68] The companies have to enter into an agreement with the Swiss Federal Office of Energy (SFOE), obliging them to become more energy efficient.[69] To this end, the energy consumer has to collaborate with one of two private organisations stipulated by the SFOE[70] The SFOE sets a final efficiency goal and then calculates a "pathway" to that goal, with annual interim goals.[71] Again, the average consumer has no choice but to bear his share of these refunds when paying his energy bill.

4.4 Exclusion of Foreign Electricity Producers from the Cost Covering Feed-in Tariff

If according to state regulation higher prices for renewable energies must be accepted by providers and, consequently, by end consumers, this attracts other producers of renewable energy from abroad trying to take advantage of these provisions. In Germany, to exclude these competitors, the cost covering feed-in tariff is only available for producers of energy from renewable energy resources, if the production takes place within the German territory (§ 5 para. 1 EEG 2017). But the legitimacy of an exclusion like that, affecting competitors from other European Union Member States, is rather doubtful under European Union law. Basically, the fundamental freedoms enshrined in EU primary law prohibit a discrimination of persons from other Member States. So at first glance, it was probable that the exclusion of companies from European Union Member States from the feed-in tariff would be declared void by the European Court of Justice, if challenged.

Only recently, a very similar issue has been brought before the European Court of Justice. In case C-573/12[72] the company Alands Vindkraft AB asked Sweden to hand out so-called green certificates for electricity from renewable sources produced in a wind farm in Aland in Finland. These certificates can be used to comply with the quota of renewable energy under Swedish laws.[73] The applicable European Union directive left it to the Member States, if they wanted to restrict advantages granted to electricity produced from renewables in their territory.[74] Acting within this margin for national consideration Sweden came under the radar of the fundamental freedom of goods, since it is settled European Union case law that electricity is regarded as a

[68] Article 15bbis(2)(c) EnG.

[69] Article 3m(1) EnV.

[70] Cleantech Agentur Schweiz (act) and Energieagentur der Wirtschaft (EnAW).

[71] For details, see SFOE (2015).

[72] ECJ, case C-573/12, ECLI:EU:C:2014:2037.

[73] ECJ, case C-573/12, para. 11 et seqq.

[74] Article 3(3) Directive 2009/28/EC, OJ 2009 L 140/16.

commercial good. Consequently, the European Court of Justice had to decide whether the Swedish law amounted to a forbidden discrimination of companies from other Member States. In a quite dubious phrase taken from the much debated PreussenElektra decision the Court stated that "in the current state of [Eu] law", it is not forbidden for Member States to promote the production of electricity from renewables only in their territory.[75] This phrase leaves a broad margin for interpreting the decision in search of the legal reasoning behind it. A thorough analysis of this decision will have to keep in mind the national interest in providing for security of energy supply and likewise the sovereign right to choose the sources of energy as stated above. At the recent state of the establishment of a European Union energy market, if a Member State would rely on the production of renewable energy from abroad, it is not in the position to secure a durable production thereof, while in its own territory it has more instruments available to promote this objective. Transposing this decision to the issue at hand, the exclusion of foreign electricity producers from the cost covering feed-in tariff seems to be justifiable under the fundamental freedoms. The example shows how strong the objective of security of energy supply and the sovereign right of choice between energy resources influence are and how they interfere with the energy market in the European Union. This leads to challenges when applying a law and economics approach to energy law.

4.5 Allocating the Exit from Nuclear Energy Costs

In an energy market, the costs of energy is set up by the production of energy, i.e. the building of the necessary installations and the costs for running the installation. Further, one must add the costs of decommissioning the installation after the end of its operation. While the latter costs are negligible for most energy resources, they are of a larger dimension in the case of nuclear energy, because of the need to safely dispose of the radioactive material. So, from a perspective of competition, the costs for decommissioning nuclear power plants are important.

It is no surprise that these costs and their allocation have come under the scrutiny by the European Union, since the regulatory design of decommissioning might influence the competition between market participants in different Member States. Despite the importance of these costs for energy prices, the European Union has only issued recommendations on this issue.[76] Specifically, it is recommended that the "polluter pays" principle is fully applied throughout the decommissioning process.[77] Also, the European Union recommends that nuclear power plant operators should set

[75]ECJ, case C-379/98, ECLI: EU: 2001: 160, para. 81.

[76]Commission Recommendation on the management of financial resources for the decommissioning of nuclear installations, spent fuel and radioactive waste, 2006/851/Euratom, OJ 2006 L 330/31.

[77]Section 3 para. 3 Recommendation 2006/851/Euratom.

up adequate decommissioning funds based on their revenues over the designed lifetime.[78] If the actual decommissioning costs exceed the estimated costs, the additional costs should be paid by the operator.[79]

The issue of costs of decommissioning nuclear power plants becomes even more important, if a state chooses an immediate opt-out of nuclear energy, like the exit from nuclear energy in Germany. In this case, producers might argue that they were not allowed to realise all their possible prospects from producing nuclear energy during the possible lifetime of their installations, thus leaving them with a financial burden because of the decommissioning. Many producers have threatened to claim for compensation under expropriation rules. This has been the case in Germany and in 2017, the German Federal Constitutional Court has ruled in favour of the producers.[80] However, the decision was based on peculiarities of the German situation. Originally there was a consensus between the ruling political parties and the energy industry that an exit from nuclear power should take place.[81] Later, this decision was reversed by the Conservative Party and specific extensions to the operational life were embedded in the Nuclear Energy Act.[82] This included a certain amount of electricity that would still be allowed to be produced by nuclear energy ("exit from the exit"). After the catastrophic events in Fukushima, the same Administration then reversed its former decision, again stipulating an exit from nuclear energy.[83] This decision frustrated the investments made by the operators in light of the formerly extended operational life and the assurances with regarded to the remaining amount of electricity to be produced.

Although the producers of nuclear energy in Germany must be compensated for the exit from nuclear energy, they further called for governmental assistance in lowering the costs of decommissioning. An economic analysis of the situation must be undertaken on an individual basis. The installations run by the Swedish owned company Vattenfall were each established as separate legal entities. So in case of insolvency because of the costs for decommissioning being too high, they would simply not be able to fulfil their obligations and in the end, the German State would have to step in. The other German producers initially did not take advantage of a legal construction like that. So later, some tried to split their enterprises into two legal entities, with one carrying the sole responsibility for all nuclear installations. This meant that they reached a similar "solution" to Vattenfall, and in the case of

[78] Section 5 para. 7 Recommendation 2006/851/Euratom.

[79] Section 6 para. 13 Recommendation 2006/851/Euratom.

[80] BVerfG, 1 BvR 2821/11, 1 BvR 321/12, 1 BvR 1456/12. The court ruled that the exit from nuclear energy was mostly in accordance with the constitution, but granted financial compensation to the operators.

[81] Agreement between the Federal Government and Electricity Supply Companies (Vereinbarung zwischen der Bundesregierung und den Energieversorgungsunternehmen vom 14 Juni 2000), http://www.bmub.bund.de/fileadmin/bmu-import/files/pdfs/allgemein/application/pdf/atomkonsens.pdf [accessed 3 October 2017].

[82] 11th Act for the revision of the Nuclear Energy Act, BGBl. 2010 I, p. 1814.

[83] 13th Act for the revision of the Nuclear Energy Act, BGBl. 2011 I, p. 1704.

insolvency they also shifted the financial burden to the German State. Instead of interfering with these plans by regulation, the German Government reached a compromise with these producers. This compromise has now become law.[84] As its main consequence, the Federal Government will take on the responsibility for the safe long-term storage of nuclear waste. In return, the nuclear power plant operators pledge to transfer roughly 23.55 billion Euros to a fund for the financing of such storage. Also, the nuclear plant operators remain responsible for the decommissioning and demolition of the plants. Again, this case is a clear example of governmental interference with the market far away from the approaches of law and economics, which promote free markets without regulation.

In Switzerland there is no immediate exit from nuclear power enacted by the legislator, but only a phasing out, which prohibits the authorisation to build any new plants, but leave existing ones untouched.[85] However, with regard to the scheduled lifetime of nuclear installations, all Swiss nuclear power plants will eventually be decommissioned over the next 2–10 years.[86] The operations of two plants have already been stopped.[87] Consequently, there is no legal issue of expropriation in Switzerland with regard to the phasing out of nuclear energy. But the general issue of bearing the costs of decommissioning of the power plants persists. In Switzerland, all the bigger energy suppliers are stakeholders in the Swiss nuclear power plants.[88] Since under the Swiss Energy Strategy 2050 these are due to be taken from the net after reaching the limit of a secure runtime without the option for replacing them by new nuclear power plants, the economic prospects of these enterprises have been in decline, since they will face costs of decommissioning without the option of selling electricity from nuclear energy any further. Unlike Germany, the Swiss Government has not entered into an agreement with the producers so far. In Switzerland, the nuclear power plant operators must be insured against damages resulting from the nuclear power plant's operation or the transport of nuclear material.[89] Also, nuclear power plant operators must make payments to a fund specifically set up to bear the costs of decommissioning and nuclear waste storage.[90]

---

[84]Gesetz zur Neuordnung der Verantwortung in der kerntechnischen Entsorgung, BGBl. 2017 I p. 14, 1222.

[85]Article 12a of the revised Nuclear Energy Act.

[86]The first decision to decommission a nuclear power plant has already been made concerning the plant Mühleberg and will take effect in 2019, see https://www.bkw.ch/de/ueber-bkw/unsere-infrastruktur/kernkraftwerk-muehleberg/stilllegung/uebersicht/#Home [accessed 3 October 2017].

[87]The nuclear power plant of Beznau I has currently halted production. The plant Leibstadt did not produce electricity for 6 months and has now started producing electricity again, see Neue Zürcher Zeitung. 20 February 2017. https://www.nzz.ch/schweiz/schweizer-atomkraftwerk-leibstadt-wieder-am-netz-ld.146724 [accessed 3 October 2017].

[88]The five commercial plants are owned by AEW, Alpiq, Axpo, BKW, CKW, EWB and EWZ. Some of the plants are co-owned by several of these companies.

[89]Article 11 Kernenergiehaftungsgesetz, SR 732.44.

[90]Verordnung über den Stilllegungsfonds und den Entsorgungsfonds für Kernanlagen, SR 732.17.

It might be tempting for the Swiss energy suppliers to take advantage of the partially liberalised energy consumption market in Switzerland by trying to gain more money from the small-scale consumers, who are currently not allowed to change their supplier. In fact, because of various different reasons, several suppliers have done so. But in 2016, this practice was stopped by the Swiss Federal Court, obligating them to allocate any rise in prices equally between small- and large-scale consumers.[91] This decision will effectively lead to further restrictions as the large-scale consumers are legally allowed to change their supplier and will not hesitate to do so. So the leeway for raising prices in practice will be rather narrow. Once the market forces are awakened they will react to market incentives. The decision of the Swiss Federal Court has been criticised by the electricity suppliers for placing disadvantages on Swiss suppliers in competition with foreign suppliers regarding large-scale consumers.[92] This argument could be persuasive regarding decommissioning, if both, Swiss and foreign suppliers include a comparable level of costs. The rules vary in all Member States of the European Union.[93] From the law and economics perspective this argument is an interesting example of industry trying to exploit market restrictions to realise equal market conditions.

5 Prospects for a Law and Economics Approach?

This overview has illustrated how much the energy sector is under the influence of interests of sovereignty, which affect the energy production and supply. In the recent past there have been some attempts to break down the monopoly-like structure of the energy grids and to introduce some competition. However, the examples show that implementing an energy transition tempts the legislator to take advantage of the not fully liberalised aspects of the energy market. From this point of view, energy policy in the European Union, Germany and Switzerland is rather far removed from the original ideas of the Chicago style law and economics. Under the circumstances resulting from the recent energy transition and the still existing fragments of the former monopoly-like structure of the energy distribution net, consumer choices are severely limited, thus hardly enabling them to enter into negotiations on the allocation of their rights as promoted by the approach of law and economics. But even the school of behavioural law and economics will have its problems in designing an alternative market in the energy sector.[94] Likewise, an economic analysis of law from the viewpoint of the individual consumer as in consumer law will have to face

---

[91] BGE 142 II 451.

[92] Cf. http://www.evupartners.ch/wie-weiter-mit-der-regulierung-der-grundversorgung/ [accessed 3 October 2017].

[93] See European Commission, SWD(2013) 59 final, p. 6 et seqq.

[94] For a discussion of behavioural law and economics in an energy market context, see Pollitt and Shaorshadze (2011).

severe shortcomings as it will struggle to take into consideration the public interests sufficiently.[95]

Notwithstanding, it must be pointed out that the interferences with the market described above mostly take place in the shadow of the monopoly-like structure of the energy distribution grid. But this does not occur to the same extent in other areas such as the production of energy, the consumption and the selling of energy, and especially not in the stock exchanges for renewables. For example, while the electricity grid itself remains a natural monopoly, many companies can now offer electricity to consumers in the same area because of third party access rules.

Furthermore, there is a certain threshold to regulatory interferences. Energy still must be affordable for private households and commercial enterprises. So all the restrictions to the energy market mentioned above should surely be analysed for their economical impacts. A cost-benefit-analysis for these interferences with the energy market is required and, indeed, in all the countries affected carried out in practice. A consumer law approach could bring some insights to this evaluation, if it introduces the effects on households in addition to the usual macroeconomic approaches.

6 The Legal Duty for an Economic Analysis

The necessity of a cost-benefit-analysis is not only a political or an academic demand, but a legal precondition: Article 89 Swiss Federal Constitution sets up the objective of an economic, cost effective supply of energy. This goal relates to the overall national economy[96] and does not imply a "cheap", but an economically optimal energy supply.[97] It considers the effects on productivity and growth, employment levels, price levels and the public finances.[98]

In the European Union, Article 194 TFEU does not explicitly provide for a similar objective. However, in developing a European energy strategy the European Commission has taken the position that a secure supply of energy must be interpreted as a secure supply at affordable costs. This means that the traditional, state-centred view on the energy market has been supplemented by a consumer-specific focus.[99]

Lastly, the German Article 1(1) Energy Economy Act (Energiewirtschaftsgesetz) calls for a reasonably priced and consumer-friendly supply of energy. The goal of a reasonably priced energy supply concerns the rational and efficient supply as promoted by sufficient competition.[100] However, some authors suggest that it does

[95]See to approaches to consumer welfare in Esposito and de Almeida (2018).
[96]Schaffhauser and Uhlmann (2014), para. 7.
[97]BBl 1988 I 337, p. 376.
[98]BBl 1988 I 337, p. 376.
[99]Heselhaus (2014a), p. 207.
[100]Theobald (2017), para. 19.

not call for specific provisions to address the socially disadvantaged and their access to affordable energy beyond the regular price levels.[101]

So in the end, although the energy sector in Europe seems to be rather remote from the approaches of law and economics, it is the law demanding an economic analysis of the impact of regulatory interferences with the energy market. And that is even more the case in countries pursuing an energy transition like decarbonisation or an additional exit from nuclear energy.

Acknowledgement The author likes to thank Ass. iur. Markus Schreiber, University of Lucerne, for assisting in research and analytical discussions.

References

Akins JE (1973) The oil crisis: this time the wolf is here. Foreign Aff 51:462–490

Baer S (1997) Zum "Recht auf Heimat" - Art. 11 GG und Umsiedlungen zugunsten des Braunkohletagebaus. Neue Zeitschrift für Verwaltungsrecht 16:27–33

Bithas K, Kalimeris P (2015) Revisiting the energy-development link. Evidence from the 20th century for knowledge-based and developing economies. Springer, Heidelberg

Buchdahl Roth M, Jaramillo P (2017) Going nuclear for climate mitigation: an analysis of the cost effectiveness of preserving existing U.S. nuclear power plants as a carbon avoidance strategy. Energy 131:67–77

Bundesamt für Energie (2016) Gesamtenergiestatistik 2015. Berne

Bundesministerium für Wirtschaft und Energie (BMWi) (2017) Energiedaten: Gesamtausgabe. Bonn, Berlin

Bundesnetzagentur (2016) Monitoringbericht 2016. Bonn

Cernoch F, Zapletalová V (2015) Hinkley point C: a new chance for nuclear power plant construction in central Europe? Energy Policy 83:165–168

Esposito F, de Almeida L (2018) A shocking truth for law and economics: consumer welfare explains the internal market for electricity better than total welfare. In: Mathis K, Huber BR (eds) Energy law and economics. Springer, Cham. (this volume)

Esposto S (2008) The possible role of nuclear energy in Italy. Energy Policy 36:1584–1588

Fraunhofer ISE (2013) Stromgestehungskosten Erneuerbare Energien. Freiburg

Heselhaus S (2014a) Aktuelle Entwicklungen im Europäischen Energierecht. Schweizerisches Jahrbuch für Europarecht 2013/2014:201–221

Heselhaus S (2014b) Differenzierungen im Klima- und Energierecht vor den europäischen Gerichten – Emissionshandelssystem und erneuerbare-Energien-Gesetz. In: Heid D, Stotz R, Verny A (eds) Festschrift für Manfred A. Dauses zum 70. Geburtstag. C.H. Beck, München, pp 137–152

International Emissions Trading Association (IETA) (2016) IETA's views on the European Commission's revision of the EU ETS Directive for the post-2020 period. Geneva

Laing T, Sato M, Grubb M, Comberti C (2013) Assessing the effectiveness of the EU emissions trading system. Centre for Climate Change Economics and Policy, Working Paper No. 126. London, Cambridge and Oxford

Lazarus RJ (1986) Changing conceptions of property and sovereignty in natural resources: questioning the public trust doctrine. Iowa Law Rev 71:631–716

[101] Theobald (2017), para. 22.

Lippert A, Kindler L (2017) Die Staatlichkeit finanzieller Mittel in Umlagesystemen. Das Urteil des EuG vom EUG 10.5.2016 zum EEG 2012 und dessen Bedeutung für Umlagesysteme. Zeitschrift für das gesamte Recht der Energiewirtschaft 6:256–262
Liu X, Zhang S, Bae J (2017) The nexus of renewable energy-agriculture-environment in BRICS. Appl Energy 204:489–496
Paetsch M, Böck R (2009) Strommarktliberalisierung in der Schweiz: Neue Strukturen und ihre Herausforderungen. St. Gallen
Plumer B (2017) The U.S. Won't Actually Leave the Paris Climate Deal Anytime Soon. The New York Times, 7 June 2017
Pollitt MG, Shaorshadze I (2011) The role of behavioural economics in energy and climate policy. EPRG Working Paper 1130. Cambridge
Schaffhauser R, Uhlmann F (2014) Art. 89 FC. In: Ehrenzeller B, Schindler B, Schweizer RJ, Vallender KA (eds) Die schweizerische Bundesverfassung, St. Galler Kommentar. Dike Verlag, Zurich
Schmocker U, Kalkhof D (n.d.) Langzeitbetrieb der Schweizerischen Kernkraftwerke. Brugg
Scholtka B, Martin J (2017) Die Entwicklung des Energierechts im Jahr 2016. Neue Juristische Wochenschrift 1370:932–936
Statistisches Bundesamt (2016) Statistisches Jahrbuch 2016. Wiesbaden
Swiss Federal Office of Energy (SFOE) (2015) Vollzugsweisung Rückerstattung Netzzuschlag. Berne, Ittigen
Theobald C (2017) § 1 EnWG. In: Danner W, Theobald C (eds) Energierecht. C.H. Beck, Munich
United Nations Framework Convention on Climate Change (UNFCCC) (2006) UNFCCC handbook. Bonn
Weitzman ML (2014) Can negotiating a uniform carbon price help to internalize the global warming externality? J Assoc Environ Res Econ 1:29–49
Winter G (2009) Das Klima ist keine Ware. Eine Zwischenbilanz des Emissionshandelssystems. Zeitschrift für Umweltrecht 20:289–298

Sebastian Heselhaus Lucerne. Professor of European Law, International Law, Public Law and Comparative Public Law at the University of Lucerne. CH-6002 Lucerne, Frohburgstrasse 3, P.O. Box 4466, Tel. +41 (0)41 229 53 84; Fax +41 (0)41 229 53 97. sebastian.heselhaus@unilu.ch. Fields of Interest: Human Rights, Environmental and Energy Law, Commercial Law and Comparative Law.

Energy Transition in Switzerland

Julia Hänni

Abstract Climate protection obligations and the current political decisions to opt out of nuclear energy programs are going to lead to fundamental changes in the energy sector. To prepare Switzerland for the intended transition, the Federal Council developed the Energy Strategy 2050. It is supposed to enable Switzerland to maintain a high standard of energy supply based on renewable energies while reducing energy-related environmental impact, in particular the adverse effects on climate. The aim of this article is to provide an overview of the major legal instruments for the promotion of renewable energies currently in force. Furthermore, it outlines the new regulatory market incentives as envisaged under the Energy Strategy 2050.

1 Introduction

1.1 Most Utilized Energy Forms

Switzerland is confronted with problems stemming from global climate change,[1] energy scarcity, as well as dependence on foreign energy supply.[2] The most utilized forms of energy are fuels (34%), followed by electricity (24%) and petroleum based

Last updated May 2017, the text refers to law in force as of 2017.

[1]According to ProClim (Academy of Natural Sciencies)/IPCC Switzerland the average annual temperature in Switzerland has risen about twice as much as the global mean in the last 150 years (the rise in global mean temperature was about 0.85 °C, whereas the average temperature rise in Switzerland was about 1.8 °C); see https://naturalsciences.ch/service/publications/81637-brennpunkt-klima-schweiz?_ga=2.218550937.1270176362.1494770701-490124639 [accessed 12 April 2017].

[2]See the overview of the Energy Strategy 2050 from the Swiss Federal Office of Energy (SFOE): http://www.bfe.admin.ch/energiestrategie2050/index.html?lang=en [accessed 12 April 2017].

J. Hänni (✉)
Faculty of Law, University of Lucerne, Lucerne, Switzerland
e-mail: julia.haenni@unilu.ch

K. Mathis, B. R. Huber (eds.), *Energy Law and Economics*, Economic Analysis of Law in European Legal Scholarship 5, https://doi.org/10.1007/978-3-319-74636-4_3

combustibles (19%), natural gas (13%) and 10% coal, wood, district heat, industrial waste and others.[3] The main consumer groups include transportation (35%), households (28%), industry (19%), services (16%) and agriculture (<2%).[4]

National providers are currently only able to supply 20% of the energy needs; the remaining 80% must be imported from abroad.[5] National energy production presently consists of 57% hydro energy, 37% nuclear energy,[6] 3% solar energy, wind, biomass and incineration power, as well as 3% from conventional thermal power plants.[7] Between 1990 and 2015, energy consumption rose by 6%. Economic fluctuations and atmospheric influences impact energy consumption on the short-term, while economic growth, combined with technological developments and change in lifestyles, influences energy consumption in the long term.[8]

1.2 Decarbonization and Withdrawal from Nuclear Energy

Swiss energy transition concentrates on two main aims: decarbonization and the withdrawal from nuclear energy. Through international climate contracts such as the United Nations Framework Convention on Climate Change (UNFCCC, 1992),[9] the Kyoto Protocol (1997),[10] and recently also the Paris Agreement (2015),[11] Switzerland has committed itself to reducing the emission of greenhouse gases.[12] In 2011, Switzerland adopted the Federal Act on the Reduction of CO_2 Emissions. The aim of the act is to limit the global rise in temperature to less than two degrees Celsius.[13] Domestic greenhouse gas emissions shall by 2020 be reduced by 20% overall compared to the 1990 levels.[14] To reach this goal, the CO_2 Act imposes a levy on

[3]Coal <1%, wood, district heat, industrial waste, other renewable energies.

[4]Dispatch Energy Strategy (Swiss Federal Council 2013), 7573.

[5]Swiss Federal Office of Energy (SFOE) 2016, http://www.bfe.admin.ch/themen/00526/00530/index.html?lang=en [accessed 12 April 2017].

[6]Other authors use the number of 33.5%, as nuclear plants were temporarily taken out of action for technical reasons; see Simona (2016), N. 4.

[7]Swiss Federal Office of Energy (SFOE), 2016, pp. 32 et seq.

[8]Swiss Federal Office of Energy (SFOE), 2016, pp. 32 et seq.

[9]United Nations Framework Convention on Climate Change, the original text is available at: http://unfccc.int/essential_background/convention/items/6036.php [accessed 4 October 2017].

[10]Kyoto Protocol, the original text is available at: http://unfccc.int/kyoto_protocol/items/2830.php [accessed 4 October 2017].

[11]Paris Agreement, the original text is available at: http://unfccc.int/paris_agreement/items/9485.php [accessed 4 October 2017].

[12]Federal Act on the Reduction of CO_2 Emissions (CO_2 Act; SR 641.71).

[13]Article 1 CO_2 Act.

[14]Article 3(1) CO_2 Act. The Federal Council may increase the reduction target to 40% to comply with international agreements; Article 3(2) CO_2 Act. To achieve reduction targets of 50% until 2030, as the Federal Council plans for the implementation of the Paris Agreement, a total revision of the CO_2 Act is necessary.

the production, extraction and importation of combustible fuels (except motor fuels).[15] A maximum of 75% of the reductions in greenhouse gas emissions may be achieved through measures carried out abroad.[16] Power plant operators and companies that commit themselves to reduce their carbon dioxide emissions ("target agreements"[17]) obtain a full refund of the CO_2 levy.[18] Furthermore, companies that operate with "high or moderate" greenhouse gas emissions can apply to participate in the Emission Trading System.[19] If they participate in the Emission Trading System they can apply to have the CO_2 levy refunded.[20]

To reach the mentioned climate protection aims is not the only task that the Swiss Energy Law faces. Following the reactor accident in Fukushima, the Federal Council decided in May 2011 to opt out of the nuclear power program.[21] The new Energy Laws prohibit the construction of new nuclear power plants.[22] The prohibition requires a large amount of electricity to be replaced by equally climate neutral renewable energy sources, such as hydropower, or so called "new renewable energy" sources such as solar- and wind energy, biomass[23] and waste.[24]

Up to now, it has been a challenge to produce energy without emitting carbon dioxide and without the risk from nuclear power. Traditional energy production has been economical with respective companies established in the market. The "new renewable energies", like solar and wind energy, biomass and waste are not yet fully developed.[25] Additionally, most of the new renewable energies are not constantly available ("energy disposability"): Switzerland is not ideally suited to produce current major forms of new renewable energies when demanded, mainly because of lack of sun, especially during winter time, and because of volatile wind conditions.[26] Serious complications result with regard to storing of energy, as well as control over productivity.

---

[15]Article 29(1) CO_2 Act; see also Rütsche (2017), p. V; Weber (2017), pp. 355 et seq.

[16]Article 3(2) CO_2 Act.

[17]Article 12a(1) Ordinance on the Reduction of CO_2 Emissions (CO_2 Ordinance; SR 641.711).

[18]Articles 25 and 31(1)(b) CO_2 Act; Article 96(2)(b) and (c) CO_2 Ordinance.

[19]Article 15(1) CO_2 Act.

[20]Article 17 CO_2 Act; Article 96(2)(a) CO_2 Ordinance. See also Stumpf (2016), pp. 1 et seq.

[21]See Weber (2016), p. 31.

[22]New Article 12a of the Swiss Federal Act on Nuclear Energy (Kernenergiegesetz [KEG] from 21 March 2003; SR 732.1). There is, however, no time limit foreseen to put the existing nuclear power stations out of action; see also Simona (2016), N. 4. For the new laws in detail, see Sect. 2.3 below.

[23]Biomass is defined as organic material produced from photosynthesis that has not been transformed through biological processes; Annex 1.5 Energy Ordinance as in force (Energieverordnung, EnV; SR 730.01).

[24]Article 1(f) EnV.

[25]Political opponents of the Energy Strategy consider nuclear energy as not fully developed yet; on this point, see http://www.forum.unibe.ch/e14354/e17270/e137360/e137364/Zusammenfassung_Energiestrategie_Schweiz.pdf, p. 3 [accessed 12 April 2017].

[26]See also Simona (2016), N. 12.

1.3 Market Challenges

This situation directly influences the Swiss energy market. New renewable energies are currently not competitive. Even if numerous consumers accept paying a higher price for electricity of renewable origin, the difference is still too substantial for these technologies to develop without state financial aid.[27] Furthermore, the international legal environment also affects the market. The European energy market is strongly subsidized, causing an excess of supply and a drop in prices.[28] Consequently, the production of hydropower, for which Switzerland would be ideally suited and which was previously successfully established in the market, is no longer profitable. Still, hydropower is planned to play a major role in the Swiss energy transition strategy. Also pumped-water storage capacity—increasingly important for new renewable energy—is affected by market distortion in particular and not profitable any more.[29] The implementation of the new energy strategy and the realization of climate protection are therefore closely connected to market-technicalities. In short: something that used to be profitable and reliable is to be replaced by something more expensive and currently less reliable, to fulfill essential environmental protection obligations.

2 Governmental Incentives

2.1 Overview

Under the obligations, according to the current law in force, to reduce carbon dioxide emissions and to promote renewable energies the national legislature faces the specific task of generating missing market incentives in favor of renewable energy.[30] To meet these obligations, the Swiss Federal Energy Act (EnG) currently in force specifically promotes (new) renewable energies by means of a levy ("Netzzuschlag").[31]

The current instruments, however, cannot achieve the ambitious long-term objectives alone. With the decision to completely withdraw from nuclear power, the 37%

---

[27] Simona (2016), N. 33; Even nuclear power is produced at loss; see Simona (2016), N. 33. The foreseen government of the electricity sector is a change to the interim intended liberalization of the energy sector; see Müller (2016), N. 20.

[28] See, for example, https://www.uvek.admin.ch/uvek/de/home/energie/energiestrategie-2050/worum-geht-es.html [accessed 12 April 2017]; see also Dispatch Energy Strategy 2050 (Swiss Federal Council 2013), p. 7585; Simona (2016), N. 33; Müller (2016), N. 19.

[29] See also Dispatch Energy Strategy 2050 Dispatch Energy Strategy, p. 7585.

[30] Article 10 et seq. Swiss Federal Energy Act (Energiegesetz, EnG; 730.0).

[31] Article 15b EnG; see also Article 35 et seq. new Energy Act of 30 September 2016 (E-EnG, not yet in force).

share of the electricity from nuclear power plants is to be replaced. Therefore, significantly more energy will have to be produced from renewable sources. Furthermore, the current promotion system has been criticized for being inappropriate in several respects.[32] The Federal Council and Parliament therefore strove towards a more promising system for the implementation of the energy transition.

To meet the long-term objectives, the Parliament and Federal Council have developed the new so-called "Energy Strategy 2050". The goals of the strategy are principally to[33]:

- Reduce end-user energy consumption
- Increase the proportion of renewable energy production
- Reduce energy-related carbon-dioxide emission
- Secure unobstructed Swiss access to international energy markets
- Expand the energy grid and energy storage capacity through grid renewal and the development of new "Smart Grids"
- Introduce a model function of the State, cities and communities
- Improve research abilities and support research of new technologies
- Intensify international collaboration.

These goals are to be achieved without endangering the supply reliability and cost-effective provision of energy in Switzerland.

The Energy Strategy 2050 is divided into three phases[34]:

- Short-term goals until 2020—so-called first measure package
- Mid-term goals until 2035
- Long-term goals until 2050 (time horizon).

In the following, I will briefly present the incentive design in force ("KEV System"[35]) and the aspects that lead to criticism. Afterwards, an overview of the new judicial incentives enshrined in the Energy Strategy 2050 shall be provided. I will do that by analyzing the newly proposed energy law draft submitted by Parliament, containing the so-called "first measure-package" until 2020, that had been accepted by popular vote on 21 May 2017. A brief outlook on the instruments planned after 2020 follows, also referred to as the "second measure-package".

2.2 *Current Feed-in Tariff System ("KEV System")*

Since 2008 the Confederation has promoted electricity production with renewable energies. Based on Article 89, section 3 of the Constitution, the Confederation is

[32] See Sect. 2.2 below.

[33] Dispatch Energy Strategy (Swiss Federal Council 2013), pp. 7565 et seq.

[34] Dispatch Energy Strategy (Swiss Federal Council 2013), p. 7565.

[35] See Sect. 2.2 below.

required to promote renewable energy sources. The Confederation is also obligated to support the development of energy technologies in the field of energy saving and renewable energy. Further basis for the promotion of renewable energy sources can be found in Article 76 (Hydropower), Article 91 (Electricity), Article 74 (Protection of the Environment) and Article 64 of the Constitution (research in general).[36]

The currently effective *Feed-in Tariff System* (Kostendeckendes Einspeisevergütungssystem; "KEV System") is a subsidy instrument for energy production from renewable sources.[37] It can basically be applied for electricity production from solar, wind, small hydro power plants, biomass, or geothermal power production.[38] With start-up financing which, under current law, is valid for a maximum of 25 years per project,[39] the difference between production costs and current market price is compensated. The companies have the possibility to produce renewable energy and sell it for compensation equal to *production costs*.[40] The system shall promote the public interest in strengthening the local production of renewable energy. The national grid operator Swissgrid is responsible for the implementation. In 2015, 11,290 plants benefitted from the KEV. The plants dependent on the feed-in tariff as the basic prices for electricity covered only 10–25% of the production costs.[41] The incentive is currently financed through a *renewable energy levy* ("Netzzuschlag"), a regulatory tax[42] imposed on consumers.[43]

Due to the numerous applications for feed-in tariffs the cost cap for the Feed-in Remuneration at cost ("KEV") was already reached in February 2009,[44] with many projects still on the waiting list.[45] For this reason, the Swiss Parliament decided to augment the renewable energy levy and raise the subsidies.[46] The increase of the levy enables a reduction of the waiting list, but still will not allow remuneration of all

[36]For a complete list of constitutional provisions that relate to energy production, see Jagmetti (2005), pp. 41 et seq.

[37]Article 15 EnG; for the calculation of the subsidies, see Annex 1/3 EnV.

[38]Article 7 et seq. EnG.

[39]Annex I.1 seqq. EnV; Simona (2016), N. 34.

[40]Article 7a EnG; Article 3 et seq. EnV.

[41]Foundation KEV (2016), pp. 3 and 8; Simona (2016), N. 34.

[42]A regulatory tax is a tax that serves to finance specific tasks of the Confederation. It can only be used to fulfill the specific tasks. Regulatory taxes are assigned revenues, cf. also Blumenstein and Locher (2016), pp. 7 and 11.

[43]Article 15b(2) EnG.

[44]Hettich and Walther (2011), pp. 144 et seq.

[45]Article 3g(2) EnV. At the end of May 2016 37,600 projects were on the waiting list; Simona (2016), N. 36.

[46]Hettich and Walther (2011), pp. 144 et seq.

projects on the list. It is expected that the respective financial resources will be exhausted by 2018, which is why new applications can no longer be considered.[47]

In 2012 the Swiss Federal Office of Energy commissioned an evaluation of the Feed-in Tariff System.[48] It concluded that the feed-in tariff was successful in implementing the goals as far as more energy from renewable energy sources was produced. Nevertheless, the existing KEV system has become subject to criticism. Besides the lack of incentive to produce under market-oriented conditions,[49] the question of a sufficient legal basis was raised also.[50] The distribution mechanism drew further criticisms. It basically operates according to a first-come first-served principle. Rapidly developed projects are considered first, whereas output performance is of subordinated priority.[51] Projects with ground-breaking technology may be lower on the waiting list and thus postponed or not remunerated at all.[52] Authors believe that under the current Feed-in Tariff System, approximately 22% of the projects had been promoted irrespective of their effective impact on energy transition ("deadweight effect"; "Mitnahmeeffekt").[53]

2.3 *New Market Incentives According to the Energy Strategy 2050*

2.3.1 Main Goals of the Energy Strategy 2050

Due to decarbonization and the entire withdrawal from nuclear carriers, as stated in the new law adopted in May 2017, the capacity of renewable energy sources must be significantly increased. Article 2 of the new Federal Energy Act (E-EnG)[54] sets the benchmark for expanding renewable energies[55]: Starting at 2831 GWh in 2015, the Parliament foresees 4400 GWh for 2020 and 11,400 GWh for 2035. For the

---

[47]Press release Swiss Federal Office of Energy SFOE 2016, available at: http://www.bfe.admin.ch/energie/00588/00589/00644/index.html?lang=de&msg-id=62433 [accessed 12 April 2017].

[48]Evaluation der kostendeckenden Einspeisevergütung (KEV) 2012, available at: http://www.bfe.admin.ch/themen/00612/02073/index.html?dossier_id=02166&lang=de [accessed 12 April 2017].

[49]See e.g. Simona (2016), N. 37.

[50]The Swiss legislator considered the Confederation competent to raise the regulatory tax and enshrined it in the formal federal act. The view is disputed by some scholars as being unconstitutional; see Hettich and Walther (2011), pp. 157 et seq.; the provision must be applied by the courts (Article 190 Cst.).

[51]Article $3g^{bis}(1)$ EnV.

[52]SFOE, www.bfe.admin.ch/energie/00588/00589/00644/index.html?lang=de&msg-id=62433 [accessed 12 April 2017]; Hettich and Walther (2011), pp. 165 et seq.

[53]On this point, see Camenisch (2016), p. 26.

[54]BBl 2016 7638.

[55]The original proposition of the Federal Council referred to objectives, not benchmarks, cf. Simona (2016), N. 5.

production of hydroelectricity the Parliament aims to attain 37,400 GWh by 2035.[56] Furthermore, the average yearly production of hydroelectricity shall increase to 44,150 GWh a year by 2050.[57] Only renewable energy produced in Switzerland counts towards this benchmark.[58] The *average overall energy consumption* per capita per year shall, compared to the year 2000, be reduced by 16% by 2020, 43% by 2035, and 54% by 2050. [59] An average of at least 24,200 GWh of electricity per year shall be *produced from renewable sources* (excluding hydropower) by 2050; this is approximately the amount currently produced by nuclear energy.[60] These concrete goals shall be reached in several measure packages.

2.3.2 First Measure Package

The goals to be reached by 2020 are listed in the first measure package and enshrined in the new Federal Energy Act adopted in 2017 (E-EnG).[61] It contains several main instruments. They include:

- Measures regarding *energy efficiency* with the aim of improving the *energy efficiency* of buildings, industries, services and vehicles.[62]
- The notion *of "national interest*" (Article 12 E-EnG): Power plants of a certain significance and a certain size—criteria to be defined by the Federal Council[63]—have a special weight when public interests conflict.[64] The provision facilitates construction and enlargement of power plants producing electricity from renewable energies. It assigns the same importance to the use of renewable energy as to objects of national interest in the sense of Article 6(2) of the Federal Act on the Protection of Nature and Cultural Heritage.[65] The notion of national interest specifically has the function of an ascertainment of the weighing of the interests,[66]

[56] Article 2(2) E-EnG.

[57] Dispatch Energy Strategy 2050 (Swiss Federal Council 2013), pp. 7647 et seq.

[58] See Simona (2016), N. 6.

[59] Article 3(1) E-EnG; Dispatch Energy Strategy 2050 (Swiss Federal Council 2013), 7648 (24.4). The average *electricity consumption* shall, compared to the year 2000, be reduced by 3% by 2020 and 13% by 2035 (Article 3(2) E-EnG).

[60] Dispatch Energy Strategy 2050 (Swiss Federal Council 2013), p. 7648.

[61] BBl 2016 7638.

[62] Article 1 E-EnG; Article 32 E-EnG; Article 44 et seq. E-EnG.

[63] Article 12(4) and (5) E-EnG. Relevant are performance and output, and the capability to produce in flexible terms (especially winter production).

[64] Article 12 E-EnG.

[65] Article 6(2) Federal Act on the Protection of Nature and Cultural Heritage (NCHA; SR 451). Examples are wetland landscapes, historical monuments, etc.

[66] On Article 6(2) NCHA, see Tschannen and Mösching (2012), 18 pp. et seq. The benchmark to expand renewable energy (Article 2 E-EnG; above Sect. 2.3.1) will in this context be important to approve also plants of smaller significance and size as in the national interest, when they substantially contribute to the envisaged expansion of renewable energies (Article 13(1)(a) E-EnG). See

but without replacing it.[67] The national interest can be decisive in court rulings when the interest to establish further plants for renewable energies and the interests of environmental protection and homeland security are at stake.[68]

- Furthermore, an *acceleration of approval procedures* by the Cantons is foreseen[69]: The new Energy Act imposes on the Cantons (and where competency requires, on the Communes[70]) to enable fast approval procedures for constructions, enlargements and renovations of renewable energy power plants.[71] Also, with the new Energy Act, the appeal concerning planning approvals/permissions for heavy and low-current installations (as well as the expropriation of such rights needed for the construction or the exploitation of such plants) will only be treated by the Federal Supreme Court when the dispute relates to a "legal issue of fundamental importance".[72]
- Measures regarding the *electricity grid* contain—besides the mentioned acceleration of planning approval procedures and of appeal procedures[73]—the creation of a legal basis for the implementation of smart meters.[74]
- Measures to optimize feed-in remuneration contain the restructuring of the current cost covering feed-in tariff to *a feed-in tariff with direct selling options*.[75] The new law states, as the law in force, a purchase obligation (feed in) for electricity products of renewable energy, biogas and cogeneration plants.[76] The purchase obligation of the network operators is limited to plants with a power of max. 3 MW or a yearly production minus self-consumption of max. 5000 MWh.[77] It explicitly excludes producers that participate in the Feed-in

---

also Simona (2016), N. 5. Furthermore, a Proposal of the siting Canton is necessary; Article 13 al. 1 lit. b E-EnG.

[67] See also Simona (2016), N. 11.

[68] See for law in force e.g. BGer 1C_79/2016 of 5 April 2017 (Grimsel).

[69] Article 14 E-EnG.

[70] Article 42 et seq. BV.

[71] A similar regulation on shortening the length of the procedure can be found in Article 18a of the Spatial Planning Act; Bundesgesetz über die Raumplanung (Raumplanungsgesetz, RPG) of 22 June 1979; SR 700.

[72] "Rechtsfrage von grundsätzlicher Bedeutung"; new Article 83 lit. w Federal Act on The Federal Supreme Court (Bundesgesetz über das Bundesgericht; Bundesgerichtsgesetz, BGG; 173.110); BBl 2016 7716. Procedures concerning the approval for constructing a new power production plant will however not change; the Federal Supreme Court receives appeals of highest Cantonal administrative courts; Articles 82 and 86 BGG in force in September 2017.

[73] Article 14 E-EnG; new Article 83(w) BGG; see above footnote 72.

[74] Article 17a new Electricity Supply Act (Bundesgesetz über die Stromversorgung; Stromversorgungsgesetz, StromVG; SR 734.7).

[75] Articles 15, 19 et seq., Article 21 E-EnG.

[76] Article 15(1)(a) and (b) E-EnG.

[77] Article 15(2) E-EnG.

Tariff System.[78] Producers of renewable energy, biogas and cogeneration plants and consumers primarily have to agree among each other about the remuneration.[79] If no agreement is reached, the law foresees remunerations according to the production type.[80]

- Article 19 et seq. of the new Energy Act introduce a new Feed-in Tariff System for *groups* of producers of renewable energy who launched their plants after 1 January 2013.[81] Eligible are producers of electricity from hydro-,[82] solar-,[83] wind- biomass[84] and geothermal power.[85] The producers of renewable electricity primarily sell their electricity directly in the market.[86] The producers receive a remuneration in the amount of the revenues reached in the market and a feed in premium ("Einspeiseprämien"),[87] corresponding to the difference between the rate of remuneration relating to production costs of reference plants[88] (fixed) and the reference market price (variable).[89] The rate of remuneration ("Vergütungssatz"; Article 22 E-EnG) orients itself to the initial costs of a reference plant. It must be concretized by the Federal Council.[90] The reference market price is an average market price over a period fixed by the Federal Council for specific plant types (Article 23 E-EnG). In particular, operators of small plants, for which direct selling would be a disproportionate burden, can be allowed to sell at a reference market price by the Federal Council (Article 21 (2) E-EnG). Their remuneration then consists of the feed in premium[91] and the reference market price.[92]

  The new Feed-in Tariff System does not necessarily correspond to the effective production costs. Unlike the KEV System in force, the new law sets an incentive to produce renewable electricity at market conditions, through the direct selling option and through the new remuneration system which refers to the market price. When more electricity can be produced at a time of higher demand

---

[78] Articles 15(4) and 19 E-EnG.

[79] Article 15(3) E-EnG e contrario.

[80] Article 15(3) E-EnG.

[81] Article 19(3) E-EnG.

[82] Hydropower plants having an output of less than 1 MW or more than 10 MW are not eligible (Article 19(4)(a) LEne, Article 19(5) E-EnG).

[83] Photovoltaic plants having an output of less than 30 kW are not eligible (Article 19(4)(b) E-EnG).

[84] Incinerators and gas plants are not eligible (Article 19(4)(c) and (d) E-EnG).

[85] Article 19(1) E-EnG.

[86] Article 21(1) E-EnG.

[87] Article 21(3) E-EnG.

[88] The rate of remuneration ("Vergütungssatz" Article 22 E-EnG) orients itself on the initial costs of a reference plant. It must be concretized by the Federal Council; Article 22(1) and (3) E-EnG.

[89] Article 21(4) E-EnG; see also Simona (2016), N. 39.

[90] Article 22(1) and (3) E-EnG.

[91] Article 21(4) E-EnG.

[92] Articles 21(3) and 23 E-EnG.

or stored for times of higher demand, the feed in remuneration will be higher (Article 21(3) E-EnG). The system therefore also favors the developing of longer storage techniques.[93]

Operators of plants that partially use fossil fuels are not eligible for the feed-in remuneration.[94] The possibility of remuneration is furthermore limited in time. Only producers who are approved within 5 years after the new law enters in force receive a feed in remuneration.[95]

- Also, the promotion of small photovoltaic plants through new *one-off contributions* is foreseen,[96] as well as a lower boundary for the subsidization of small hydropower plants.[97] Furthermore, an expansion of financing guarantees, to protect funds for *geothermal energy projects,* is included.[98]
- Investment contributions are foreseen for photovoltaic-, hydropower- and biomass plants (Articles 24–29 E-EnG).[99] Investment contributions are awarded once and contain a potentially higher risk in comparison with the feed in tariff.[100] Also, investment contributions are limited in time (until 2030).[101]
- Notably, with the energy levy ("Netzzuschlag"), the feed in premium (Einspeiseprämie; Article 21 E-EnG), the investment contributions (Article 26 et seq. E-EnG) and geothermal exploration contributions (Article 33 E-EnG) are funded.[102] It is presently fixed at 1.5 centimes/kWh and can, under the new law, be increased to 2.3 centimes/kWh when the new law enters into force.[103] The tax will have an impact on major consumers.[104] The legislator therefore spares enterprises consuming large amounts of energy from the energy levy ("Netzzuschlag").[105]

The list of instruments set out in the first measure package shall enable the ambitious goals of the Strategy to reduce overall energy consumption by more

[93] Article 23(2) E-EnG; see also Simona (2016), N. 41.

[94] Article 19(4)(e) E-EnG.

[95] Article 38(1)(a) E-EnG.

[96] Article 24(1)(a) E-EnG.

[97] Article 19(4)(a) E-EnG; see also Article 24(1)(b)(2) E-EnG; Dispatch Energy Strategy 2050 (Swiss Federal Council 2013), 7526, 7596.

[98] Article 33 E-EnG.

[99] Cf. Article 7a^{bis} EnG as in force ("Einmalvergütung").

[100] Simona (2016), N. 50.

[101] Article 38(1)(b) E-EnG.

[102] Article 35 et seq. E-EnG. See in this context Draft "Verordnung über die Förderung der Produktion von Elektrizität aus erneuerbaren Energien" (Energieförderungsverordnung, EnFV): UVEK (2017), pp. 1 et seq.

[103] Article 35(3) E-EnG.

[104] Simona (2016), N. 60.

[105] Article 39 et seq. E-EnG.

than half by 2050. But they will not by themselves be sufficient; the sector must achieve significant technical advances to reach the ambitious long-term goals.[106] Further legal instruments to improve innovation are foreseen and currently causing many controversial discussions (second measure package).

2.3.3 Second Measure Package (2021–2050)

As part of the second energy policies package the Federal Council first intended to establish a transition of the promotional system to a steering system.[107] It foresaw a new constitutional provision—Article 131a E-Cst—that should serve as a basis for the introduction of a climate and energy steering tax (so-called "KELS").[108]

The Federal Council saw several advantages for achieving the goals of the strategy, specifically the encouragement of innovation, the freedom of choice of consumers, and increased efficiency.[109] Market-based legal instruments do not, however, automatically entail fairer distribution keys: steering taxes are often criticized for putting a heavier burden on financially weaker entities, whereas richer entities receive freedom of choice of whether to adjust their behavior or not.[110]

The specific proposition of the Federal Council introducing a steering tax for the second measure-package was only agreed to in principle by the Parliament—as a concept to pursue—but not in the proposed form. The proposition was considered to be insufficiently elaborated. The National Council, as first chamber, for this reason did not further discuss the new draft articles of the steering tax in the March 2017 session. Nevertheless, it accepted that solutions with even more market-incentivizing instruments must be developed for the period after 2020.[111] Recently discussed additional incentives for investments are e.g. capacity mechanisms ("Kapazitätsmechanismen"), bonuses for the supply of capacities, and quota models ("Quotenmodelle") for certificates of power production that can be traded with the aim of generating additional income for the producers.[112]

---

[106] Simona (2016), N. 3; Müller (2016), N. 21.

[107] In the sense of the first measure package; see Sect. 2.3.2.

[108] Dispatch KELS (Swiss Federal Council 2015), pp. 7877 et seq.

[109] Dispatch KELS (Swiss Federal Council 2015), p. 7889.

[110] See also Camenisch (2016), pp. 27 et seq.

[111] AB 2017 N. 283 et seq.

[112] In this context see also UVEK (2016), pp. 1, 5 et seq., 21 et seq., 31 et seq. The incentives refer to subsidization and are not further developed yet, nor has the compatibility with international law been fully researched, see SPOE 2016, p. 33.

3 Appraisal

Since the first implementation of the Feed-in Tariff Subsidization System in 2008, under the law already in force, more renewable energy has been produced. The Federal Council could therefore assume a significant impact when evaluating the current promotion system. The promotional incentives of the European market, led especially hydropower (production and storage), a power source that had been economically successful for many years in the past, to become unprofitable. According to the new energy strategy, large hydropower plants will therefore be eligible for subsidies under the new laws.

The first measure package of the Energy Strategy 2050 intends to further adjust the energy policy to climate policy through market based legal instruments. The strong subsidization of solar and wind energy, hydropower, biomass and waste combined with market-based legal instruments sets considerable incentives in favor of the production of renewable energy. The new Federal Act on Energy encourages the production of renewable energies in the planning approval procedures and foresees stronger subsidization. It is to be expected that, with the new incentives, the level of self-sufficiency will increase. The energy levy ("Netzzuschlag"), carried by the consumers, will be increased significantly to finance the transition. At the same time, some articles of the new Energy laws seem to be contradictory, as for example enterprises that consume large amounts of energy, shall be—for reasons of competition—spared from the energy levy.[113] The new provisions (as is already the case with the current law in force) substantially increase the burden on all other contributors. Furthermore, some instruments that help to expand the production of renewable energy are in direct conflict with environmental and heritage protection aims. Delicate court cases on major conflicting state interests are to be expected.[114]

The goal of the second measure package will be to replace the current financial support program with a new steering tax.[115] Whether and how the Federal Council will concretize the intended steering tax, or if it will introduce other market based steering instruments, has not been decided yet.[116] The full bandwidth of legal instruments that Switzerland is going to use to fulfill energy transition goals and climate protection obligations in their entirety is still in development.

Acknowledgments Many thanks to Tania Cucé, MLaw, Ralph Hemsley, MLaw, and Sarah Kehl, MLaw, Scientific Research Assistants at the University of Lucerne, for valuable research contributions.

---

[113]Article 40 et seq. E-EnG. See Sect. 2.3.2 above.

[114]Article 12 E-EnG. For law in force see Abegg (2016), pp. 1 et seq.; and under current law the case BGer 1C_79/2016 from 5 April 2017 (Grimsel).

[115]Dispatch Energy Strategy 2050 (Swiss Federal Council 2013), p. 7599.

[116]Report of the Swiss Federal Office of Energy (SFOE), Electricity Market after 2020, pp. 1 et seq.; see Sect. 2.3.3 above.

References

Abegg A (2016) Energiewende im Konflikt mit Natur- und Heimatschutz: Anwendbarkeit des Natur- und Heimatschutzgesetzes des Bundes auf Anlagen zur Erzeugung von erneuerbarer Energie: ein Kommentar zu Art. 2 NHG. Zürich Dike Verlag, Zurich

Blumenstein E, Locher P (2016) System des Schweizerischen Steuerrechts, 7th edn. Zurich, Schulthess Verlag

Camenisch L (2016) Klima- und Energielenkungssystem: normative Überlegungen zu Art. 131a E-BV. Zürich Dike Verlag, Zurich

Foundation KEV (2016). Annual report. http://www.stiftung-kev.ch/berichte/jahresberichte.html

Hettich P, Walther S (2011) Rechtsfragen um die kostendeckende Einspeisevergütung (KEV) für Elektrizität aus erneuerbaren Energien. Schweizerisches Zentralblatt für Staats- und Verwaltungsrecht 3(2011):143–171

Jagmetti R (2005) Energierecht. Helbing & Lichtenhahn, Basel

Müller RP (2016) Liberalisierung des Strommarkts – Rolle rückwärts? Jusletter, 19 December 2016

Rütsche B (2017) Foreword. In: Mathis K, Huber BR (eds) Environmental law and economics. Springer, Cham, p V et seq

Simona M (2016) La Loi fédérale sur l'énergie (LEne) du 30 septembre 2016. Jusletter, 19 December 2016

Stumpf S (2016) Das Klima als globales öffentliches Gut? – Fragen der ökonomischen Theorie an die Rechtswissenschaft. Juwiss.de, 2016 (76)

Swiss Federal Council (2013) Botschaft zum ersten Massnahmenpaket der Energiestrategie 2050 (Revision des Energierechts) und zur Volksinitiative «Für den geordneten Ausstieg aus der Atomenergie (Atomausstiegsinitiative)» vom 4. September 2013. BBl 2013:7561–7562 (Dispatch Energy Strategy)

Swiss Federal Council (2015) Botschaft zum Verfassungsartikel über ein Klima- und Energielenkungssystem vom 28 Oktober 2015. BBl 2015:7877–7878 (Dispatch KELS)

Swiss Federal Department of the Environment, Transport, Energy and Communications (DETEC [UVEK]) (2016) Auslegeordnung Strommarkt nach 2020. Bericht zu weitergehenden Massnahmen für bestehende Kraftwerke und Erneuerbare Energien vom 23 Dezember 2016. http://www.bfe.admin.ch/energiestrategie2050/06449/index.html?lang=de&dossier_id=06748

Swiss Federal Department of the Environment, Transport, Energy and Communications (DETEC [UVEK]) (2017) Erläuternder Bericht. Erstes Massnahmenpaket zur Energiestrategie 2050. Verordnung über die Förderung der Produktion von Elektrizität aus erneuerbaren Energien (Energieförderungsverordnung, EnFV). https://www.admin.ch/ch/d/gg/pc/documents/2833/6_Bericht-EnFV_de.pdf

Swiss Federal Office of Energy (SFOE) (2015) Overall energy statistics. http://www.bfe.admin.ch/themen/00526/00541/00542/00631/index.html?lang=de&dossier_id=00763

Tschannen P, Mösching F (2012) Nationale Bedeutung von Aufgaben- und Eingriffsinteressen im Sinne von Art. 6 Abs. 2 NHG, Gutachten im Auftrag des Bundesamtes für Umwelt (BAFU). Berne

Weber RH (2016) Energy law in Switzerland, 2nd edn. Stämpfli Verlag AG, Bern

Weber RH (2017) Emission trading schemes: a Coasean answer to climate change? In: Mathis K, Huber BR (eds) Environmental law and economics. Springer, Cham, pp 355–377

Julia Hänni Lucerne. Assistant Professor of Public Law at the University of Lucerne. CH-6002 Lucerne, Frohburgstrasse 3, P.O. Box 4466, Tel. + 41 (0)41 229 53 83; Fax + 41 (0)41 229 53 97. julia.haenni@unilu.ch. Fields of Interest: Public Law, European Law (European Union law; bilateral relations between Switzerland and the European Union), International Climate Change and Energy Law, Philosophy of Law (theories of justice; phenomenology; global justice).

The Interplay Between Liberalization and Decarbonization in the European Internal Energy Market for Electricity

Anna-Alexandra Marhold

Abstract This contribution explores the interplay between liberalization and decarbonization in the European electricity market. The focus of this chapter is to see whether liberalization of the EU electricity market, in Europe realized by means of the unbundling regime, inherently promotes decarbonization of the grid. In other words, it seeks to explore if decarbonization of the electrical grid is a positive externality of liberalizing the market, absent of any other policies promoting the scale up of renewables in the grid. To this end, it examines existing economic and econometric literature on the issue and places it in the greater context of internal energy market legislation and European energy policy.

1 Introduction

Consumer protection lies at the heart of the European Union (EU) competition law system. EU energy policy is *de facto* an extension of competition law to the EU energy sector. For business and consumers, this means that guaranteeing a reliable energy supply at reasonable prices is paramount. In this spirit, the EU has been progressively working towards the completion of the Internal Energy Market and a coherent EU energy policy since the 1980s, increasingly liberalizing European electricity and gas markets.[1] Ownership Unbundling and Third Party Access, set out in 2009 in the Third Energy Package legislation, are key elements with a dual goal in this respect: they facilitate liberalization, as well as a Europe-wide integration of energy markets.[2] These legal instruments essentially mandate the breaking up of

[1]European Commission 2017, 'A Fully Integrated Internal Energy Market'.

[2]Ownership unbundling is taken up in Article 9(1) of the Electricity (2009/72/EC) and Gas Directives (2009/73/EC); Third Party Access is taken up in Article 32 of the Directives.

A.-A. Marhold (✉)
Tilburg Law and Economics Center, Tilburg University, Tilburg, The Netherlands
e-mail: a.marhold@uvt.nl

K. Mathis, B. R. Huber (eds.), *Energy Law and Economics*, Economic Analysis of Law in European Legal Scholarship 5, https://doi.org/10.1007/978-3-319-74636-4_4

previously vertically integrated energy companies and allow the introduction of competition in the market where possible.

In its efforts to decarbonize its economy and increase its security of supply, the EU further promotes the scaling up of clean energy and energy efficiency.[3] This can be understood from the perspective of mitigating the adverse effects of climate change and CO_2 emissions: the Union must meet its obligations undertaken under international climate agreements, such as the recent 2015 Paris Agreement.[4] To this end, the Union has extensive legislation in place to legitimize support schemes for renewable energy under EU law, i.e. by means of the Renewable Energy Directive, 2014 EU Guidelines on State Aid for Environmental Protection and Energy, the EU General Block Exemption Regulation and supporting case law.[5] In the wake of the imminent energy transition, the Commission furthermore released legislative proposals for a new 'clean' energy package to replace the current Third Energy Package legislation in late 2016. The focus of the new proposals, presently under negotiation, is on decarbonizing the economy and the promotion of sustainable development.[6]

It therefore comes as no surprise that in achieving a greater energy security for the Union the EU must walk on a tightrope between the two objectives; competitiveness and attaining a clean energy transition. While not conflicting objectives in and of themselves, it has proven to be challenging to reconcile liberalization on the one hand, while meeting climate targets and decarbonizing the electricity grid on the other.

This chapter is interested in exploring the interplay between liberalization and decarbonization of the European electricity market. The focus of this piece is to see whether liberalization of the EU electricity market, in Europe realized by means of the unbundling regime, inherently promotes decarbonization of the grid. In other words, it seeks to explore if decarbonization of the electrical grid is a positive externality of liberalizing the market, absent of any other policies promoting the scale up of renewables in the grid. We will limit ourselves to discussing the electricity grid, as the electricity sector is at the center of many clean and renewable energy support schemes, as opposed to gas or nuclear.

After this introduction, Sect. 2 will first provide some background and economic rationales of the Internal Energy Market. Section 3 will explore the interplay between liberalization and decarbonization. It will reveal that there is indeed a causal link between them, to certain degree. However, as the chapter will determine in

---

[3]EU 2020 Climate and Energy Package 2017.

[4]COP21 Paris Agreement: United Framework Convention on Climate Change (UNFCCC), UN Doc FCCC/CP/2015/L.9/Rev. 1 'Adoption of the Paris Agreement' (12 December 2015).

[5]European Commission, Guidelines on State aid for environmental protection and energy 2014–2020 (2014/C 200/01) C 200/1. 28 June 2014 and European Commission, Commission Regulation (EU) No 651/2014 of 17 June 2014 declaring certain categories of aid compatible with the internal market in application of Articles 107 and 108 of the Treaty Text with EEA relevance; OJ L 187, 26 June 2014, pp. 1–78.

[6]DG Energy, 'Commission Proposes New Rules for a Consumer Centered Clean Energy Transition', 30 November 2016.

Sect. 4, liberalization legislation alone is not enough to enable clean energy to compete with fossil fuels in the EU electricity market. Understandably, EU renewable energy policy attempts to correct these market failures. By means of a conclusion, Sect. 5 will recap the issues discussed.

2 The Materialization of the EU Internal Energy Market

By way of background and understanding the economic rationale of the EU energy system and the place of support schemes for clean and renewable energy, this section will lay out some fundamentals of EU Internal Energy Market legislation pertaining to electricity. Subsequently, it will examine whether, and to what extent, decarbonization of the European electricity grid can be considered an inherent positive externality of liberalization legislation, ignoring any additional measures to scale up renewable energy.

The EU Internal Market for Electricity, part of the EU Internal Energy Market is the result of gradually introducing a more coherent EU-wide energy legislation and policy from the 1980s onwards. The culmination of the process has—so far—been the launch of the Energy Union package in 2015 and the Clean Energy Package proposed by the European Commission in 2016.[7] The ultimate objective is to have a fully interconnected EU energy market, that is at the same time liberalized, decarbonized and can guarantee 'security of energy supply' for Europe's citizens.

'Security of energy supply' is an elusive term. In fact, there is no clear-cut and legally binding definition of 'security of supply', neither on the international level, nor in the context of EU law.[8] In the words of the EU itself:

> DG Energy undertook steps to ensure that the assessment of security of supply becomes more quantifiable and transparent. This overview shows that although there is no clear definition at the EU level of what security of supply means, there is a clear focus on measures to establish security of supply.[9]

---

[7]European Commission, 'Energy Union Package – A Framework Strategy for a Resilient Energy Union with a Forward-Looking Climate Change Policy', 25 February 2015, and DG Energy, 'Commission Proposes New Rules for a Consumer Centered Clean Energy Transition', 30 November 2016.

[8]The EU in its energy security strategy in so many words confirms that there is no legal definition of energy security on the European level, see European Commission (2014), p. 166; European Commission, 'European Energy Security Strategy', COM(2014) 330 final, Brussels, 28 May 2014.

[9]Despite a lacking legal definition on EU level, the Union believed the concept of energy security was clear an important enough to put forward a European Energy Security Strategy, preceding its Energy Union Package, European Commission, European Energy Security Strategy, Brussels, 28 May 2014, COM (2014)330; This strategy was accompanied by an in-depth study of Europe's energy security European Commission (2014), p. 3.

While the EU has elaborated on some criteria in its Energy Security Strategy (to be discussed below), a clear legal definition of the term is lacking.[10] The status quo is that a vast number of academics and policy makers have been vigorously discussing and trying to frame the definition of 'energy security' and 'energy security of supply' legally or otherwise, albeit without a clear consensus.[11]

The most straightforward point of reference then is International Energy Agency, which describes the concept of 'energy security' in the broadest sense as 'the uninterrupted availability of energy sources at an affordable price'.[12] The United Nations offers an additional description and characterizes 'energy supply security' as *"the continuous availability of energy in varied forms, in sufficient quantities, and at reasonable prices"*.[13] One can further distinguish two dimensions of energy security: long-term energy security, which implies timely investments taking into account sustainable development needs, and short-term energy security, implying that the system should react adequately to sudden changes in supply and demand.[14]

Despite the fuzziness of the concept of energy security, it is commonly understood that energy security covers elements of: (1) a reliable supply that is, (2) accessible, and, (3) affordable. A fourth, overarching element is brought forward, which is that the supply should be sustainable. It follows that by guaranteeing energy security, energy markets should be resilient in the event of shocks (in the European context, one could e.g. think of the recurring gas transit disputes between Russia and Ukraine that took place in the 2000s that affected a great number EU Member States directly).[15] Notwithstanding the absence of a legal definition, it is obvious that security of supply is of vital importance for the EU. The EU has therefore put forward an Energy Security Strategy.[16] Several elements of this strategy are highly relevant for the completion and liberalization of the internal market for electricity. These are, amongst others: moderating energy demand, building a well-functioning and fully integrated internal market, increasing energy production in the Union, further developing energy technologies and improving coordination of national energy policies.[17]

The dimension of liberalizing the energy market for electricity and gas can be understood as extending the idea of the European single market by breaking up vertically integrated energy companies and introducing competition to these

[10]European Commission, European Energy Security Strategy, Brussels, 28.5.2014, COM (2014) 330; European Commission (2014), p. 3.

[11]Energy Charter Secretariat (2015), p. 10 et seq.; The Council of European Energy Regulators (CEER) (2010), Dreyer and Stang (2013), p. 1 et seq.; and generally, Lilliestam and Patt (2012) and Metais (2013).

[12]International Energy Agency, 'What is Energy Security?'.

[13]Energy Charter Secretariat (2015), p. 113 et seq.

[14]Energy Charter Secretariat (2015), p. 113 et seq.; International Energy Agency (2016), p. 86 et seq.

[15]See e.g. on this generally Marhold (2011).

[16]European Commission (2014).

[17]European Commission (2014), p. 3.

industries where possible.[18] The consumers, in the form of EU citizens, are ultimately at the heart of EU competition policy, and this is one of the underlying rationales for liberalization policies in the energy market: by making companies compete fairly with one another, efficiency is encouraged, quality and innovation increases, prices decrease and consumers have an overall broader choice, apart from a more secure supply.[19] Through Internal Energy Market legislation, two policy goals thus merged into one: the completion of the EU single market by means of extending competition policy to the energy market, on the one hand, and, introducing and advancing a coherent Union-wide, increasingly integrated energy policy, on the other.[20]

There were many reasons for introducing liberalization and interconnection of network industries later to the energy sector than to most other goods and services sectors in the EU: first, energy was, for decades, a purely national matter linked to state security and security of energy supply of the separate EU Member States. Second, there were historically relatively little cross-border interconnections of electricity grids and gas pipelines across Europe. And third, until today, energy remains a shared competence between the Union and its Member States, as is evidenced by Article 4.2(i) of the Treaty on the Functioning of the European Union (TFEU).[21] This entails that both the EU and Member States may legislate in this area, as long as they respect the 'duty of sincere cooperation' among themselves flowing from Article 4(3) of the Treaty on the European Union (TEU).[22] In short, the duty of sincere cooperation entails that the EU and its Member States must refrain from acting against each other's respective interests.

The specific article setting out EU energy policy is taken up in Article 194 TFEU.[23] The Article lays out the objectives of EU energy policy in paragraph one, while paragraph two subsequently determines that the European Parliament and the Council can establish the measures necessary to achieve these objectives. Paragraph two of this article further emphasizes the shared nature of the competence: the EU may, for instance, not determine the internal energy mix of its Member States.[24] It states that "*Such measures shall not affect a Member State's right to*

[18]Pollitt in a brief paper provides a historical overview of the 'liberalization era' and its effects: Liberalization is characterized by its attention for competition, and unbundling is one of the tools. Privatization is often an effect of liberalization but not always, and part of the reason liberalization is not yet complete is that governments are afraid to lose the control or the power to cross-subsidize, see Pollitt (2012), p. 128 et seq.

[19]DG Competition 2017, 'Why is Competition Policy Important for Consumers?'.

[20]See for an overview Marhold (2016), pp. 250–254; Also see European Commission (DG Energy) 2017, 'Markets and Consumers – Integrated Energy Markets for European Households and Business'.

[21]Consolidated Version of the Treaty on the Functioning of the European Union, 2008 O.J. C 115/47 (hereafter: TFEU).

[22]Consolidated Version of the Treaty on European Union, 2010 O.J. C 83/01 (hereafter: TEU).

[23]Article 194 TFEU.

[24]Article 194(2) TFEU.

determine the conditions for exploiting its energy resources, its choice between different energy sources and the general structure of its energy supply, without prejudice to Article 192(2)(c)."[25] This is somewhat paradoxical, at minimum, as the Union has set binding targets for shares of renewable energy in its Member States, although justification for this can be partially found in mentioned Article 192(2)(c) TFEU for environmental protection.[26] We can nevertheless discern a tension here between the targets and requirements set out in the EU Renewable Energy Directive discussed in this contribution and Member States' sovereignty (including sovereignty over their natural resources) to decide their energy mix. Regarding renewable energy, we can conclude that while the EU at Union level may prescribe overall renewable energy targets, the Union is not in a position to decide on the actual energy mix of its Member States, nor does it have a say in what energy resources Member States can and should use.[27] Perhaps this is one of the motives why the Commission in the new Clean Energy Package has proposed to do away with binding renewable energy targets on the national level, instead solely providing a binding target on the EU level, as a possible compromise to Member States in this area.[28]

A second reason why liberalization was introduced later into the European energy sector (though connected to the previous point), is that the electricity and gas industry has traditionally either been state-owned and/or operated by vertically integrated companies, often behaving as a natural monopoly owing to the sunk cost connected to energy production and infrastructure investments.[29] It thus became evident that the breaking up of these industries was to be a challenging process that could only succeed if implemented in phases. It should be noted that while the electricity and gas sector differ significantly from one another, certain core legislative changes in EU law (such as Ownership Unbundling and Third Party Access) were designed to apply to both sectors. This is simply because the electricity, as well as the gas industry, have certain characteristics in common, i.e. they are 'network-bound', tied to fixed infrastructures, and their operational processes, from energy production to transmission and distribution, where historically heavily regulated on state level.

---

[25]Article 194(2) TFEU.

[26]Art 192(2)(c) TFEU: "*By way of derogation from the decision-making procedure provided for in paragraph 1 and without prejudice to Article 114, the Council acting unanimously in accordance with a special legislative procedure and after consulting the European Parliament, the Economic and Social Committee and the Committee of the Regions, shall adopt: measures significantly affecting a Member State's choice between different energy sources and the general structure of its energy supply.*".

[27]See on this e.g. Sveen (2014), p. 157 et seq.

[28]European Commission, Proposal for a Directive of the European Parliament and of the Council on the promotion of the use of energy from renewable sources (recast), COM/2016/0767 final/2 - 2016/0382 (COD), 23 February 2017, under 1.1.

[29]Daintith and Hancher (1986).

During the first phase of implementing the IEM in the late 1980s, cross-border transit opened for both electricity and gas, implying that Member States could no longer oppose transnational flows of energy. In the early 2000s, the Second Energy Package introduced the legal unbundling of gas and electricity sectors, mandated the minimum threshold of legal separation of the production and sale of energy from transmission and distribution activities of energy.[30] By 2009, the Commission adopted the Third Energy Package in the form of an Electricity and Gas Directive (2009/72/EC and 2009/73/EC respectively), introducing the most stringent form of unbundling, known as Ownership Unbundling. The new Clean Energy Package proposed by the Commission in the fall of 2016 attempts to take this a step further by emphasizing the need to introduce flexibility onto the grid, *inter alia* to accommodate prosumers and smart energy systems into the existing structure.[31]

As the 2016 package is merely a set of proposals on the negotiation table at present, we take a step back to the Third Energy Package that is currently still in force. Ownership Unbundling, set out in Article 9 of the 2009 Electricity Directive, prescribes the complete separation of companies' electricity generation and sales activities from their transmission network activities, requiring them to be operated by strictly independent entities.[32] Although all EU Member States must attain full Ownership Unbundling in both their electricity and gas sectors, it remains difficult to realize this in all Member States in a timely manner today and milder forms of unbundling are still accepted (the case in the gas sector in e.g. Hungary, Croatia and Lithuania).[33] Unbundling and integrating energy markets is additionally accompanied by significant challenges: it for instance exposes the need to attract sufficient infrastructure investments in the European electricity market and the need to manage capacity remuneration mechanisms that Member States have in place.[34]

---

[30]Directives 2003/54/EC for electricity and 2003/55/EC for gas, OJ 2003 L 176.

[31]European Commission, Communication on 'Clean Energy For All Europeans' Brussels, 30 November 2016 COM(2016) 860 final, 8.

[32]Johnston and Block (2012), p. 73; ECJ, C-439/06 *Citiworks* AG (22 May 2008) and Article 9 of the Electricity Directive 2009/72/EC.

[33]In fact, none of Member States has managed to fully transpose the Electricity and Gas Directives (due date for transposition of the Directive was 2011). Note in this respect that while 'full ownership unbundling' remains the basic model and target for EU MS, vertically integrated energy companies can resort to two other alternatives: the independent system operator (ISO) and independent transmission operator (ITO) model. Under the former model, the transmission network can remain in the ownership of the energy company. Nevertheless, the transmission network itself must be managed by an ISO, which must perform all day-to-day network operator functions and must be completely separated from the energy company. In the ITO scenario, the transmission networks can also remain under the ownership of an energy consortium, but the transmission subsidiaries would be set up as independent joint stock companies carrying their own brand name and subject to stringent regulatory control. Most EU Member States whose transmission systems are controlled by vertically integrated undertakings prefer this last scheme of unbundling to comply with the Third Energy Package.

[34]See e.g. European Parliament Briefing, *Understanding the Electricity Markets in the EU* (Brussels, November 2016) and Glachant et al. (2014).

Another cornerstone of liberalization of the energy market the EU introduced in the Third Energy Package, is the concept of Third Party Access, taken up in Article 32 of the Electricity Directive.[35] Third Party Access ensures that Member States have a system in place where third parties (usually competitors to the natural energy monopoly) can access the transmission and distribution grid under objective, transparent and non-discriminatory terms.[36] One of the essential components of Third Party Access is the regulation of tariffs, which have to be published, *"applicable to all eligible customers, including supply undertakings, and applied objectively and without discrimination between system users."*[37] Transmission System Operators, as well as Distribution System Operators, are the guarantors, i.e. the entities tasked with guaranteeing Third Party Access.[38] In the electricity sector, for instance, there is currently an emphasis on building more cross-border capacity by direct current interconnectors (Article 17 of Regulation 714/2009) in view of enhancing Third Party Access to the grid.[39]

3 Liberalizing the EU Electricity Sector: Decarbonization as a Positive Externality?

After laying out the rudiments of the European energy landscape above, we now turn to the essential question on the nexus between liberalization legislation and decarbonization of the electricity grid. What we are particularly interested in is to discover whether liberalization policies in the electricity sector are inherently accompanied by the positive externality of leading to more clean energy inputs on the supply side of the market. We choose to address this question with respect to the electricity sector only, as this sector, as opposed to the gas sector, is dealing with a secondary energy commodity in the sense energy statistics.[40]

This proposition demands some elaboration. While electricity can certainly be classified as 'energy', in the sense that it provides power input, it is only a 'secondary

---

[35] Article 32 of Electricity Directive 2009/72/EC.

[36] Article 32 of Electricity Directive 2009/72/EC; See also Article 37(6) on the regulation of tariffs. The European Court of Justice (ECJ) in *Citiworks* confirmed that TPA is paramount and essential for both competition to function in the market, as well as completing the internal electricity market, ECJ, C-439/06 *Citiworks AG* (22 May 2008), paras 40 and 44.

[37] Article 32(1) Electricity Directive 2009/72/EC.

[38] Johnston and Block (2012), p. 75 et seq. However, since a right balance must be attained between competition policy and attracting sufficient investments in energy infrastructure, the EU maintains an exemption policy to TPA. In the electricity sector, for instance, there is currently an emphasis on building more cross-border capacity by direct current interconnectors (Article 17 of Regulation 714/2009), meaning that these can qualify if it meets certain conditions). Article 17, Regulation 714/2009/EC. See for a more in-depth analysis Van der Vijver (2012), p. 336 et seq.

[39] Article 17 Regulation 714/2009/EC.

[40] OECD, International Energy Agency and Eurostat (2005), p. 18 et seqq.

energy commodity' in that it needs to be generated by means of transforming a primary energy commodity first. Primary energy commodities are either clean, also known as 'green' (sun, wind, hydro), or non-renewable, also known as 'brown' (e.g. fossil fuels such as coal and petroleum).[41] As opposed to natural gas, which is a primary, non-renewable energy commodity by definition, measuring changes in the supply side of the mix in the electricity sector is therefore considerably easier.

It is for this reason that the electricity sector provides a suitable case study for exploring our question, the relevance of which is twofold: first, it helps us to understand if we can identify a causal link (based on economic and econometric studies) between liberalization and decarbonization (i.e. an increase of clean energy feeding into the grid as a positive externality, by creating more space on the grid for clean energy producers), and to what extent. Second, in case this question can be answered in the affirmative, it may additionally provide some indicators on why liberalization legislation alone is not enough for clean energy to compete with 'brown' inputs in the electricity sector.

When considering the policies, the EU has taken up in its energy directives over the past two decades, especially regarding Ownership Unbundling and Third Party Access in the electricity sector, one could make the following assumption: through the implementation of this legislation (1) a larger share of producers of clean electricity can access the grid more easily; (2) thereby increasing the share of clean electricity in the energy mix. This way, it could be argued, unbundling and Third Party Access policies have a positive externality, namely contributing to the decarbonization of the grid by means of the diversification of energy inputs into the grid, by increasing the share of clean sources for the generation of electricity (e.g. wind, solar, hydro-electric, etc.). It could thus be argued that if this is the case, liberalization legislation would simultaneously serve a public interest goal, namely contributing to a cleaner environment and sustainable development.

There is mixed evidence in economic and econometric literature to support this assumption. A branch of literature exploring the interplay between market liberalization and innovation provides some interesting insights on these matters. Jamasb and Pollitt, for instance, have studied the patenting activities of transmission and distribution companies in the UK, by collecting data on renewable and non-renewable energies in the 2000s.[42] Their research demonstrates that while there was first a downward trend with respect to patenting activities at the start of liberalization policies, this was followed by an surge in these activities during the 2000s.[43] Nevertheless, at the same time, Jamasb and Pollitt concluded that liberalization as such was accompanied by a decline in overall R&D expenditures and cuts in the public budget.[44] Nemet and Kammen, furthermore, found a negative

[41]This distinction is widely used in economics literature.

[42]Jamasb and Pollitt (2011), p. 309.

[43]Jamasb and Pollitt (2011), p. 309.

[44]Jamasb and Pollitt (2011), p. 309.

correlation between liberalization and an increase in patents for wind and solar power technologies in the US in the mid-2000s.[45]

Concerning the scale-up of renewable technologies specifically, Jamasb and Pollitt in their subsequent research contradict their earlier outcomes and conclude that an increase in environmental policies and support schemes introduced by the government does lead to an inherent growth in public R&D spending and the patenting of renewables.[46] Furthermore, other studies have indicated that innovation in clean energy was more likely to thrive in countries with more liberalized markets and that there was a causal link between the degree of liberalization and the success rate of clean energy policies.[47] Nesta, Vona and Nicolli, for instance, observe that

> In particular, the combination of environmental policies and market liberalization is the most effective method of inducing innovation in renewable energy, particularly near the technological frontier. This finding corroborates the complementarity hypothesis that environmental policies are more effective in competitive markets.[48]

This indicates that while liberalization of the market may contribute to increasing the share of renewables in the grid, it may not be enough to correct sufficiently for market failures.

Analogous studies have been conducted in the European 'brown' electricity sector. In a 2016 study, Cambini, Caviggioli and Scellato studied EU electricity market regulation and innovation in the period form 1990–2009 by considering the growing number of patents in the traditional energy sector, based on Eurostat and International Energy Agency Data.[49] The authors indeed found an increase in patent activities in the traditional electricity sector because of market liberalization, measured along the three factors of entry barriers, public ownership and vertical integration.[50] Especially, the econometric results found that policies aimed at reducing vertical integration, i.e. unbundling, have a positive influence on innovation in the European electricity sector.[51] However, a further 2014 study by Nicolli and Vona points out that lowering entry barriers is in fact a more significant force in facilitating renewable energy innovation, than privatization and unbundling.[52] Notwithstanding, they also conclude that this varies heavily across technologies (e.g. the well-developed wind industry profits from this).[53] Finally, the introduction of a more stable regulatory framework, in this particular study the Kyoto Protocol, amplifies the inducement effect of energy policies and privatization.[54]

---

[45]Nemet and Kammen (2007), p. 746.

[46]See generally Jamasb and Pollitt (2011, 2015).

[47]Nesta et al. (2014), p. 396.

[48]Nesta et al. (2014), p. 409.

[49]Cambini et al. (2016), p. 734.

[50]Cambini et al. (2016), p. 734.

[51]Cambini et al. (2016), p. 734.

[52]Nicolli and Vona (2016), p. 190.

[53]Nicolli and Vona (2016), p. 190.

[54]Nicolli and Vona (2016), p. 190.

What can we conclude from this evidence? Although the results point in various directions and are primarily deduced from using patents as a variable for measuring innovation in (renewable) energy, we can nevertheless draw some relevant inferences. It seems that in the primary phases of applying liberalization policies such as unbundling, patents in renewables and R&D spending first decrease. However, we also observe that subsequently, the market regains itself. Then, we witness an increase in innovation, especially in combination with governmental environmental policies and support schemes for renewables, by a growing number of patents in the 'green' and 'brown' European electricity sector alike. Especially policies promoting vertical unbundling appear to promote innovation in the sector, which seems to correspond with the fact that most energy industries have been historically vertically integrated. From this information, one can conclude that liberalization of the EU electricity market inherently promotes innovation, also in the renewable energy industry, measurable in the form of more patents in renewable energy technology. This given is notwithstanding any additional legislation for the scale up of clean and renewable energies.

However, the evidence also points to the fact that this is the most effective in countries where environmental *and* liberalization policies are combined. Moreover, while there may be strong indicators that liberalization *per se* does contribute, at least to some extent, to more clean energy technology innovation in the European electricity sector, this does not mean that it corrects for market failures adequately (e.g. correcting for climate change and the greenhouse gas externality).

Despite liberalization legislation, clean energy is still not on par with 'brown' energy in the electricity grid. Several causes for this are discussed here. First, the prices for fossil fuels (especially petroleum) vis-à-vis those for clean energy, while fluctuating over the decades, were considerably low overall.[55] This fact was coupled with the reality that Europe was growing increasingly dependent on imported fossil fuels.[56] Second, the traditional 'brown' industries have a first-mover advantage because of the early investments these firms have made to suit their production and transmission activities, vis-à-vis access for the producers of clean and renewable energies.[57] While the number of players in the market may actually be increasing, it remains more challenging to change supply side of electricity mix and for clean energy firms to access the market.[58] Furthermore, there is a whole string of other, non-cost barriers that prevent clean energy capacity to compete with fossil fuels on a level playing field in the energy market in general. These are comprised of both regulatory and non-regulatory barriers, e.g. administrative, physical, social (information asymmetry), financial barriers etc.[59]

[55] Johnston and Block (2012), p. 303.

[56] Johnston and Block (2012), p. 306.

[57] See also generally Petropoulos and Willems (2017).

[58] Johnston and Block (2012), p. 304.

[59] Johnston and Block (2012), p. 320.

4 EU Renewable Energy Policy: Legal Instruments Correcting for Market Failures

As the EU has undertaken binding commitments under international climate treaties (most recently under the 2015 Paris Agreement), it must make active efforts to curb emissions to prevent the further heating up of the earth.[60] The previous section demonstrated that there is indeed a causal link between liberalization and innovation, more precisely with respect to an increase in patents for clean and renewable energy technology, in the EU energy market. While liberalization by means of unbundling is one of the cornerstones of the Union's energy policy evidently, it is not enough to realize a significant decarbonization of the European energy sector by means of scaling up the share of renewables in the market. Additional regulation to mitigate the negative externalities of CO_2 emissions is thus clearly necessary.

Liberalization of the electricity market does correct adequately for market failures and allows renewable energy to compete with energy from brown energy sources in the grid on a level playing field. EU legislation to support renewable energy has been put in place with exactly this rationale in mind, to balance out this inequality and promote the share of renewables in the IEM.

The EU Renewable Energy Directive 2009/28/EC, also known as the Second Renewables Directive, is still the central legal instrument therein.[61] It sets ambitious goals for Member States, for instance that the share of renewables in the overall EU energy mix should be 20% or even 30% by 2020 (Article 3).[62] Moreover, it, among others, offers a framework for promoting renewable electricity, sets out mandatory national action plans for its 27 Member States to ensure they reach their goals through binding renewable energy targets (Articles 4 and 5), rules to overcome barriers to the development of renewable energy and ensure access to the grid (Articles 13 and 16).[63] More importantly, the Directive recognizes that for Member States to meet their renewable energy targets, the need for support schemes to foster this goal be implemented and this is therefore recognized and supported in various articles of the Directive as a legitimate means to an end.[64] The 20% target of renewable energy in the overall EU energy mix by 2020 that is set by the EU is a complex construct by its conception and design: First, the 20% target is an aggregate

[60] Paris Agreement 2015.

[61] EU Renewable Energy Directive 2009/28/EC.

[62] Article 3, EU Renewable Energy Directive 2009/28/EC.

[63] Article 3, EU Renewable Energy Directive 2009/28/EC.; Johnston and Block (2012), pp. 307–308.

[64] Article 2(k): *"support scheme' means any instrument, scheme or mechanism applied by a Member State or a group of Member States, that promotes the use of energy from renewable sources by reducing the cost of that energy, increasing the price at which it can be sold, or increasing, by means of a renewable energy obligation or otherwise, the volume of such energy purchased. This includes, but is not restricted to, investment aid, tax exemptions or reductions, tax refunds, renewable energy obligation support schemes including those using green certificates, and direct price support schemes including feed-in tariffs and premium payments'.*

target for the whole EU, not for individual Member States separately.[65] The Directive in its Preamble states that:

> Member States have different renewable energy potentials and operate different schemes of support for energy from renewable sources at the national level. The majority of Member States apply support schemes that grant benefits solely to energy from renewable sources that is produced on their territory. For the proper functioning of national support schemes it is vital that Member States can control the effect and costs of their national support schemes according to their different potentials.
>
> [...]
>
> In order to ensure the effectiveness of both measures of target compliance, i.e. national support schemes and cooperation mechanisms, it is essential that Member States are able to determine if and to what extent their national support schemes apply to energy from renewable sources produced in other Member States and to agree on this by applying the cooperation mechanisms provided for in this Directive.[66]

Complex calculations were made to reach the overall Union total of 20%. The percentage of renewable energy targets each of the Member States must reach is taken up in their individual national action plans, ranging from 10% (for Malta) to 49% (for Sweden).[67] Elements that were considered were: the starting situation of each Member State in 2005, plus an assessment of what percentage was possible to reach considering its fuel mix, economic development and realistic potential. Two remarks must be made in this respect. First, it should be mentioned that although the targets set by the EU for each of the Member States are binding, it is unclear what repercussions (apart from possible infringement proceedings by the Commission) follow in case the targets are not met. While the Commission requires Member States to report on their progress every 2 years and the Commission itself engages in monitoring and reporting, nowhere in the Directive itself does it state what the consequences are of non-compliance and/or a failure to meet the targets.[68] It is therefore quite remarkable that Member States have taken their commitments so seriously, as Eurostat has indeed reported a steady increase in the energy mix of renewables since the introduction of the binding targets.[69]

Support schemes for the scale up of clean energy in the EU come in various forms, such as investment aid, tax exemptions or reductions, tax refunds, renewable energy obligation support schemes including those using green certificates, and direct price support schemes including feed-in tariffs and premium payments.[70]

---

[65] EU Renewable Energy Directive, Preamble para 17.

[66] EU Renewable Energy Directive 2009/28/EC, Preamble para 25.

[67] See EU Renewable Energy Directive, Annex I, 'National overall targets for the share of energy from renewable sources in gross final consumption of energy in 2020'.

[68] Articles 22 and 23, EU Renewable Energy Directive.

[69] See Eurostat news release, 'Renewable energy in the EU: Share of renewables in energy consumption in the EU still on the rise to almost 17 per cent in 2015' (14 March 2014).

[70] Eurostat news release, 'Renewable energy in the EU: Share of renewables in energy consumption in the EU still on the rise to almost 17 per cent in 2015' (14 March 2014).

The feed-in tariff is by far the most popular support scheme for increasing the share of clean energy in the electricity grid up until now, although the EU plans to phase this instrument out over time.[71] Through the feed-in tariff, producers of clean energy receive a fixed, long-term guaranteed price per unit of energy fed into the grid. At present, there is a multiplicity of support schemes in the EU, differing in design, set-up and goal. There is no harmonization across Member States of these schemes, resulting in a plethora of successful and less successful examples of the scale up of clean energy in the electricity grid.[72] There seems to have been a conscious decision to not harmonize the various EU's clean and renewable energy support schemes across Europe. One reason for this may be the fact that both the schemes and renewable energy technologies as such are in the early stages of development that it would be premature to harmonize them across Member States on an EU level.[73] While it is this certainly a valid reason, for this Chapter it means that the schemes are difficult to map and monitor comprehensively at present.[74]

Nevertheless, disregarding international commitments, on EU level, support schemes for clean energy generally must abide by EU State Aid legislation.[75] According to EU state aid rules, the Treaty generally prohibits state aid unless it contributes to certain areas of economic development of a Member State. It is defined as an advantage in all forms conferred on a selective basis to undertakings by national public authorities according to Article 107(1) TFEU.[76] If found to be in violation of EU state aid law, the Member State in question must abolish the aid.[77] However, some categories of state aid, specified by decision of the Council, may be compatible with EU law.[78] Moreover, Article 109 TFEU stipulates that the Council may determine that certain aid is exempted from regular state aid rules.[79]

As discussed above, the EU allows support schemes for the scaling up of renewable energy to correct for market failures. As the Renewable Energy Directive in Annex 1 states:

[71] Johnston and Block (2012), p. 332 et seq.; the EU wants to move away from FIT schemes towards Feed in premia.

[72] One could think of the FIT scheme in Germany, that was constructed as an add-on to the consumer's bill. At the other spectrum there is Spain, where after initial subsidization of the renewable energy sector, the country had to cut back on support and incurred large amounts of debt because of, inter alia, the financial crisis and the design of the scheme.

[73] Johnston and Block (2012), pp. 339–340.

[74] The most comprehensive effort is the Beyond 2020 project, researching the design and impact of a harmonized policy for renewable electricity in Europe. Their comprehensive final report discusses pathways and possibilities for the harmonization of renewable energy across Europe, see Beyond 2020 (2014).

[75] Articles 107–109 TFEU.

[76] Article 107(1) TFEU.

[77] Article 108(2) TFEU.

[78] Article 107(3)(e) TFEU.

[79] Article 109 TFEU.

> In order to be able to achieve the national objectives set out in this Annex, it is underlined that the State aid guidelines for environmental protection recognize the continued need for national mechanisms of support for the promotion of energy from renewable sources.[80]

Moreover, two more sets of regulations dating from 2014 are relevant in this respect: The 2014 Block Exemption Regulation Declaring Certain Categories of Aid Compatible with the Internal Market, and the Commission Guidelines on State Aid for Environmental Protection and Energy.[81] The first document determines that state aid for environmental protection, including that for early adaptation to future Union standards, investment aid for energy efficiency measures, aid for high-efficiency cogeneration, investment aid for the promotion of energy from renewable sources, operating aid for the promotion of electricity from renewable sources, including those in small scale installations *"[...] shall be compatible with the internal market within the meaning of Article 107(3) of the Treaty and shall be exempted from the notification requirement of Article 108(3) of the Treaty, provided that the conditions laid down in this Article and in Chapter I are fulfilled."*[82] The Guidelines on State Aid for Environmental Protection and Energy sets out additional rules for these types of state aid to be compatible with the rules, with a higher goal of reaching the 20/20/20 targets.[83]

5 Conclusion

The evidence discussed in this chapter shows that liberalizing the Internal Marker for Electricity by means of unbundling and Third Party Access requirements in the energy sector inherently contributes to decarbonization of the electricity grid.[84] Unfortunately, we have also come to the straightforward conclusion that liberalization legislation alone does not correct enough for market failures such as curbing CO_2 emissions by scaling up the amount of clean energy producers on the grid or active in the energy mix. Notwithstanding unbundling, clean energy is still not on par with traditional, non-renewable energy. While it could be argued that liberalization legislation contributes to decarbonizing the grid by facilitating innovation, this has not been enough to correct for the negative externalities of carbon emission and it has not been able to make renewable energy compete with brown energy on

[80]EU Renewable Energy Directive 2009/28/EC, Annex 1, footnote 1.

[81]EC, Commission Regulation No 651/2014 of 17 June 2014 declaring certain categories of aid compatible with the internal market in application of Articles 107 and 108 of the Treaty, OJ L187/1 (26 June 2014) (hereafter: Block Exemption Regulation) and Guidelines on State aid for environmental protection and energy 2014–2020, 2014/C OJ C200/1 (28 June 2014).

[82]General Block Exemption Regulation, Section 7, Articles 36–43.

[83]Guidelines on State Aid for Environmental Protection and Energy, Preamble, under (3).

[84]See *supra* Sect. 2.

the grid on a level playing field.[85] Generally, intervention from above is thus necessary to scale up the share of clean energy in the electricity grid on the supply side, while simultaneously developing policies to incentivize energy efficiency on the demand side.

For the EU to meet both objectives of liberalization and decarbonization, legislation supporting the scale up of clean energy is thus necessary. Since 2009, the Commission has introduced binding targets for Member States for the share of renewables in their energy mix through the Renewable Energy Directive, to 20% or even 30% by 2020.[86] The introduction of these binding targets in 2009 has caused a steady rise in the share of renewables in their energy mix, evidences by data from Eurostat.[87] Aside from these binding targets, EU law moreover provides for legal and policy space under state aid law, by means of the European Commission, Guidelines on State aid for environmental protection and energy and the General Block Exemption Regulation.[88] It is our good hope that, once adopted, the new clean energy package will step up the efforts in this direction and will deliver a set of rules allowing Europe to leapfrog to a truly decarbonized European electricity grid.

References

Beyond 2020 (2014) Final report of the beyond 2020 project – approaches for a harmonisation of RES(-E) support in Europe. Intelligent Energy Europe, Vienna

Cambini C, Caviggioli F, Scellato G (2016) Innovation and market regulation: evidence from the European electricity industry. Ind Innov 23:734–752

Council of European Energy Regulators (2010) Energy Regulation and Security of Supply – The European Regulators' Approach (presentation of 8 March 2010) <ceer.eu>

Daintith T, Hancher L (1986) Energy strategy in Europe – the legal framework. De Gruyter, Berlin

Dreyer I, Stang G (2013) What energy security for the EU. Eur Union Inst Secur Stud:1–4

Energy Charter Secretariat (2015) International energy security – a common concept for energy producing, consuming and transit countries. Energy Charter Secretariat, Brussels

European Commission (2014) Commission Staff Working Document, In-depth study of European Energy Security, SWD(2014) 330final, 2 July 2014. Brussels

Glachant J-M, Saguan M, Rious V, Douguet S (2014) Incentives for investments: comparing EU electricity and TSO regulatory regimes. EUI Robert Schuman Centre for Advanced Studies Research Report: 1–101

International Energy Agency (2016) World Energy Outlook 2016. International Energy Agency, Paris

[85] See on this specifically Struckmann and Sapi (2017), p. 663 et seqq.

[86] EU Renewable Energy Directive 2009/28/EC.

[87] Eurostat, 'Energy from Renewable Sources'.

[88] European Commission, Guidelines on State aid for environmental protection and energy 2014–2020 (2014/C 200/01) C 200/1. 28 June 2014 and European Commission, Commission Regulation (EU) No 651/2014 of 17 June 2014 declaring certain categories of aid compatible with the internal market in application of Articles 107 and 108 of the Treaty Text with EEA relevance; OJ L 187, 26 June 2014, pp. 1–78.

Jamasb T, Pollitt M (2011) Electricity sector liberalisation and innovation: an analysis of the UK's patenting activities. Res Policy 40:309–324

Jamasb T, Pollitt M (2015) Why and how to subside energy R+D: lessons from the collapse and recovery of electricity innovation in the UK. Energy Policy 83:197–205

Johnston A, Block G (2012) EU energy law. Oxford University Press, Oxford

Lilliestam J, Patt A (2012) Conceptualising energy security in the European context. Smart Energy Eur Work Pap 4:1–13

Marhold A-A (2011) The Russo-Ukrainian gas disputes, the Energy Charter Treaty and the Kremlin proposal – is there light at the end of the gas pipe? Oil Gas Energy Law J 3:1–114

Marhold A-A (2016) EU Regulatory private law in the energy community – the synergy between the CEER and the ECRB in facilitating costumer protection. In: Cremona M, Micklitz HW (eds) Private law in the external relations of the EU. Oxford University Press, Oxford, pp 249–272

Metais R (2013) Ensuring energy security in Europe: the EU between a market-based and a geopolitical approach. College of Europe EU Diplomacy Paper 03: 1–32

Nemet G, Kammen D (2007) US energy research and development: declining investment, increasing need, and the feasibility of expansion. Energy Policy 35:746–755

Nesta L, Vona F, Nicolli F (2014) Environmental policies, competition and innovation in renewable energies. J Environ Econ Manag 67:396–411

Nicolli F, Vona F (2016) Heterogenous policies, heterogenous technologies: the case of renewable energy. Energy Econ 56:190–204

Organisation for Economic Co-operation and Development, International Energy Agency and Eurostat (2005) Energy statistics manual. OECD/IEA; Eurostat, Paris

Petropoulos G, Willems B (2017) Providing efficient network access to green power generators: long term property rights. Tilec Discussion Paper 007: 1–28

Pollitt M (2012) The role of policy in energy transitions: lessons from the energy liberalisation era. Energy Policy 50:128–137

Struckmann K, Sapi G (2017) Energy and environmental aid. In: Werner P, Verouden V (eds) EU state aid control – law and economics. Kluwer Law International, Alphen aan den Rijn, pp 663–714

Sveen T (2014) The Interaction between Article 192 and 194 TFEU. EU renewable energy law: legal challenges and perspectives: Scandinavian Institute of Maritime Law Year Book 2014. Oslo University, pp 157–182

Van der Vijver T (2012) Third party access exemption policy in the EU gas and electricity sectors: finding the right balance between competition and investments. In: Roggenkamp M, Barrera-Hernandez L, Zillman D, del Guayo I (eds) Energy networks and the law – innovative solutions in changing markets. Oxford University Press, Oxford, pp 333–352

Anna-Alexandra Marhold Tilburg. Assistant Professor of Law at the Tilburg Law and Economics Center, Tilburg University. PO Box 90153, 5000 LE Tilburg, the Netherlands, Tel. +31 628 788 966; a.marhold@uvt.nl. Fields of Interest: International Economic Law, International Trade Law, International and European Energy Law, Environmental Law, Climate Change and Sustainable Development, Public International Law, Competition Law, Economic Analysis of Law.

The Temperature Target of the Paris Agreement and the Forgotten Aspects of a Meaningful Energy Transition

Felix Ekardt and Jutta Wieding

Abstract The starting point of this paper is the energy transition currently taking place in Europe (and beyond) and the drastic temperature target set by Article 2 (1) Paris Agreement (although the agreement remains vague regarding other aspects). In view of the temperature limit, the energy and climate transition (globally and in Europe) is, by all means, insufficient. Especially as it requires the immediate and complete phase out of fossil fuels is not obvious. In addition, energy transition is often mistaken for a power transition, wholly relying on technical approaches and neglecting the necessary sufficiency measures. Existing policy approaches fail because of lacking ambition in their targets, as well as rebound and shifting effects (understood in a broad sense). But there are promising alternative policy approaches, especially on a Law and Economics basis.

1 Problem

For some time, the general issue of an energy and climate transition has become a point of discussion, as the continuing climate change will be of existential and economic consequence for humankind. According to a broad scientific consensus, it is estimated that the earth is approaching severe global warming of 3–6 °C (compared to pre-industrial level) within the twenty-first century. This phenomenon is caused by the high greenhouse gas emissions induced by humans, at the core of which are besides aspects of land use the use of fossil fuels in areas like energy production, industry, agriculture, domestic heating, power and transportation. This dimension of climate change will, according to present knowledge of natural science and economics, lead to vast economic damage, increased levels of forced migration, existentially threatened existence for millions of people, and, as a final consequence armed conflict over scarce resources such as food and water.

F. Ekardt (✉) · J. Wieding
Forschungsstelle Nachhaltigkeit und Klimapolitik, Leipzig, Germany
e-mail: mail@sustainability-justice-climate.eu; jutta.wieding@posteo.de

K. Mathis, B. R. Huber (eds.), *Energy Law and Economics*, Economic Analysis of Law in European Legal Scholarship 5, https://doi.org/10.1007/978-3-319-74636-4_5

Meanwhile, the current energy and climate transition in Europe and worldwide raises many doubts. This paper will therefore show the following: the Paris Agreement (PA) intends a zero-emissions target, which is far lower than the current global strategies aim for. There is no practical commitment to the inevitable phase out of fossil fuels, and the debate is focused only on technical solutions. Many measures taken so far miss the nature of the energy and climate issue, which is rooted in a problem of quantity. Therefore, they only achieve fragments of their original purpose, as they are prone to cause rebound effects (including growth effects) and shifting effects to other regions, sectors or environmental problems. At the same time, behaviour-orientated and policy-instrument orientated research in Law and Economics in particular has shown that there are solutions to gradually (on a broad scale both geographically and sectorally) phase out fossil fuels of the market. If the phase out of fossil fuels was seriously addressed—and not reduced to a (rather moderate) energy transition regarding electric power only—other environmental problems such as biodiversity loss, soil degradation and disturbed nitrogen cycles would also be approached. In doing so, it would be possible to assess the issues, which need to be structurally tackled with further economic or other instruments.

2 The Paris Temperature Limit and the Structure of the Paris Agreement

In December 2015, states across the world have agreed on a new climate change agreement. The signing of the Paris Agreement was enthusiastically welcomed by everyone, because it was doubtful whether it would be possible to come to an agreement at all. Based on the agreement, all states are obligated to increase their efforts to reduce global warming. Furthermore, they must adopt unavoidable measures to address climate change (adaptation) and provide restitutions to those states most affected by climate change (loss and damage).

The Paris Climate Agreement lacks ambition in most of its details and is, as such, disappointing.[1] At the same time, it contains a very ambitious target, which is unfortunately frequently overlooked. It determines that global warming needs to be limited to well below (!) 2 °C, and even undertake efforts to limit it to 1.5 °C. For an industrialised country such as Germany with high per capita emissions, this requires zero greenhouse gas emissions and no usage of fossil fuels in power, heating, fuels and material use by around the year 2038. However, this is the bottom-line for every country. These steps should limit global warming to well below 2 °C according to the data of the Intergovernmental Panel on Climate Change (IPCC). To achieve the limit to 1.5 °C, the global phase out of greenhouse gas emissions would need to be reached by the end of the 2020s. This assumes that

[1]On the following details of this chapter see Ekardt (2016), and Ekardt and Wieding (2016b), inter alia based on IPCC data.

negative emissions technologies are not technically feasible or extremely dangerous. The climate debate in Europe and the world largely neglect that (see next Sect. 2).

The Paris temperature limit is convincing, given its basis in human rights,[2] as on-going climate change would mean that the physical basis for freedom and democracy might come to collapse. It does however, overstep the democratic margin of appreciation to accept this. The margin of appreciation originates at the junction between "ecological" freedom rights (to the fundamental preconditions of freedom: life, health, and minimum subsistence level) and "economic" freedoms of corporations and consumers. This is usually overlooked by those who only consider economic freedom, as well as those who fail to realise that freedom also includes taking precautions against irreversible dangers such as climate change.

The ambitions of the Paris Agreement's overarching targets stand in stark contrast to the various individual national reduction targets.[3] After the failed climate negotiations in Copenhagen 2009, the drafters of the Paris agreement used that experience and turned towards voluntary commitments. This seemed the only way to reach a consensus among the wide range of interests between the involved parties. However, a consensus between the parties is necessary in international law. The results of this compromise and thus the operational requirements of the Agreement are stated in Article 4(2-19) PA. Every state party must freely determine and submit their reduction targets in the form of National Determined Contributions (NDCs). Despite the remarkable length of the article, there are no concrete terms on how to achieve the reduction targets. Consequently, there was never a doubt—not even during the negotiations—that the submitted NDCs will not meet the ambitious long-term target for global warming. This applies before considering that not all NDCs will be fulfilled, which is possible as there are loopholes to their legally binding nature:

- Many NDCs include conditions such as a requirement for appropriate financial support by other parties. However, following current indications, it is improbable that finances will be provided in the required amounts, or under the conditions determined in the NDCs.[4]
- The Paris Agreement does not include concrete sanctions in case that the NDCs are not completely put into action.
- Although Article 4(3) PA states that each NDC "will" be more ambitious than the previous ones, this increase in ambition might be marginal because of missing requirements set forth in the Paris Agreement. Again, the only clearly defined requirement is the overall target set in Article 2(1) PA.
- Article 14(2) PA requires an evaluation of the NDCs every 5 years starting in 2023 (and in 2018 before the PA enters into force). However, no explicit indicators are given which could easily be evaluated in terms of compliance.

[2]See Ekardt (2016), §§ 4 E. III., 7 C.; Ekardt et al. (2015a, b), pp. 579 et seq.; Skillington (2012), pp. 1196 et seq.; Sterk et al. (2013); OHCHR (2015); OHCHR (2014).

[3]See Ekardt and Wieding (2016b) and Averchenkova and Bassi (2016).

[4]For more on this see Averchenkova and Bassi (2016).

- Article 13 PA establishes a transparency framework, which serves to lighten the responsibility for states not only about the primary commitments, but also regarding measuring and procedures of emissions reductions. It establishes evaluation of states in a "non-intrusive, non-punitive manner, respectful of national sovereignty" and in consideration of the specific conditions of a country. This has rather little to do with the customary understanding of transparency.
- Even beyond the transparency framework, the NDCs are subjected to other measures undermining their binding nature. Articles 4(4-5), 9(1) PA indicates that developed countries "should continue" taking the lead. The obligation for countries in transition such as China, South Africa, India or Brazil to act remains even more vague.
- As if to increase flexibility further, every party may leave the Paris Agreement after a while without giving reasons (Article 28 PA).
- Certain types of emissions are exempt from emission reduction obligations from the start. This regards emissions from the fast-growing sectors of international aviation and marine traffic. Also, the role of emissions from land-use related emissions and sinks[5] is not completely apparent (Article 5(1) PA), neither of those from agriculture nor those from other land-use changes and deforestation (below more on this). Although these are hard to measure exactly, they make up large quantities of global emissions.

This shows that the vagueness of individual measures and instruments of the Paris Agreement stands in contrast to the legally binding global temperature limit in Article 2(1) PA. It is however undoubtedly admissible to interpret regulation details considering the target of the regulation (systematic interpretation). Article 2(1) PA therefore suggests that there is a criterion to measure when evaluating National Determined Reduction Plans—the global temperature target. Therefore, it will become mandatory that NDCs must continually show great increase in ambition levels—but this will be ignored by most of the parties (including EU-Member States like Germany), thereby ignoring all consequences (of climate change).

3 Frictions with the Current Energy Transition

Taking the prescribed Paris temperature limit as point of reference, key governance deficiencies in the current energy transition become apparent. The EU and Germany will drastically fail to meet the ambitious temperature limits with their climate targets so far and the instruments currently in place. Since according to Article 3 PA NDCs are the sole implementation tool to meet the temperature limit, the Agreement would be set up for failure in view of insufficient NDCs (on this in Article 4(2-19)). However, the Agreement calls for later improvement of NDCs which, after all that

[5]Forests, fenlands and pastures can absorb and store greenhouse gas emissions, eliminating them from the carbon cycle. Therefore, they are valued as so-called "sinks".

has been said, would need to happen both very fast and drastically. Even when looking at the past, the label as climate forerunner attributed to the EU or Germany[6] has less merit than generally thought. One indicator for this is, that neither party actively contributed much for a better outcome of the Paris negotiations. The EU pledged an emissions reduction of 40% by 2030 as (supra-)national contribution in terms of Article 4(2) PA.[7] This is far too little to meet the temperature limit set in Article 2 PA, which had also been proposed and supported by the EU. If developed countries had committed to more ambitious reduction targets and more financial support for developing countries in terms of mitigation, adaptation, as well as compensating for losses and damages, other countries globally might have followed with their own stronger commitments. Furthermore, despite the self-proclaimed positive role, per capita emissions remain a multiple of the requirements of the temperature limit. Even the (on a high level) achieved emissions reductions since 1990 are predominantly statistical sugar-coating. They occurred largely because of the shift of production of EU-consumer goods abroad. EU-wide, these shifting effects alone account for more than the statistical emission reduction of 10% compared to 1990.[8] In the context of this paper, it is this overall balance that shines a rather dim light on the European energy transition; this cannot be overruled by claiming the quantitative number of legislative norms in Europe.[9]

The European energy transition, as currently implemented (almost everywhere), is basically a power transition. Heating, transport and material use of fossil fuels e.g. fertilizer (and causes of climate emissions besides fossil fuels, which mostly occur in the agricultural sector) are neglected. Policy measures taken so far in Europe and elsewhere are nor in the least enough to induce a speedy and complete phase out of fossil fuels—not even remotely in the power sector, and especially not in other mentioned sectors. It is not only other sources of emissions, but also other environmental problems, which receive very little attention. Therefore, despite all intellectual and technical opportunities, the claim that Europe is an environmental forerunner in comparison to the allegedly lagging developing countries, seems quite far-fetched. Because at the end of the day, it is not nice speeches that count, but the ecological footprint.

---

[6]See Elmer et al. (2015), pp. 18 et seq.; Enquête-Kommission (2010), p. 497; Böcher and Töller (2012), pp. 22 et seq.; explicitly critical Becker and Richter (2015), pp. 3 et seq.; partially also Moreno et al. (2015), pp. 13 et seq.

[7]See overview of legal documents on www.bmwi.de/DE/Themen/Energie/Europaische-und-internationale-Energiepolitik/europaeische-energiepolitik,did=648682.html [accessed 24 August 2017].

[8]See on phenomena which are difficult to exactly calculate Peters et al. (2015), pp. 8903 et seq.; even more radical Hoffmann (2015), p. 20, furthermore Becker and Richter (2015), pp. 3 et seq.

[9]For a more detailed account of instruments in EU energy law see Hennig (2017), Ekardt (2016), and von Bredow (2013).

4 Purely Technical Approaches Versus Sufficiency

It is however ambiguous, whether environmental protection will be successful if purely based on technical solutions. Renewable energies and energy efficiency as technical perspectives might, by themselves, not be enough to meet the above-mentioned global temperature limit. To address various problems associated with the current energy supply system, sufficiency (respectively behavioural change) as an additional (!) strategy might become necessary, although purely technical solutions seem appealing to solve environmental problems such as climate change. New technologies create new markets and employment, whereas behavioural change often means eliminating a good from the market and eventually question an economic model, which is based on growth. Also, a purely technical transformation can be more convenient and therefore easier to implement than changing behavioural patterns.[10] There are different aspects however, which speak against exclusive (!) technical problem-solving. This is true for climate change, but even more so regarding other environmental problems[11]:

1. The scope of problems caused e.g. through climate change must be considered. Considering the speed of innovation so far, it seems highly improbable that a transformation to increased renewable energies and energy efficiency will reduce greenhouse gas emissions to zero in 10 or 20 years.[12] It remains uncertain whether the potential of renewable energies is always estimated correctly by their proponents.[13] Note that the scope of the problem requires a global view, so the question is if consumption wishes can be met purely technically in a world society built on economic growth and increasing prosperity. New findings of resources will merely put off the problem; in the case of climate change they even aggravate the situation.
2. Essential is also that some problems cannot be solved by technology, for example those regarding food. Most of produced emissions in the food sector can be allocated to products from animals. This is because the long chain from animal feed to animal calories leading to human nutrition requires a multiple of plant production (for animal feed) and therefore a multiple of fertilizer, land use, as well as other emission sources, such as the notorious methane flatulencies of cattle.[14] This can be avoided by reducing consumption of meat and other animal products. This however requires a behavioural change and cannot be solved by a technical measure.

---

[10]Therefore, one-sided Paech (2012); Sommer and Welzer (2014), pp. 72 et seq.

[11]On all this Hennig (2017) and Ekardt (2016).

[12]See for details Jackson (2013); Ekardt et al. (2015a), pp. 15 and 27 et seq.; in this direction also Stengel (2011), pp. 131 et seq.

[13]See Hänggi (2011), pp. 131 et seq.; Bürkle (2015); DLR (2006).

[14]See Heinrich-Böll-Stiftung et al. (2015), pp. 20 et seq.; Stoll-Kleemann (2014).

3. This leads to an issue, which might be the most important one: to sustain living conditions (as well as the economy and to preserve world peace) other environmental problems besides climate change must be tackled. However, for many of them, technical solutions are much less available than they are for climate change. Key examples are damaged eco-systems and the loss of biodiversity, disturbed nitrogen cycles and soil degradation.[15] Solutions will require mankind to retreat from land use and to restrain agriculture. This further implies putting a stop to ever growing personal living space and continuously growing consumption of animal products; likewise, it will not be possible to compensate the omission of mineral fertilizers by constantly expanding land use etc. It will also not be possible to replace all materials used for goods in wealthy societies with materials from renewable or quasi infinitely available resources.[16]
4. Remember furthermore that shifting of emissions, land use etc. to other countries is not a long-term option and must be stopped under normative considerations.[17]
5. Also, options of renewable-energy and efficiency options are finite. Even if energy were infinitely available, limits result from other finite resources without which energy is useless. For example, rare earths are necessary to produce cell phone, flat screens, or batteries for electric cars. The amount of energy a product needs in production and use, accounts only for a fraction of its environmental pollution.[18]
6. The debate is even stronger dominated[19] by the following issue: Technical improvements so far have the tendency to trigger rebound effects that make up for savings by increased energy efficiency. Rebound effects occur through more frequent or more intense use of a product. More efficient cars for instance are driven longer distances and in general, the number of cars on the road is constantly increasing. Therefore, the point is that there are no emission reductions. At least, technical innovation will not avoid that growing wealth will take up all savings in emissions—or that there will be shifting into other areas of life. Effective sustainability politics will have to address this problem.[20] This however, can only serve as proof that sufficiency really is imperative, if technical innovation is not fast enough to outrun rebound effects. Or that capital seeking to be invested will not trigger overusing other resources (this would result in

[15]For more see Ekardt (2016), § 6 E. V. 2.

[16]Especially since most of them will compete with food production and cause further problems: Ekardt (2016), § 6 E. V. 1.

[17]See Ekardt (2016), §§ 1 B. II., 5 C. IV., 6 E. III. 2.

[18]Schmidt-Bleek (2014), p. 65; Hoffmann (2015), p. 20; Hehn (2015), pp. 79 et seq.

[19]Visible in e.g. Heyen et al. (2013), p. 9; Paech (2012), pp. 69 et seq.; Hoffmann (2015), pp. 17 et seq.; Becker and Richter (2015), pp. 3 et seq.; Santarius (2015), pp. 273 et seq.; Klingholz (2014), pp. 100 et seq.; Stengel (2011), pp. 134 et seq.; Reimer and Tölle (2013), p. 589 (597); von Bredow (2013), pp. 66 et seq.; Voget-Kleschin (2013), pp. 97 et seq.

[20]For more details on rebound and shifting effects see Ekardt (2016), § 6 D. IV.; for possible solutions see Ekardt (2016), § 6 E. III.

efficiency simply being equivalent to expansion[21]). This would lead right back to the arguments previously made.

7. Even if all points made above were void, and there actually was a purely technical way (and therefore by maintaining constant economic growth) to solve the climate crisis and other environmental problems, the unsolvable problem remains that technical options will have to continue improving infinitely (!) and hence not only the energy demands of today would need to be met but the ever-growing demands. If all others fail, this endless spiral will exceed the capacities of a physically finite world. Therefore, the question is much less "if" than "when" sufficiency will become inevitable.

So, we do see the so-called decoupling of growing wealth and nature exploitation through technological innovation, but just not on a sufficient level in view of the temperature limit set in Article 2 PA.[22] The doctrine of decoupling, which economists also known as Kuznets curve, was not even valid at the time of its development. Even when it was developed at the beginning of the twentieth century, Kuznets was aware of the partial randomness of his calculations.[23] Of course, neither the future in general, nor technical innovation specifically can be predicted with certainty, not even when the limits of human knowledge are disregarded. Furthermore, the development of environmental problems, not only climate change, are highly uncertain. Normatively, it is possible to debate the necessary scope of action in detail, however, targets like far-reaching greenhouse-gas-emission reductions, stabilising eco-systems, stop of soil degradation and the like, will remain reasonable from an ethical and legal point of view.[24] It remains therefore the tendency to include behavioural change and sufficiency as key strategy (beside consistency and efficiency) in environmental policy. This does not only imply talking about social infrastructure to implement new technologies.[25] While, indeed, we must analyse conditions of societal change, both technological change and behavioural change must be included. Also, the analysis cannot end—as often done—with merely naming stakeholders and institutions.

If, as seen, sufficiency needs to play a crucial part in the sustainability transition, less goods and services will be sold (e.g. less holiday flights). This could, if taken to a considerable scope, lead to an unplanned transition towards a post-growth society,

---

[21]Which is the (overly) strong turn of Santarius (2015), p. 273.

[22]Hoffmann (2015), pp. 12 et seq.; Luks (2013), pp. 23 et seq. and 65 et seq.; Santarius et al. (2016), pp. 81 et seq.; Jackson (2013), pp. 81 et seq.; Heyen et al. (2013), p. 8; Becker and Richter (2015), pp. 3 et seq.; Bauriedl (2016), pp. 217 et seq.; Paech (2012), pp. 69 et seq.; Voget-Kleschin (2013), pp. 97 et seq.; on the data basis of very limited absolute decoupling see www.umweltbundesamt.de/tags/energieverbrauch [accessed 24 August 2017]; missing the point Handrich et al. (2015), p. 27; Paqué (2010), pp. 72 et seq. and 96 et seq.; Liebe and Preisendörfer (2013), p. 239 (242).

[23]With a detailed calculation Piketty (2015), pp. 29 et seq.; Moreno et al. (2015), p. 28; disregarded in Liebe and Preisendörfer (2013), p. 239 (242); Paqué (2010), pp. 96 et seq.

[24]See Ekardt (2016), § 5 C. IV.

[25]Neglected e.g. in Schmid et al. (2016), pp. 263 et seq.

meaning to a society that must cope without growth or even with degrowth eventually.[26] Surely, it is possible to derive business ideas from the concept of sufficiency being based on sharing economy, regional and slow products, service orientation or education and courses and so on. This would allow certain industries to grow.[27] Real sufficiency however would, when reaching ecological targets without jeopardising them through rebound effects or problem shifting into other sectors or other environmental issues, most probably lead to selling and buying less. This will hardly allow for the current growth orientated society to remain the way it works so far. Consequently, there are already businesses which consciously decide against growing—and even more businesses which exist involuntarily without growth.[28] This is not about deliberately avoiding growth. The transition towards a degrowth society could be the side effect of adequate sustainability politics if they include considerable sufficiency measures.

Imagining continued economic growth despite the above named long-term (!) and world-wide (!) problems means the world implicitly or explicitly ignores those issues.[29] This implies using only technical measures for sustainability, which will not be enough because of the mentioned frictions (scope of the problem, other environmental problems than climate change, danger of overestimating technology, rebound and shifting effects with continuously growing wealth, etc.). Regarding scope of the problem, the possible scope of damage is often not reflected adequately. Steering the world into the danger of wars and civil wars, the age of growth will rather obviously end, despite all problems associated with quantifying this in detail. A problematic solution could be to normatively proclaim that economic growth must be maintained and therefore accepting considerable environmental damage. In other words, in a finite world, growth will physically encounter limits eventually.[30]

[26]See Jackson (2013); Paech (2012); Schulz and Bailey (2014), pp. 277 et seq.; Scheidler (2015), pp. 205 et seq.; Jensen and Scheub (2014); Miegel (2010); unclear Muraca (2015), pp. 59 et seq.; Stengel (2011), pp. 163 et seq.

[27]Examples for that—without clearly distinguishing from macroeconomic development—in Posse (2015), pp. 59 et seq.; Heyen et al. (2013), p. 18; Wilts and von Gries (2015), pp. 41 et seq.

[28]Examples for that Liesen et al. (2013), pp. 5 et seq.

[29]E.g. Stern (2009), p. 11 or 92; Radermacher et al. (2011), pp. 105 et seq.; Handrich et al. (2015), p. 27; Paqué (2010), pp. 72 et seq.; Fücks (2013), pp. 69 et seq.; Enquête-Kommission (2010), pp. 430 et seq.; Sukhdev (2013), pp. 209 et seq.; Schmidt-Bleek (2014), pp. 126 et seq.; see also Weimann (2009), p. 26 and Nordhaus (2008), pp. 32 et seq.; not with sufficient scepticism in UNEP (2010), passim and Kaven (2015), pp. 176 et seq. (in naming other authors like Jänicke, Altvater and Rifkin); explicitly contra Stern (2009) (in the spirit of the discription in this paper) Helm (2008), pp. 24 et seq. and Hänggi (2011), pp. 182 et seq.; left open in Ott (2011), pp. 54 et seq.; on empirical growth over decades and centuries Piketty (2015), pp. 105 et seq.; rightly on the problem Posse (2015), p. 59.

[30]See Tichy (2009), pp. 4 et seq.; Paech (2005), pp. 84 et seq.; Hinterberger and Pirgmaier (2009), pp. 58 et seq.; Lutter and Giljum (2009), pp. 12 et seq.; Tichy (2009), pp. 4 et seq.; left open in Grunwald and Kopfmüller (2012), pp. 48 et seq.; more optimistic Kettner (2009), pp. 77 et seq.; Schneider (2009), pp. 71 et seq.; see also Kesselring (2015), pp. 1 et seq. These thoughts are not rendered wrong by the famous sociologist Werner Sombart, who declared "sustainability and "stationary" economy along with criticism of capitalism in the 1930s to be Nazi positions.

Disrespecting the physical limits of this world will most probably end in a disaster either environmentally or impacting global food security or resulting in violent encounters, as predicted by the Club of Rome 1972.[31] In short: forcing new products in to the market and healing the worst does not make for a sustainability strategy. Long-distance flights will not be an environmental gain just because the jets are constructed relatively energy efficiently.

One could think: If sufficiency will lead to the end of a growth society, and an energy and climate transition, it cannot be economically sensible.[32] This however might be because of a misunderstanding. Carefully planned, step-by-step transformation of the economy might after all be economically smarter than a world of drastic climate damage and climate wars.[33] Furthermore, sufficiency will help avoid social costs and conflicts related to technical options (including wind power).

5 Motivations for Energy Transition

Policy instrument proposals require verified assumptions on how norm addressees are behaving and how they will react to governance incentives. Economists rely on the behavioural model of homo oeconomicus, which critics consider out-dated and therefore consider price incentives as overestimates. The commonly cultivated perception is that economic instruments especially, such as levies or cap-and-trade schemes are only effective if people act as homo oeconomicus; however, this is not true, as will be shown below. Findings from more complex behavioural research will rather support the expectable effectiveness of those instruments. Note that the findings below are not limited to a certain character type, but include citizens,

References in Luks (2013), p. 42. Very elaborate theoretical economic criticism of growth is provided by Paech (2005), pp. 193 et seq.; on the connection to economic theory of decreasing marginal benefits Hänggi (2011), pp. 28 et seq.; unclear Radermacher and Beyers (2011), passim (on one side rightly observing that growth can also mean "0.1%" and then gradually even less, but at the same time predicting de facto a "ten times" richer world). On the defensive role of most NGOs in these debates Stoll (2014), pp. 124 et seq.

[31]The technological potential was underestimated in Meadows et al. (1972), passim, at the same time, the environmental situation is also seen too optimistically (also because of lack of knowledge of climate change); rightly on this Klingholz (2014), passim; one-sided on the deficiencies Fücks (2013), pp. 81 et seq.; out-dated scepticism of Malthus (1977), passim, the substantial technological dynamic has been wrongly estimated.

[32]On the uneconomic nature of sufficiency options Jakob and Edenhofer (2014), pp. 447 et seq.; (too) open in our opinion Pissarskoi (2014), pp. 235 et seq. There in our view neglecting that purely technical options are not enough, if 95% emissions reductions for climate protection, the shifting of problems in other countries reversed and other environmental problems (biodiversity, nitrogen cycles etc.) must be tackled at the same time. It seems furthermore improbable that—as claimed—there are more sufficiency measures in planning than are necessary to complement technological options. Same problems in Fücks (2013), pp. 69 et seq.; correctly Stengel (2011), p. 163.

[33]In favour of considering all actual costs of growth Seidl and Zahrnt (2010), pp. 179 et seq.

politicians, entrepreneurs, NGO activists etc. Also, they are not limited to a certain nationality. The aim is to integrate findings from behavioural science in various disciplines like sociology, economics, psychology, socio-biology, anthropology and ethnology; and of course, the field of behavioural economics.[34]

Based on pluralistic methodological approaches, it was shown elsewhere[35] that non-sustainable and non-sufficient behaviour has various sources in different actors and that it should therefore be avoided to focus relevant aspects on behavioural science only. Pure knowledge of facts has proven to be only a small part in triggering behaviour. It is more important to understand how actors are interdependent. The behaviour of, for example, citizens is influenced by politicians and vice versa. The same applies to the dependency between enterprises and consumers. It is part of a certain economic system to constantly acquire customers that buy more and new products without caring about the means of production and that are inclined to find products, which are produced exemplary from a social and ecological perspective, too expensive. But it also requires enterprises which offer—or in fact do not offer—customers products to trigger needs and thus constantly increasing their profits,[36] ergo keeping up the spiral of growth and high resource intensity. It would be misleading however to simply talk in Marxian tradition of exploitation and estrangement, particularly since many liberties have been installed in modern societies at the same time.[37] As suggestive many offers might be, production and consumption are not forced by just one side and many individual suppliers and demanders make their contributions.[38] The role of factors such as self-interest, the dilemma of public goods, path dependencies and conceptions of normality as aspects of motivation in this interaction, especially looking from an economic point of view has been described by many.[39] Two aspects crucial to comprehensively explaining the reluctance to act on sufficiency are however frequently neglected.

One of which are common conceptions of normality as shown by many.[40] Despite all intellectual recognition of climate change and the associated problems, we continue to live in a high-emission world. When you set aside this article, the next meat buffet, the next car drive to work or the next holiday flight is not far. These things are just ordinary nowadays, if one can afford them financially. Dismissing

---

[34]More on this perspective in Ekardt (2016) with several references.

[35]Most recently by Ekardt (2016), § 2.

[36]See Gronemeyer (2002), pp. 173 et seq. and passim.

[37]See Ekardt (2016), § 1 A.

[38]This is still true if supposed that people nowadays are determined by many very subtle mechanisms in jobs, leisure, romantic relationships, emotions, identities etc., even if this external determination utilises the illusion of individual autonomy. One-sidedly therefore Schreiner (2015), pp. 104 et seq.; Schridde (2014); Gorz (2009), pp. 7 et seq. building on Sartre (1943), as well as Foucault (1973), pp. 30 et seq.; precise Fücks (2013), pp. 73 et seq.; Stengel (2011), p. 259; Prakash et al. (2016), pp. 288 et seq.

[39]Summarized by Ekardt (2016), § 2.

[40]See also Deutscher Bundestag (2013), pp. 438 et seq.; Stengel (2011), pp. 183 et seq.; Schützenmeister (2010), pp. 267 et seq. und 275 et seq.; Ekardt (2016), § 2; Welzer (2013).

flying as a form of travel completely might lead to social pressure and an image as a "weirdo". Lifestyle is also relevant to social standing, in any given situation one's social surroundings requires a certain apartment, cars and travels, to belong. This is increasingly true for countries outside the Western hemisphere, which follow the role models of industrialised countries. Especially decision-makers in politics and enterprises are often used to entertaining a lifestyle that includes frequent flights, opulent buffets, global friendships, regular meat consumption, and suddenly now they are required to think about abolishing this type of lifestyle (with foreseeable results?). Concepts of normality vary significantly nowadays; however, the fact that we develop them (unconsciously) to simplify ordinary activities seems to be a biological invariable.

Human emotions are likewise relevant for all of us, including entrepreneurs, politicians, civil servants etc.[41] Damage because of climate change is geographically and temporally distant, invisible, with highly complex causalities which make it hard to imagine caused by an ordinary activity and therefore not usually emotionally accessible to people (citizens, politicians, entrepreneurs).[42] On the other hand, a daily car drive to work and the next holiday flight are in the here and now and therefore very well visible. Time-space abstraction massively reduces empathy, which is also recognised in experimental psychology, e.g. in the notorious Milgram experiment and from holocaust research.[43] Additionally, mankind has a remarkable talent in emotionally preferring the comfortable, the dwelling in the accustomed, the denial of unpleasant interconnections etc. Another typical component of the high levels of emissions is a justifying mechanism: "others are even greater contributors" (SUV drivers, other political parties, other industries). The tendency to increase what is mine (in terms of votes, profits or personal belongings), sometimes going overboard towards greediness, also seems to be equally innate to mankind. A trait which can probably be traced back to evolution. The same might be said for the fundamental human pursuit of appreciation from other people, e.g. through "status goods", which also determine one's identity and place in social networks—by striving for goods which show to myself and others that I am a well-off, nice, open-minded person. This is complemented by other, empirically well founded human inclinations[44] which also turn out to be rather fatal in the context of sustainability and climate change: inability to believe that future catastrophes will happen; notoriously underestimating moderate risks, as well as the allegedly "only small" contribution to big, highly complex occurrences; tendency to solve problems with already known

[41]While the different aspects cannot be precisely differentiated; Ekardt (2001), § 13. 3.c; Entzian (2016), pp. 32 et seq. and 187 et seq.; Wilson (2015), pp. 185 et seq.; Kuckartz (2010), pp. 144 et seq.; Ernst (2010), pp. 128 et seq.; Klöckner (2015), pp. 153 et seq.; Deutscher Bundestag (2013), pp. 438 et seq.; Bruppacher (2014), pp. 51 et seq.; Blöbaum (2012), pp. 233 et seq.; Beckenbach (2003), pp. 13 et seq.

[42]Beyerl (2010), pp. 247 et seq.

[43]See Milgram (1974), p. 183; Welzer (2013).

[44]See Klöhn (2006), pp. 95 et seq.; Stoll-Kleemann et al. (2001), pp. 107 et seq.; more references in Ekardt (2016), § 2.

measures (which just might have caused the problem); tendency to judge big problems by way of personal experience, as well as prominent or dramatic events (leading at times to major distortions); tendency to unrealistically positive perceptions of one's own efforts, as well as shifted perception of some maybe less important risks compared to others. Such emotions towards climate change are well documented; also in focus-group experiments.[45]

Whether the listed aspects should be categorised as "individual actions" or "collective structures" is a discourse in behavioural science disciplines and especially in sociology since Weber and Durkheim who thought contrarily.[46] The controversy is however questionable since this would express concrete motivations of people, respectively interacting groups of people, or at least the side-effects and aggregated consequences. All aspects are encountered both in the individual and in structures—of course in human—forms. "Self-interest", "conceptions of normality" or "emotions" are not only visible in individuals but are also shaping higher structures; so, in the end, retention of power or accumulation of capital are collectivised variations of self-interest and path dependencies. Those who prefer to identify e.g. "capitalism" as driver for developments in society as a whole, fail to define what constitutes society and if all aspects of that are influenced by capitalism. This leads to the here proposed position that it does not make sense to distinguish between "anthropology" and "social theory". At least, if not every social situation is deliberately brought about by an individual. There are unexpected or unintended consequences to actions, and of course, individuals aggregate to structures. Individuals act, as already discussed, by no means always rationally and deliberately.[47] This paper will therefore not give way to methodological collectivism, nor methodological individualism, but much rather assume that this confrontation is empirically inadequate.[48]

Non-sustainable behaviour is therefore easy to explain. At the same time, these findings hint at the fact that a fundamental turn towards sustainability, and specifically sufficiency, might be very hard to achieve, as there is reason to assume that emotions especially are part of a core biological configuration, which cannot be eliminated. To achieve sustainability, it is however essential that different actors will move together as a whole—and that aspects, which can be changed are in fact changed, e.g. self-interest calculations or path dependencies. These necessary

[45]See Stoll-Kleemann et al. (2001), pp. 107 et seq.

[46]On the more recent debate Giddens (1988), pp. 51 et seq.; Gimmler (1999), pp. 27 et seq.; Pogge (2007), pp. 967 et seq.; Habermas (1981); Blöbaum (2012); Greve (2015), pp. 9 et seq.; Mead (1968), pp. 187 et seq.; Soff (2010), pp. 85 et seq.

[47]Explicitly on this: Greve (2015), p. 20, who on p. 26 points out that individual actions cannot be allocated to "collective attributions" alone, because these attributions would again be actions, therefore leading to an infinite regress.

[48]Similar in its intention: Habermas (1981); Giddens (1988), pp. 51 et seq.; Mead (1968), pp. 187 et seq.; Soff (2010), pp. 85 et seq.; and at last also Greve (2015), pp. 26 et seq.

changes can be influenced through new political frameworks such as levies or caps on fossil fuels. Pricing will also support a change in conceptions of normality.[49] However, it will hardly be possible to discuss change as a matter of politicians, because of the interdependencies of actors; it is of particular importance to have groups and individuals in society *demanding* and fighting for new policies. Bluntly speaking, what politicians do depend on the citizens and the other way around. The key however is not just discourse, but *practicing* new and more sustainable normalities.

6 Governance Problems

The effect of existing national and transnational sustainability instruments is limited, when considering the results of per capita emissions as stated earlier. In view of the massive body of regulations, this must be explained, when considering human motivation (which includes politicians). Sustainability politics and (also) energy and climate law so far frequently operates with substantial regulation for individual products, plants or actions. This applies to cars, buildings or other individual areas of life, which are determined and maybe, in case of an offense, sanctioned. However, modern resource and sink (meaning the capacity to absorb, regenerate or reform a substance) problems are quantity problems. This means that usually it is not an individual action but rather a total quantity of input or removal of resources is relevant. This is particularly obvious for climate change and the finite resources. But for loss of biodiversity, pollution, radiation or noise, the total amount of disturbances is relevant. However, as opposed to climate change, local exposure also matters (local exposure—hot spots—are often fit to be regulated by command-and-control measures). Quantity aspects of a problem are, in current debates, mostly neglected as they lead to governance problems. Quantity problems cannot be solved by regulation that targets single products, plants, individual sectors or even isolated geographical spaces. Therefore, a broad sector and substantial scope is needed. It is important to note that the above-mentioned insufficiencies also occur with voluntary actions of businesses, also known as self-regulation—and lastly also with voluntary actions of consumers.[50] To put it in more detail:

---

[49]More in Ekardt (2016), § 2 G.

[50]On the following Ekardt (2016); Hennig (2017); similar von Bredow (2013). A brief version of the following list in Ekardt (2014), chapter IV, as well as in Hennig (2017), chapter 3.1.2.2; furthermore, von Bredow (2013), pp. 121 et seq.; an example for the transition of these points into the mainstream debate Pufé (2014), pp. 231 et seq.; Bauknecht et al. (2015), pp. 38 et seq.; Radkau (2011), pp. 580 et seq.; often, these problems are touched upon in Linz (2015), p. 10, only to be "forgotten" later. One aspect of the quantity problem is that many rather harmless individual activities add up to a harmful total. The typical focus of command-and-control law in individual activities suggests that some of those actions are "still okay".

1. An effective[51] instrument approach for sustainability (or other political targets) must be substantially strong enough to meet the target to be achieved (target adequacy). European instruments are currently not designed to reach zero emissions soon. Therefore, they are set up to fail in achieving the target set in Article 2 (1) PA and therefore infringe on the human rights the target is based upon. Symptomatic for this climate policy is that certain sectors such as food, domestic heating in old buildings or transportation are scarcely regulated. Neither in terms of renewable energies, nor regarding energy efficiency let alone sufficiency. The focus of existing law is the introduction of renewable energy into the power market. This has partially been successful. Other sectors, besides power, the increase of energy efficiency, and sufficiency have been neglected for the most parts. Same goes *prima facie* for other resource and sink problems which are beyond the scope of this chapter. Policy instruments to tackle loss of biodiversity, soil degradation etc. do not consistently target the harmful factors.[52]
2. Command-and-control approaches could be improved in terms of target adequacy, but an effective policy approach also must have an effective enforcement. In this regard, current sustainability efforts are deficient as well, as is proven by their results. Not all legal standards are kept in practice (and it is very difficult to substantially improve that given a large number of detailed norms in command-and-control law). For example, insulation in new buildings is not installed consistently by builders and construction workers, unless an authority steps in. Another vivid example is nature conservation, which works rather poorly in practice despite a large policy body consisting of compensation for disruptions.[53]
3. Given the behavioural analysis (Sect. 5) and empirical data, regulations and efforts addressing only parts or single sectors or areas (such might be federal law, regional measures, individual or commercial activities) tend to trigger (a) sectorial, (b) resource-related and (c) geographical shifting effects regarding production and/or consumption. In most literature, only geographical shifting is mentioned.[54] Because of policy measures, resource use and emissions by businesses and citizens is shifted to different areas of their lives, different places or simply encouraged to use other resources or produce different emissions even more intensely. All these shifting effects are possibly not only a direct reaction to policy measures, they may occur independently, however they are all part of the same ecologically dysfunctional processes (weak leakage). Just to give some examples: when transitioning from fossil fuels to bio fuels, or other (sometimes only alleged) climate protection measures in agriculture, the strain on soils, water,

[51]On the term see Ekardt (2016), § 1 D. III. 2.

[52]For more see Ekardt (2016), §§ 6 E. V. 3., 6 E. VI. 1.

[53]Also see Ekardt (2016), § 6 E. VI. 1.

[54]See e.g. SRU (2012), Tz. 13 et seq.; Hey (2014), p. 632; Heyen et al. (2013), p. 18; clearer in that regard Schmidt-Bleek (2014), pp. 80 et seq.; Santarius (2015), pp. 185 et seq.; von Bredow (2013), pp. 125 et seq. In terms of climate change missing the point, when discussing possible different results of "regulation competition": Giegerich (2010), p. 57 (80); and Mehde (2005), pp. 94 et seq.

and nature in general rises.[55] New energy technology such as electro-mobility can cause a massive use of rare soil and produce huge amounts of waste,[56] if the total amount of cars is not limited (sufficiency). Shifting effects are not only the result of avoiding regulation, but also a good indicator that there is more investment capital in other sectors e.g. due to energy efficiency.[57] Shifting effects can therefore be empirically observed. They also logically follow the behavioural findings discussed above, which implicates that fully calculated and moreover altruistic behaviour in favour of reducing environmental pollution and abstaining from using ideal material options for a particular action is very often improbable. In summary, this shows a strong interdependence between different environmental problems.[58] Generally, savings in expenses e.g. for energy can be easily transformed, geographically, as well as materially: Whoever owns a well-insulated home because of command-and-control requirements, can use money saved from the cheaper heating costs for an additional leisure flight. Not all savings are shifted, but this is mostly because not all (!) people act egoistically.[59] Claiming that it is hardly possible to cause shifting effects with some activities, e.g. because commuting by car in the mornings is unavoidable, cannot serve as viable explanation, since expenses saved by taking public transport can easily be used for holiday flights. Claiming, shifting effects have the positive side-effect of combating poverty in the Global South by enhancing economic activity, is also not convincing. Poverty eradication is better constructed within ecological limits; and the only emission that are not harmful when accepting a global quantity control are those not emitted in the first place.

4. Rebound effects, a concept discussed since the nineteenth century, are frequently confused with shifting effects.[60] Command-and-control law or voluntary action triggers technological improvements[61] leading to higher resource efficiency or use of renewable energy in production and/or (!) consumption of a product.[62]

[55]More on that Hennig (2017); Ekardt (2016), § 6 E. V. 1.-2.

[56]In detail shown in Schmidt-Bleek (2014), pp. 80 et seq. (however missing the crucial points when talking of policy instruments and explaining human motivation.).

[57]With detailed empirical literature Santarius (2012), pp. 185 et seq.

[58]More on this Hennig (2017); Ekardt (2016), § 6 E. V. 3.

[59]See Ekardt et al. (2015b), chapter 2.3.2 and 2.4; Gesang (2011), pp. 210 et seq.

[60]See Fischer et al. (2013), pp. 12 et seq.; Santarius (2012), pp. 9 et seq.; Hoffmann (2015), pp. 17 et seq.; Santarius (2012), pp. 39 et seq.; Becker and Richter (2015), pp. 3 et seq.; von Bredow (2013), pp. 121 et seq.; Klingholz (2014), pp. 100 et seq.; now also Buhl (2017), pp. 327 et seq.; the discourse in political science largely overlooks rebound and shifting effects; see e.g. Jänicke and Lindemann (2009), pp. 171 et seq. (who instead emphasise the incentive-giving character of environmental policy and IASS (2011), pp. 18 et seq.

[61]In contrast to Santarius (2012), p. 48 the problem should not be analysed limited to energy efficiency or even efficiency at all; see reference above on renewable energies, which are introduced into the market in addition to fossil energies.

[62]In contrast to the debate that focuses on the end-user only, Santarius (2012), pp. 168 et seq. Shows in empirical depth that there are also rebound effects on the production side (contributing in total more than user behaviour). See also Peters et al. (2015), pp. 30 et seq.

Best examples are buildings and cars. Often however, this will not, or only marginally, lead to *de facto* savings in resources or emissions (and sometimes even cause an increase of the problem, so-called "backfire"). There are four reasons that may cause this rebound effect: (a) Technical improvement like increased energy efficiency, maybe because of legal requirements, might directly (because of reduced costs) lead to an increase in consumption of a product or a service. Or the product or service is produced or consumed with higher productivity. Both leads to a compensation of the ecological savings. (b) Sometimes, the effect occurs (mostly in addition to (a)) when technical improvement of a product or service goes hand in hand with increased wealth, leading to higher production and/or consumption. (c) Along with all this, human behaviour may shift in favour of raised consumption (e.g. in travelling farther or driving bigger cars), encouraged by the clear conscience of seemingly having improved the ecological footprint (by driving a new electric car).[63] (d) Part of the rebound effect in a broader sense is the phenomenon that more ecologically friendly products are purchased and used not instead but in addition to other products. E.g. the old refrigerator in the basement—or renewable energy in addition to fossil energy.[64] Rebound effects are empirically evident[65]—otherwise, the continuous improvement of technology would reduce the ecological footprint—and are plausible looking at above-mentioned findings of behavioural sciences. They show that both self-interest, and perceptions of normality, as well as the feeling that there is a limited contingency of "good deeds" play essential roles in influencing human behaviour. It is also known that, similarly to shifting effects, it is impossible to exactly determine the causalities of motivations for a certain behaviour. Methodological problems and the enormous varieties of relevant (often globalised) factors and alternatives cannot be overcome (so far). Incidentally, referring to geographical or sectorial shifting effects as indirect rebound effects should be avoided.[66]

5. All these sustainability problems are increased by the difficulties to measure, calculated and observe sustainability inventory and consequences of disturbances. Inevitably this leaves room for euphemistic and inadequate observations and reactions (depicting problems). This has been discussed in detail concerning bioenergy, land-use emissions and biodiversity.[67]

[63]"Psychological" rebound effects occur in Santarius (2012), pp. 87 et seq., 132 et seq., 211 et seq.; and Paech (2012), pp. 69 et seq.; see also Peters et al. (2015), pp. 30 et seq.

[64]See in this context also Binswanger (2006), pp. 107 et seq.

[65]See also findings in Santarius (2012), pp. 68 et seq. and passim.

[66]On this kind of talk pars pro toto Santarius (2015), p. 50.

[67]See Hennig (2017) and Ekardt (2016).

7 Economic Governance Approaches

Governance instruments so far, such as command-and-control law, informational law, or nudging[68] address problems on a sectorial and geographical limited scope. Therefore, they encounter discussed governance deficiencies, which can be both empirically observed and explained by the behavioural analysis delivered above. Thus, it is necessary to identify alternative instruments. Alternatives and weaknesses of existing approaches are discussed elsewhere in detail,[69] which is why this paper will only briefly sketch out options. An alternative approach at the level of a Paris Agreement would introduce global quantity limits. More realistic seems an introduction of this approach on a lower level as forerunner initiative. Combined with certain mechanisms, which create openness on one side and avoid shifting effects outside of participant territory, this will give the ability to gradually increase the number of participating states.

In looking for more effective policy instruments, a key starting point should be the core factor of several environmental problems, with are fossil fuels. They are, especially in fertilizers, key drivers of modern agriculture, and address as such not only climate change but also biodiversity, as well as disrupted nitrogen cycles. The target according to the Paris Agreement is the total phase out of fossil fuels of the markets in all sectors (also in transportation, heating, agriculture) gradually in 10 or 20 years. If done with a global or at least a European cap (absolute quantity control), this would result in far-reaching consequences. To be clear, this system would not in the least resemble the existing EU ETS (emissions trading scheme), because it would target a strict cap (including the elimination of old certificates), as well as a complete inclusion of all fossil fuels uses. Justification of this approach is primarily its ecological effectiveness and not its possible cost-efficiency (while there is a good chance that might also be achieved).

A cap does not have the problems of price elasticity—the unwanted substance will be reliably taken out of the market. This fact is neglected by many parts of the current research on economic instruments. If applied to a broad geographical scope and all industries, caps eliminate typical problems of public goods by forcing all to act. Incidentally, other factors are also addressed, which are not considered in the model of the homo oeconomicus. For example, new conceptions of normality are established; the assumption that nature can be deliberately used up is step by step—for this is the most probable form of social change[70]—replaced with a more careful use of scare environmental resources. All this does not exclude the use of complementary e.g. educational and planning measures (e.g. to transform towards cities of short distances), which might prove to be necessary.[71]

[68] On the latter see Ekardt and Wieding (2016a).

[69] E.g. Ekardt (2016); Hennig (2017); von Bredow (2013), each with suggested further reading.

[70] See Ekardt (2016), § 2 G.

[71] More in Ekardt (2016), § 6 E. VI.

Renewable energies, energy efficiency and sufficiency would replace fossil fuels for power, heating and transportation. The amounts of fossil fuels on the market would simply decrease until finally they are no longer available on the market in 10–20 years. The thereby increasing scarcity will lead to dramatically increasing prices. The materially and geographically broad approach is crucial for the effectiveness of the instrument—specially to avoid rebound and shifting effects. Conventional agriculture would gradually see a transition to ecological agriculture. Also, the production of animal products would become less attractive overall; production of animal products would increasingly shift towards low-emission pastoral farming. Consequently, this would also result in less production quantities and decreasing disposal rates.

Problems caused by conventional agriculture, which are not climate related, such as biodiversity loss, soil degradation, water pollution, air pollution and disrupted nitrogen cycles, are also addressed. By gradually removing nitrogen mineral fertilizers from the market, an incentive towards organic farming and using smaller machines in the transition towards small-scale farming is created. This approach would at the same time reduce cases of illness (including health costs) caused by air pollution.

However, it has already been mentioned that not all greenhouse gases are fossil fuel induced. These other gases are not directly accounted for in this approach. The described approach will massively increase prices for mineral fertilizer and therefore the production of animal products, which lies at the core of several environmental problems. Relying on a fossil fuel cap alone, a reduction of land use might not be achieved if (because of less mineral fertilizer) yields per acre decrease. One approach could be to add livestock to an emissions trading system. This will however not address the whole problem. The necessary additional approach should therefore also target a substance easy to measure and trace. One way would be to apply a tax to agriculture as additional environmental economic instrument. This will reduce those emissions not caused by fossil fuels and will at the same time decrease the incentive to use more land, while also strengthening climate protection and environmental conservation. Designing a progressive tax, small-scale farming is incentivised and—in combination with a cap on fossil fuels—organic farming, which is more environmentally friendly thus avoiding other current environmental problems.

It is crucial to tax imported goods with the additional costs of energy and land-use pricing by means of an eco tax; exported goods should be exempt at least partially from the additional costs. Those so-called border adjustments will prevent that production, for instance steel industry or production of animal feed, is moved outside the system. This will also create an incentive to change production methods outside the participating countries and avoids competitive drawbacks for European corporations. Developing countries, which join the EU system can use the revenues of the certificate auctioning to decrease poverty and finance technical environmental protection. Additional policy instruments are beyond the scope of this paper. The instruments described will be sufficient to provide the key incentive for change. The often-described variety of prohibitions of e.g. suburban vehicles and other luxury goods, would not be necessary anymore.

The notion that economic instruments will not affect aspects like the availability of alternatives or "the situation" is therefore not accurate as such. It is also not true that price effects have been exhaustively proven to be limited in practice.[72] Firstly, this is because of the fact that practical experiences with economic instruments in environmental policy are only based on small price effects, not however on prices which increase by a multiple as would be appropriate to meet targets e.g. as formulated in the Paris agreement. Secondly, the notion that price effects in a cap-and-trade system are not effective is in the proposed system (differently from levies and taxes) void since caps give no leeway to the citizens. Especially, cutting emissions down to zero based on Article 2 PA leaves no room for price elasticity. Equally, there is no evidence supporting the idea that intrinsic moral motivation for action is destroyed by economic instruments.[73] It is much rather an assumption which might or might not turn out to be valid. The question whether pricing will erase altruistic motivation to act is moot, as such motivation regarding sustainability is rather weak anyhow.

References

Averchenkova A, Bassi S (2016) Beyond the targets: assessing the political credibility of pledges for the Paris Agreement. Climate Change and the Environment

Bauknecht D et al (2015) Gesellschaftlicher Wandel als Mehrebenenansatz. UBA-Texte, Dessau-Roßlau

Bauriedl S (ed) (2016) Wörterbuch Klimadebatte. transcript, Bielefeld

Beckenbach F (2003) Kognitionswissenschaftliche Erweiterung der ökonomischen Analyse von Umweltproblemen? In Jahrbuch Ökologische Ökonomik 3, ed. Frank Beckenbach, pp 13–40

Becker B, Richter C (2015) Klimaschutz in Deutschland – Realität oder Rhetorik? Momentum Q: 3–19

Beyerl K (2010) Der Klimawandel in der psychologischen Forschung. In: Voss M (ed) Der Klimawandel. Sozialwissenschaftliche Perspektiven. Springer VS, Heidelberg, pp 247–265

Binswanger M (2006) Die Tretmühlen des Glücks. Herder, Freiburg

Binswanger M (2012) Sinnlose Wettbewerbe. Warum wir immer mehr Unsinn produzieren. Herder, Freiburg

Blöbaum A (2012) Barrieren für weibliches Engagement im Naturschutz? Ein empirischer Blick auf naturwissenschaftliche und Naturschutzvereine. In: Frohn J, Rosebrock H-W (eds) Ehrenamtliche Kartierungen für den Naturschutz? Historische Analysen, aktuelle Situation und Zukunftspotenziale. Landwirtschaftsverlag, Münster, pp 203–225

Böcher M, Töller AE (2012) Umweltpolitik in Deutschland. Eine politikfeldanalytische Einführung. Springer, Wiesbaden

Bruppacher S (2014) Den inneren Schweinehund überwinden. Individueller Klimaschutz. Politische Ökologie 139(2014):51–57

Buhl J (2017) Rebound-Effekte im Steigerungsspiel. Zeit- und Einkommenseffekte in Deutschland. Nomos, Baden-Baden

Bürkle D (2015) Noch ein Kraftwerk in der Wüste: Atacama 1. DLR-Blogs, 14 October 2015. http://www.dlr.de/blogs/de/desktopdefault.aspx/tabid-6192/10184_read-856/

Deutscher Bundestag (2013) Schlussbericht der Enquete-Kommission, 3 May 2013. bpb, Bonn

---

[72] Lenz (2015), p. 357 and passim.

[73] With barely any empirical evidence Menges (2006), pp. 61 et seq.; and Binswanger (2012), pp. 99 et seq.

DLR (2006) Trans-Mediterraner Solarstromverbund (TRANS-CSP). Berlin. www.dlr.de/dlr/Portaldata/1/Resources/documents/TRANS-CSP_Zusammenfassung.pdf. Accessed 3 Mar 2018
Ekardt F (2001) Steuerungsdefizite im Umweltrecht: Ursachen unter besonderer Berücksichtigung des Naturschutzrechts und der Grundrechte. Zugleich zur Relevanz religiösen Säkularisats im öffentlichen Recht. Pro Universitate Verlag, Sinzheim
Ekardt F (2014) Jahrhundertaufgabe Energiewende. Ein Handbuch. Links, Berlin
Ekardt F (2016) Theorie der Nachhaltigkeit. Ethische, rechtliche, politische und transformative Zugänge – am Beispiel von Klimawandel, Ressourcenknappheit und Welthandel, 3rd edn. Nomos, Baden-Baden
Ekardt F, Wieding J (2016a) Nudging and environmental law: perspectives and examples. In: Mathis K, Avishalom T (eds) Nudging – possibilities, limitations and applications in European law and economics. Springer, Cham, pp 247–262
Ekardt F, Wieding J (2016b) Rechtlicher Aussagegehalt des Paris-Abkommens: Eine Analyse der einzelnen Artikel, ZfU Sonderheft: 36–58
Ekardt F, Neumann W, Wieding J, Schmidt-Kanefendt H-H (2015a) Grundlagen und Konzepte einer Energiewende 2050. BUND-Hintergrund
Ekardt F, Klinski S, Schomerus T (2015b) Konzept zur Fortentwicklung des deutschen Klimaschutzrechts. Metropolis, Marburg
Elmer C-F, Faulstich M, Hey C (2015) Der Klimabeitrag als Teil des Paradigmenwechsels der internationalen Klimapolitik. Ökonomisches Optimum oder Realweltanalyse? ifo-Schnelldienst 14(2015):18–20
Enquête-Kommission (2010) "Wachstum, Wohlstand, Lebensqualität" des 17. Deutschen Bundestages: Schlussbericht. BT-Drs. 17/13300
Entzian A (2016) Denn sie tun nicht, was sie wissen. Eine Studie zu ökologischem Bewusstsein und Handeln. oekom, München
Ernst A (2010) Individuelles Umweltverhalten: Probleme, Chancen, Vielfalt. In: Welzer H, Soeffner H-G, Giesecke D (eds) Klima Kulturen. Soziale Wirklichkeiten im Klimawandel. Campus, Frankfurt, pp 128–143
Fischer C, Grießhammer R et al (2013) Mehr als nur weniger. Suffizienz – Begriff, Begründung und Potenziale. Öko-Institut, Freiburg. http://www.oeko.de/oekodoc/1836/2013-505-de.pdf
Foucault M (1973) Wahnsinn und Gesellschaft. Suhrkamp, Frankfurt a.M.
Fücks R (2013) Intelligent wachsen. Die grüne Revolution. Hanser, München
Gesang B (2011) Klimaethik. Suhrkamp, Berlin
Giddens A (1988) Die Konstitution der Gesellschaft. Campus, Frankfurt
Giegerich T (2010) Gemeinwohl durch Wettbewerb? VVDStRL: 243–283
Gimmler A (1999) Institution und Individuum. Zur Institutionentheorie von Max Weber und Jürgen Habermas. Campus, Frankfurt
Gorz A (2009) Auswege aus dem Kapitalismus. Beiträge zur politischen Ökologie. Rotpunktverlag, Zurich
Greve J (2015) Reduktiver Individualismus. Springer VS, Wiesbaden
Gronemeyer M (2002) Die Macht der Bedürfnisse. Überfluss und Knappheit, 1st edn. WBG, Darmstadt
Grunwald A, Kopfmüller J (2012) Nachhaltigkeit. Eine Einführung, 2nd edn. Frankfurt a.M.
Habermas J (1981) Theorie des kommunikativen Handelns, vol 1: Handlungsrationalität und gesellschaftliche Rationalisierung; Bd 2: Zur Kritik der funktionalistischen Vernunft. Suhrkamp, Frankfurt a.M.
Handrich L, Kemfert C et al (2015) Turning point: decoupling greenhouse gas emissions from economic growth. Heinrich-Böll Foundation, Berlin
Hänggi M (2011) Ausgepowert. Das Ende des Ölzeitalters als Chance, 1st edn. Rotpunktverlag, Zurich
Hehn N (2015) Postfossile Stadtentwicklung. Rechts- und Steuerungsprobleme einer Umsetzung kommunaler Energiewende- und Klimaschutzkonzepte im Rahmen der Stadtplanung. Metropolis, Marburg
Heinrich-Böll-Stiftung, IASS, BUND, Le Monde diplomatique (2015) Bodenatlas: Daten und Fakten über Acker, Land und Erde, 1st edn. Berlin

Helm D (2008) Climate-change policy: why has so little been achieved? Oxf Rev Econ Policy:24–30

Hennig B (2017) Nachhaltige Landnutzung und Bioenergie Ambivalenzen, Governance, Rechtsfragen. Metropolis, Marburg

Hey C (2014) Das 7. Umweltaktionsprogramm – ein Interimsprogramm. In: Ewer W et al (eds) Methodik – Ordnung – Umwelt, Festschrift für Hans-Joachim Koch. Duncker & Humblot, Berlin, pp 617 et seqq

Heyen D et al (2013) Mehr als nur weniger. Suffizienz: Notwendigkeit und Optionen politischer Gestaltung. Öko-Institut Working Paper 3/2013. http://www.oeko.de/oekodoc/1837/2013-506-de.pdf

Hinterberger F, Pirgmaier E (2009) Die ökonomischen Grenzen des Wachstums. Kann unsere Wirtschaft anhaltend wachsen? Wissenschaft & Umwelt interdisziplinär: 58–66

Hoffmann U (2015) Can green growth really work – and what are the true (socio-)economics of climate change? Heinrich-Böll Foundation, Berlin

IASS (2011) Transgovernance. The quest for governance of sustainable development. Springer, Potsdam

Jackson T (2013) Wohlstand ohne Wachstum- Leben und Wirtschaften in einer endlichen Welt. oekom, München

Jakob M, Edenhofer O (2014) Growth, degrowth, and the commons. Oxf Rev Econ Policy:447–458

Jänicke M, Lindemann S (2009) Innovationsfördernde Umweltpolitik. In: Eifert M, Hoffmann R (eds) Innovationsfördernde Regulierung. Duncker & Humblot, Berlin, pp 171–195

Jensen A, Scheub U (2014) Glücksökonomie. Wer teilt, hat mehr vom Leben. oekom, München

Kaven C (2015) Transformation des Kapitalismus oder grüne Marktwirtschaft? Oekom, München

Kesselring T (2015) Experimentieren wir mit dem Kollaps? Wachsende Zweifel am Wachstum. IABLIS. https://www.iablis.de/iablis_t/2015/kesselring15.html

Kettner C (2009) Wachstum "light"! Qualitatives Wachstum muss keine Utopie bleiben. Wissenschaft & Umwelt interdisziplinär: 77–84

Klingholz R (2014) Sklaven des Wachstums. Die Geschichte einer Befreiung. Campus, Frankfurt a.M.

Klöckner CA (2015) The psychology of pro-environmental communication. Beyond standard information strategies. Palgrave Macmillan, London

Klöhn L (2006) Kapitalmarkt, Spekulation und Behavioral Finance. Eine interdisziplinäre und vergleichende Analyse zum Fluch und Segen der Spekulation und ihrer Regulierung durch Recht und Markt. Duncker und Humblot, Berlin

Kuckartz U (2010) Nicht hier, nicht jetzt, nicht ich. Über die symbolische Bearbeitung eines ernsten Problems. In: Welzer H, Hans-Georg S, Giesecke D (eds) Klima Kulturen. Soziale Wirklichkeiten im Klimawandel. Campus, Frankfurt, pp 143–160

Lenz C (2015) Zur Durchsetzungsfähigkeit von Suffizienzstrategien. Eine Analyse auf der Grundlage von Ansätzen der Neuen Politischen Ökonomie. Metropolis, Marburg

Liebe U, Preisendörfer P (2013) Für oder wider die Natur? ZfU 3(2013):239–260

Liesen A, Dietsche C, Gebauer J (2013) Wachstumsneutrale Unternehmen. Pilotstudie zum Postwachstumsdiskurs in Unternehmen. IÖW 205/13

Linz M (2015) Suffizienz als politische Praxis. Ein Katalog. Wuppertal-Institut, Wuppertal

Luks F (2013) Die Zukunft des Wachstums. Theoriegeschichte, Nachhaltigkeit und die Zukunft einer neuen Wirtschaft, 2nd edn. Metropolis, Marburg

Lutter S, Giljum S (2009) Ökologische Wachstumsgrenzen. Die Notwendigkeit eines Systemwechsels im Umgang mit natürlichen Ressourcen. Wissenschaft & Umwelt interdisziplinär: 12–20

Malthus T (1977) Das Bevölkerungsgesetz. dtv, München

Mead GH (1968) Geist, Identität und Gesellschaft aus der Sicht des Sozialbehaviorismus. Suhrkamp, Frankfurt a.M.

Meadows D et al (1972) Die Grenzen des Wachstums. DVA, Stuttgart

Mehde V (2005) Wettbewerb zwischen Staaten. Mohr Siebeck, Tübingen

Menges R (2006) Freiwillige, verursacher- oder gemeinlastfinanzierte Beiträge zum Klimaschutz? Eine Kategorisierung umweltpolitischer Instrumente auf Basis der Kostenträgerschaft. Zeitschrift für Umweltpolitik und Umweltrecht 2006:61–80

Miegel M (2010) Exit. Wohlstand ohne Wachstum. Propyläen, Berlin
Milgram S (1974) Obedience to authority. An experimental view. Harper Perennial, New York
Moreno C, Chassé DS, Fuhr L (2015) Carbon metrics. Global abstractions and ecological epistemicide. Berlin. https://www.boell.de/sites/default/files/2015-11-09_carbon_metrics.pdf
Muraca B (2015) Gut leben. Eine Gesellschaft jenseits des Wachstums. bpb, Bonn
Nordhaus WD (2008) A question of balance – weighing the options on global warming policies. Yale University Press
OHCHR (2014) Mapping human rights obligations relating to the enjoyment of a safe, clean, healthy and sustainable environment. Focus report on human rights and climate change. Geneva
OHCHR (2015) The effects of climate change on the full enjoyment of human rights. Geneva
Ott K (2011) Vier Pfade ins Postwachstumszeitalter. Vorgänge 3(2011):54–68
Paech N (2005) Nachhaltiges Wirtschaften jenseits von Innovationsorientierung und Wachstum. Eine unternehmensbezogene Transformationstheorie. Metropolis, Marburg
Paech N (2012) Befreiung vom Überfluss. Auf dem Weg in die Postwachstumsökonomie. Oekom, München
Paqué K-H (2010) Wachstum! Die Zukunft des globalen Kapitalismus. Oekom, München
Peters A et al (2015) Rebound-Effekte – ihre Bedeutung für die Umweltpolitik. UBA-Texte, Dessau-Roßlau
Piketty T (2015) Das Kapital im 21. Jahrhundert. C.H.Beck, Bonn
Pissarskoi E (2014) Gesellschaftliche Wohlfahrt und Klimawandel. Umgang mit normativen Annahmen und Ungewissheiten bei der klimaökonomischen Politikberatung. Oekom, München
Pogge T (2007) Weltarmut als Problem globaler Gerechtigkeit. Deutsche Zeitschrift für Philosophie 55(6):967–980
Posse D (2015) Zukunftsfähige Unternehmen in einer Postwachstumsgesellschaft Lehren aus dem Ernährungssektor. Uwf 23(1):59–67
Prakash S et al (2016) Einfluss der Nutzungsdauer von Produkten auf ihre Umweltwirkung. UBA-Texte, Dessau-Roßlau
Pufé I (2014) Nachhaltigkeit, 2nd edn. UVK, Konstanz
Radermacher FJ, Beyers B (2011) Welt mit Zukunft. Die ökosoziale Perspektive, 2nd edn. Murmann, Hamburg
Radermacher FJ, Riegler J, Weiger H (2011) Ökosoziale Marktwirtschaft. Historie, Programm und Perspektive eines zukunftsfähigen globalen Wirtschaftssystems, München
Radkau J (2011) Die Ära der Ökologie. Eine Weltgeschichte. Oekom, München
Reimer F, Tölle S (2013) Ressourceneffizienz als Problembegriff. Zeitschrift für Umweltrecht 2013:589–597
Sachverständigenrat für Umweltfragen (SRU) (2012) Umweltgutachten 2012. Berlin
Santarius T (2012) Der Rebound-Effekt. Über die unerwünschten Folgen der erwünschten Energieeffizienz. Wuppertal-Institut, Wuppertal
Santarius T (2015) Der Rebound-Effekt. Ökonomische, psychische und soziale Herausforderungen für die Entkopplung von Wirtschaftswachstum und Energieverbrauch. Metropolis, Marburg
Santarius T, Walnum HJ, Aall C (eds) (2016) Rethinking climate and energy policies. New perspectives on the rebound phenomenon. Springer, New York
Sartre J-P (1943) Das Sein und das Nichts. Paris
Scheidler F (2015) Das Ende der Megamaschine. Geschichte einer scheiternden Zivilisation. Promedia, Wien
Schmid E, Brigitte K, Anna P (2016) Putting an energy system transformation into practice: the case of the German Energiewende. Energy Res Soc Sci:263–270
Schmidt-Bleek F (2014) Grüne Lügen. Nichts für die Umwelt, alles fürs Geschäft – wie Politik und Wirtschaft die Welt zugrunde richten. Ludwig, München
Schneider F (2009) Ökonomische Wachstumsgrenzen: Sollen wir sie zur Kenntnis nehmen und für erstrebenswert halten? Wissenschaft & Umwelt interdisziplinär: 71–78
Schreiner P (2015) Unterwerfung als Freiheit. Leben im Neoliberalismus, 2nd edn. PapyRossa, Köln
Schridde S (2014) Murks? Nein danke! Was wir tun können, damit die Dinge besser werden. oekom verlag, Munich

Schulz C, Bailey I (2014) The green economy and post-growth regimes: opportunities and challenges for economic geography. Geografiska Annaler: Ser B, Hum Geogr 96(3):277–291
Schützenmeister F (2010) Hybrid oder autofrei? – Klimawandel und Lebensstile. In: Martin V (ed) Der Klimawandel. Sozialwissenschaftliche Perspektiven. Springer VS, Heidelberg, pp 267–281
Seidl I, Zahrnt A (2010) Staatsfinanzen und Wirtschaftswachstum. In: Seidl I, Angelika Z (eds) Postwachstumsgesellschaft. Konzepte für die Zukunft. Metropolis, Marburg, pp 179–200
Skillington T (2012) Climate change and the human rights challenge. Extending justice beyond the borders of the nation state. Int J Hum Rights 16:1196 et seq
Soff M (2010) Vorsatz, Wille, Bedürfnis. Nachhaltige Schlussfolgerungen aus Kurt Lewins Motivationspsychologie. Vortrag bei der Tagung der Interdisziplinären Studiengesellschaft (ISG. Essen)
Sommer B, Welzer H (2014) Transformationsdesign. Wege in eine zukunftsfähige Moderne. oekom, München
Stengel O (2011) Suffizienz: Die Konsumgesellschaft in der ökologischen Krise. Wuppertaler Schriften zur Forschung für eine nachhaltige Entwicklung. oekom, München
Sterk W et al (2013) The international climate regime and extraterritorial human rights obligations. Status Quo and Future Prospects, Darmstadt
Stern N (2009) A blueprint for a safer planet: how to manage climate change and create a new era of progress and prosperity. Cambridge
Stoll G (2014) Die Rolle der NGOs in der Degrowth-Diskussion: Da wäre mehr drin. Politische Ökologie 139/2014
Stoll-Kleemann S (2014) Fleischkonsum im 21. Jahrhundert – ein Thema für die humanökologische Forschung. GAIA: 366–372
Stoll-Kleemann S, O'Riordan T, Jaeger C (2001) The psychology of denial concerning climate mitigation measures: evidence from Swiss focus groups. Glob Environ Chang:117–130
Sukhdev P (2013) Corporation 2020. Warum wir Wirtschaft neu denken müssen. Oekom, München
Tichy G (2009) Nachhaltiges Wachstum?, Wissenschaft & Umwelt interdisziplinär: 4–10
UNEP (2010) Green economy report. A preview. New York
Voget-Kleschin L (2013) Sustainable food consumption? Claims for sustainable lifestyles in between normative and eudaimonistic issues – the example of food production and consumption. Manuskript, Greifswald
von Bredow H (2013) Energieeffizienz als Rechts- und Steuerungsproblem. Unter besonderer Berücksichtigung der erneuerbaren Energien. Metropolis, Marburg
Weimann J (2009) Die Klimapolitik-Katastrophe. Metropolis, Marburg
Welzer H (2013) Selbst denken. Eine Anleitung zum Widerstand, Frankfurt
Wilson EO (2015) Der Sinn des menschlichen Lebens. C.H.Beck, München
Wilts H, von Gries N (2015) Europe's waste incineration capacities in a circular economy. Proc ICE – Waste Resource Manag 168(4):166–176

Felix Ekardt Leipzig/Berlin. Director of the Forschungsstelle Nachhaltigkeit und Klimapolitik (Research Unit Sustainability and Climate Policy) in Leipzig/Berlin and Professor of Public Law and Legal Philosophy at the University of Rostock. D-04229 Leipzig, Könneritzstraße 41, Tel. + 49 (0)341 492 77 866; Fax + 49 (0)341 246 59 876. mail@sustainability-justice-climate.eu. Fields of Interest: Environmental Law and Policy, Theory of Justice, Human Rights Governance, Sustainability Issues.

Jutta Wieding Dresden. Master of Arts and PhD student at Research Unit Sustainability and Climate Policy Leipzig/Berlin. D-01097 Dresden, Fritz-Hoffmann-Str. 5, Tel. +49 (0)351 329 50 101. jutta.wieding@posteo.de. Fields of Interest: International and German environmental policy, climate and energy policy.

A Shocking Truth for Law and Economics: Consumer Welfare Explains the Internal Market for Electricity Better Than Total Welfare

Fabrizio Esposito and Lucila de Almeida

Abstract This chapter challenges the use of total welfare as the axiological assumption adopted by economically-informed legal scholarship in the field of electricity. To do so, it demonstrates that the efficiency hypotheses can be grounded in two different economic rationales: the traditional one based on total welfare; and an alternative one based on consumer welfare. To challenge the uncritical endorsement of total welfare, the chapter chooses the competition pillar for the EU internal market for electricity as a case study and shows that consumer welfare better explains its economic rationale. This finding proves that the economically-informed legal scholars are wrong in considering total welfare an unquestionable starting point for their research. This will likely be a 'shocking truth' for law and economics scholars. The argument is articulated in four steps. The first step builds the methodological foundations. It describes two types of explanatory claims, one external and the other internal to legal discourse, and discusses the superior relevance of the latter to legal practice. The second step lays the analytical framework. It identifies points of divergence between the two efficiency hypotheses, total and consumer welfare, with a focus on electricity markets. The third step reviews the economically-informed legal scholarship and the economic one on the regulation of electricity markets. It shows that scholars endorse total welfare, consumer welfare, and even both. The fourth and final step enters the realm of the EU internal market for electricity and proves that the economic rationale of legal materials and legal discourse is better explained by consumer welfare. This finding supports our alternative efficiency hypothesis based on consumer welfare.

F. Esposito (✉)
European University Institute, Florence, Italy
e-mail: fabrizio.esposito@eui.eu

L. de Almeida
Faculty of Law, University of Helsinki, Helsinki, Finland
e-mail: lucila.dealmeida@helsinki.fi

K. Mathis, B. R. Huber (eds.), *Energy Law and Economics*, Economic Analysis of Law in European Legal Scholarship 5, https://doi.org/10.1007/978-3-319-74636-4_6

1 Introduction

Economic theories have provided an important contribution to the re-regulation of electricity markets over the last decades. Already in 1983, the landmark work *Markets for Power* by Joskow and Schmalensee rejected proposals to deregulate the electricity sector and, instead, called for a re-regulation founded on economic efficiency as the primary objective,[1] the so-called maximisation of welfare.[2] Normative and positive regulatory theories have thereafter proposed regulatory frameworks with the aim of granting economic efficiency in emerging markets for electricity. Meanwhile, liberalisation and re-regulation have attracted the attention of economically-informed legal scholars[3] towards the regulation of markets for electricity. These scholars typically take total welfare as the axiological (that is, about value) assumption in their analytical framework. This chapter challenges the practice in economically-informed legal scholarship of taking for granted that total welfare maximisation is the market rationale in both normative and explanatory claims in law. It answers Calabresi's call for reviving the explanatory project in law and economics and it does so by showing the potential of consumer[4] welfare maximisation as the core of an alternative efficiency hypothesis of law. We also address a concern of legal scholars about economic explanations of the law: they must take legal discourse seriously; conversely, economic explanations must be internal and not external explanations of the law.

The EU internal market for electricity is a very attractive area of law for testing the explanatory power of the efficiency hypotheses. Electricity is an industry that has experienced strong and very recent liberalisation processes across the world. Thus, there have been rich discussions about the interplay between the market and the law—typically captured by referring to a process of liberalisation, privatisation or by opposing deregulation to something else: re-regulation, antitrust or competition or contract. While we find some of these expressions more accurate than others, they all try to emphasise the increase in the trust, reliance, confidence shown by the legal

[1]Joskow and Schmalensee (1983), p. 8.

[2]We use the term "welfare" to cover the uses of a variety of terms that while theoretically distinguishable, are often used interchangeably, such as wealth, surplus, well-being. Similarly, "total" welfare covers expressions like "social", "societal", "overall" and "aggregate" welfare.

[3]As we accept the linguistic regimentation proposed by Calabresi (2016) concerning the use of the expressions "economic analysis of law" and "law and economics", we use the adjective "economically-informed" to cover both. While this adjective is not popular (the only other occurrence we can think of is in Sanchez-Graells 2018) we consider it accurate and it is also the parallel of the more popular adjective "behaviourally-informed".

[4]We use the term "consumer" consistent with Article 101 Treaty on the Functioning of the European Union (TFEU). This meaning is thus broader than the use of "consumer" in EU consumer protection, which is typically restricted to contracting parties acting outside their professional activity. Therefore, in the context of the EU internal market for electricity, "consumers" refers to contracting parties at the end of the electricity supply chain (final customers, household customers), wholesale customers, as well as network users in the transmission or distribution bilateral agreements with the network grid operators.

system to the market as a means for the allocation (production and distribution) of electricity.

In this context, our research question is: Does consumer welfare provide an internal economic explanation of the law that is better than the one founded on total welfare? To test the explanatory power of these efficiency hypotheses, we assess whether consumer welfare is better than total welfare at explaining the competition pillar of the EU internal market for electricity. What we find is that, not only it is possible to formulate an efficiency hypothesis grounded in consumer welfare, but also that it is indeed the case that consumer welfare clearly has a superior explanatory power of the competition pillar of the EU internal market for electricity. With this basis, we challenge the assumption of total welfare, which is typically taken as a truism in economically-informed legal research. Our findings are innovative, and we provocatively call it a 'shocking truth' because we aim to draw the attention of legal scholars and invite them to be more critical to the axiological foundations they import from economic theory.[5]

The chapter is structured as follows. Section 2 describes the economic explanatory project, calls for its revival and stresses the critical importance of distinguishing external from internal explanations but also the higher value of the latter for legal practitioners and scholars. Section 3 details what disagreements are helpful to answer our research question. Section 4 shows that there is a disagreement on the microeconomic rationale of the market in the economic literature on networks in general and on electricity in particular. Interestingly, this disagreement is largely ignored by economically-informed research in law. Section 5 develops a coherent description of the normative system of EU energy law over three decades of positive integration, pointing out the importance of consumer welfare in this regard. Section 6 concludes by stressing that searching the microeconomic rationale from the internal point of view is attractive for both legal and economic research.

2 Efficiency Hypothesis as Internal Explanation of the Law

Economically-informed research in law is commonly divided into normative and positive approaches. However, this distinction is inadequate to capture the variety of questions economically-informed research has been answering. Melissa Hart, Jon and Kathleen Hanson offer a more nuanced account, distinguishing two normative questions: "[S]hould efficiency be the goal of law? And, second, if so, how should the law be reformed to best serve that goal?" and three positive questions: "What are a policy's behavioural effects, and would that policy leads to the efficient [...]

[5]The findings of the current research are consistent with similar recent findings in other areas of economic theory and EU law, namely principal-agent theory and EU consumer and company law. See Esposito and Grundmann (2017).

outcome? [. . .] [W]hat would the law look like if efficiency were its sole purpose, and does the law, in fact, look like that?".[6] Following Posner, who has greatly contributed to the related research, the last question can be called the efficiency hypothesis of the law.[7]

Hart and the Hansons emphasise the original success and historical importance of the efficiency hypothesis for the establishment of economically-informed legal scholarship, but also its growing unpopularity. The claim about the unfashionable character of the efficiency hypothesis of law was made in both editions (1996, 2010) of *The Blackwell Companion to Philosophy of Law* and it is still accurate—with perhaps one exception, namely behavioural analysis.[8] An illustrative example of the state-of-the-art is Sanchez-Graells' recent contribution to *Research Methods in Law*.[9] The author distinguishes a "normative framework" from "a methodology for the analysis of the legal reality".[10] This methodology "helps to describe and explain how the law is and what effects it creates or can be expected to create."[11] Although the expression "describe and explain how the law is" suggests that there is room for an efficiency hypothesis of law in his overview, actually the author provides no discussion of the matter.

The reluctance to engage in explanatory projects is arguably based on the tension between two different commitments of mainstream economically-informed research. The first is the axiological commitment to total welfare, the second is the effort to provide analyses that do not engage in axiological argumentation. Sanchez-Graells' chapter is again illustrative of this point. The author observes that "the normative dimension of the economic analysis of law . . . ultimately rests on the pursuit of economic efficiency as a proxy for the maximisation of social welfare" which, he observes, is an axiologically controversial criterion.[12] However, this critique does not persuade him because the purpose of economic analysis is "to ensure that the legal system is both effective in achieving its goals (which are by no means predetermined by the law and economics approach), and efficient in doing so."[13] The tension is obvious: what if the legal system is not pursuing total welfare? When this is not the case, a critique of the law in terms of total welfare maximisation does

[6]Hanson et al. (2010), p. 300.

[7]Posner (1975). Seminal in this regard is also Coase (1960).

[8]In fact, in behaviourally-informed scholarship, at least in Europe, there is a growing interest for understanding the extent to which the content of the law is "behaviourally-aligned" (Almeida et al. 2016). See, for example, in this book series, Sibony (2015).

[9]Sanchez-Graells (2018). We refer to Sanchez-Graells' chapter to illustrate the tensions in mainstream economically-informed legal scholarship. We want to emphasise that we have chosen to use Sanchez-Graells' chapter because we found it exceptionally clear and well-made (updated, rich of carefully chosen references, etc.) and it is because of these properties that the choice was made.

[10]Ivi, p. 2.

[11]Ibidem.

[12]Ibidem.

[13]See also Posner (2015).

not contribute to achieving the goals of the legal system, but substitutes total welfare maximisation to the goals of the legal system.

Hart and the Hansons also draw our attention on the peculiar nature of the efficiency hypothesis. On the one hand, it is based on an analysis of legal materials that is dismissive of the language, concepts, rhetoric used by judges. On the other hand, it does not present the efficiency hypothesis as a realistic account of judicial opinions. This second feature of the efficiency hypothesis is at the core of a radical critique to the hypothesis, powerfully articulated by Dworkin. His critique holds that an efficiency hypothesis not warranted by the analysis of legal reasoning, does not describe legal practice because it is blind to its argumentative or discursive dimension.[14] Put differently, an explanation of the law external to legal practice is useless for knowing what the law of a jurisdiction is. At most, this explanation is useful to identify the effects of the law on behaviour.[15]

The externalist critique requires careful consideration. In fact, from a legal point of view, knowing the law of a jurisdiction is the starting point of many important activities of a practitioner. To name the most common ones: advising a client, litigating a case, negotiating a settlement. To perform these activities, legal practitioners need internal explanations of the law. If the externalist critique is found convincing, the legal relevance of any economic external explanation becomes unclear. In this regard, it is important to consider that even Jody Kraus, one of the most sympathetic legal philosophers to mainstream economically-informed research in law, has accepted the critique as potentially disruptive.[16] His attempt to deflect it consists in arguing that concepts used by judges that apparently are deontological can have a consequentialist meaning. We find this defence unsatisfactory at the conceptual level for two reasons, but in any event irrelevant for current purposes. The first problem of this defence is that it is conceptually too crude in that it presupposes an unconvincing clear-cut distinction between deontological and consequentialist language.[17] The second problem is that the defence is at the conceptual level, while Posner's efficiency hypothesis is empirical. Nonetheless, the crucial limitation of this defence is that it is completely unhelpful to discriminate between the two maximands identified in our research question because consumer welfare maximisation is a consequentialist criterion as well.

In addition, the justification for the focus on external explanations given by Posner is suspicious. Posner is certainly right in observing that "the true grounds of legal decisions [can be] concealed rather than illuminated by the characteristic rhetoric of judicial opinion."[18] To circumvent this problem, his analysis relies

[14]Dworkin (1980), pp. 219–223.

[15]Małecka (2017) rightly criticises Posner for claiming that Kelsen's theory of law has opened the way to the use of economics in legal scholarship.

[16]Kraus (2007).

[17]See, in this book series, Mathis (2012) and Cserne (2012).

[18]Quotation taken from Hanson et al. (2010).

conspicuously on regulatory capture approaches.[19] These approaches are based on the idea of bargains between regulators and powerful addressees—bargains that are very unlikely to leave explicit traces in public speech acts. However, one cannot avoid the thought that if the public speech acts seem "consumerist",[20] perhaps a consumerist explanation is useful. This is particularly the case since, in the heydays of the efficiency hypothesis also Posner was sceptical about the extension of regulatory capture considerations to "consumerist" law. In fact, he observed that "[t]he 'consumerist' measures of the last few years . . . are not an obvious product of interest group pression, and the proponents of the economic theory of regulation have thus far largely ignored them."[21] In our view, this argument counts as a strong reason for taking the plain meaning of legal materials quite seriously in this area, without the need to engage in a deeper discussion of the usefulness of regulatory capture approaches for the analysis of legal materials.[22] Ultimately, while Posner is right that we cannot always take legal discourse at its face value, Dworkin is also right: ignoring the speech acts of legal officials amounts to the proverbial mistake of throwing away the baby with the bath water.

In any linguistic practice (and therefore also in legal discourse), speakers can be confused, unclear, mistaken—possibly even lying—about their understanding of their own speech acts. For example, judges may want to conceal their exercise of discretion—that is to say, the political character of (at least some of) their decisions.[23] However, also economists can be imprecise when they speak about the law or lawyers when they speak about economics. For example, Cole and Grossman have criticised several economic conceptions of property rights because they "bias economic analyses and create the potential for cross-disciplinary misunderstanding".[24] At the same time, Williamson lectured Posner very harshly for the latter's dismissive account of the post-Coasian developments in transaction-cost economics.[25] Thus, while the speech acts of legal practitioners have to be analysed with caution, ignoring them sounds more like the attitude of an attorney trying to exclude

[19]Posner (1974). For a review, den Hertog (2012).

[20]Posner (1974), p. 353.

[21]Posner (1974), p. 353. The efficiency hypothesis went together with the claim that common law judges are better protected from regulatory capture than both legislative bodies and agencies.

[22]See Sect. 4.2 for a brief overview of some attempts by economists to give a political explanation of consumerist law.

[23]See Kraus (2007). These considerations are also at the centre of another debate sprung by Dworkin—the debate on the explanation of theoretical disagreements among legal practitioners. The core of that debate is how to give a theoretical account of the fact that when legal practitioners disagree on what the law is they seem to disagree on matters of fact. For a review of the claims and further references, see Esposito (2017b).

[24]Cole and Grossman (2002), p. 318.

[25]See Williamson (1993) and Posner (1993).

evidence damaging the client rather than the attitude of someone interested in discovering to what extent economic theory explains legal practice.[26]

Like Cole and Grossman, we consider interdisciplinary coherence valuable. In fact, we believe that economics and law can help each other in addressing their respective concerns for the clarity, completeness and lack of contradictions of conceptual structures. Indeed, we concur with Wagner's recent observation that Posner, in his textbook, "claims that the entire body of common law rulings can be rendered coherent by recognising that those rulings promote economic efficiency".[27] However, we doubt the capacity of total welfare maximisation to deliver this interdisciplinary coherence. Take two quick but illustrative examples. First, "a more economic approach" is a term of art in EU competition law. It is clear that the maximand of the Commission's more economic approach is not total welfare.[28] We thus face two alternatives. On the one hand, we can criticise the Commission for using the expression "more economic" to refer to something that is not aligned with mainstream economics. On the other hand, we can search for a more nuanced economic theory that fits and is coherent with the conceptual framework introduced by the Commission. Second, EU law shows a strong concern for contractual fairness. There are references to fairness in Articles 101 and 102 TFEU, and more generally, unfair contractual terms are unfair because they create an imbalance between the performances of the parties, to the detriment of the consumer.[29] Thus, an economic framework capable of incorporating concerns for contractual unfairness is obviously desirable as a matter of interdisciplinary research. However, total welfare has typically been considered an obstacle to this outcome.[30] With the present research, we try to contribute to this quest for interdisciplinary coherence.

What is the way out of the tension between giving an economic explanation and taking legal discourse seriously? A way out is an efficiency hypothesis of law immune from Dworkin's critique. In fact, if the law tries to pursue an economic goal—say, total welfare maximisation—a legal practitioner can formulate legal arguments based on this goal.[31] On the contrary, if an efficiency hypothesis does not offer an internal explanation, it can describe the economic consequences, function, effects of legal practice in the light of a certain economic theory, but it does not give an account of its legal goal, purpose, function, or end.

To sum up, in this section we have argued that the economic explanatory project deserves to be restored because it is an important line of interdisciplinary research. Moreover, we answer the call for economically-informed internal explanations of the law for three reasons. First, internal explanations are more useful to legal

[26]Haack (2014), p. 12 similarly distinguishes between 'inquiry' and 'pseudo-inquiry' (not only in law).

[27]Wagner (2016), p. 17.

[28]See Hildebrand (2016) and Witt (2016).

[29]See, for example, Article 4 Directive 93/13/EEC.

[30]See, for example, Gordley (2006), pp. 18–25.

[31]Possibly, the best articulation of these considerations can be found in Calabresi (1982).

practitioners and officials engaging in legal reasoning and argumentation. Second, only an economically-informed legal scholarship that does not impose on the law axiological assumptions because they are mainstream in economics can avoid the tension between offering a value-free analysis and assuming total welfare maximisation as axiological assumption. Third, identifying points of interdisciplinary coherence cannot but facilitate the cross-fertilisation between legal and economic research.

In this context, we could try to corroborate the mainstream efficiency hypothesis as an internal explanation. However, for the reasons sketched in Sect. 1 and in this section, we do not have much confidence in the success of such a research question. It is for this reason that we formulate an alternative efficiency hypothesis, according to which efficiency is about the maximisation of consumer welfare. Then, we identify points of divergence between a total and a consumer welfare approach and finally we look at actual legal discourse to see which hypothesis fits better with it. In so doing, we follow Calabresi's recent methodological directive that if one finds "rules and practice that economic theory cannot explain," he must search for a "more nuanced theory" that is explanatorily superior.[32]

3 Parallel Circuits: Building Blocks for Total and Consumer Welfare

The core of our analysis is thus the comparison between internal explanations based on total and consumer welfare maximisation, our two efficiency hypotheses. In this section, we explain how we intend to offer an internal efficiency hypothesis of the competition pillar of the EU internal market for electricity. More precisely, the purpose of this section is threefold. First, we make some methodological remarks. Second, we spell out in detail the divergence between an efficiency hypothesis based on total welfare and one based on consumer welfare. Finally, we relate our efficiency hypotheses with typical issues of the electricity market.

3.1 Preliminary Remarks

We have three preliminary remarks: (1) we abstract from the 'maximand controversy'; (2) how we analyse unclear or untruthful speech acts; (3) we distinguish propositions about value and propositions about means.

First, we abstract from the 'maximand controversy'—that is, the controversy on how to measure "welfare".[33] We can do so because the two efficiency hypotheses we

[32]Calabresi (2016), pp. 3–4.

[33]See Esposito (2017c) for an account and for references.

consider are compatible with any number of solutions to this controversy. In fact, for our purposes, the key point of disagreement is whether "consumer" instead of "total" welfare ought to be maximised, not how to measure welfare.

A second consideration relates to the observations by Posner, Dworkin, and Kraus (among others) on the unavoidable limitations of the analysis of speech acts for explanatory purposes. The problem is that the face value of these speech acts can be questioned by pointing to the possibility of unclear or untruthful communication. In this regard, our analysis is guided by the following methodological principles. Our general strategy to reconcile two apparently conflicting speech acts is questioning their plain meaning.[34] Our guiding principle is (unsurprisingly) the internal coherence of the discourse.[35] Thus, the account that results in the greatest overall coherence is the one we will prefer. Typically, this means that less explicit, more vague statements must adapt to more explicit, less vague ones.

Third, we distinguish two types of propositions: propositions about value and propositions about means. Propositions about value or axiological propositions describe the value the norms of a legal system are designed to pursue. Propositions about means describe the norms a legal system would have to include to pursue a given value. Thus, propositions about means connect legal values and an understanding of reality to norms that are considered as means to those legal values.[36]

The distinction between propositions about value and about means is important because our research question focuses on an axiological disagreement—that is, on the conflict between two propositions about value. More precisely, we are interested in the disagreement between assuming total and consumer welfare maximisation as the microeconomic rationale of the market.[37] Thus, instrumental disagreements are not directly relevant to our research question. In fact, two speakers can agree at the axiological level while disagreeing at the instrumental one, to the effect that they will disagree on what norms are justified instrumentally. For example, it is possible to disagree on the desirability of price caps *vis-á-vis* rate regulation regardless of whether the maximand is total or consumer welfare.[38] At the same time, the opposite is also true: even in case of axiological disagreement, instrumental agreement can follow from the convergence on the desirable norm and/or outcome. For example, in

[34]In the literature referred to in the previous footnote, the distinction is sometimes made between disagreement, agreement and mere convergence. Convergence is an agreement based on different reasons that happen to lead to—to make converge—on the same outcome.

[35]For a general theory of discursive coherence, see Kehler (2002).

[36]It must be noted that building axiological hierarchies between different instrumental propositions can be considered a purely instrumental exercise only under very specific circumstances, namely, the lack of trade-off between different values. For example, if norm N_1 satisfies goal G_1 more than norm N_2 but N_2 satisfies goal G_2 more than N_1, the choice between N_1 and N_2 is not merely technical. This is the central insight behind Vilfredo Pareto's ordinalist project. Calabresi (2016) discusses extensively the risk of hiding axiological judgments behind Paretian critiques.

[37]For the concepts of disagreement and axiological proposition, see Esposito (2017b).

[38]See, for example, Clemenz (1991) who applies both welfare maximands.

ideal market conditions, perfect competition maximises both consumer and total welfare in comparison to a non-discriminating monopolist. Building on this consideration, it is possible to reach a certain degree of convergence, as beautifully summarised by Kahn: "[T]he single most widely accepted rule for the regulated industries is regulate them in such a way as to produce the same results as would be produced by effective competition if it were feasible."[39] Indeed, both consumer and total welfarists can agree with this claim.

Disagreements about means are nevertheless an important source of information to us. Propositions about means connect normative speech acts to axiological propositions and therefore allow us to infer axiological commitments from the interplay of instrumental commitments and norms. For example, if one holds that 'from a welfarist point of view, there is no need to regulate a perfectly discriminating monopolist that is productively efficient,' the plain meaning of the speech act does not indicate whether the maximand is consumer or total welfare. However, we can unambiguously infer this speaker is committed to total welfare at the axiological level in the light of the instrumental proposition connecting the market behaviour of such a monopolist to maximum total welfare and zero consumer welfare. As we shall see, these considerations will be useful for the review of both the economically-informed literature and EU legal materials.

Bearing these considerations in mind, we can move to the identification of divergences between the two efficiency hypotheses we consider.

3.2 *Distribution, Deadweight Loss, and Productive Efficiency*

We look at three main points of divergence between an efficiency hypothesis based on total welfare and one based on consumer welfare: (1) disinterest for distribution; (2) the focus on the deadweight loss[40] in welfare analysis; (3) the type of interest for productive inefficiency. Note that the second and third points of divergence between the two efficiency hypotheses are derivative from the first. Disregarding the axiological relevance of distributive effects implies focusing only on the deadweight loss in welfare analyses and by extension on the dimension of the output (because less-than-optimal-output implies a deadweight loss) and considering productive inefficiencies intrinsically bad because they reduce total welfare.

Disinterest in the distribution of welfare, wealth, and income[41] is without doubt a central feature of the brand of economics fashionable among economically-informed

[39]Kahn (1988), p. 17. Quoted also by Tardiff (2000), p. 170. See also Esposito (2017a), who offers an analysis of the impact of behavioural insights on economically-informed consumer policy without taking sides in the total-consumer welfare controversy.

[40]In a monopoly, the deadweight loss is the part of social welfare that would be created in perfect competition lost by consumers without being transferred to the monopolist.

[41]Note that concerns about the reliability of willingness to pay and to be paid as welfare indicator are beyond the scope of this inquiry. Nevertheless, we are conscious of the axiological implications

legal scholars. It is, additionally, the source of fundamental disagreement between the total and the consumer welfare criteria. However, there is a distributive concern for which total and consumer welfare approaches would converge over the same outcomes. The concern is about the imposition of a cost to some consumers to grant an allegedly higher benefit to other consumers. However, the reasons for convergence are different because in one case the justification is merely instrumental, while in the others the distributive outcome is the purpose of the intervention. This insight will be relevant for the discussion of consumer vulnerability.

Whether the focus is on the deadweight loss only is arguably the easiest and most important test for our research. Typically, in fact, it is sufficient to check the considerations about the effects of monopolistic behaviour to understand an author's position. Which market variable is considered more important between prices and quantities is quite telling too. In fact, if one is concerned only with the variation of quantities, then he is concerned only with the size of the pie and thus committed to a total welfare approach. On the contrary, if one is concerned with the consequences of the variation of prices for consumers, then there is a distinctive pro-consumer concern that is incompatible with total welfare. Indeed, there can also be unclear references to prices and quantities because variations of quantities and prices can simply be signalled to justify concern for the evolution of a market, without any specification of the axiological grounds for the concern. Formalisations of axiological propositions into goal functions are revealing because they show that statements apparently suggesting a total welfare approach are expressing a consumer welfare one. In fact, the consumer welfare approach requires that the interest of undertakings is merely instrumental. For example, a total welfare standard designed to minimise production costs and to grant zero economic profit to undertakings is a consumer welfare standard.

Beside distribution and the deadweight loss, another valuable source of insights is the attitude towards productive inefficiency—that is, against the unnecessary use of resources in a line of production. Here, the positions of the two hypotheses tested by our research question is opposite to the one regarding distribution. In fact, from a total welfare perspective, the waste of resources is relevant regardless of its effect on consumer welfare; those resources could have been used somewhere else. From a consumer welfare perspective, whether undertakings prefer a 'quiet life' is relevant only to the extent that it implies a reduction in consumer welfare.

A final point needs to be discussed. It consists in the objection that unless it is proven that a certain outcome is desirable according to one approach but not to the other the research question of this chapter is uninteresting. To this objection, we raise here three general orders of considerations. First, unless we consider the possibility that the two standards lead to diverging judgments, we cannot know if the judgments

of any position in this regard. Importantly, while a consumer welfare approach typically goes together with a critical attitude against wealth effects much more easily than a total welfare approach, this tendency is by no means conceptual and it is thus largely unhelpful for current purposes.

diverge. Thus, our research is already valuable in that it signals to economists the importance of checking whether certain conclusions based on a total welfare assumption would hold also with a consumer welfare one, and vice versa. Second, even if the two approaches converge from an economic point of view, Dworkin's critique would still apply. The approach that is more in line with legal discourse is more valuable for legal practitioners and officials. In this hypothetical scenario, choosing one criterion over does not change much as a matter of economic method. However, choosing the assumption that fits better with legal practice makes interdisciplinary discourse much easier, without compromising the integrity of the economist as a scholar. Third, there are reasons to believe that the choice between the two axiological assumptions does make a difference also in terms of outcomes. We consider here two of these reasons, regarding enforcement costs and price variations with negligible effects on exchanged quantity.

To see why the difference between a total and a consumer welfare approach matters when it comes to enforcement costs, consider a market where a price fixing cartel leads to a consumer welfare loss of EUR 15 mil, divided in a transfer of EUR 10 mil from consumers to producers and a deadweight loss of EUR 5 mil. Adopting total welfare as standard, the harm amounts only to EUR 5 mil—the deadweight loss. On the contrary, with consumer welfare as the standard, the harm is EUR 15 mil—the deadweight loss plus the transfer. Suppose, for the sake of simplicity, that the legal system can only choose between a fully effective intervention that could eliminate the cartel's practice at the cost of EUR 10 mil, and inaction (at null cost). From a total welfare perspective, if the intervention costs EUR 10 mil and the harm is EUR 5 mil, the intervention brings a net loss of EUR 5 mil and it is thus undesirable. From a consumer welfare perspective, the result is the opposite. If the intervention costs EUR 10 mil and the harm EUR 15 mil, enforcement brings a net benefit of EUR 5 mil and it is thus desirable.

A divergence in outcomes can also be seen when applying different prices does not lead to variations in quantities and therefore there is no deadweight loss. In fact, from a total welfare perspective, in such circumstances the actual price is irrelevant, because it leads only to a transfer of welfare. On the contrary, from a consumer welfare perspective the lower the price the seller is willing to offer, the better. Let us consider a concrete example from the wholesale electricity market. Suppose there is a wholesale customer willing to pay up to 100 EUR/MWh and to buy 1000 MWh and there are two wholesale producers both willing to sell 1000 MWh for no less than 5 and 5.5 EUR/MWh respectively.[42] From a total welfare point of view, who the seller is and whether the price is 5, 5.5, or even 100 EUR/MWh is irrelevant. Total welfare is the same in any case. What changes is only its distribution. From a consumer welfare point of view, instead, the most desirable price is 5 EUR/MWh. With any price higher than 5 EUR/MWh, consumer welfare is reduced.

[42]Example inspired by PCR PXs (2016), pp. 29–30.

On the grounds of these considerations, we can move to identify the points of the economic theory of electricity markets that are more relevant for current purposes.

3.3 The Focus on Energy-Only Pricing Methods

In discussions about the electricity markets worldwide, it is common to distinguish three main topics, pillars, or sector-oriented policies: (1) the design of regulatory mechanisms to construct, enhance or maintain competition; (2) security of supply; and (3) environmental sustainability. As we shall see in Sect. 5, the same trichotomy also informs EU law and the project of building the EU internal market for electricity. At face value, these policies appear to be autonomous and sometimes conflicting. But are they indeed autonomous or even conflicting policies? Their interplay is complex and the resulting conflicts have been appropriately characterised as a trilemma.[43] Nevertheless, policies that seem to conflict could be in axiological relation (one being more valuable than the other) or in instrumental relation (one being instrumental to the other).

One implication of our research question consists in developing a more nuanced understanding of these issues. However, this chapter can only be a first contribution to such a broad project. Therefore, we must determine the scope of our inquiry. To do so, we first exclude environmental policies. We do so because environmental issues are a classic case of negative externalities that the market is commonly recognised to be poor at dealing with. Arguably then, they are largely irrelevant to our purpose. Within the pillars of market design and security of supply, we identify three areas that in our view are particularly relevant for answering our research question. These areas are: the pricing methods of electricity in supply contracts along the supply chain, investments in infrastructure (e.g. generation or transmission systems), and the concern for access to electricity grids (e.g. transmission, distribution, and interconnector systems). Given these three areas are too broad for being analysed in this chapter, we reluctantly focus only on pricing mechanisms of electricity in contractual transactions for the supply of electricity along the production chain. And ultimately, even about pricing methods, we narrow the study to 'energy-only' methods thereby excluding 'energy-and-capacity' methods.[44] The reason is that extending the discussion to 'energy-and-capacity' methods would imply including in the analysis issues relevant also to security of supply and access to electricity grids. Therefore, extending the study beyond 'energy-only' methods would defeat the purpose of reducing the scope of the analysis.

The discussion of pricing methods is very important for our research because of the peculiarities of the electricity industry. In fact, it is common to distinguish two types of electricity producers—low load and peak load producers—and two related

[43]Röpke (2013).

[44]Joskow and Tirole (2007); Gonzàlez-Diaz (2015).

electricity markets—low load and peak load. Low load producers have considerably lower marginal costs and higher fixed costs compared to peak load producers. The consequence is that the economic rule of a market clearing price equal to marginal costs can lead the price of electricity to sky-rocket during a peak up to five hundred times the low load price.[45] Even worse perhaps, in some cases even if all the possible generation capacity is employed, the market does not clear and some consumers must be left off the grid. The management of these issues is very delicate. On the one hand, the increment of prices during a peak is very important to low load producers to recoup fixed costs. A constant policy concern is in fact the financial sustainability of the investment in new electricity plants, sometimes referred to as the 'missing money problem'.[46] On the other hand, given the (wide-spread assumption of) price inelasticity of electricity demand, marginal cost pricing can have extraordinary distributive effects from consumers to undertakings. Think of the California electricity crisis of 2000–01. It was calculated that, at the time, peak load management in California led to a redistribution of approximately USD 40 billion and to a loss because of power interruptions of USD 250 million.[47] Thus, the deadweight loss was equal to only the 0.625% of the transfers. It is worth noting that according to an operational assumption often made in the literature, the deadweight loss is typically estimated as amounting to around 50% of the transfers.[48] Thus, from a total welfare perspective, the California electricity crisis was arguably no crisis at all. Yet, there has been great concern, even among economists, about the situation and its impact on consumers.[49]

Economists have long studied the price mechanisms applicable in the electricity market. The features of this market that make it particularly problematic are the (near) impossibility of storing electricity, the high fixed and sunk costs[50] and the existence of two products (low and peak[51] load electricity) with different demand and supply schedules. Regarding energy-only prices, the theoretical benchmark is typically the so-called Ramsey or Ramsey–Boiteux pricing, and then other

[45] Stoft (2002) offers a clear, mathematically non-challenging and widely quoted description of these phenomena. Joskow and Tirole (2007), p. 74 refer to sky-rocketing prices.

[46] The missing money problem is in part a consequence of the long-term investment in a plant and the possibility of technological developments jeopardising the financial plan of the investment. This part of the problem is often referred to in economic contract theory as hold-up problem (Schmitz 2001) or as the economic rationale of the "right to serve" (Goldberg 1976, pp. 432–434). In the electricity sector, the subsidies to renewable energy plants have exacerbated this financial technological risk (see Röpke 2013; Gonzàlez-Diaz 2015).

[47] De Nooij et al. (2007), p. 286.

[48] Easterbrook (1985).

[49] See, for example, Wolak (2003) and Manifesto (2003).

[50] The difference basically consists in their short-run avoidability, see Braeutigam (1989), pp. 1303–1304. For an excellent introduction to the problem associated to the determination of costs, see Conkling (2011).

[51] Conkling (2011), pp. 100 et seqq. points out that "peak" is ambiguous, as it is possible to distinguish coincident and non-coincident demand peaks. As the author explains, this has implications for cost-based pricing techniques.

mechanisms—especially rate of return regulation and price capping—are discussed as proxies for it.[52] The key economic problem is that short-run marginal cost pricing does not allow to cover long-run fixed costs. Thus, the question becomes how to calculate the 'optimal' prices for covering these costs. Very briefly, Ramsey–Boiteux prices are designed in such a way that the price of the good with less elastic demand subsides the more elastic one. However, they are of limited practical relevance because their information requirements are formidable, which causes a serious problem in monitoring the actions of the undertakings allegedly using them. This fact has prompted economists to come up with incentive-compatible price mechanisms. One option is rate of return regulation, which pays an undertaking an amount based on production costs or invested capital. The greatest risk of this method is incentivising productive inefficiencies, in particular in the form of an excessive use of capital—sometimes called the Averch–Johnson effect.[53] Another option is price capping, which consists in imposing a maximum price for electricity during peak loads. Its main problem is whether it gives enough incentives to invest in innovation and/or new generation capacity or, in other terms, whether it causes a missing money problem.

As we shall see in the next section, the discussion of these pricing techniques offers valuable insights to answer our research question because it shows what makes the pricing mechanisms 'optimal' for the authors discussing them.

4 Alternating Currents in Economically-Informed Research

We now use the analytical framework of the previous section to build the economic premise of our research question, namely that there is axiological disagreement on the microeconomic rationale of the market and that therefore economic analysis does not require necessarily to assume total welfare as a maximand. Conversely, we point out that there is a gap in economically-informed legal research: the assumption of total welfare maximisation is not universally accepted in the economic analysis of electricity markets. This is crucial, in our view, because the challenge we move here to total welfare cannot be labelled as a moral or philosophical critique to be thus (once again) dismissed because it lacks economic grounds. Even economically-informed legal scholars rejecting any explanatory project are—at the very least—in need of some argument to support their choice of incorporating a total welfare approach instead of a consumer welfare one. In fact, as both are used by economists,

[52]The name refers to Ramsey (1927) and Boiteux (1960). For a fuller conceptual and historical account, see Baumol (2008).

[53]Averch and Johnson (1962). For a recent discussion, see Netz (2012), pp. 104–111.

the commitment to offering an economic perspective does not justify by itself the assumption of total welfare. Moreover, basic norms of academic transparency[54] imply these economically-informed legal scholars owe their audience (academic colleagues, students, policy-makers, judges, lawyers, etc.) an explanation of why they never discuss the theoretical availability of a different axiological foundation for their analyses.

The section is structured as follows. First, we review the economically-informed legal scholarship on network industries and in particular on electricity to see if there is any room for a consumer welfare approach. We take instead for granted that in general discussions of mainstream economically-informed legal scholarship this is the stated view.[55] Second, we review an illustrative portion of economic literature related to the issues identified in Sect. 3.3.

4.1 *Axiological Commitments in Legal Economically-Informed Research in Electricity Market(s)*

In this review, we first offer a few illustrative examples of individual research, but then we focus our attention on the content of literature reviews. In fact, we consider the second type of source a more illustrative indicator of whether there is consensus or not in mainstream literature at the axiological level.

In his early research on natural monopolies, Posner clearly takes a total welfare approach.[56] His main concern is with problems of productive efficiency.[57] In his view,

> [the] market power [of a natural monopolist] flows from the cost and demand characteristics of the market in which he is selling, rather from unfair or restrictive tactics or from legal privileges. Moreover, . . . the natural monopolist is well situated to adopt a method of pricing – discrimination – that maximizes profit without necessarily restricting output.[58]

As pointed out in Sect. 3.2, Posner's disregard for distributive concerns (so that price discrimination is acceptable as long as it does not restrict output) confirms his endorsement of the total welfare standard. More recently, Ølikke and Møllgard use a

[54]For a recent call for transparency in legal scholarship by an economically-informed researcher in law, see De Geest (2015).

[55]This is the case in both Hanson et al. (2010) and Sanchez-Graells (2018). See however Esposito (2017c), pointing out that a confusion regarding the maximand is an underdiscussed feature of the behavioural turn and Esposito and Grundmann (2017), pp. 8–11 and 14–18, pointing out similar ambiguities in the use of the concepts of consumer sovereignty and of principal and agent relations.

[56]Posner (1999), pp. vi and 3.

[57]Posner (1999), pp. 31–53.

[58]Posner (1999), p. 19.

total welfare approach in their attempt—in our view almost an internal explanatory project[59]—to give an economic definition of the EU concept of services of general economic interest.[60] Sidak and Spulber offer conflicting statements because acting in the "public interest" means "maximizing social welfare", but a few pages later the "appropriate objective" for a public utility becomes "advanc[ing] economic efficiency and consumer welfare".[61] Bellantuono also takes a total welfare approach as the basis of a comparative law and economics approach to energy markets.[62]

The *Economics of Regulation and Antitrust* by Viscusi, Vernon and Harmington requires a deeper reconstruction. The book reached the fourth edition in 2005, and we consulted the second (1995) and the fourth ones. In fact, the book literally endorses every possible axiological position we have encountered in the review, including the claim that economic analysis is free from value choices.[63] And it does so several times even if the analysis is limited to the areas of more direct relevance for current purposes. Interestingly, this fact has passed unnoticed in book reviews.[64] The very first observation about the microeconomic rationale is a cheer to convergence between total and consumer welfarism:

> [i]f we existed in a world that functioned in accordance with the perfect competition paradigm, there would be little need for antitrust policies and other regulatory efforts.[65]

A few pages later, the problem of monopoly pricing is that "there are economic efficiency losses to society", but in the following section monopolies cause "efficiency and equity problems" so that—same paragraph—the "monopoly will not best advance the interests of society as a whole."[66] After introducing the conflict between short-run and long-run consumer welfare, the authors give what we think is a very clear articulation of the consumer welfare standard:

> [t]he overall object of [economic] analyses is to determine how we can best structure the price and incentive schemes for these firms so that we protect the interests of electricity

[59]See, however, below Sect. 5.

[60]Ølikke and Møllgard (2016), p. 219. See also Davies (2012), pp. 576–580. A twofold limitation of Ølikke and Møllgard (2016) for current purposes is that on the one hand it offers a definition of services of general economic interests on which total and consumer welfare approaches can converge and second it focuses only on the concern for consumers' access: "The strengthening of a component of a network that underprovides services to a significant share of the population of a Member State" (p. 218).

[61]Sidak and Spulber (1997), pp. 134, 139, see also p. 325, where the "welfare benefits of entry equal the change in consumer surplus owing to competition."

[62]Bellantuono (2013). Note that the claim of the author is not explicit, but can be inferred by his references and by the connection of efficiency to the level of transaction costs (p. 238) and of static efficiency to increases in production capacity (p. 250).

[63]Viscusi et al. (1995), p. 79. As we have consulted both the second and fourth edition of this book, pages between brackets refer to the fourth edition.

[64]Benjamin (1997) and Waller (2006).

[65]Viscusi et al. (1995), p. 2.

[66]Viscusi et al. (1995), pp. 5–6.

consumers while at the same time providing incentives and a reasonable return to the firms involved.[67]

While the conflicting statements recur,[68] in the light of this block quotation a plausible reconciliation is the following: the convergence between consumer and total welfare, united with the desire to offer arguments minimising one's axiological commitments, leads to the endorsement of a total welfare standard; however, the concern for consumers resurfaces either explicitly or in the form of fairness considerations. Interestingly, in some statements "social" is best understood as "consumer". In any case, this reconciliatory attempt is only partially successful and some incoherencies in the text remain.

We now move to chapters in sources that, by their nature, advance a claim to comprehensiveness in their account of the debate. In the 2007 *Handbook of Law and Economics* edited by Polinsky and Shavell, the chapter on "natural monopolies" is written by Paul Joskow. Joskow here[69] takes first a total welfare approach, in which he emphasises the importance of high barriers to entry, productive inefficiencies and rent-seeking expenditures to justify legal intervention.[70] However, Joskow recognises the existence of "additional normative public policy goals". Among them, there is "the distribution for surplus between consumers and producers."[71] In the 2012 *Encyclopedia of Law and Economics*, three chapters are particularly relevant; they focus on theories of regulation in general, and then more specifically on natural monopolies and on the electricity sector. They all accept a total welfare approach.[72] However, den Hertog recognises the importance, in practice, of equity considerations beside total welfare maximisation and Netz qualifies as "fair" the earnings of undertakings under price regulation.[73] Only de Hauteclocque and Perez are consistent total welfarists. However, de Hauteclocque has also written—notably, with Glachant the year before and alone the following year—that "competition policy is about maximizing long-term social welfare, with sometimes a bias in favour of consumer welfare."[74]

---

[67] Viscusi et al. (1995), p. 7.

[68] Viscusi et al. (1995): convergence pp. 76–78 (82–84), p. 309 (358–359), p. 360 (410–411), pp. 365–366 (415–417); social or total welfare approach pp. 73–74 (79–80), pp. 76–78 (82–84), pp. 83–84 (89–90), p. 367 (417), p. 377 (429), p. 393 (444); concern also for equity or fairness p. 79 (85), p. 81 (86–87), pp. 83–84 (89–90), p. 308 (n.a.), p. 379 (429), p. 386 (n.a.); consumer welfare approach p. 379 (429), pp. 400–401 (452).

[69] However, see below footnotes 87–88 and accompanying text.

[70] Joskow (2007), pp. 1249–1253.

[71] Joskow (2007), p. 1256.

[72] den Hertog (2012), p. 31; Netz (2012), pp. 102–103; de Hauteclocque and Perez (2012): most clearly at p. 395.

[73] den Hertog (2012), p. 35; Netz (2012), p. 103.

[74] de Hauteclocque and Glachant (2011), p. 202; de Hauteclocque (2013), p. 27.

4.2 Axiological Commitments in Economic Research in Electricity Market(s)

Also in the case of economic literature, we start with the Chicago School. Here, we find axiological agreement in the articles of the 1960s by Williamson and Demsetz, although later they had instrumental disagreements. Williamson is adamant in his total welfarism: he draws the readers' attention to the fact that in his welfare analysis "benefits and costs are weighted equally 'to whomsoever they may accrue'," and thus "society is indifferent to the income redistribution".[75] Demsetz introduced in the debate the idea that a periodic competition for the electricity market (competition for the market) would have been a reliable proxy for the price mechanism of a competitive market. For most of the article, Demsetz is concerned only with designing a proxy for the competitive outcome regardless of who benefits from it. However, Demsetz explicitly rejects the relevance of distributive concerns and overlooks the fact that these concerns are part of the public debate over the electricity market.[76] It is interesting to observe that, a few years earlier, in *The Journal of Law and Economics* Stigler and Friedland were well aware of the pro-consumer orientation of electricity regulation—but they pointed out its ineffectiveness, without offering considerations that are relevant for the total-consumer welfare axiological disagreement.[77]

If we broaden our perspective, we can see that—unsurprisingly—total welfare is explicitly and coherently assumed in the literature as the welfare standard.[78] But beside this approach, there is a variety of other—not necessarily mutually exclusive—positions. Some authors have an explicitly agnostic approach between standards. They either analyse both[79] or build general welfare functions that allow them to assign variable weights to consumers' and undertakings' welfare.[80] There are even some apparent consumer welfarists who justify this standard on total

[75]Williamson (1966), p. 813.

[76]Demsetz (1968), pp. 58, 61–65. Note that at the instrumental level, there were notable disagreements between Williamson and Demsetz et al., as summarised in Crocker and Masten (1996), pp. 10–12.

[77]Friedland and Stigler (1962).

[78]Braeutigam (1989), pp. 1300–1301; Armstrong and Vickers (1991); Pfaffenberger (2008), pp. xxxv and xli; Willems (2015), p. 142. Particularly telling is Prieger (1996), pp. 307 and 313 et seqq., where the author builds a "partially regulated optimal price vector" based on total welfare and then labels as "myopic" and "short-sighted" a regulator "who fails to account for the feedback effect" of the price mechanism and curiously also "seeks to maximize the benefits to consumers of the dominant firm's goods." We add to this list also Crocker and Masten (1996) who take a transaction costs minimisation approach (p. 10) on the grounds of the identification, based on Coase (1960), of cost minimisation and welfare maximisation as two sides of the same coin in the transaction costs literature.

[79]Clemenz (1991), p. 398.

[80]Arrow and Kalt (1979), pp. 16–17; Lee and Thakor (1987), pp. 722–723; Cowan (2002), p. 174; Armstrong and Sappington (2006), p. 331.

welfare grounds. For example, for Armstrong and Sappington "society values consumer welfare at least as highly as the welfare of shareholders, perhaps because consumers are less wealthy than shareholders or because many shareholders reside in another jurisdiction".[81] To these considerations de Nooij et al. add the tentative observations that "electricity consumers are voters and producers are not," and that redistribution of wealth would have negative aggregate welfare effects or it would benefit foreigners.[82]

In other cases, it is just extremely difficult to point out what the welfare standard is. Sometimes it remains so implicit that in our view any attempt of classification would risk distorting the source.[83] In other cases, there is a laundry list of conflicting considerations. In his widely cited *Power System Economics*, Stoft first defines efficiency in total welfare terms, then observes that "almost universally", but not in "economic dictionaries", "allocative efficiency" is concerned with the "demand-side", then explains why competition is "good for consumers" but later he suggests that there is no reason to prefer one side of the market to the other.[84] While Stoft is consistent in his total welfare perspective, it is clear that his position is the result of a choice among options. But it does not end here.

What starts to be surprising is that some total welfarists 'hedge their bets', so to speak, by watering down their totalitarian approach with a recognition of the concerns for equity, fairness, and distribution.[85] Crew and Kleindorfer do this with great transparency. Economics "provide[s them] an analytical basis for public policy evaluation" and a total welfare approach can be "modified by introducing equity constraints."[86] This is crucial because, as seen in Sect. 3.2, a purely distributive concern is incompatible with a total welfare standard. In their influential *Markets for Power*, Joskow and Schmalensee base their analysis on "economic efficiency, the efficiency with which society employs the scarce material resources at its disposal" but they do so while being aware that "economic efficiency is just a means toward more basic ends, including justice, national security, and quality of life."[87] Moreover, evaluating the economic efficiency of the electricity industry requires to assess if the supply is made "at the minimum possible cost" and if "the prices charged consumers of electricity appropriately reflect the costs of electricity supply, so that consumer decisions about electricity use also reflect those costs appropriately."[88]

[81]Armstrong and Sappington (2006), p. 331.

[82]de Nooij et al. (2007), p. 285.

[83]For example, Ramsey (1927), Boiteux (1960), Bradley and Price (1988), Lyon (2000) (who at p. 58 observes that "[t]o protect consumers, regulators also imposed price and profit controls"); Conkling (2011); Kaminski (2012).

[84]Stoft (2002): total welfare terms (p. 69), the observation that "allocative efficiency" is concerned with the "demand-side" (p. 72), competition "good for consumers" (p. 78), no reason to prefer one side of the market to the other (p. 116).

[85]Kahn (1988), p. 16, fn 46; Röpke (2013), p. 6; de Nooij et al. (2007), pp. 279, 291–292.

[86]Crew and Kleindorfer (1986), pp. 10 and 14–21.

[87]Joskow and Schmalensee (1983), p. 8; see also pp. 154–155.

[88]Joskow and Schmalensee (1983), p. 9; see also p. 137.

Notably, the first definition of "economic efficiency" suggests a total welfare approach, but it does so only instrumentally to other axiological concepts. More interestingly, the considerations about prices reflecting minimal costs are at the core of a strong idea of sovereign consumers, the satisfaction of whose interests is the purpose of the market mechanism.[89] In other terms, these considerations seem to us in line with a consumer welfare approach. Nonetheless, the view they express is not idiosyncratic.

Part of the literature explicitly takes a consumer welfare perspective. And importantly it does so with the same levity total welfarists show in adopting a total welfare approach. In their influential 1979 article, Vogelsang and Finsinger explain that "[t]he firm's social objective as pursed by the regulatory agency is the maximization of welfare," where "[w]elfare is supposed to be given by consumers' surplus" only.[90] Also Riordan simply "[a]ssume[s] that the welfare criterion of the regulator is maximization of consumer surplus, subject to the constraint that expected profits are nonnegative".[91] Similarly, for Joskow and Tirole the social optimum is based on the maximisation of the net surplus of consumers.[92]

An important share of the literature is not explicitly interested in consumer welfare, but a closer look reveals a clear commitment to it. This happens in a variety of studies interested in price mechanisms that can lead a monopolist to make an exogenously determined level of profit while maintaining incentives to cost reduction.[93] Often, the level of profits is zero or close to zero.[94] This attitude is very important for our purposes. In fact, it implies a distributive concern against the undertaking who is rewarded with no more than a certain amount, to the effect that all the remaining welfare is captured by consumers. In Sect. 3.2 we explained that this approach is incompatible with total welfarism.

Sometimes, the closer look reveals a tension between the claim made in natural language and the one made with the aid of mathematic formalisations. In fact, in some cases "social welfare" and associated expressions boils down to "consumer welfare" in the formalisation. For example, Hagerman builds a "total surplus maximization problem", but then imposes a profit cap so that he maximises consumer

---

[89] See Esposito and Grundmann (2017), pp. 8–11 for an analysis of the concept and the distinction from the very weak notion of consumer sovereignty as respecting consumer preferences.

[90] Finsinger and Vogelsang (1979), p. 158.

[91] Riordan (1984), p. 110.

[92] Joskow and Tirole (2007).

[93] For Greenberg et al. (1981), p. 909 this is the "traditional regulatory framework" and the "return on invested capital (is) commensurate with the risk"; Sherman (1981), p. 477, fn 5 points out that social welfare could be reached even without the profit constraint. Clemenz (1991), p. 395 observes that "what the regulator (presumably) really cares for is not the amount invested in cost reduction, or not even the actual cost reduction, but the consumers' net utility over the planning period." Crew and Kleindorfer (1986), p. 23 explain price caps as an "attempt to regulate the level of profits to some 'fair' level."

[94] Stefos (1990); Cowan (2002), p. 174; Höffler (2006), p. 29.

welfare.[95] In other cases the tension is internal to the natural language. Clemenz argues that "in general [price cap] regulation yields higher social welfare than can be achieved in a [rate of return] regime," but "social welfare" must be understood in the light of the previous observation that "the socially optimal price cap" is the one that "is better for consumers".[96]

4.3 Axiological Commitments, Economics and Electricity Market(s): Concluding Remarks

The reviews in Sects. 4.1 and 4.2 have identified three types of axiological commitments. According to the first position, the microeconomic rationale is total welfare maximisation and distribution between consumers and undertakings does not matter. According to the second, intermediate position, the microeconomic rationale is total welfare maximisation but distribution between consumers and undertakings matters for non-economic (moral, political) reasons. According to the third, the microeconomic rationale is consumer welfare maximisation, to the effect that the concern for distribution between consumers and undertakings is internal to economic reasoning. In terms of diffusion, total welfarism appears to us to be the strongest in economically-informed legal research (Sect. 4.1), but also stronger there than in the economic literature reviewed in Sect. 4.2. The intermediate position appears roughly equally strong in the two sub-sections, while consumer welfarism appears to be the weakest in Sect. 4.1 but becomes much stronger in Sect. 4.2. Obviously, the reliability of these considerations is limited, given the limited extension of the analysis. Another interesting finding is that some of the sources reviewed in Sect. 4.1 refer to sources reviewed in Sect. 4.2 ignoring the fact that they have an axiological disagreement.[97] The most interesting case of hidden axiological disagreement is however offered by Joskow's scholarship: while endorsing the intermediate position in *The Handbook of Law and Economics*, equally naturally in other cases he supports consumer welfarism.

Nevertheless, the finding of an intermediate position requires some comment since our research question considers explicitly only the first and third positions. We have therefore to specify the relation of the second position with our research question. Upon little reflection, we see that the intermediate position embodies

[95] Hagerman (1990), p. 76. See also Cowan (2002), abstract and p. 174.

[96] Clemenz (1991), p. 392. At page 398 and following Clemenz formalises both a total and a consumer welfare standard and uses both.

[97] We prefer not to make explicit references because we are not engaging personally with any specific author. Note also that we did not make a systematic review of all the sources quoted in Sect. 4.1, but we recognise it would be an interesting extension of our inquiry—issues of personal engagement aside.

exactly that distributive concern total welfarism denies. Therefore, the intermediate position is more compatible with consumer welfare than with total welfare. It opens the way to the question whether a consumer welfare approach may contribute to clarify the meaning of "fairness" in contract law issues.[98] However, for current purposes, we are satisfied with the conclusion that the second position fits better with consumer welfarism than with total welfarism.

5 EU Electricity Law as a System: Revealing the Value of Consumer Welfare in Positive Integration

As we have seen in Sects. 3 and 4, total and consumer welfare are two different microeconomic rationales for the market mechanism. The question then becomes which of these two microeconomic rationales can be used to offer a better internal explanation of the EU internal market for the electricity. In search for the internal explanation of EU law, the question then becomes: does EU law endorse axiological propositions aimed at increasing the pie (total welfare) only or also at giving it to consumers (consumer welfare)? This last and final session analyses the impact of EU law in the electricity market. It considers EU law as a set of valid rules created by supranational authorities with delegated power to legislate or adjudicate disputes. Therefore, these are rules enshrined in the provision of the Treaty, secondary legislation, and the judgments of the Court of Justice of the European Union (CJEU).

Over the last three decades, the regulatory framework of EU law applied to the electricity sector has passed through three regulatory reforms known as the energy packages. The Commission has proposed the fourth regulatory reform, the so-called the Clean Energy Package, but most of the Directives and Regulations are still legislative proposals and, therefore, it will not be included in the analysis. Considering the regulatory frameworks over the last three decades, each of the three packages has been approved by fully revoking the prior regulatory framework, whose reforms change obligations to assure the accomplishment of EU values. This wealth of legal materials is very useful to answer our research question, and in particular to understand if EU electricity law can be better explained as trying to maximise total or consumer welfare.

The impact of EU integration on the electricity sector has moved through two phases. In the first phase, it moved from the original inapplicability of the Treaty's provisions to the creation and enforcement of a distinct set of rules imposing obligations on Member States and, most importantly, electricity undertakings and customers. This phase lasted until the 1980s, when EU law stopped considering the electricity industry as conducting "activities of non-economic interest".[99] The CJEU,

---

[98]See above, Sect. 2. Note that Esposito and Grundmann (2017) point into this direction concerning financial investments and consumer credit contracts.

[99]Judgment of the Court of 15 July 1964, C-6/64, *Flaminio Costa v E.N.E.L.* ECLI:EU:C:1964:66.

by reviewing its precedents and recognising the economic interest of providing universal services like postal services[100] and telecommunication,[101] also exposed electricity undertakings to the enforcement of the entire corpus of provisions in the Treaty. Of particular significance were provisions on non-discrimination, the four freedoms and, most importantly, competition law. Since the early 1990s, the Treaty provisions on the four freedoms and non-discrimination have been applied to Member States and national laws, while duty-imposing rules of competition have targeted market actors. In parallel, the Commission released the first Green and White Papers on the regulation of energy markets. The Treaty provisions later gained substance and effectiveness in the electricity market with EU secondary legislation, which was later approved as the 1st energy package.

By looking at the three decades of integration project, this section claims that EU electricity law is a system of norms that undoubtedly endorses consumer welfare more than total welfare as a market rationale. This claim is supported by observing the EU legal framework of the liberalisation of electricity markets step-by-step, or more accurately, package-by-package. Considering the analysis in Sect. 2, the focus is narrowed to two rights that in principle might appear contradictory, but as we shall see are not. These are the qualification of competitive prices and competitive markets, and affordable and reasonable prices as individual consumer rights.

Beginning with the application of the provisions of the TFEU to electricity markets, two provisions—Articles 101 and 106 TFEU—are of particular interest. While the first concerns anti-competitive behaviour, the latter regards Services of General Economic Interest (SGEI). In Article 101 TFEU, the EU original legislator makes the political choice of endorsing consumer welfare quite clear. It is important to stress the wording of the command in Article 101(3) TFEU, stating explicitly that an efficiency defence under EU competition law requires that an agreement "contributes to improving the production or distribution of goods ... while allowing consumers a fair share of the resulting benefits." The clearness of the legislator's command requires no further comment. Competition law being the set of rules for which the codes of law and economics are more connected, this is particularly telling for our research question.

Concerning, SGEI (and before that, Public Service Obligations), Article 106 TFEU might appear to support a total welfare approach, but this is not sustained if this provision is read in conformity with Protocol 27. There is indeed an affinity between the expressions "total welfare" and "general economic interest" in the Treaty. It is in fact undeniable that the idea of a service in the general economic interest calls to one's mind the idea of the interest of society and ultimately total welfare on the grounds of an association like the following: general economic interest—social welfare—total welfare. Moreover, the final sentence of Article 106 (2) TFEU refers to the "development of trade", which again might suggest a total

[100]Judgment of the Court of 19 May 1993, C-320/90 Corbeau. ECLI:EU:C:1993:198.

[101]Judgment of the Court of 13 February 1990, C-202/88, France v Commission, ECLI:EU:C:1990:64.

welfare approach, especially if effects on trade are measured in terms of quantity variations.[102] Nonetheless, all doubts vanish in front of Protocol 27. Article 1 of the Protocol very emphatically establishes that SGEI must be operated "as closely as possible to the needs of the users" and ensure "a high level of quality, safety and affordability" for them, among others.

While the provisions of Articles 101 and 106 TFEU have passed through few amendments over more than six decades, the same cannot be said for the provision of EU law directly addressed to the market for electricity. Since 1996, EU legislation has passed through substantial reforms considering the first, second, and third packages. Yet the Commission is now advancing the negotiations of the fourth regulatory framework: the Energy Union. Besides secondary legislation approved in these packages, in between the second and the third package, the trichotomy of electricity policy—competition and integration, security of supply, and environmental sustainability—was lifted to constitutional status when the TFEU replaced the Treaty of Rome in 2006. The TFEU in fact includes Article 194, which could be aligned with total welfare since there are no references to consumers. However, Article 194 TFEU simply promotes to the level of primary EU law the three pillars of energy policies already introduced in Sect. 3.2, which were already embodied in the secondary legislation. The secondary legislation thus needs an in-depth investigation.

If one analyses the EU secondary legislation regulating the internal market for electricity from the first to the third package, over three decades of liberalisation and (re)regulation, he or she will conclude that there is no space to counter-argue the statement that EU pursues consumer welfare. The reason that justifies so strong a claim is that the EU legislator has carefully inserted explicit assertions about the political choice for consumer welfare since the 1st Directive, but not only. This lawmaker has carefully emphasised in more passages and with more explicit terms in the Directives and Regulations about the commitment to consumer welfare. In fact, each package contains norms enshrining rights for consumers (i.e. wholesale customers, final customers, household customers) and duties for undertakings and Member States in which the axiological ground is explicitly the right of consumers to fair and competitive prices.

Through the 1st and 2nd Electricity Directives, the liberalisation of the electricity market has relied on two regulatory strategies to create competition involving two key market transactions: the supply of electricity and the transmission service. The first strategy grants rights to access the network system to electricity undertakings on a non-discriminatory basis by advancing a system of tariffs with close monitoring of third party access rights. The second regulatory strategy deals more directly with energy-only prices paid by market players located on the demand side. Although tariff design for transmission and distribution systems is relevant for economically efficient allocation, energy-only price has been the focus of this research.

---

[102] See above, Sect. 3.2.

Looking at regulations affecting the energy-only price of electricity in supply contracts, the EU legislator created rights and duties that could be conflicting at first blush, but with deep and systematic understanding of the regulations are clearly not. On the one hand, Directives have granted the rights for consumers to recognised as what EU law calls "eligible customers".[103] On the other hand, the lack of competition in the early stages of liberalisation reasoning provisions that granted certain categories of consumers the right to a "reasonable price".[104] The creation of the competitive and internal market occurs heavily through the implementation of those two rights: the right to "reasonable price" and the right to be "eligible customer".[105] While the latter imposed on Member States the obligation to boost competition from the wholesale to retail market, the former granted protection to consumers as far as the liberalisation did not extend economic benefits to the very bottom of the supply chain: household customers. The goal of creating gradual competitive and integrated electricity markets all the way from the wholesale to retail transactions lasted for two decades. In this scenario, the purpose of the right to a "reasonable price" granted consumers benefits that they could not obtain directly by competitive markets.

If one compares provisions granting rights to the status of eligible customer and rights to a reasonable price, they could be understood as contradicting each other, but this would be an erroneous understanding. Eligible customers are defined in Article 2(9) of the 2nd Directive as "customers who are free to purchase electricity from the supplier of their choice." While eligible customers in the 1st Directive were necessarily "final customers consuming more than 100 GWh,"[106] Article 23(1) of the 2nd Directive sets out the target of converting all "non-household customers" into eligible customers by 1 July 2004 and also all "household customers" by 1 July 2007.[107] Concerning reasonable prices, Article 3 of the 1st, 2nd, and 3rd Directives established that "household customers . . .have the right to be supplied with electricity of a specified quality within their territory at reasonable [. . .] prices." If one tries to develop a systematic interpretation of these provisions, Articles 23(1) of the 2nd Directive and Article 3 of all three Directives might appear to conflict. Price regulation is often criticised as a regulatory strategy that precludes competition in liberalised markets. However, this reading amounts to a mistaken interpretation, as the legislator refers to the rights to a "reasonable price". As seen above, eligible customers have the right to be "free to purchase from suppliers of their choice." This right refers to the power of certain consumers to choose between two or more suppliers rather than be supplied by the incumbent. Therefore, the right to be "free to purchase", which cannot be understood as the right to a "freely determined price" or a "free market", does not conflict with rights to "reasonable prices". These rights

---

[103]Directive 96/92/EC Article 7(7), Directive 2003/54/EC Article 9.

[104]Directive 96/92/EC, Article 3(2). Directive 2003/54/EC Article 3(3), Directive 2003/54/EC Article 3(3).

[105]De Almeida (2017), pp. 237–241.

[106]Directive 96/92/EC, Article 19(3).

[107]Directive 2003/54/EC Article 23(1).

are ultimately focused on two different aspects of the electricity market. The right to be eligible is meant to contribute to the competitiveness of the market. The right to a reasonable price focuses instead to an outcome, a state of affairs or a result, but it is silent on the means to achieve it. Considering this clarification, the second question in need of an answer refers to the relation of these rules with consumer and total welfare.

It could be argued that rights to reasonable prices were transitory rights, a sort of political compromise in the process of liberalisation of the market. This reading suggests the ancillary character of these consumer rights, thereby challenging their importance for the identification of the legal rationale of the EU electricity market. This line of argument cannot be convincingly sustained. In fact, in the last 5 years, the CJEU has confirmed that electricity prices in the retail market can continue to be based on temporary referential prices insofar as Member States have a plan to enhance competition and assure consumers receive the benefits. This was the decision of the Court in the *Federutility case* that, although interpreting Article 3 (3) of the 2nd Gas Directive, can comfortably be applied analogically to the electricity market considering the similarity between the provisions in the Electricity and Gas Directives.[108] The judgement clarified the content of the semantically vague rules on "reasonable prices". The Court established that household customers' right to "reasonable prices" is a proxy for their right to a "competitive price". Therefore, "referential prices" or regulated prices set by Member States are compatible with EU law only if they are a temporary measure substituting the market mechanism when the latter is not working properly. Moreover, though the *Federutility case* refers to the 2nd energy package, the interpretation given to Article 3(3) is aligned with the recitals of the 3rd Electricity Directive. Differently from the prior Directives, where the commitment to consumer welfare could be grasped mainly through a systematic understanding of the Articles, the 3rd Directive moved this commitment to the front page of the legal text. Numerous recitals were dedicated to express the will of the EU legislator regarding the welfare of consumers. Starting with Recital (1), which informs that the internal market of electricity "aims to deliver real choice for consumers"; moving to Recital (9), asserting cross-border interconnection should be developed to secure transactions "at the most competitive price to consumers", and Recital (51) stating that "consumer interest should be at the heart of this Directive." Above all, Recital (57) leaves no space for controversies:

> Promoting fair competition and easy access for different suppliers and fostering capacity for new electricity generation should be of the utmost importance for Member States in order to allow consumers to take full advantage of the opportunities of a liberalised internal market in electricity.

Notably, one could claim that Recitals (1) and (9) of the 3rd Directive can be explained also from a total welfare point of view. In fact, the references to consumers could be taken as merely instrumental to the creation of a competitive market, which can then be understood as instrumental to total welfare maximisation. However,

---

[108] Judgment of the Court of 20 April 2010, C-256/08, *Federutility v AEEG*, ECLI:EU:C:2010:205.

Recital (57) explicitly states that consumer must "take full advantage of the opportunities of a liberalised internal market in electricity." This concern for consumers taking "full advantage" clearly concerns a concern in favour of consumers. These considerations about the recitals are particularly important given that recitals play a crucial role in EU law in that they have to explain the rationale of the secondary law.[109] Thus, if one could have claimed there was room for discussion on whether the normative system of EU law was commitment to the maximisation of total welfare, this disagreement can no longer be held since the 3rd Directive.[110] Even the subsequent EU Regulation governing energy wholesale market is carefully drafted with emphasis on the political choice for consumer welfare. Although the subject of the REMIT is rather addressed to regulate market behaviour of trader and brokers rather than energy-price, the lawmaker does not hesitate to reinforce that "the goal of increased integrity and transparency of wholesale energy markets should be to foster open and fair competition in wholesale energy markets for the benefit of final consumers of energy."[111]

Besides rights relating to price mechanisms, the observation of the dynamic change of rules also drew our attention to another set of rules, which has gained space since the 2nd Directive; namely, rules protecting vulnerable consumers. Though vulnerability does not explicitly grant individual rights to consumers, the obligations of Member States to protect vulnerable consumers is important for reasons discussed in Sect. 2. As Article 3(7) of the 3rd Electricity Directive defines consumer vulnerability in terms of energy poverty, it reassured the pecuniary dimension of the protection granted to this category of customers. In fact, there is no indicia suggesting that the protection of vulnerable consumers is justified as merely instrumental to the maximisation of total welfare instead of being considered an intrinsically valuable goal. Thus, the duty of protecting vulnerable consumers reinforces the proposition of this chapter.

The resulting image is that of a market created and opened to competition gradually but steadily, in which the active role of the State at the retail level becomes increasingly difficult to justify on the grounds of the increasing effectiveness of the market mechanism. As a key component for establishing this effectiveness is the extent to which consumers are benefitting from the process, we conclude that the microeconomic market rationale of EU electricity law is more plausibly taken to be consumer rather than total welfare maximisation.

---

[109]The CJEU has the tendency to interpret the recitals according to their plain meaning and to use them to give a teleological interpretation to the articles of secondary legislation. For an analysis, see Klimas and Vaičiutaitė (2008).

[110]If the proposal of the 'New Deal for Consumers' becomes law in the framework of Energy Union, the consumer welfare approach of EU law will become even clearer.

[111]Regulation 1227/2011 Recital (2).

6 Conclusion: The 'Shocking Truth' Revealed by the Internal Explanation of EU Electricity Law

This chapter has challenged the apparently uncontroversial assumption among economically-informed legal scholars that the maximisation of total welfare is the microeconomic rationale of the market. It has done so in four steps, which are the contents of Sects. 2–5, respectively. Section 2 advocated in favour of internal explanations of the law from both legal and economic points of view. Section 3 discussed points of convergence and divergence between explanations grounded in two alternative efficiency hypotheses, the mainstream one based on total welfare and the alternative one we introduce based on consumer welfare. Section 4 has shown that, contrary to the narrative of mainstream economically-informed legal scholars, total welfare is simply one of several possible microeconomic rationales of the market. This finding then implies that one needs a reason to choose among the alternatives. In this chapter, we have taken the view that an interesting reason is the degree of fitness with the content of the analysed legal system. This reason is interesting from a legal point of view because knowing what the law is, is an important starting point for many activities of legal practitioners and scholar. It is also interesting from an economic point of view because it allows us to solve axiological disagreements without engaging in axiological argumentation, which is something economists are typically reluctant to do. On these grounds, in Sect. 5 we have offered an internal explanation of the competition pillar of the EU internal market for electricity.

What we found is—in our opinions, at least—a shocking truth for economically-informed legal scholars. Contrary to their usual narrative, the analysed sub-system of rules of EU electricity law can be understood as endorsing an economic axiological proposition, but this proposition is about the maximisation of consumer welfare, not of total welfare.

From a legal perspective, law being a phenomenon made through and by legal interpretation and legal argumentation, it is important to enhance the awareness of legal scholars and practitioners that the economic assumptions of economic models harbour axiological choices and that there is room for choosing among alternatives. In this context, searching for the fitness of economic concepts with the law by searching for internal explanations of the law can hopefully enhance the awareness of both lawyers and economists about the values implied in the use of certain equations, graphs, and numbers instead of others. Therefore, while we think that the shocking truth we find is intrinsically important, we are tempted to suggest that the method used is perhaps even more important. Searching for internal explanations of the law is in fact an attractive way for lawyers and economists to discuss with each other, in full respect of their own prerogatives, strengths and weaknesses.

Also from an economic perspective, searching for internal explanations of the law is an attractive line of inquiry. Accepting the authority of the law implies accepting the axiological choices made by institutions legitimised to make these choices, which in turn is arguably more value-free than adopting an axiological assumption simply because it is used by many economists. Furthermore, Sect. 4 has shown that economists are not particularly precise in articulating their axiological positions, these positions often diverge, and furthermore they are typically not supported by axiological argumentation. On these grounds, our analysis in Sect. 5 implies that, when dealing with the analysed materials recalled in the previous paragraph, the assumption of total welfare is axiologically in contrast with the content of the law, which is a condition that is clearly very far from the ideal of a value-free inquiry.

Acknowledgments We thank Hans-W. Micklitz, Charlotte Sieber-Gasser and Lynn Gummow for the comments on earlier drafts. We are also thankful to Klaus Mathis and Bruce Huber for the invitation to the 6th Law and Economics Conference held on 7–8 April 2017 at University of Lucerne, and Régis Lanneau for his comments during the conference. Any remaining errors are ours. The research leading to these results has received funding from the European Research Council under the European Union's Seventh Framework Programme (FP/2007–2013), ERC Grant Agreement n. [269722], and the Academy of Finland under the Finland Distinguished Professor programme (FiDiPro) [283002].

References

Almeida SR, Ciriolo E, Lourenço JS, Troussard X (2016) Behavioural insights applied to policy: European Report 2016. Publications Office, Luxembourg

Armstrong M, Sappington DEM (2006) Regulation, competition, and liberalization. J Econ Lit 44 (2):325–366

Armstrong M, Vickers J (1991) Welfare effects of price discrimination by a regulated monopolist. Rand J Econ 22(4):571–580

Arrow KJ, Kalt JP (1979) Why oil prices should be decontrolled. Regulation 3:13–17

Averch H, Johnson LL (1962) Behavior of the firm under regulatory constraint. Am Econ Rev 52 (5):1052–1069

Baumol R (2008) Ramsey pricing. In: The New Palgrave Dictionary Online

Bellantuono G (2013) The comparative law and economics of energy markets. In: Eisenberg T, Ramello G (eds) Handbook of comparative law and economics. Edward Elgar, Cheltenham, pp 236–261

Benjamin L (1997) Book review of economics of regulation and antitrust. J Media Econ 10 (2):41–42

Boiteux M (1960) Peak-load pricing. J Bus 33(2):157–179

Bradley I, Price C (1988) The economic regulation of private industries by price constraints. J Ind Econ 37(1):99–106

Braeutigam RR (1989) Optimal policies for natural monopolies. In: Schmalensee R, Willig RD (eds) Handbook of industrial organization, vol 2. Elsevier, Amsterdam, pp 1289–1346

Calabresi G (1982) The new economic analysis of law: scholarship, sophistry, or self-indulgence? Proc Br Acad 1982:85–108

Calabresi G (2016) The future of law and economics: essays in reform and recollection. Yale University Press, New Haven

Clemenz G (1991) Optimal price-cap regulation. J Ind Econ 39(4):391–408

Coase RH (1960) The problem of social cost. J Law Econ 3:1–44

Cole DH, Grossman PZ (2002) The meaning of property rights: law versus economics? Land Econ 78(3):317–330

Conkling RL (2011) Energy pricing. Springer, Dordrecht

Cowan S (2002) Price-cap regulation. Swed Econ Policy Rev 9(2):167–188

Crew MA, Kleindorfer PR (1986) The economics of public utility regulation. Palgrave Macmillan UK, London
Crocker KJ, Masten SE (1996) Regulation and administered contracts revisited: lessons from transaction-cost economics for public utility regulation. J Regul Econ 9(1):5–39
Cserne P (2012) Consequence-based arguments in legal reasoning: a jurisprudential preface to law and economics. In: Mathis K (ed) Efficiency, sustainability, and justice to future generations. Springer, Dordrecht, pp 31–54
Davies G (2012) Freedom of movement, horizontal effect, and freedom of contract. Eur Rev Private Law 20(3):805–828
De Almeida L (2017) Integration through self-standing European private law: insights from the internal point of view to harmonization in the energy market. PhD Dissertation, European University Institute, Florence
De Geest G (2015) Any normative policy analysis not based on Kaldor-Hicks efficiency violates scholarly transparency norms. In: Hatzis A, Mercuro N (eds) Law and economics: philosophical issues and fundamental questions. Routledge, Abingdon, pp 183–202
de Hauteclocque A (2013) Market building through antitrust: long-term contract regulation in EU electricity markets. Edward Elgar, Cheltenham
de Hauteclocque A, Glachant J-M (2011) Long-term contracts and competition policy in European energy markets. In: Glachant J-M, Pinon D, de Hauteclocque A (eds) Competition, contracts and electricity markets. Edward Elgar, Cheltenham, pp 201–232
de Hauteclocque A, Perez Y (2012) Electricity regulation. In: Van den Bergh R, Pacces A (eds) Regulation and economics. Edward Elgar Publishing, Cheltenham, pp 377–405
de Nooij M, Koopmans C, Bijvoet C (2007) The value of supply security. Energy Econ 29 (2):277–295
Demsetz H (1968) Why regulate utilities? J Law Econ 11(1):55–65
den Hertog J (2012) Economic theories of regulation. In: Van den Bergh R, Pacces A (eds) Regulation and economics. Edward Elgar Publishing, Cheltenham, pp 25–95
Dworkin R (1980) Is wealth a value? J Leg Stud 9(2):191–226
Easterbrook FH (1985) Detrebling antitrust damages. J Law Econ 28(2):445–467
Esposito F (2017a) A dismal reality: behavioural analysis and consumer policy. J Consum Policy 40 (2):193–216
Esposito F (2017b) Alcune Note sui Disaccordi Teorico-Interdisciplinari del Diritto con l'Economia. Rivista Internazionale di Filosofia del Diritto S5(1):91–117
Esposito F (2017c) How behavioural law and economics vindicate the new haven school. In: Oeconomia. Special issue on Behavioural Law and Economics: History, Methodology and Philosophical Evaluations
Esposito F, Grundmann S (2017) Investor-consumer or overall welfare: searching for the paradigm of recent reforms in financial services contracts. Working papers of the Law Department of the EUI, 2017/5
Finsinger J, Vogelsang I (1979) A regulatory adjustment process for optimal pricing by multiproduct monopoly firms. Bell J Econ 10(1):157–171
Friedland C, Stigler GJ (1962) What can regulators regulate? The case of electricity. J Law Econ 5:1–16
Goldberg VP (1976) Regulation and administered contracts. Bell J Econ 7(2):426–448
Gonzàlez-Diaz FE (2015) EU policy on capacity mechanisms. In: Hancher L, De Hauteclocque A, Sadowska M (eds) Capacity mechanisms in the EU energy market: law, policy, and economics. Oxford University Press, Oxford, pp 3–31
Gordley J (2006) Foundations of private law: property, tort, contract, unjust enrichment. Oxford University Press, Oxford
Greenberg E, Marshall WJ, Yawitz JB (1981) Optimal regulation under uncertainty. J Financ 36 (4):909–1021
Haack S (2014) Evidence matters: science, proof, and truth in the law. Cambridge University Press, New York

Hagerman J (1990) Regulation by price adjustment. Rand J Econ 21(1):72–82
Hanson J, Hanson K, Hart M (2010) Law and economics. In: Patterson D (ed) A companion to philosophy of law and legal theory, 2nd edn. Blackwell, Chichester, pp 299–326
Hildebrand D (2016) The role of economic analysis in EU competition law: the European school, 4th edn. Kluwer Law International, Alphen aan den Rijn
Höffler F (2006) Monopoly prices versus Ramsey-Boiteux prices: are they "Similar", and: does it matter? J Ind Compet Trade 6(1):27–43
Joskow PL (2007) Regulation of natural monopoly. In: Polinsky M, Shavell S (eds) Handbook of law and economics, vol 2. Elsevier, Amsterdam, pp 1227–1248
Joskow P, Schmalensee R (1983) Markets for power. An analysis of electric utility deregulation. The MIT Press, Cambridge
Joskow P, Tirole J (2007) Reliability and competitive electricity markets. Rand J Econ 38(1):60–84
Kahn AE (1988) The economics of regulation. The MIT Press, Cambridge
Kaminski V (2012) Energy markets. Risk Books, London
Kehler A (2002) Coherence, reference, and the theory of grammar. CSLI, Stanford
Klimas T, Vaičiutaitė J (2008) The law of recitals in European Community legislation. ILSA J Int Comp Law 15(1):1–33
Kraus JS (2007) Transparency and determinacy in common law adjudication: a philosophical defense of explanatory economic analysis. Va Law Rev 93(2):287–359
Lee WY, Thakor AV (1987) Regulatory pricing and capital investment under asymmetric information about cost. South Econ J 53(3):720–734
Lyon TP (2000) Preventing exclusion at the bottleneck: structural and behavioural approaches. In: Crew MA (ed) Expanding competition in regulated industries. Springer, Boston, pp 55–82
Małecka M (2017) Posner versus Kelsen: the challenges for scientific analysis of law. Eur J Law Econ 43(3):495–516
Manifesto on the California Electricity Crisis (2003) Available at https://www.hks.harvard.edu/hepg/Papers/Ad-hoc.energy.professionals_California.Manifesto_1-30-03.pdf
Mathis K (2012) Consequentialism in law. In: Mathis K (ed) Efficiency, sustainability, and justice to future generations. Springer, Dordrecht, pp 1–30
Netz JS (2012) Price regulation: a (non-technical) overview. In: Van den Bergh R, Pacces A (eds) Regulation and economics. Edward Elgar, Cheltenam, pp 99–137
Ølikke GS, Møllgard S (2016) What is a service of general economic interest? Eur J Law Econ 41:205–241
PCR PXs (EPEX SPOT – Nord Pool– OMIE – OPCOM – GME – OTE – TGE) (2016) EUPHEMIA Public Description. PCR Market Coupling Algorithm
Pfaffenberger W (2008) Preface. In: Sioshansi FP (ed) Competitive electricity markets: design, implementation, performance. Elsevier, Amsterdam
Posner RA (1974) Theories of economic regulation. Bell J Econ Manage Sci 5:335–358
Posner RA (1975) The economic approach to law. Texas Law Rev 53:757–782
Posner RA (1993) The new institutional economics meets law and economics. J Inst Theor Econ 149:73–87
Posner RA (1999) Natural monopoly and its regulation. Cato Institute, Washington
Posner RA (2015) Norms and values in the economic approach to law. In: Hatzis A, Mercuro N (eds) Law and economics: philosophical issues and fundamental questions. Routledge, Abingdon, pp 1–15
Prieger JE (1996) Ramsey pricing and competition: the consequences of myopic regulation. J Regul Econ 10(3):307–321
Ramsey FP (1927) A contribution to the theory of taxation. Econ J 37(145):47–61
Riordan MH (1984) On delegating price authority to a regulated firm. Rand J Econ 15(1):108–115
Röpke L (2013) The development of renewable energies and supply security: a trade-off analysis. Energy Policy 61:1011–1021
Sanchez-Graells A (2018) Economic analysis of law, or economically-informed legal research. In: Watkins D, Burton M (eds) Research methods in law. Routledge, Abingdon, pp 170–193

Schmitz PW (2001) The hold-up problem and incomplete contracts: a survey of recent topics in contract theory. Bull Econ Res 53(1):1–17

Sherman R (1981) Pricing inefficiency under profit regulation. South Econ J 48(2):475–489

Sibony A-L (2015) Can EU consumer law benefit from behavioural insights? An analysis of the unfair practices directive. In: Mathis K (ed) European perspectives on behavioural law and economics. Springer, Dordrecht, pp 71–106

Sidak JG, Spulber DF (1997) Deregulatory takings and the regulatory contract: the competitive transformation of network industries in the United States. Cambridge University Press, Cambridge

Stefos T (1990) Regulating without cost information: a comment. Int Econ Rev 31(4):1021–1025

Stoft S (2002) Power system economics: designing markets for electricity. IEEE Press; Wiley-Interscience, Piscataway, NJ: New York

Tardiff TJ (2000) Cost standards for efficient competition. In: Crew MA (ed) Expanding competition in regulated industries. Springer, Boston, pp 169–190

Viscusi WK, Vernon JM, Harrington JE (1995 and 2005) Economics of regulation and antitrust, 2nd and 4th edns. The MIT Press, Cambridge

Wagner RE (2016) Economic efficiency and the law: distinguishing form from substance. In: Marciano A, Ramello GB (eds) Law and economics in Europe and the U.S. The legacy of Juergen Backhaus. Springer, Dordrecht, pp 17–30

Waller SW (2006) Book review: economics of regulation and antitrust. World Compet 29(3):504

Willems B (2015) The generation mix, price caps, and capacity payments. In: Hancher L, De Hauteclocque A, Sadowska M (eds) Capacity mechanisms in the EU energy market: law, policy, and economics. Oxford University Press, Oxford, pp 149–154

Williamson OE (1966) Peak-load pricing and optimal capacity under indivisibility constraints. Am Econ Rev 56(4):810–827

Williamson OE (1993) Transaction cost economics meets Posnerian law and economics. J Inst Theor Econ 149:99–118

Witt AC (2016) The more economic approach to EU antitrust law. Hart studies in competition law, vol 14. Hart Publishing, Oxford, Portland and Oregon

Wolak FA (2003) Diagnosing the California electricity crisis. Electr J 2003:11–37

Fabrizio Esposito Florence. PhD Researcher in Law at the European University Institute. Florence 50139, Via Bolognese 160, Villa Salviati. fabrizio.esposito@eui.eu. Fields of Interest: Theory of EU Economic Law (Consumer Law, Competition Law, Sector-specific regulation), Law and Economics, Legal Theory and Legal Reasoning.

Lucila de Almeida Helsinki. Postdoctoral Researcher Fellow at Institute of International Economic Law at the University of Helsinki. Helsinki, Yliopistonkatu 3, P.O. Box 4, FI-00014. lucila.dealmeida@helsinki.fi. Fields of Interest: Private Law Theory (Contract Law), Economic Law, Energy Law; and Legal Theory.

Part II
Investment in Infrastructure

Paying for Energy

Bruce R. Huber

Abstract The energy sector is amid an expensive transformation, especially in the United States and Europe. As aging coal and nuclear power plants are replaced by natural gas and renewable energy, it is worth asking how energy consumers will pay for the infrastructural overhaul that lies ahead. The way that energy costs are borne has important consequences: some technologies are underused because agreement about how to pay for them cannot be secured, while others are overused simply because their costs may easily be imposed on ratepayers or taxpayers. This article begins with a brief historical survey of energy policy to demonstrate the importance of the various ways to pay for energy. It then moves to an analysis of some of today's most vexing energy problems, and demonstrates that the adoption of acceptable cost-sharing mechanisms is crucial to the upgrade of energy infrastructure. To identify such mechanisms, one must look not only to the distribution and magnitude of costs—who will pay, and how much—but also to the operation of the relevant political, legal, and regulatory institutions. The key point is that superior technologies are not self-executing. Clean, safe and abundant energy depends not simply on technological improvement, but on securing a viable way to pay for it.

1 Introduction

Much of the world's energy infrastructure is due for a makeover. Coal-fired power plants, which for many years have generated the lion's share of global electricity, are rapidly being retired. In the West, nuclear power is also in a tight spot because of economic and safety concerns, as well as aging plants. In the United States, many nuclear power plants are nearing the end of their useful lives: some have already

B. R. Huber (✉)
Notre Dame Law School, Notre Dame, IN, USA
e-mail: bhuber@nd.edu

K. Mathis, B. R. Huber (eds.), *Energy Law and Economics*, Economic Analysis of Law in European Legal Scholarship 5, https://doi.org/10.1007/978-3-319-74636-4_7

been shuttered, and the operating licenses for dozens more will expire in the next 20 years.[1] Coal and nuclear power have together accounted for a sizeable share of the world's electricity generation. As these sources decline they will have to be replaced.[2] In Europe and the United States, this replacement will most likely require an increase in electricity generated by wind, solar, hydropower, and natural gas.[3] The shift from coal and nuclear to natural gas and renewables will require major infrastructural changes. The best renewable energy resources, especially in the United States, tend be in rural areas hundreds of miles from the centers of energy demand, and burgeoning natural gas development will require a great deal more pipeline capacity than is currently available. Bringing this new energy to market will involve not only new generation facilities, but also substantial additions to the power grid and pipeline networks that serve as the backbones of the domestic energy system. Even the projected growth in "distributed generation"—on-site forms of electricity generation like rooftop solar cells—will necessitate considerable improvements to the grid alongside the deployment of generating equipment.[4]

New power generation facilities, new transmission lines, new gas pipelines—these are expensive propositions. As energy policy makers debate various aspects of energy policy, it is worth paying attention to how policy makers plan to pay for the upcoming overhaul. Every bit as important as the raw physical technology of energy is the way that societies foot the bill for it, for the way that costs are borne will have important consequences.

What sorts of consequences? First, and most importantly, infrastructure simply will not be built if no way can be found to pay for it.[5] In most Western economic sectors, the market organizes capital investment. We tend to assume that if there is sufficient demand for something, market forces will provide it: new cars, new toys, new books make their way into the marketplace as if automatically, conjured into existence by the "invisible hand." But in these instances, investment is premised on a prospective revenue stream that will flow between buyers and sellers in market transactions. In other sectors, however—including energy—market forces are channeled and constrained by governmental intervention. Certain kinds of infrastructure would almost certainly be underdeveloped but for state action.[6] Regulators

[1]U.S. Nuclear Regulatory Commission (2016), p. 49 (Table 7, listing year of expiration of operating licenses for all nuclear power plants currently in operation). The licenses of all currently operating nuclear power facilities will expire by 2049 unless changes are made to current regulations.

[2]Overall demand growth for electricity has and may continue to decline in recent years. U.S. Energy Information Administration (2015), p. 8. Although some regions now predict negative growth in demand in the short term, the upcoming wave of plant retirements will not be offset entirely by reduced demand and a great deal of new generating capacity will nonetheless be required.

[3]U.S. Energy Information Administration (2015), p. 24 (projecting that "natural gas fuels more than 60% of the new generation needed from 2025 to 2040, and growth in generation from renewable energy supplies most of the remainder").

[4]Fucci (2011).

[5]Frischmann (2005), pp. 924–925.

[6]Standard economic theory posits that a fundamental market failure exists with respect to "public goods," goods jointly consumed by all without possibility of exclusion. Paul Samuelson is often

are involved at every part of the energy system, from the extraction of natural resources to the generation of energy to its distribution and eventual sale to end users.[7] Thus the organization of massive expenditures is a much more public and political process than in most other contexts. Paying for infrastructure requires political agreement on not only the target of investment but also the means of bearing its costs. This agreement can be difficult to achieve.

Subtler are the systemic consequences of individual decisions about paying for energy. Many energy investments, whether in energy efficiency or distributed generation, are cost-effective overall but entail high up-front costs. Research demonstrates that consumers irrationally avoid such up-front costs, with significant implications for the build-out of energy infrastructure.[8] A great deal of work has been devoted to understanding this problem and solving it with public policy.[9]

Similarly, when a mode of payment has been identified and agreed upon—when paying for infrastructure is "easy"—there can be unintended consequences. Widespread political acceptance of the basic utility model, in which utilities pass along capital costs to captive ratepayers, almost certainly led to an overinvestment in certain forms of energy infrastructure. Similarly, congressional "logrolling" practices in the United States kindled the era of "big hydro," a dam-building spree that brought cheap hydropower but also ecological devastation. Many dams in America are now being torn down as their environmental consequences become known. Moreover, just as consumers sometimes find themselves "stuck" with outdated devices, so too do utilities sometimes find themselves saddled with infrastructure that impedes their flexibility later. Infrastructure is durable, so investment decision reverberates into the future for years to come.[10]

This essay directs attention to the ways that paying for energy is structured by law and regulation, using examples drawn from the United States. It begins in Sect. 2 with a short example intended to frame the discussion that follows. Section 3 offers some historical examples to demonstrate that the development of energy infrastructure is shaped, sometimes dramatically, by the way its costs are borne. In Sect. 4, the discussion turns to current issues in energy and an examination of various tactics that policy makers have employed recently to address problems associated with paying for upgrades to energy infrastructure. Ultimately, the essay concludes that those concerned about cleaner, safer, or more abundant energy, whether consumers or scholars or activists, must work to enable not only the development of new resources and technology, but also the institutional mechanisms that will help pay for them

credited with key developments in public goods analysis (Samuelson 1954) although Samuelson's work built on the innovations of economists such as Eric Lindahl and Ugo Mazzola.

[7]U.S. Federal Energy Regulatory Commission (2012).

[8]This is the so-called "energy efficiency gap." Early and seminal analysis include Jaffe and Stavins (1994) and Brown (2001).

[9]For example, see Baker (2012), Michelsen and Madlener (2016), and Arimura et al. (2012).

[10]Decisions may also distort incentives downstream as actors seek to protect existing investments. Owners of coal-fired power plants in the United States, for example, have been very successful in winning grandfathered exemptions from Clean Air Act regulations. Hsu (2006).

most effectively. Careful analysis can shed light on which policy tools, and indeed which policy institutions, are best suited to the accomplishment of these energy goals.

2 Paying for Energy: An Example

Consider Sally, a hypothetical tenant in an apartment building. Like many tenants, Sally never sees her own energy bill; her landlord simply pays for the energy for the entire building and folds that cost into the rent. Sally's monthly rental payment does not go up or down depending on how much energy she uses, so she does not have much of a direct financial incentive to reduce her energy consumption. If Sally reduces her consumption, it is not likely because of a financial incentive; it is likely to occur for some other reason. On the other hand, if Sally were billed directly for her energy usage, her bill would reflect her own usage. If she chose, she could take steps to reduce her consumption and thus reduce the amount of money she spends on energy.[11]

On one hand, this example illustrates the importance of *who pays* for energy—in this case, is it landlord or tenant? We might expect less energy consumption from tenants who pay for their energy individually.[12] More generally, the issue of who pays is quite important in energy policy. Many ratepayers, and the utilities that serve them, understandably resist the idea of paying for someone else's energy. One often hears rhetoric opposing the "socialization" of energy costs, which refers to the spreading of costs beyond merely the entities who will directly benefit from particular expenditures.[13]

The distribution of energy costs is important, to be sure, but just as important is the issue of *how much* must be paid. In our example, Sally is unlikely to confront her landlord to explain that she consumes very little energy and that she would prefer that her rental payment not be affected by her neighbor, who sets his furnace too high in the winter and his air conditioner too low in the summer.[14] Relatively few people, we can be confident, have ever refused to rent an apartment because they did not wish to subsidize their neighbor's energy consumption. Only a small amount of money is at stake. Thus, the magnitude of a shared cost often affects one's willingness to pay it. *Contra* the rhetoric of socialization mentioned above, plenty of people

---

[11]Flynn and McManus (2010). For a leading account of the role of individual behaviours in shaping overall energy consumption and thus environmental outcomes, see Vandenbergh (2004).

[12]Levinson and Niemann (2004) note, for example, that tenants set their thermostats between one and three degrees warmer during winter months when the landlord pays for energy directly, all else being equal. See also Davis (2011) and Jaffe (2012).

[13]See, e.g., Follett (2016).

[14]Levinson and Niemann (2004), p. 51 (noting the persistence of inefficient arrangements even when they are clearly to the detriment of both tenant and landlord).

are, in fact, willing to pay for someone else's energy if it is only a small amount of money.

The reader might protest that this example is trivial and not at all analogous to the infrastructural investments mentioned at the start of the Article. But if the landlord-tenant distinction is multiplied over a large territory, the aggregate difference in energy demand represents some very expensive infrastructure. "Direct-metered" tenants attuned to energy costs will not only tend to consume less energy overall, but also will almost certainly purchase more energy-efficient goods than a "master-metered" counterpart. These goods will remain a part of the energy consumption picture for their useful lives.

More to the point, we can now see that behind the questions of *who pays?* and *how much?* is another exceedingly important question that is often hidden from view: namely, *who decides* who pays? In many U.S. states, landlords are prohibited from sub-metering their electricity.[15] Sally's landlord might well wish to bill individual tenants based on their consumption, but cannot if the state will not permit it. A rule allowing or even requiring sub-metering could have a substantial impact on residential energy consumption in a given jurisdiction. To focus on rules of this sort is to focus on the institutions that make such rules. Legislatures, agencies, and sometimes courts establish and interpret the rules and regulations that govern the field of energy. Advocates who seek to change the rules must understand how these institutions work, how change comes about, and what sorts of rule changes are likely to lead to desired outcomes. Different institutions function differently; a state legislature may respond to a very different set of forces and interests than a federal agency.

Who pays? How much? Who decides? These questions, though rudimentary, can direct our attention to some fundamental patterns that have arisen in the energy sector. The remainder of this essay examines these patterns in a handful of historical and current situations.

3 Historical Examples

A careful look at history reveals that the ways that energy costs have been structured and allocated are important to the story of energy—perhaps just as important as technological innovations and resource discoveries. We can see an example of this almost immediately following Thomas Edison's pioneering work with electricity.

[15] Ferrey (2011), p. 227. See also Matter of Campo Corp. v. Feinberg, 279 A.D. 302 (N.Y. 1952) (upholding decision by New York's Public Service Commission to disallow submetering).

3.1 The Insull Era

Edison's fame is well deserved, but it was one of Edison's subordinates, Samuel Insull, who was largely responsible for the business innovations necessary to deliver electricity to the masses. Here we must oversimplify a long and incredibly rich story.[16] Insull arrived in the city of Chicago before the regulation of electric utilities. Electricity companies in their infancy faced severe competition. Each company required its own generators and power lines, but this redundancy made the enterprise so expensive that only a few customers could afford a connection to an electric system. Sam Insull quickly realized that the only way to make electricity cheap enough to sell to average consumers and small businesses, was by eliminating competition to achieve economies of scale.[17]

There were important technological innovations that helped propel Insull: the switch to alternating current (AC) rather than direct current (DC) allowed power to be transmitted over longer distances, and the steam turbine drastically reduced the size and eventually the cost of power generating facilities.[18] These developments facilitated greater economies of scale, but alone they would likely have been insufficient to allow for the rapid expansion of electric service. Competition had to be stifled.

So Insull used all means necessary, scrupulous or not, to take out his competitors. He acquired some of them; others he ruthlessly forced out of business.[19] Eventually, however, Insull succeeded in convincing Illinois state legislators that the electricity industry could only become viable if it was treated as a regulated monopoly.[20] And ever since then, the electricity sector has indeed been thoroughly regulated. The idea of the "natural monopoly" evolved from a descriptive idea—that certain industries will gravitate towards monopoly—into a prescriptive one. The "utility consensus," as Richard Hirsh has labelled it, formed around the idea that the electricity sector had to be structured as a regulated, monopoly utility to operate efficiently.[21] This

[16]Some leading historical accounts are McDonald (2004), Wasik (2008), Platt (1991), Klein (2008), and Jonnes (2004). In McDonald's words, "[Insull], more than any other man, was responsible for founding the business of centralized electric supply; ... he either formulated or borrowed from others and first successfully applied on a large scale the concepts of the load and diversity factors (on which all utility rates are based); ... [and he] was the father of effective governmental regulation of public utilities and a progenitor of rural electrification..." Supra at pp. vii–viii.

[17]McDonald (2004), p. 57 ("Insull knew ... that the only sensible way to sell electric lighting was to have no competition ... [His competitors believed] that electricity should be considered as a luxury product that t should be sold at the highest possible price. Insull's thinking ... was based on the premise that electricity should be considered as for everybody, 'even the smallest consumer,' and that it should be sold at the lowest possible price.").

[18]King (2011) and Hughes (1993).

[19]Platt (1991), pp. 77–78 (see especially Table 7, listing competitors purchased by Insull's Chicago Edison Company).

[20]Platt (1991), p. 87; McDonald (2004), pp. 113–128.

[21]See generally Hirsh (1999).

consensus spread rapidly around the United States and facilitated enormous growth in electricity usage, especially in urban areas; gone was the fierce competition that prevented emerging electricity firms from finding their feet under them.

Insull was responsible for several other innovations bearing on the structure of payment for energy. He recognized that the crucial attribute of electricity, from a business standpoint, is that it cannot be stored. Even now, electricity must be generated exactly when it is needed, and demand for energy varies throughout the day. Thus, an electricity provider must have enough generators to satisfy peak demand, yet those same expensive generators could well sit idle during off-peak times. Insull devised new pricing structures to make his investments more efficient by shifting demand to those off-peak times, enabling his generating facilities to be up and running and turning a profit for a greater portion of each day.[22]

Much more could be said, but let us pause to analyze briefly this period. Who paid for energy? The decision to purchase electricity was made by businesses and consumers—by individual market actors. The amount that they paid largely depended on how widely the costs of infrastructure could be spread. These costs could be spread more widely if the number of purchasers increased, which was most easily accomplished by reducing competition. When the state sanctioned utility monopolies that could achieve significant economies of scale, the price of electricity went down, purchases went up, and infrastructure expanded quite rapidly.[23] One important lesson of this era, then, is that the rapid growth of energy infrastructure that characterized the early twentieth century depended on finding an acceptable legal and social mechanism to share and spread costs. State regulatory bodies—today's public utility commissions (PUCs) and their kin—and cost of service regulation became that mechanism.

3.2 *The Expansion Era*

After the forging of the "utility consensus" in Insull's day, state regulation of electric utilities became the norm and utilities flourished. In fact, they probably expanded too much—and the problem arose largely because of the way that the costs of energy were collected and paid.

To understand why, we need to look under the hood of cost-of-service regulation. Public utility commissions allow utilities to recover revenue sufficient to cover certain costs. The conventional formula used to calculate this "revenue requirement" is $R = O + B(r)$. R is the utility's revenue requirement; O represents the firm's operating expenses; B represents the rate base; and r represents a rate of return. The crucial distinction embedded within this formula is between O and B. Operating

[22]Platt (1991), pp. 83–87.

[23]Platt (1991), p. 121 (see Chart 6, showing exponential growth in electricity generated in Chicago between 1898–1912).

expenses are reimbursed dollar-for-dollar and earn no return. Capital costs, on the other hand, are allowed into the rate base and earn the rate of return, *r*, allowed by law and designated by the commission. Investors, therefore, are granted a guaranteed return on capital expenditures, but none on operating expenses.

For utility investors, this guaranteed return is the central feature of cost-of-service regulation. It requires no financial genius to note that investors have a substantial incentive to enlarge the rate base as much as possible because the rate base earns a guaranteed return, so long as *r* exceeds the investors' cost of capital. As early as the 1960s, economists began to notice that this form of cost-of-service regulation created an incentive to overinvest in capital.[24] The primary check on this tendency should have been the state regulatory commissions, which were generally charged by their legislatures with the task of approving rate base treatment only for those capital expenditures that were in the public interest.[25] Over the decades, however, these state commissions became accustomed to more-or-less rubber-stamping utilities' requests; the "public interest" became equated with low rates for consumers rather than a broader understanding of the public good. Thus, nearly any capital investment that was likely to result in lower rates for electricity customers was likely to be approved by the relevant regulatory commission.

To be sure, this mode of regulation allowed utilities to achieve economies of scale. There were enormous efficiencies to be gained by expanding and interconnecting the grid and by allowing large geographical regions to share huge generating facilities.[26] Cost-of-service regulation allowed utilities to reap many of these benefits, all of which turned on large infrastructural investments for which it would otherwise have been difficult to assemble the requisite capital.

But with the benefit of hindsight, we can see that this system created or contributed to several major problems. Most analysts would agree that utilities did, in fact, over-invest in expensive capital projects—principally, in coal and nuclear-powered electric generating facilities.[27] Coal-fired generation facilities were constructed *en masse*, leading not only to what was probably too much generation capacity, but also to our current dependence on a very dirty fuel.[28] The legacy of this generation of coal plants has haunted us ever since, for these plants have caused enormous air pollution issues including the acid rain scares of the late 1900s.[29] Of the over two hundred nuclear generating facilities that were approved for construction before 1980, roughly half were mothballed before completion. Utility commissions had approved these plants, caught up in the belief that nuclear power would make electricity "too cheap to meter;" thus in most instances, ratepayers were left holding the bag. As a further consequence of abundant coal and nuclear energy, America became quite

[24]This phenomenon is known as the Averch-Johnson Effect after Averch and Johnson (1962).

[25]Phillips (1993), pp. 340–342.

[26]Breyer and MacAvoy (1974).

[27]Pierce (1984).

[28]Ackerman and Hassler (1981).

[29]Revesz and Westfahl Kong (2011).

accustomed to cheap electricity. Inexpensive power bred inefficient patterns of usage, increased consumption, and lifestyles and business practices premised on an endless supply of inexpensive electricity. And because demand for energy, once established, is relatively inelastic, subsequent energy shortages—whether in oil, natural gas, or otherwise—contributed to increasing inflation.

In short, the utility consensus and the mode of regulation it presupposed led to the construction of too many generating plants, built too quickly. Cost-of-service regulation encouraged large capital investments by essentially assuring investors a guaranteed return, secured by a smooth revenue stream from ratepayers. Conversely, the system made it relatively easy for massive investments to be spread out over populations and over time. In hindsight, such investments were made with too much ease; had regulators allowed investors to bear greater risk, the expansion of American power infrastructure would likely have been more measured.

3.3 The Big Dam Era

Although investor-owned utilities depended principally on fossil fuels for electricity generation during the twentieth century, hydroelectric power also had a substantial footprint. Small hydropower facilities, of the sort that provide power principally to a single user or a small cluster of users, were among the most common type of power generator in the late 1800s and early 1900s. Usually built by private landowners, they could be found throughout the country. The large dams that now emblemize especially the American West were too large and risky for private investors acting alone.[30] These dams were typically funded in the first instance by Congress, which either guaranteed its investment with future tax receipts or chartered power marketing firms that would have the ability to pass costs along to captive ratepayers. In both cases, the costs of these dams were spread widely, financed through small per capita payments by myriad ratepayers and taxpayers.

Extraordinary capital investment was required for dams on the scale of the Bonneville Dam on the Columbia River or the Hoover Dam on the Colorado River. Few engineers, let alone financiers, dared to contemplate such extravagant projects. Yet for all their risk and difficulty, grand hydroelectric projects held appeal for national policy makers for many reasons. Early in the century, they epitomized the sort of large public works projects that the federal government endorsed to increase employment and stimulate the national economy.[31] In certain watersheds, such as the Columbia, they also offered the possibility of enormous quantities of continuous power. Such sources were extraordinarily valuable to the war effort in the 1940s because of massive energy demands associated with the construction of

[30]Reisner (1993).

[31]White (1991), pp. 484–487 (characterizing large dams like the Hoover as a "symbol of the New Deal in the West").

aircraft and the production of nuclear materials.[32] Whole cities were built around the abundance of inexpensive power. Many hydropower facilities also served irrigation purposes and therefore dovetailed nicely with other federal goals.[33]

Today, large federal projects are a sign of political power. In the early twentieth century, however, many politicians initially opposed large-scale federal spending programs of the kind represented by hydropower. Legislators from western states, if left to their own political principles, preferred state or private investment to "socialized" federal projects.[34] Yet many of these legislators were persuaded to support the dam-building campaign by receiving projects in their home states. Marc Reisner, in his epic book *Cadillac Desert*, refers to federal dam-building legislation as the first pork-barrel spending programs.[35] Again, the cost of these dams was huge in the aggregate, but small on a per capita basis—especially when that cost was spread out over several years. The political opposition that one might ordinarily expect in resistance to big spending projects was thereby diffused. Politicians persuaded voters that the benefits of big dams outweighed the detriments and that the financing risk was minimal. Legislators logrolled their way to national agreement.

The consequence of "easy" cost-spreading by way of federal taxation was that the government built, by almost any measure, too many large dams: too many in terms of existing demand for energy; too many in that they have fostered a national dependence (some might say addiction) to low-cost energy; too many in terms of their environmental repercussions.[36] Federal dams have left a dubious legacy across, especially, the American west. Historical fish runs, long a mainstay of Western economies, have been decimated.[37] Sediment accumulation behind dams has not only damaged downstream habitat, but has rendered many dams' lifespans much shorter than expected.[38] Because of their exceedingly low operating costs, dams have provided low-cost power—a good thing, to be sure, but also a phenomenon that has fostered an indifference to energy efficiency and conservation measures in those locales where hydropower dominates.[39]

Again, let us pause to analyze in broad stroke the era of big hydropower. Who paid? A large captive audience of federal taxpayers. How much? A very little bit, per capita. Who decided who paid? Congress—an institution that, like utility commissions at the local level, is structured in a way that allows it to spread costs more widely than a conventional market system would allow.[40] The lesson—again, in

[32]Reisner (1993).

[33]Reisner (1993), pp. 134–144.

[34]For a sense of the nature of the opposition, see, e.g., Russell (1949).

[35]Reisner (1993), pp. 167 et seq. (noting that "[w]ater projects came to epitomize the pork barrel").

[36]White (1995), p. 50 (noting that The Dalles Dam in central Oregon generates fully 13 times the electricity demanded by the city of Portland).

[37]Blumm et al. (2006).

[38]Reisner (1993), pp. 473–475.

[39]See generally Manganiello (2015).

[40]See Lowi (1964). In this seminal piece, the eminent political scientist Lowi explains the preponderance of what he terms "distributive policies" from Congress—policies whose hallmark is the distribution of money and other "goodies" to various jurisdictions.

very crude form—is that if costs can be spread easily, there is a risk that the development of energy generation resources will outpace not only demand, but also the collective ability to understand the systemic impacts of such development.

4 Current Issues and Applications

Today, the world of energy policy is a complicated, fragmented, and rapidly-changing one. The last several decades have brought profound changes in energy technologies, policy objectives, and regulatory strategies.[41] In many parts of the country the traditional utility model has been restructured. With expanded authority from the U.S. Congress, the U.S. Federal Energy Regulatory Commission (FERC) has aggressively enabled the creation and growth of wholesale power markets.[42] Many states have required local utilities to sell off their generation facilities and offer choices to consumers in their service territories.[43] There are increasing opportunities for buyers of energy to reduce their dependence on the grid altogether, whether by investments in efficiency or in on-site power generation. State and federal regulators operate in an increasingly politicized space, pressured not only by their political principals but also by social activists. There are, in short, many moving parts at every level of the energy system.

In this context of disruption and rapid evolution, there are many opportunities for improving the way purchasing decisions and investments are made.[44] There remain many situations like Sally in her apartment building—situations in which the structure of purchasing decisions has a great bearing on the behaviors of actors within the system. For those who are concerned about the deployment of renewable energy, the reduction of greenhouse gas emissions within the energy sector, the reduction of our dependence on foreign energy resources, or simply the long-term price of domestic power, analytical attention should be fixed squarely on the decision-making processes within the institutions that decide how the costs of energy are paid.

The following examples explore several contexts in which problems of payment structure have been addressed. The first subsection examines the problem of

[41]Elliott (2013).

[42]The key pieces of legislation were the Public Utilities Regulatory Policies Act (PURPA) of 1978, 16 U.S.C. § 2601; the Energy Policy Act of 1992, Pub. L. No. 102-486 (Oct. 24, 1992); and the Energy Policy Act of 2005, Pub. L. No. 109-58 (Aug. 8, 2005). Among the key FERC Orders were No. 888, 61 Fed. Reg. 21,540 (1996) and No. 2000, 65 Fed. Reg. 810 (2000).

[43]NCSL (2001).

[44]Indeed, the entire restructuring movement can be thought of as a response to the inefficiencies of the regulatory model and an attempt to create cost savings through greater competition. The changes I have in mind are oriented towards a broader set of goals beyond simply the consumer price of energy.

interstate transmission lines while the second looks to on-site power consumption and generation.

4.1 Transmission

The construction of new transmission lines is one of the biggest infrastructural challenges facing the American energy industry today. Several developments are driving this issue to the forefront. One is the deregulation of the electric power sector, which has entailed the creation of regional wholesale markets for electricity. Such markets cannot function effectively without an interconnected and reliable transmission grid.[45] Many experts argue that at present, additional transmission capacity is necessary to alleviate system bottlenecks and improve the reliability and efficiency of the power grid.[46] But perhaps the most important recent development is the rapid increase in demand for renewable energy.[47] A number of U.S. states have enacted renewable portfolio standards (RPSs), which require electricity suppliers within the state to purchase a certain percentage of renewable energy.[48] In many of these states, compliance with the RPS will require purchases of out-of-state energy. Yet the areas best suited to the generation of renewable energy—places like the windswept Great Plains and the sunny deserts of Southeastern California and Nevada—lie relatively far from urban demand centers. As renewable energy production has grown and continues to grow, new transmission lines, therefore, have been and will be necessary to bring renewable energy to the market, both as a general matter and to satisfy state RPS demands.

Transmission lines are expensive.[49] The physical components of transmission infrastructure are costly, and siting a line also requires the procurement of a lengthy right-of-way. Each segment must be obtained from an individual landowner, and although lines are sited to avoid expensive urban areas, the aggregate expenditure required to obtain property rights may dwarf the cost of physical construction.

But the high cost of transmission lines by itself is not the primary impediment to their construction. Rather, the biggest problems have to do with the way that government processes allocate that cost. Jurisdiction over siting transmission lines

[45]Benjamin (2007), p. 36 (the author, a FERC commissioner, notes that "transmission networks provide the foundation for wholesale electricity market competition").

[46]NAERC (2001), p. 5; Shahidehpour (2004), p. 15 (noting that "current transmission and distribution systems were designed primarily for the industrial era of the 1950s and 1960s," and that under-investment in grid improvements has led to higher costs and more frequent service interruptions).

[47]Klass and Wilson (2012), pp. 1809–1811.

[48]Some 38 U.S. states now have RPS laws in place, although these laws vary significantly from state to state; see Fershee (2011), pp. 80–83.

[49]Planned upgrades in the Western Interconnection alone are estimated to cost at least $200 billion. Klass and Wilson (2012), p. 1812.

lies with state governments,[50] yet many of the lines that will be necessary in the coming years are interstate. State processes address regional transmission needs only with great difficulty.

Here is why. In the early stages of the development of American energy infrastructure, electric generation stations were generally located close to the urban demand centers they served.[51] Transmission lines were constructed by conventional, vertically-integrated utilities and financed in the same way as generation facilities: costs were recovered from ratepayers as the state utility commission allowed. The movement to "interconnect" local grids, and to create regional grids that could share generating facilities and thereby achieve greater economies of scale, led to increased construction of interstate transmission lines.[52] Interstate transmission transactions were (and remain) regulated by the U.S. Federal Energy Regulatory Commission (FERC). Individual utilities filed transmission tariffs with FERC and, assuming FERC found the rates to be "just and reasonable" and not unduly discriminatory or preferential,[53] charged these rates for third-party transmission. Conversely, captive ratepayers footed the bill for transmission infrastructure, which was not problematic as long as all entities involved were benefiting from the expansion of transmission capacity, which was generally the case.

In the new world of restructured utilities and increasing demand for renewable energy, however, things are very different. These differences make paying for new transmission lines more difficult in several respects. The following stylized example, depicted in Fig. 1, illustrates some of the new complexities. Suppose that State A is a low population state with a great deal of potential for wind power. States C and D are high population states with little internal wind energy potential. State B is between State A on the west and States C and D on the east. Suppose now that State C has adopted an RPS requiring a great deal of wind energy to be imported from State A. (State D remains legally indifferent between renewable and conventional energy sources.)

In this situation, State C's legal mandate to import wind energy—let us assume that it must come from State A—may impact all the other states in the scenario. Officials in State A may not wish to develop more energy resources than are needed in-state; officials in State B may not like having transmission lines run through its state that will provide no benefit to state residents. In fact, both States A and B may

[50]Many believe that a larger federal role is appropriate. "Federal law governing the responsibility for siting transmission facilities was written in 1935. At the time, transmission facilities were not interstate, and there was virtually no interstate commerce in electricity." Shahidehpour (2004), p. 16; Klass and Wilson (2012), pp. 1859–1867; Ostrow (2011).

[51]Furthermore, "[t]ransmission lines were historically built to link large stationary power plants to nearby electricity demand centers like cities." Klass and Wilson (2012), p. 1802.

[52]The interconnection push led to only a relatively small increase in transmission links between vertically-integrated power systems. This is because interconnection was not principally a vehicle for delivering power across a regional market, but only a backstop to address temporary shortfalls in generation. Benjamin (2007), pp. 36–37.

[53]16 U.S.C. § 824–825.

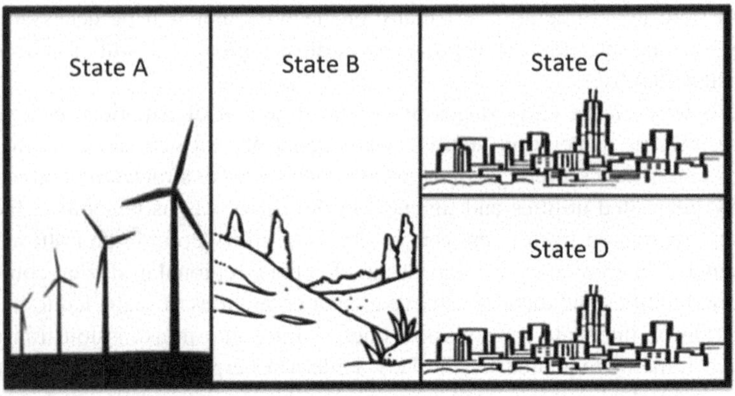

Fig. 1 Infrastructural challenges

have laws that require their state utility commissions to consider only the benefits accruing to residents as they decide whether to approve projects or not.[54] Conversely, these commissions may be legally barred from approving projects that principally benefit other states. As one FERC commissioner has noted, "regulators in low-cost states have a statutory obligation to guard the interest of their consumers. They cannot legally support a policy that will lower electricity prices in other states if doing so disadvantages their state's consumers."[55] Put into terms of our example, State A's and State B's regulators may be required by law to reject a new transmission line if it will lead to price increases for state residents.

Considering these sorts of collective action problems among the states—situations in which multiple states have the power to essentially veto a new transmission project—FERC in the 1990s took steps to incentivize regional governance. FERC authorized utilities to set up large regional transmission organizations (RTOs) to conduct regional planning processes, facilitate regional transmission cooperation, and create a regional pricing market for electricity.[56] Thus, to return to our example, utilities in States A, B, C and D may now be covered under the same RTO, in which case transmission markets are regionally controlled. The RTO may choose to authorize a new transmission line running from State A to State C and to allocate the costs to all its members. If so, ratepayers in States A, B, and D will be paying for transmission lines that do not provide them with any electricity at all. State D may get some electricity from the line, but because such electricity could be purchased

---

[54]Dworkin et al. (2011), pp. 538–541.

[55]Benjamin (2007), p. 41.

[56]See, e.g., Inquiry Concerning the Commission's Pricing Policy for Transmission Services Provided by Public Utilities Under the Federal Power Act, FERC Stats. & Regs. 31,005 (1994), *clarified*, 71 FERC 61,195 (1995) (this document is often called the "Transmission Pricing Policy Statement"); Order No. 888: Promoting Wholesale Competition Through Open Access Non-Discriminatory Transmission Services by Public Utilities; Recovery of Stranded Costs by Public Utilities and Transmitting Utilities, 75 FERC 61,080 (1996).

more cheaply from closer conventional power generation facilities, its customers are essentially subsidizing the public policy goals of State C, with its RPS.

With or without the RTO, the collective action problem is caused by the mismatch between the scale of problem and the interests of the actors who can solve it.[57] Localized actors often oppose regional actions that do not benefit them, and if those localized actors can essentially veto the action, it will not proceed. Precisely these sorts of issues have presented major challenges to transmission development in recent years.[58] Transmission shortfalls have on occasion led to curtailment of renewable energy production, and yet agreement on the construction of new lines has been wanting. The RTO process has been successful in some instances,[59] but there has been a good deal of litigation over the methods that RTOs use to allocate costs among their participants.[60]

As FERC has recognized, the problem is much more easily solved at the regional level.[61] But the American political and legal system does not easily lend itself to regional governance. Regional governance institutions are nearly always voluntary[62]; RTO membership, in fact, is always in flux. Even if the members of an RTO can devise a way to share the costs of new transmission that is acceptable to enough members to satisfy its governance requirements, there is no guarantee that a member opposing a particular proposal will remain in the RTO. Thus far, it appears that RTO membership brings with it enough benefits that even those members who oppose a particular cost-sharing agreement are willing to stay put, rather than abandon the RTO. As a matter of institutional design, the objective is to structure cohesive regional decision making in such a way as to preserve group membership while securing agreement on regional projects.

[57]It is in this sense that the problem is multi-scalar, as many scholars have noted. See Osofsky and Wiseman (2013).

[58]Klass and Wilson (2012), p. 1830.

[59]News Release, PJM, *PJM Grid Operator Plans Billions In Transmission Improvements To Meet Massive Generator Fuel Shift* (7 March 2013) (crediting a planning process, the PJM Regional Transmission Expansion Plan, with successfully managing fuel shifts).

[60]Illinois Commerce Comm'n v. FERC, 576 F.3d 470 (7th Cir. 2009); Illinois Commerce Comm'n v. FERC, 721 F.3d 764 (7th Cir. 2013).

[61]Some have gone further and advocated the nationalization of the grid, e.g. Carpenter and Prevost (2012).

[62]Regional greenhouse gas trading programs, for example, have struggled to maintain cohesiveness. The Regional Greenhouse Gas Initiative (RGGI) in the northeastern U.S. has endured numerous threats of departure from member states; thus far, New Jersey in the only state of the original ten to formally withdraw.

4.2 Distributed Generation

The previous section described challenges in paying for transmission resources that span jurisdictional lines. A different set of difficulties arises in the context of distributed generation.

Much of the energy distributed over the grid is ultimately used in buildings and households where individual managers and users make piecemeal decisions that, in the aggregate, are crucial to infrastructural development. A great deal of research has explored how buildings could require less energy from the electric grid.[63] The most substantial reductions would involve substantial investment by homeowners and building owners, in the form of efficiency upgrades or the installation of distributed generation equipment.

These kinds of investments generate two sorts of payment problems. The first has to do with the high upfront costs associated with efficiency upgrades and distributed generation, which can create financing problems for certain building owners, especially homeowners. The second problem arises when sites shift towards on-site power generation and decrease their dependence on the grid. The concern is that the flight of users away from the grid will increase the per capita costs of those who remain connected to the grid, thereby creating the possibility of a "death spiral" among utility customers. The remainder of this section will discuss each of these problems in turn.

Upgrades to existing appliances and lighting can entail thousands of dollars of investment; solar or geothermal power installations can easily run into the tens of thousands. Such high upfront costs represent an enormous obstacle especially to homeowners, who may reason that the break-even point on such investments is many years away—so many years, in fact, that the homeowner is uncertain whether he or she will still occupy the home. The owner may be further dissuaded by the belief that energy improvements may not be fully incorporated into the resale value of the building.

More generally, although many homeowners regard their homes as their most important investment, household decision makers often make energy-related decisions that are irrational and ill-suited to beneficial long-term infrastructural development. One of the most persistent "mistakes" in individual behavior has to do with the time value of money.[64] Consumers generally seek to minimize up-front or short-term expenditures even if greater up-front expenditures would significantly decrease long-term costs. An obvious example is light bulbs: consumers have not adopted energy efficient light bulbs as rapidly as might seem rational given the available cost savings.[65] Similar behaviors arise with large appliances which, like lighting, represent a sizeable share of household energy consumption. There have been significant efforts to increase and improve the information available to consumers at the time of

[63] Sartori et al. (2012).

[64] Hassett and Metcalf (1993).

[65] Di Maria et al. (2010), pp. 48–50.

purchase to help make them aware of the long-term cost savings available with energy efficient bulbs.[66] These efforts appear to have created some changes in consumer attitudes.[67]

Against this backdrop, municipalities in the U.S. began to experiment with ways to incentivize local home and building owners to make investments in energy efficiency and distributed generation. They sought to take advantage of municipal access to tax-exempt financing to provide accessible financing to owners, and to provide a financing mechanism that would bridge the present owner to a potential buyer in the future. One solution relied on local governments' ability to place tax assessments on real property. These governments could act as lending bodies to owners and recover the periodic repayments through property tax assessments. Because these repayment obligations would be passed on even to future purchasers, current owners could make capital improvements with the knowledge that they would not be personally liable for loan repayment after the sale of the building. Programs such as these came to be known as Property-Assessed Clean Energy or "PACE" programs. First implemented by Berkeley, California, other municipalities across the country rapidly followed suit. It appeared that this policy device addressed many owners' concerns over high up-front costs.

PACE programs suffered a crushing blow when the U.S. Federal Housing Finance Agency (FHFA) in 2011 advised Fannie Mae and Freddie Mac, the federally-chartered mortgage organizations, to avoid buying mortgages on properties with PACE-related property tax assessments. The FHFA's concern was that by employing tax liens, PACE programs placed clean energy loans above mortgages in terms of repayment priority, because tax repayment obligations are considered senior to mortgage obligations. As a matter of policy, FHFA was concerned that mortgages would be subordinated to voluntary investments by building and home owners.[68] Although the Agency's maneuver was litigated, the federal courts upheld the decision, and residential PACE programs have been all but frozen ever since.

In the wake of this setback, clean energy proponents have pushed another proposal: on-bill repayment programs offer private financing to building owners, but attach the repayment obligation to regular utility billing.[69] The loan travels "with the meter," just as with PACE financing, and loans are generally offered only when they meet a "bill neutrality" test: i.e., the regular loan payment must be less than the anticipated energy savings, so that the customer's utility bill is the same or less than it was before incurring the loan.[70] The regular outlay to the owner, therefore, is less than the previous utility bill even during the repayment period; after the loan is paid

[66]Gillingham et al. (2006), pp. 175–180.

[67]*Id.* Financial incentives may be superior to information campaigns, however; see Kaufman (2014), pp. 497–499.

[68]FHFA argued that PACE assessments are unlike routine tax assessments in that they are voluntary and longer in duration.

[69]Ottinger and Bowie (2015), p. 725.

[70]NRDC (2014).

off, the bill is much lower. This test bars any investments in which the cost of financing exceeds the immediate energy savings, which is a substantial shortcoming; many cost-effective projects remain uncovered by programs such as these.

Payment mechanisms like PACE and OPR are made more important by the fact that other, more direct forms of support for renewable development have receded in recent years. States in particular, which had put in place net metering policies—policies which allowed building owners to sell back to the grid any excess power they were generating on site, often at a premium—have been hit with a backlash from local utilities.[71] As customers have adopted distributed generation, and solar installations in particular, utilities have argued that the beneficiaries of net metering policies are not paying their fair share for grid resources.[72] Because the costs of maintaining grid infrastructure have historically been folded into electric rates, ratepayers whose purchases from the grid are reduced by self-generated energy pay less for that infrastructure, although they continue to depend on its availability just as much as other ratepayers.

Utilities' concerns have grown louder as solar installations increase in number across the U.S. and especially in Hawaii, the Southwest, and the Sun Belt states. Continued growth in solar could cause other ratepayers to bear the burden of grid maintenance, although most solar users rely on the grid to back up their on-site generation. On the other hand, charging an additional fee to those who have installed solar power could drive some customers off the grid entirely, leaving the utility with even less revenue and fewer captive customers left to support the grid.

5 Conclusion

The point of these examples is to demonstrate that there are substantial and unresolved questions about how energy users in the United States and Europe will bear the costs of the infrastructural overhaul required by upcoming shifts in the energy sector. These questions demand as much attention and ingenuity as the more visible and obvious questions about which resources and technologies will be deployed to satisfy energy needs. In the short run at least, the implementation of new generation and transmission facilities will turn on securing agreement about cost sharing. There are difficulties associated with the decision-making mechanisms in all the political and regulatory institutions tasked with allocating the costs of energy infrastructure. We have seen, for example, how state regulators can frustrate regional transmission development, and how federal mortgage lenders can impede local efforts to finance capital improvements. Advocates for infrastructural development, therefore, must be prepared to move nimbly among these institutions to accomplish their goals.

[71] Davies and Carley (2017).

[72] Rule (2015), pp. 116 and 125.

References

Ackerman B, Hassler WT (1981) Clean coal/dirty air: or how the clean air act became a multibillion-dollar bail-out for high-sulfur coal producers. Yale University Press, New Haven
Arimura TH et al (2012) Cost-effectiveness of electricity energy efficiency programs. Energy J 33 (2):63–99
Averch H, Johnson LL (1962) The behavior of the firm under regulatory constraint. Am Econ Rev 52:1052–1069
Baker E (2012) Option value and the diffusion of energy efficient products. Energy J 33(4):49–59
Benjamin R (2007) Principles of interregional transmission expansion. Electr J 20:36–47
Blumm MC, Thorson EJ, Smith JD (2006) Practiced at the art of deception: the failure of Columbia Basin Salmon recovery under the endangered species act. Environ Law 36:709–810
Breyer S, MacAvoy P (1974) Energy regulation by the Federal Power Commission. Brookings Institution, Washington, D.C.
Brown MA (2001) Market failures and barriers as a basis for clean energy policies. Energy Policy 29:1197–1207
Carpenter DW, Prevost R (2012) Toward further development of the U.S. electrical transmission system: my grid, your grid, our grid. Electr J 25:10–20
Davies L, Carley S (2017) Emerging shadows in national solar policy? Nevada's net metering transition in context. Electr J 30:33–42
Davis LW (2011) Evaluating the slow adoption of energy efficient investments: are renters less likely to have energy efficient appliances? In: Fullerton D, Wolfram C (eds) The design and implementation of U.S. climate policy. University of Chicago Press, Chicago, pp 301–316
Di Maria C, Ferreira S, Lazarova E (2010) Shedding light on the light bulb puzzle: the role of attitudes and perceptions in the adoption of energy efficient light bulbs. Scottish J Polit Econ 57 (1):48–67
Dworkin M et al (2011) Energy transmission and storage. In: Gerrard M (ed) The law of clean energy: efficiency and renewables. American Bar Association Press, Chicago, pp 531–558
Elliott ED (2013) Why the U.S. does not have a renewable energy policy. Environ Law Rev 43:10095–10101
Ferrey S (2011) Sale of electricity. In: Gerrard M (ed) The law of clean energy: efficiency and renewables. American Bar Association Press, Chicago, pp 217–240
Fershee JP (2011) Renewables mandates and goals. In: Gerrard M (ed) The law of clean energy: efficiency and renewables. American Bar Association Press, Chicago, pp 77–93
Flynn WM, McManus JT (2010) Inside the world of residential electricity submetering. New York Law Journal, 15 March 2010
Follett A (2016) Supreme Court allows 'Socialized Electricity' to make green energy profitable. Daily Caller, 25 January 2016
Frischmann BM (2005) An economic theory of infrastructure and commons management. Minn Law Rev 89(4):917–1030
Fucci FR (2011) Distributed generation. In: Gerrard M (ed) The law of clean energy: efficiency and renewables. American Bar Association Press, Chicago, pp 345–358
Gillingham K et al (2006) Energy efficiency policies: a retrospective examination. Annu Rev Environ Resour 31:161–192
Hassett KA, Metcalf GE (1993) Energy conservation investment: do consumers discount the future correctly? Energy Policy 21(6):710–716
Hirsh RF (1999) Power loss: the origins of deregulation and restructuring in the American electric utility system. MIT Press, Cambridge
Hsu S-L (2006) What's old is new: the problem with new source review. Regulation 29(1):36–43
Hughes TP (1993) Networks of power: electrification in western society, 1880–1930. The Johns Hopkins University Press, Baltimore

Jaffe AB, Stavins RN (1994) The energy-efficiency gap: what does it mean? Energy Policy 22 (10):804–810
Jaffe E (2012) Why renters waste more energy than homeowners. The Atlantic
Jonnes J (2004) Empires of light: Edison, Tesla, Westinghouse, and the race to electrify the world. Random House, New York
Kaufman N (2014) Overcoming the barriers to the market performance of green consumer goods. Resour Energy Econ 36(2):487–507
King G (2011) Edison v. Westinghouse: a shocking rivalry. Smithsonian.com
Klass AB, Wilson EJ (2012) Interstate transmission challenges for renewable energy: a federalism mismatch. Vanderbilt Law Rev 65(6):1801–1873
Klein M (2008) The power makers: steam, electricity, and the men who invented modern America. Bloomsbury Press, London
Levinson A, Niemann S (2004) Energy use by apartment tenants when landlords pay for utilities. Resour Energy Econ 26:51–75
Lowi TJ (1964) American business, public policy, case-studies, and political theory. World Polit 16 (4):677–715
Manganiello CJ (2015) Southern water, southern power: how the politics of cheap energy and water scarcity shaped a region. University of North Carolina Press, Chapel Hill
McDonald F (2004) Insull: the rise and fall of a billionaire utility Tycoon. Beard Books, Washington, D.C.
Michelsen CC, Madlener R (2016) Switching from fossil fuel to renewables in residential heating systems: an empirical study of homeowners' decisions in Germany. Energy Policy 89:95–105
North American Electricity Reliability Council (2001) Reliability Assessment 2001–2010
National Conference of State Legislatures (2001) Restructuring in retrospect
Natural Resources Defense Council (2014) On-bill financing programs: overview and key considerations for program design
Osofsky HM, Wiseman HJ (2013) Dynamic energy federalism. Maryland Law Rev 72(3):773–843
Ostrow AP (2011) Process preemption in federal siting regimes. Harv J Legislation 48(2):289–341
Ottinger RL, Bowie J (2015) Innovative financing for renewable energy. Pace Environ Law Rev 32 (3):701–755
Phillips CF Jr (1993) The regulation of public utilities: theory and practice. Public Utilities Reports, Arlington
Pierce RJ Jr (1984) The regulatory treatment of mistakes in retrospect: canceled plants and excess capacity. Univ Pa Law Rev 132(3):497–560
Platt H (1991) The electric city: energy and the growth of the Chicago Area, 1880–1930. University of Chicago Press, Chicago
Reisner M (1993) Cadillac desert: the American west and its disappearing water, revised edn. Penguin Books, New York
Revesz RL, Westfahl Kong AL (2011) Regulatory change and optimal transition relief. Northwest Univ Law Rev 105(4):1581–1634
Rule T (2015) Solar energy, utilities, and fairness. San Diego J Clim Energy Law 6:115–148
Russell D (1949) The TVA idea. Foundation for Economic Education, Irvington-on-Hudson
Samuelson P (1954) The pure theory of public expenditure. Rev Econ Stat 36(4):387–389
Sartori I et al (2012) Net zero energy buildings: a consistent definition framework. Energy Buildings 48:220–232
Shahidehpour M (2004) Investing in expansion: the many issues that cloud transmission planning. IEEE Power & Energy Magazine
U.S. Energy Information Administration (2015) Annual Energy Outlook 2015
U.S. Federal Energy Regulatory Commission (2012) Energy primer: a handbook of energy market basics
U.S. Nuclear Regulatory Commission (2016) 2016–2017 Information Digest

Vandenbergh MP (2004) From Smokestack to SUV: the individual as regulated entity in the new era of environmental law. Vanderbilt Law Rev 57(2):515–628
Wasik J (2008) The merchant of power: Sam Insull, Thomas Edison, and the creation of the modern metropolis. St. Martin's Griffin, New York
White RW (1991) It's your misfortune and none of my own: a new history of the American West. University of Oklahoma Press, Norman
White RW (1995) The organic machine: the remaking of the Columbia River. Hill and Wang, New York

Bruce R. Huber Notre Dame, IN, USA. Professor of Law and Robert and Marion Short Scholar at Notre Dame Law School. 2143 Eck Hall of Law, Notre Dame, Indiana, 46556, USA, Tel. +1 574 631 2538. bhuber@nd.edu. Fields of Interest: Environmental Law, Property Law, Natural Resources Law, Energy Law.

Energy Market and Policy Revolutions: Regulatory Process and the Cost of Capital

James W. Coleman

Abstract As the world embarks on a transition toward a low-carbon economy, one common characteristic of alternatives to fossil fuels has gone surprisingly unexamined: the cost of these alternative sources is disproportionately concentrated in capital expenses, rather than operating expenses. Solar, wind, and hydro power have very low operating expenses: the cost of these power sources is largely in their construction. Even nuclear power has low fuel costs compared to fossil fuel power sources. So as the world decarbonizes the power grid and electrifies the transportation sector, capital costs will grow increasingly important in the energy sector. At the same time, several trends in energy law have been conspiring to raise the cost of capital. First, privatization and deregulation of electric utilities mean that energy investors are less certain of recovering their capital investments. Second, a push for more public participation in decision-making on energy infrastructure has, at times, resulted in delays and uncertainty that make private companies even more wary of long-term capital investments in new energy facilities. Third, the drive for more careful and holistic environmental assessments of new energy facilities has, in some cases, further delayed new infrastructure, again making private investors wary of large, new investments. This Article considers how to manage these conflicting trends, describing how governments can achieve public participation and improved environmental assessment while, at the same time, ensuring the predictability that can support capital investment in a new energy economy. It also explores particular areas where these tensions may be irreconcilable, suggesting ways that governments may be able to serve the goals of expanded participation and assessment, while providing private capital with traction to achieve a transition away from fossil fuels.

J. W. Coleman (✉)
Southern Methodist University Dedman School of Law, Dallas, TX, USA
e-mail: jwcoleman@smu.edu

K. Mathis, B. R. Huber (eds.), *Energy Law and Economics*, Economic Analysis of Law in European Legal Scholarship 5, https://doi.org/10.1007/978-3-319-74636-4_8

1 Introduction: Attracting Capital to Build the New Energy Economy

The world is facing two monumental challenges that are in tension: maintaining broad-based economic growth while, at the same time, decarbonizing the world economy to meet global climate goals. To meet these challenges, the world will need to attract massive investment in new sources of power to expand electricity access in developing countries and replace coal power fleets in the world's major economies. The International Energy Agency predicts that this task will require more than two trillion dollars of new investment.[1] Achieving these twin goals is made more difficult by another emerging tension in energy investment: low carbon energy investments are increasingly capital-intensive but, at the same time, several developments in energy law are making returns on investment more uncertain, raising the cost of capital.

The United States Clean Power Plan (Plan)—the first attempt to control greenhouse gas emissions from the existing power sector in the world's largest economy—demonstrates how low carbon polies will require major capital investments. The Plan, recently withdrawn by the Trump administration, envisioned replacing the U.S. coal fleet with a mix of increased power from solar and wind and natural gas power.[2] Despite the massive environmental downsides of coal power, it minimizes capital costs: it is easy and cheap to transport to the places it is needed and to store where it is needed, which are major challenges for both natural gas and renewable power. In the run up to the Plan, in November 2014, the U.S. electric power reliability watchdog, the North American Electric Reliability Corporation warned that the Plan would endanger the reliability of electric service unless it was accompanied by a massive build out of gas and electricity transport and storage.[3]

The electricity system must constantly match electricity supplied with electricity demanded. However, solar and wind power cannot be dispatched on demand—they are produced only when the sun shines or the wind blows and thus far we do not have ways to economically store electric power until it is needed. Natural gas can back up solar and wind, but it is a gas, which makes it expensive to transport and store. Power is also expensive to transport and store, so a transition from coal to renewables and natural gas would require expensive investments in both gas and power transport and storage.

While this need for new transport infrastructure is building, there is increased uncertainty attached to energy investment around the world. First, privatization and

---

[1]International Energy Agency (2014).

[2]The Supreme Court prevented the Plan from taking effect, West Virginia v. Envtl. Prot. Agency, 136 S. Ct. 1000, 1000 (2016), and thus far the courts have, at the request of the Trump administration, agreed to keep the Plan in limbo while the administration works to repeal it. Timothy Cama, Court suspends case over Obama climate rule, The Hill, 28 April 2017, http://thehill.com/policy/energy-environment/331060-court-suspends-case-over-obama-climate-rule.

[3]North American Electric Reliability Corporation (2014).

deregulation of electric utilities has meant that less and less of power sector investment by companies is made based on a guaranteed rate of return through a regulatory compact. Second, increasing interest and activism focused on energy infrastructure has, at times, resulted in delays and uncertainty that made private companies even more wary of long-term capital investments. Third, a trend toward more wide-ranging environmental assessments of new energy facilities—embodied in the Keystone XL precedent and its application to facilities across the world, as explained in Sect. 3 of this chapter—has further delayed new infrastructure, again making private investors wary of large, new investments. Together these three trends are raising the cost of capital for investing in new energy infrastructure, and thus raising the cost of achieving the world's environmental goals.

This Article proceeds in four further sections. Section 2 describes why ongoing revolutions in energy markets and policy call for massive new capital investments in low carbon power production and transport. Section 3 describes how trends in energy law and policy are, at the same time, increasing the uncertainty and cost of long-term investment in the energy industry. Section 4 evaluates possible methods of encouraging more investment in the industry while accommodating the policy concerns that are resulting in increased delay and uncertainty for energy investors. Section 5 concludes.

2 Transitioning to a Low Carbon Economy Will Require Massive Long-Term Energy Investment

As mentioned above, the transition to a low carbon economy requires massive capital investment in the energy system. Renewable power must be not only built but, potentially even more challenging, carried to centers of power demand by new power transmission. A natural gas boom will complement expanded renewable power better than coal, but it will require more pipelines to carry it to market and more storage to ensure that it is available when non-dispatchable wind and solar power fails. And to move transportation and other sectors away from oil, the economy will require more electricity and a more flexible electrical distribution grid.

Renewable sources such as wind and utility-scale solar power are easiest to site in low-population density areas, which are often also the deserts and plains where these resources are richest. That power must be transmitted to the urban centers of electricity demand. This in turn requires multi-billion dollar investments in long-distance power transmission.

At the same time, transitioning to a low carbon economy will require closing coal plants. So until electricity storage becomes widely available and affordable, increased natural gas power will be required as a replacement to back up renewable sources that only provide power when the sun shines and the wind blows. And natural gas is a better complement for renewable power sources because it can easily be ramped up and down to balance solar and wind sources—offering little power when the sun is shining and the wind is blowing but providing a lot of power when those sources fail and consumers demand power.[4]

But one persistent advantage of coal has been its ease of transport and storage. In much of the industrialized world towns grew up near coal mines and rivers that could transport coal and the existing railroad infrastructure was, in large part, designed to facilitate movement of coal to centers of electricity demand.

By contrast, gas will require much more expensive infrastructure to ensure that the precise amount of gas is constantly being delivered to exactly the places that it is needed to accommodate spikes in electricity demand or dips in renewable power supply. As a gas, it is more expensive to transport: long haul, air-tight pipelines are multi-billion dollar projects, liquefaction facilities to bring gas to overseas markets cost tens of billions, and even the liquefied natural gas ships that shuttle between these facilities cost a quarter of a billion dollars each.[5]

Storing gas also requires major capital investments. Coal can simply be stored in piles, but to store natural gas, a company must find an air-tight aquifer, depleted reservoir, or salt cavern that can hold the gas until it is needed. The difficulty of finding suitable storage locations was dramatically illustrated in 2016 when the Southern California Gas Company overfilled a storage reservoir at Aliso Canyon, creating a major leak that took 4 months to plug and forced thousands of citizens to abandon their homes.[6]

As the world's carbon reduction goals grow more ambitious, the need for capital investment will simply grow more pressing. For now, countries and regions that pursue climate regulation often limit their costs by relying on countries with lower ambitions for carbon regulation. For example, they can purchase emission reductions from foreign countries where they are cheap because those nations have not yet pursued inexpensive low-hanging-fruit reductions.[7] Or they can import lower-price electricity or commodities from these less-ambitious countries.[8] But as climate targets grow stronger across the world, countries will increasingly be forced to close fossil-fuel plants and connect to new sources of renewable power that will often be far away. And they will be forced to build out electricity and natural gas storage to ensure that their grid remains reliable at high penetrations of renewable power.[9]

Even further investments in power transmission infrastructure may be one important strategy to increase the reliability of intermittent sources like wind and solar power. If a regional grid can diversify the geographic area powering its renewable

---

[4]Coleman (2018).

[5]U.S. Department of Energy (2015).

[6]U.S. Energy Info. Admin. (2016).

[7]Coleman (2014b).

[8]Coleman (2014b).

[9]The most plausible alternatives to a major build out in renewable power, such as nuclear power and carbon capture, would also require massive capital investment. Woite (1978) and Rubin et al. (2007).

sources, they may provide more reliable power. Even if the sun is not shining in one region, it may be shining in a neighboring state or country.[10]

Finally, the most difficult stage in decarbonization—moving away from oil—will require further capital investments. Oil is the most energy dense fossil fuel and it is easy to move because, as a liquid, it can be pumped by pipeline or be easily placed on ships, trucks, or rail cars. As we try to electrify our transport system we will need to expand power generation to accommodate this new demand and expand power transport to make sure that quick charging stations are widely available to support a flexible transportation network.

3 Energy Law Trends Are Raising Uncertainty for Energy Investors and Increasing the Cost of Building the Energy Future

At the same time, other trends in energy law are conspiring to raise uncertainty for energy investors. The transmission to competitive markets has meant that fewer investors can be certain that their energy investments will receive a steady stream of income that justifies the initial capital investment. At the same time, increased public focus on energy infrastructure has repeatedly delayed energy infrastructure projects, increasing the risk that a project will never even be completed. Finally, expanded environmental assessments have raised new hurdles to constructing new energy transport facilities.

The most significant trend of the past 30 years in energy law is restructuring—creating competition in markets through a combination of breaking down vertically-integrated utilities and more surgical rate regulation of energy transport bottlenecks that could otherwise exercise monopoly power.[11] In many of the jurisdictions that have pursued this restructuring—often described as "deregulation"—these policies are seen as encouraging static efficiency, ensuring that power is provided by low cost facilities.

However, the persistent concern is that deregulated markets do not provide sufficient incentive to encourage new power sources. Jurisdictions have turned to several methods of supplementing power provider's revenues from power auctions, such as capacity markets, long-term power purchase agreements, and specific credits for favored sources such as natural gas and nuclear power.[12] If competitive markets are having difficulty motivating construction of conventional energy sources, how can they be expected to encourage an entirely revamped market driven by renewable power?

[10]Roques et al. (2010).

[11]Sioshansi and Pfaffenberger (2006).

[12]*Von Talen Energy Marketing, LLC*, 136 S.Ct. 1288 (2016).

In more recent years, the growing profile of the energy industry and increased focus on climate change have encouraged regulators at all levels of government to exert influence on energy infrastructure decisions. Increased awareness of global energy markets and the environmental consequences of energy production has created unprecedented interest in the energy system and a demand for recognition of the legitimate and varied interests of national, subnational, and local stakeholders in energy decisions.

This demand often manifests as a push for each level of government—federal, state, indigenous, and local—to have a say in decisions on energy transport. This enthusiasm has sometimes produced overlapping authorities and confused standards that have left the process for approval of energy facilities in flux.[13] For example, in the United States, the separate long-standing approval processes for interstate oil pipelines, gas pipelines, and power transmission are all currently in flux.

The federal government's long-term practice has been to leave approval of interstate oil pipelines mostly to the states—a pipeline company may build a pipeline as long as it has certificates or permits from all the states along the pipeline route.[14] But at the end of President Obama's administration, the government announced that it would consider changing this standard and declared that it would do a full federal environmental review of the Dakota Access pipeline—a reversal of the usual federal policy. That decision was reversed by the incoming Trump administration and is now being litigated in the courts.[15] Consequently, there is continuing uncertainty about whether the federal government will be required to approve future oil pipelines.

Similarly, the states have long had control over interstate power transmission siting. Again, in its last year, the Obama administration announced a new policy, declaring that the federal government would partner with private transmission companies that wanted to build interstate transmission to support wind power.[16] The new administration has not yet suggested whether it will abide by this policy and it may, again, ultimately be decided by the courts, leaving investors uncertain about whether states or the federal government has final say on new transmission projects.

Finally, interstate natural gas pipelines, unlike oil and power transport, have long been regulated by the federal government.[17] But opposition to fracking has made U.S. states increasingly frustrated with their inability to stop pipeline projects that would cross their borders. New York may have hit upon an innovative solution—denying a local Clean Water Act permit to a pipeline that had already been approved by the U.S. Federal Energy Regulatory Commission. That decision, too, is being challenged in court.

[13]Coleman (2014a).

[14]Klass and Meinhardt (2015).

[15]Coleman (2018).

[16]Klass and Rossi (2017).

[17]Klass and Meinhardt (2015).

Even when it is clear who the appropriate regulator is, new environmental review standards and methods have created deep uncertainty about when energy projects will be approved. The success of environmental groups in delaying the Keystone XL project, a proposed pipeline that would carry oil from the Canadian oil sands to Steele City, Nebraska, has made it a model for environmental movements around the world, who are increasingly challenging energy transport projects across the fossil fuel supply chain: gas pipelines, port facilities, liquefied natural gas projects, and power transmission.[18]

But it remains unclear what rule the Keystone XL precedent stands for. Keystone XL was initially proposed in 2008 and the 7-year environmental review of the project focused on how it would affect oil production in Canada: President Obama said that if it increased oil production in Canada, he would deny it.

This focus was surprising for several reasons. First, the long-standing policy of the United States had been not to consider foreign impacts that were properly under the control of authorities in another country. Second, even in theory, it is very hard to say what the impact of a single pipeline facility will be on international energy markets. Third, the implied standard that energy projects should be denied if they will help an industry in a U.S. energy trading partners is, to say the least, diplomatically awkward. Fourth, the Keystone XL standard seems to be in direct conflict with the usual standard for approving pipelines, which is that they should be approved *only if* they would connect new sources of supply and demand. Even more confusing, the Obama administration's decision on Keystone XL stated that (1) it was unlikely to have any impact on oil production in Canada, but (2) it would nevertheless be perceived as increasing oil production and so (3) should be denied notwithstanding the lengthy analysis that had delayed the project.[19]

Despite the difficulty in understanding what principal the Keystone XL precedent stands for, it is becoming increasingly important worldwide, with environmental groups pushing for what they call "a climate test" for energy transport projects.[20] In the U.S., the Trump administration quickly reversed the previous administration's decision, approving the pipeline, but again, the propriety of this decision has been challenged by several anti-pipeline groups and will be resolved in court. In the meantime, Canada has adopted its own version of the Keystone-like climate test, but is struggling with some of the same questions about how such a test can be implemented.

These expanded climate assessments are, if anything, more dangerous to transportation infrastructure of lower carbon sources such as electricity and gas. After all, even if no new pipelines are built, oil can be transported through the existing infrastructure such as rail, barge, trucks, and ship. Gas and renewable power, by contrast, must have new dedicated transmission facilities. Following the Keystone XL precedent energy transport opponents have grown much savvier about

[18]Coleman (2017).

[19]U.S. Department of State (2015).

[20]Coleman (2017).

challenging these transmission projects because they will encourage energy production and consumption and all the externalities associated with that production—water and air quality for natural gas production and land use and bird kills for wind projects.

Each of these trends have, at times, resulted in overlapping authority and shifting standards that can make investors wary of the energy transport projects, such as gas pipelines and electricity transmission, required to drive a transition to a low-carbon economy. This kind of regulatory uncertainty is particularly dangerous to energy transport projects because they are capital intensive—most of their costs are up front and they only pay off over time—which makes them particularly vulnerable to regulatory uncertainty.[21]

4 Principles Toward Encouraging Investment in the Energy Future

There has never been more need for energy investment but investors have never faced such uncertainty about whether their investments will pay off. If policymakers could lessen this uncertainty, they could lower the economic cost of meeting their goals for encouraging an energy transition. How can policymakers increase certainty while respecting the legitimate concerns of stakeholders that are intensely interested in regulatory approvals?

4.1 Principle 1: Wide Participation, One Decision-Maker

Governments must accommodate increased interest in energy projects. Stakeholder interest in the global energy industry, both within and beyond their jurisdiction, is entirely appropriate because carbon emissions from the energy industry affect all parts of the globe. Consumer interest in energy supply chains is here to stay and local, subnational, and national politicians will naturally be interested in what the industry does beyond their borders. To that end, governments should make increased provision for wide participation in approvals of energy infrastructure, including facilitating input from all levels of government.

At the same time, ultimate decision-making authority on energy projects should, to the extent possible, be centralized. It is natural that policymakers frustrated at one level of government should seek to relitigate the issue at another level. But overlapping decision-makers is a recipe for uncertainty and there is no a priori reason to think that subjecting each proposed project to multiple veto gates would improve the overall economic and environmental result. Multiple veto gates just

[21]Teisberg (1993) and Yang et al. (2004).

mean more opportunities to kill proposed investments—and that is true whether those investments are in oil, in gas, or in renewable power. So long as we believe more energy investment is necessary, we should have a unified decision-making structure that allows such investments.

Similarly, energy transport projects should not be used as opportunities to relitigate disputes about energy production that is decided by another governmental entity. If the energy transport project presents issues that are intimately connected with approval of energy production, then perhaps the two issues can be decided in a single procedure. But the transport decision should not be used after the fact with the goal of hampering a decision that has already been made about production.

Canada's traditional system of energy regulation may be a helpful model here. Canada has traditionally left the issue of energy production (and, to an extent, local pollution) to each province's sole authority. Interprovincial issues, by contrast, are for the federal government to decide; provinces have input, but cannot veto interprovincial projects. This overall system, sometimes known as "water-tight compartments" allows for wide participation in energy decision-making but ensures that each issue is ultimately decided by a single responsible government.[22]

4.2 *Principle 2: Prospective Rulemaking for Environmental Reviews*

To the extent possible, changes to the rules of environmental assessment and the standards for approval should be implemented only prospectively, so that the goalposts are not moved half-way through the review process. This would allow continued improvement in environmental assessment while providing a measure of certainty to investors in interstate energy transport.

For example, scientists continue to improve techniques for assessing the "life cycle" impacts of energy production—showing the net impact of a fuel over the full cycle from production to transport to consumption. However, these techniques do not yet provide resolution to determine the impact of any single energy project (and may never be able to provide this resolution). Governments should continue attempting to improve this method of environmental assessment but should not impose it as part of existing reviews. Developing experimental methods of study within an environmental review process simply imposes too much delay and uncertainty on the environmental review process.

[22]Lucas (2007).

5 Enabling the Energy Future

The next decades will be crucial for answering the twin challenges of global energy policy: massively expanding energy access to support increased living standards across the world while, at the same time, transitioning to forms of energy that have less impact on the air, water, and the climate. Meeting these challenges will require an unprecedented build out of long-lived energy infrastructure: new zero carbon power generators, transmission to carry renewable power to market, and pipelines, storage and liquefaction facilities for natural gas to support that transition. Society will bear the cost of these investments, and this cost will be far smaller if investors can be sure that stable policies will ensure that they can recover their investment over many, many years. And these investments must not be delayed given the inter-generational cost of delay in moving to a new, low-carbon energy system. Thus, it has never been more crucial to find ways to accommodate increased interest and public participation in energy transport decisions without introducing uncertainty into the investment process.

References

Coleman JW (2014a) Importing energy, exporting regulation. Fordham Law Rev 83(3):1357–1399

Coleman JW (2014b) Unilateral climate regulation. Harv Environ Law Rev 38:87–126

Coleman JW (2017) Investing in the shadow of the law: how agencies are using proposed rules to transform industry long before final rules are tested in court. George Mason Law Rev 24:497–532

Coleman JW (2018) Beyond the pipeline wars: reforming environmental assessment of energy transport infrastructure. Utah Law Rev 2018:119–167

International Energy Agency (2014) World Energy Investment Outlook

Klass AB, Meinhardt D (2015) Transporting oil and gas: U.S. infrastructure challenges. Iowa Law Rev 100(3)

Klass AB, Rossi J (2017) Reconstituting federalism battles in energy transportation. Harv Environ Law Rev 41:424–491

Lucas AR (2007) Mythology, fantasy and federalism: Canadian climate change policy and law. Pacific McGeorge Glob Bus Dev Law J 20:41–62

Roques F, Hiroux C, Saguan M (2010) Optimal wind power deployment in Europe—a portfolio approach. Energy Policy 38(7):3245–3256

Rubin E, Chen C, Rao A (2007) Cost and performance of fossil fuel power plants with CO2 capture and storage. Energy Policy 35(9):4444–4454

Sioshansi FP, Pfaffenberger W (2006) Electricity market reform: an international perspective. Elsevier, Oxford

Teisberg EO (1993) Capital investment strategies under uncertain regulation. RAND J Econ 24 (4):591–604

U.S. Department of Energy (2015) Natural gas infrastructure implications of increased demand from the electric power sector

U.S. Energy Information Administration (2016) Today in energy: Southern California natural gas inventories nearly flat this injection season. https://www.eia.gov/todayinenergy/detail.php?id=27432

U.S. North American Electric Reliability Corporation (2014) Potential reliability impacts of EPA's proposed clean power plan: initial reliability review
United States Department of State (2015) Record of decision and national interest determination
Von Talen H (2016) Energy Marketing, LLC, 136 S.Ct. 1288
Woite G (1978) Capital investment costs of nuclear power plants. Int Atomic Energy Agency Bull 20(1):11–23
Yang B, Burns ND, Backhouse CJ (2004) Management of uncertainty through postponement. Int J Prod Res 42(6):1049–1064

James W. Coleman Dallas. Assistant Professor of Law at Southern Methodist University Dedman School of Law. 3315 Daniel Ave., Dallas, TX 75205, U.S.A. Tel. + 1 214-768-4037. jwcoleman@smu.edu. http://www.EnergyLawProf.com/. Fields of Interest: Energy Law, Oil & Gas Law, Environmental Law, Empirical Legal Studies, International Trade & Corporate Law, Administrative Law, Regulatory Theory, Economic Analysis of Law.

Intergenerational Choice Under Uncertainty: The Case of Future Energy Technologies—Legal and Economic Perspectives

Stephan Meyer

Abstract Should we care about future generations? This question has been plaguing philosophy, economics, and the law for a long time. At least in practical terms, agreement seems to exist today that governments should indeed pursue intergenerational sustainability. This article focuses first on some remarkable similarities between legal and economic reasoning when it comes to justifying this contemporary policy goal. It discusses necessary features of sustainability policy, chief among which is "keeping options open". Subsequently, a particularly intricate issue of sustainable public policy is presented, using electric transportation in Germany as a contemporary example. As it turns out, keeping options open for future generations (through climate protection, for instance) may require diminishing future options elsewhere. It seems the present generation simply cannot "do it right", despite best efforts. This article finally explores how to deal with this dilemma.

1 Some Brief Interdisciplinary Remarks on Intergenerational Sustainability

1.1 Law as a Policy Tool for Achieving Intergenerational Sustainability?

1.1.1 The Future-Orientated Nature of Law

At first glance, law seems like a perfect candidate to factor in future generations. It is the very idea and nature of law to preserve past decisions and reproduce them in the future.

S. Meyer (✉)
University of Applied Sciences Wildau, Wildau, Germany

University of Erfurt, Erfurt, Germany
e-mail: stephan.meyer@th-wildau.de

K. Mathis, B. R. Huber (eds.), *Energy Law and Economics*, Economic Analysis of Law in European Legal Scholarship 5, https://doi.org/10.1007/978-3-319-74636-4_9

Consequently, law that is passed today will benefit not only the present, but, possibly, the generations to come as well. A striking example for there being some truth to that is the German health care system. Created by a federal act in 1883, its basic structure has remained unchanged until today. It has survived one revolution, two Constitutional Acts and the Nazis. Although prone to justified criticism as to its efficiency, it is one of the most effective health care systems in the world and covers over 90% of the German population. We, being the "future generation", can be happy with what was passed as law in 1883.

Of course, I have been painting an unbearably simplistic picture here.

Democratic decision-making tends to be myopic.[1] People often care most about their own present needs, and representative government will be happy to oblige. Herein lies the very reason intergenerational sustainability proves so difficult to achieve. However, law itself provides some remedy for this issue. Constitutionalism, more specifically the hurdles to constitutional amendments, may be employed to insulate long-term protective goals "from the vicissitudes of political controversy".[2] Of course, it will require a sort of anti-myopic moment of enlightenment on the part of the constitution-amending majority in the legislature to provide for sustainability-aware provisions in the first place. Germany, for instance, added the protection of natural foundations of human and animal life in the Constitution, expressly being mindful of the responsibility toward future generations.[3] And, somewhat even more impressive, limits to borrowing were introduced binding the federal and the state level.[4] Rolling back from this state of affairs would require gathering a Constitution-amending majority once more to repeal the clause, which seems—at least for the foreseeable future[5]—extremely unlikely.

So, if used wisely, law, thanks to its inherent longevity, does indeed serve to safeguard the interests of future generations—so it would seem.

1.1.2 Democracy as a Possible Limit to Permissible Sustainability Policy

Even if we mean well, who are we to make decisions for future generations? The issue of democratic legitimacy looms large. Law—possibly passed generations ago—remains in force and binds present and future generations without their having

[1] *See*, e.g., Kleiber (2014), pp. 5–6.

[2] Justice Robert Jackson, *W. Va. State Bd. of Educ. v. Barnette*, 319 U.S. 624, 638 (1943), referring to the purpose of the Bill of Rights.

[3] Article 20a of the German Constitution [Grundgesetz]. However, the precise legal relevance of the express mentioning of future generations remains somewhat dubious, *see* Kleiber (2014), pp. 30–36.

[4] Article 109(3) of the German Constitution [Grundgesetz]. Mückl (2007), pp. 189–193 for an overview. *See also* Kleiber (2014), pp. 19–21, 36–38.

[5] However, in a very long term, *any* predictions about future preferences are not in order. See the remainder of the article for a more thorough examination of this point.

had any say in its creation. This obvious tension between democracy and constitutionalism is much debated.[6]

Legitimacy seems less intricate with ordinary law. Simple revisability accounts for future changes of the majority opinion. However, ordinary law, too, sometimes turns out to be permanently binding. Unlike with constitutional law, this sort of bindingness is not a *de jure*, but a *de facto* one. Empirical effects created by state regulation may be largely irreversible.

The German public health care system serves as an example once more. As mentioned, it is highly effective, but inefficient. Fundamental organisational changes that would increase efficiency are practically impossible for actuarial reasons.[7] As a result, we are stuck with the 130-years-old system. Were our great-great-grandparents therefore wrong to establish it? Intuitively, the answer is: "probably not". (I will get back to that point in a moment.) Generally, law will quiet often have long-term, possibly irreversible effects, be those *de jure* (constitutional law) or *de facto* (ordinary law). This being inevitable, a rational response cannot be to purport an obligation to avoid impacts on future generations altogether. Rather, a balance needs to be achieved between the present and the future generation's ability to democratically arrange their own circumstances of life. Thus, some limits to the present generation's responsibility for the future are in order. It has been suggested that the "fundamental anthropological attributes" of human societies may serve foremost to delineate such limits.[8] Among those attributes is the need for essential requisites like oxygen, water, absence of (severe) environmental hazards. This approach seems basically agreeable. It should be noted, however, that it bears a great risk of unbounded interpretation when put in practice. Practically anything can somehow be tied to relevant detrimental effects. Therefore, the "fundamental anthropological attributes"-standard needs to be handled extremely restrictively.

When applied to the health care system, the standard demonstrates that our ancestors did not wrong us when they (somewhat inadvertently) acquiesced in the long-term effects of the system they established. While relevant to human health, the system or its inefficiency does not directly diminish any of the essential requisites.[9]

The standard does require the present generation to avoid or at least minimise direct detrimental impacts on essential requisites. This rule appears to be a plain

---

[6]Mückl (2007), pp. 200–201; Appel (2005), pp. 77–78 for a brief discussion.

[7]Currently, a specific period's public health care expenditure is covered by the total fees paid during that very period. Thus, no capital stock is ever built. In contrast, *private* health insurance commonly employs a capital funded system. Relatively high premiums—as compared to the individual's actual health costs—at young age allow for savings that will cover health costs at old age. In essence, each generation is self-sustaining. Converting German public health insurance into the latter system would require a transition period during which insurants pay twice: The traditional fees *and* payments that start create a capital stock. Therefore the transition period would have to be extraordinarily long. One estimate states 50 years, Henke and Borchardt (2003), p. 7; *see also* Grabka et al. (2003).

[8]Birnbacher (2008), p. 26; *see also* Barry (1977), pp. 274–275.

[9]It could be argued that the money wasted on the system's inefficiency could otherwise be spent on environmental protection or the like. However, such reasoning would keep the present generation from pursuing any resource-consuming policy and miss the balance described in the text above.

"Conserve resources!"-directive and therefore simple to follow. However, resources can not only be conserved through mere abstinence but through active action as well. And that is when things quickly turn paradoxical. Germany's stance towards nuclear energy provides a nice example. The introduction of nuclear energy in the 1950s was greeted with hooray and heavily promoted by the government. If environmental awareness had already existed back then, people would probably have praised the technology as a perfect instrument of intergenerational sustainability. It is practically emission-free, does not consume fossil fuel, is practically inexhaustible and made Germany independent of its sparse natural resources (coal).

In our days, Germany has reached a different democratic decision on nuclear energy, which, however, will make neither the nuclear waste nor the opportunity costs of not having invested earlier in alternative energy disappear.[10] Whatever a generation does, the future may not like it for it. This calamity paves the way for an economic look at intergenerational sustainability.

1.2 Economic Aspects and Caveats

1.2.1 Modelability of Sustainability

I choose Pareto efficient[11] allocation as the common measure of optimal social welfare. The better the conditions of perfect competition are approximated, the more the state of the economy will gravitate toward an efficient equilibrium. Thus, maximising social welfare remains a continuous process. Policy measures targeted at further approximating perfect competition and implemented today will only gradually take full effect and thus improve welfare in the future. The rigorous and ideal nature of the conditions of perfect competition forecloses optimal efficiency ever be fully attained.

Market-based governance thus shares law's inherently future-oriented nature, albeit not by preserving and reproducing beneficial choices of the past, but—ideally—by sustaining an asymptotical beneficial dynamic.

However, similarities go beyond these general future-oriented properties. Just as law can *specifically* be employed to enable (constitutional law) or implement (ordinary law) consideration of intergenerational sustainability in present-day policy design, so the market, too, can specifically be defined as to encompass utility of future generations as well. Economic modeling of intergenerational equilibrium

[10]A similar paradox is attached to safe nuclear waste disposal. Such disposal is a means of protecting future generations; however, once a disposal site is chosen and waste being dumped, this decision is practically irreversible, *see* for discussion Bundesverfassungsgericht [BVerfG] [Federal Constitutional Court], 10 November 2009, NEUE ZEITSCHRIFT FÜR VERWALTUNGSRECHT [NVwZ] 114 (116, para. 30), 2010 (Ger.).

[11]Potential Pareto efficiency (a.k.a. Kaldor-Hicks) will do.

exists,[12] albeit the proper path to present consideration of future benefit is proving hard to come by.

1.2.2 Ignorance of Future Preferences as a Source of Uncertainty

Hyperbolic Discounting: Harm or Benefit for Future Generations?

Commonly, *exponential* discounting of future benefit is suggested, accounting for people's time preference. Benefits at a later point in time are generally valued less than at an earlier point in time. Time preference appears to be an anthropological constant, what makes it—at first glance—a suitable candidate for adequate incorporation of future needs in present-day market-based governance. However, behavioural economics notoriously describes that humans rather demonstrate *hyperbolic* discounting. In fact, empirical evidence indicates that this holds true for intergenerational discounting also.[13]

Exponential discounting is time-consistent. Delaying consumption from the present moment to 1 month in the future, for example, will result in the same utility loss as will delaying it from 1 month in the future to 2 months.

In contrast, hyperbolic discounting is present-biased. The prospect of instant gratification in the case of a good that is immediately available for consumption results in a drastically increased preference for the good in this present moment. Therefore, the utility loss associated with an initial delay is much greater than the loss between any two future periods. This is often explained as a lack of human self-control. Although the individualistic methodology in economics forecloses any "objective" verdict of irrationality—preferences are to be taken as they are—it is important to note that in case of hyperbolic discounting, the individual will deem the present bias, and a choice made upon it, as rational only at that very moment in the present. At any other moment in time (when looking back at such a past choice, for instance), he or she will consider it a mistake. This is not so with exponential discounting, where judging one's own choice to be rational does not depend upon the point in time the judgment is made.

The question remains, should policy makers take this quality of hyperbolic discounting as a reason for paternalistic intervention, protecting people from their own lack of self-control, or should they accept hyperbolic discounting as an anthropological fact of human utility assessment and indeed discount future benefit hyperbolically?[14] Things get even messier as soon as we pay attention to the fact that hyperbolic discounting may serve the purpose of future generations. Despite

[12] *See*, e.g., the contributions in Roemer and Suzumura (2007). It is another story whether the regulator possesses the proper policy tools for exacting behaviour from economic agents necessary to approximate this equilibrium, *see* Lind (1990), pp. 20–21; *see also* Beaucamp (2002), pp. 57–70.

[13] Henderson and Bateman (1995); cf. Cropper et al. (1992); *contra* Frederick (2003).

[14] Suggested, e.g., in Henderson and Bateman (1995).

there being a substantial utility loss *initially*, the present (discounted) value of utility enjoyed in a *more distant* future declines slower over time than with exponential discounting. As a general[15] result, distant benefits of environmental projects are presently valued higher than in the case of exponential discounting.

Randomness of Preference Change

Unfortunately, trouble does not stop there. So far only time delay has been considered as an influential factor for present utility assessment. This implies that, aside from discounting, the set of an individual's preferences remains basically the same over time. Such stable preferences are one of the neoclassic key conditions of perfect competition. However, the "nuisance"[16] of behavioural economics includes preferences not being stable, but erratic. An individual may, for instance, stumble across a randomly available anchor (of judgment) and spontaneously alter his preferences significantly.[17]

The relevance for predicting future utility is obvious. Economically speaking, a person may not be the same individual that he or she was a minute ago. Any statement depending on future preferences becomes dubious. Nevertheless, taking into account the existence of more permanent personality traits, normatively postulating individual integrity as a prerequisite of economic reasoning may not seem entirely unwarranted. That does not bar from accounting for the results of behavioural economics when appropriate.

1.2.3 Non-identity as Barring from Intergenerational Discounting

However, matters get completely out of hand as soon as we drop another major similarity with law into the equation. Above I discuss the absence of democratic legitimacy for making decisions that will bind future generations. We face the exact same problem in economics. As stated above, it does not seem entirely unreasonable to normatively postulate the integrity of *individuals* over time. In comparison, such course of action in the case of separate generations, possibly hundreds of years apart, would seem absurd. Therefore, any imposing of present-day assumptions about future utility appears to be without basis. Indeed, some theorists therefore reject,

---

[15]This only holds true if the same discount rate is used for exponential and hyperbolic discounting.

[16]Loewenstein and Thaler (1989), p. 192, citing an alleged economists' view of the research on the psychology of decision-making.

[17]*See* Felser (2010) for an overview of anchoring and other cognitive biases. For example, an experiment found that participants are willing to spend significantly more money for a meal in a restaurant named "Studio A, 97th Street" then in a restaurant named "Studio A, 17th Street", the street number being the random anchor for judging how much an acceptable bill would be. The number 97 sets a relatively high anchor, so a higher bill seems acceptable, Dogerlioglu-Demir and Koçaş (2015), p. 611.

for example, the notion of intergenerational discounting entirely.[18] While an individual may be entitled to deem benefits that he or she will personally gain in the future as less valuable than benefits that are presently available to him or her, the notion of discounting seems unjustified from the outset for non-identical agents. A similar view is featured prominently in moral thinking.[19] A general prospect of economic growth seems unfit to counter this objection, for spreading it across centuries does not seem viable.[20]

But not only discounting becomes doubtful. The set of preferences may change entirely from one generation to another. Two-hundred years ago, the sight of smoking chimneys warmed people's hearts, for it made them think of progress, future, technology, growth, prosperity, work, the dawn of a new age. Today for most people the sight of smoking chimneys is just hurtful. It has become a symbol of everything that is wrong with our modern civilisation.

While another reversal of this thinking may seem unlikely at first glance, there is no means of telling whether in a couple of hundred years from now people might adopt a defeatist attitude and will not care about resources or protecting the environment. And as already stated above, economics' individualistic methodology requires us to treat anything as providing positive utility that an individual values as providing him or her with positive utility. From a purely microeconomic view, one stance is as good as another.

> Let us [...] [not] weakly believe that one generation is not as capable as another of taking care of itself, and of ordering its own affairs. [...] Each generation is as independent as the one preceding, as that was of all which had gone before. It has then, like them, a right to choose for itself the form of government it believes most promotive of its own happiness [...],[21]

What follows is the same as was already concluded for the legal view. We should abstain from predictions of future utility whatsoever[22] and simply keep options open as best as possible,[23] at least when it comes to the essential requisites. However, as already seen with law, keeping options open may require to act. I already illustrated possible paradoxical consequences for the past case of nuclear energy. Next, I wish to examine a more contemporary issue: electric transportation in Germany.

---

[18]Discussion at Cansier (2008), pp. 65–67; Kleiber (2014), p. 189 et seq; Mathis (2011), pp. 169–171.

[19]*See*, e.g., Parfit (1984), p. 357: "At a discount rate of five per cent, one death next year counts for more than a billion deaths in 500 years. On this view, catastrophes in the further future can now be regarded as morally trivial. As this case suggests, the social discount rate is indefensible."; *see also* pp. 480–86. *See also* Davidson (2008), p. 472.

[20]*See* Mathis (2011), pp. 168–169.

[21]Pres. Thomas Jefferson: Jefferson (1816).

[22]*Contra* d'Arge et al. (1982), p. 251.

[23]*Cf.* Cansier (2008), p. 59.

2 Electric Transportation in Germany: An Overview

2.1 Electric Transportation as a Policy Goal

Further diffusion of electric vehicles on the German market is "an issue of major strategic importance for the German Federal Government".[24] Germany seeks to become a lead market for electric transportation. The goal is to put one million electric vehicles on the road by 2020[25] through an instrument mix of direct funding and incentives.

To be sure, electric transportation is a global effort. The United States of America, too, seek to have one million electric vehicles on the road by 2020.[26] Other major contenders are China and Japan.[27]

2.2 Key Instruments

2.2.1 Direct Research and Infrastructure Funding

- A "Lithium-ion Battery Innovation Alliance" has been initiated and co-funded with 60 million Euros by the Federal Government (private funding: 360 million).[28] In total, it is planned to spend two billion Euros of public funding on battery research.[29]
- Starting March 2017, 300 million Euros will be spent on the "measure to support the installation and upgrade of electric charging infrastructure across Germany", providing public grants to individuals and private business enterprises.[30]
- Several pilot regions received a total support of approximately 130 million Euros.[31]
- Further infrastructure and research projects by municipalities and private business enterprises receive support from another federal grant programme.[32]

---

[24]German Federal Government (2009), p. 3.

[25]German Federal Government (2009), pp. 8, 17.

[26]GIZ GmbH (2016), p. 34.

[27]GIZ GmbH (2016), pp. 34–53; Berger (2015).

[28]German Federal Government (2009), p. 19.

[29]https://www.bundesregierung.de/Webs/Breg/DE/Themen/Energiewende/Mobilitaet/mobilitaet_zukunft/_node.html [accessed 28 February 2017].

[30]European Commission, State Aid SA.46574 (2016/N)—Germany, C(2017)753 final (not yet published in the Official Journal) ("Förderrichtlinie Ladeinfrastruktur für Elektrofahrzeuge", ["Funding Guidelines for Electric Vehicle Charging Infrastructure in Germany"]).

[31]NOW GmbH (2011), p. 10.

[32]Förderrichtlinie Elektromobilität [Funding Guidelines Electric Transportation], 9 June 2015, Bundesanzeiger Amtlicher Teil (Federal Gazette Official Section) 29 June 2015 B3.

- The Federal Government pursues a multi-technology approach and therefore also funds hydrogen and fuel cell technology. The National Innovation Programme Hydrogen and Fuel Cell Technology (NIP) I + II provides a total amount of public funding of approx. one billion Euros.[33]

2.2.2 Consumer Incentives

- Since May 2016, buyers of electric vehicles receive a grant of 3000 or 4000 Euros ("environmental bonus"), depending on the electric drive technology. Half of the amount is publicly funded. A total of 600 million Euros will be spent,[34] supporting the purchase of at least 300,000 vehicles.
- Vehicles with an exclusively electric propulsion are exempt from motor vehicle tax for 10 years if licensed before the year 2021.[35]

3 Economic Justifiability of Public R&D Funding in the Electric Transportation Sector

Public funding of technological innovation is economically debatable. Generally, a competitive market is a superior discovery procedure for more effective and/or more efficient solutions. State intervention would only disrupt the optimal innovation process, possibly enforcing diffusion of a less adequate technology. While justifiability of public R&D activities cannot be fully explored here, it can at least be said that—to possibly be viable at all—such activities—like any state intervention in the market – presuppose some sort of market failure.

Market failure in R&D predominantly comes in the guise of positive externalities. Knowledge spillover benefits competitors without any monetary reimbursement of the innovator. Patents or compensatory state subsidies are the common policies to internalise those benefits.[36]

---

[33]Förderrichtlinie für Maßnahmen der Forschung, Entwicklung und Innovation im Rahmen des Nationalen Innovationsprogramms Wasserstoff- und Brennstoffzellentechnologie. Phase II (Schwerpunkt Nachhaltige Mobilität) [Funding guidelines for measures in the areas of research, development, and innovation within the framework of the National Innovation Programme Hydrogen and Fuel Cell Technology. Phase II (focus sustainable mobility)], 26 September 2016, Bundesanzeiger Amtlicher Teil (Federal Gazette Official Section) BAnz AT 29 September 2016 B4.

[34]Richtlinie zur Förderung des Absatzes von elektrisch betriebenen Fahrzeugen (Umweltbonus) [Funding Guidelines for the Support of the Marketing of Electric Vehicles (Environmental Bonus)], 29 June 2016, Bundesanzeiger Amtlicher Teil (Federal Gazette Official Section) 1 July 2016 B1.

[35]Sec. 3d Kraftfahrzeugsteuergesetz [KraftStG] [Motor Vehicle Tax Act], 26 September 2002, BGBl. I at 3818, last amended by Gesetz [G], 23 December 2016, BGBl. I at 3234, art. 19 para. 8 (Ger.).

[36]*See*, e.g., OECD (2008), pp. 22–23.

I abstain from further examining externalities for they present the major aberrancy of *any* R&D activity. The remainder of the article will instead focus on reasons for market failure that are—or at least could be—specific to electric transportation.

In particular, two such reasons conspire to bring about market failure: uncertainty and indivisibility.

3.1 Uncertainty and Indivisibility as Reasons of Market Failure

3.1.1 Research Risk and Market Risk

At this time, it is yet to be seen which propulsion technology will be most suitable. Battery operated electric vehicles possess high energy efficiency (at least internally; overall efficiency depends also on how the nation produces its electric energy in the first place—i.e., renewable, nuclear, fossil). On the other hand, at a comparable range the battery weighs about three times as much as a fueled-up hydrogen tank of a fuel cell electric vehicle. Besides efficiency, a key factor of marketability is, in my opinion, the refueling/recharging time. Fuel cell vehicles, fueled by liquid hydrogen, match conventional combustion engine vehicles in that respect (3–5 min). In comparison, even Tesla's Supercharger (120 kW) needs 30 min for a recharge equivalent of 270 km.[37] This seems like a major nuisance for potential buyers of a multipurpose vehicle (city and long-distance). A third option are exchangeable batteries ("battery swap"), which is unfortunately not pursued by the German Government or by private business enterprises (I shall explain my regrets in a moment). Ninety seconds to five minutes for the battery swap in abandoned pilot projects by Tesla and "Better Place" are reported, easily matching pumping (fossil) fuel.[38]

The subject matter holds uncertainty in two respects. The research risk refers to technological success (for example, will a significant increase of energy density in batteries be achievable). The market risk refers to consumer acceptance. These types of risk are evidently intertwined here. Consumer acceptance will mostly depend on reliability, long range, quick refueling/recharging and pricing.

It is important to note, first, that uncertainty itself does not imply market failure. It is rather an inherent property of the market itself. However, misallocation may occur when there is a significant mismatch of the overall economic risk preference and the risk preference of private business enterprises potentially pursuing the project. In

[37] https://www.tesla.com/de_DE/supercharger?redirect=no [accessed 1 March 2017].

[38] https://www.tesla.com/videos/battery-swap-event?redirect=no; https://www.tesla.com/de_DE/blog/battery-swap-pilot-program; http://www.jpost.com/printarticle.aspx?id=213562 [accessed 1 March 2017].

that case, the project may seem macro-economically desirable but is still dropped by the industry.[39]

The German policy instruments as described above serve to reduce uncertainty.[40] Funding research is supposed to expedite the creation of innovative knowledge and thus the identification of the most apt propulsion technology, reducing research risk. Infrastructural subsidies and consumer incentives should reduce market risk. Considering that market risk does not imply market failure anyway, and that policy action is already reducing existent market risk, any further state intervention does not seem in order. The issue so far resembles the introduction of competing new consumer electronics. More recently than the notorious VHS introduction in the 1970s, HD for home use was introduced with Blu-ray and HD-DVD simultaneously, causing some reluctance to buying any one of the two new expensive players. However, the market sorted this out and HD-DVD vanished.

3.1.2 Indivisibility as a Reinforcer of Uncertainty

Is the situation different for electric transportation after all? In fact, here, consumers have at their disposal a fully operative and individually satisfactory alternative, that is, conventional combustion engine vehicles.

It could be said that electric vehicles do provide *some* extra utility in the form of positive emotions (knowing to act environmentally responsible; having a somewhat more pleasant driving experience like less noise, full torque at low revolution).

However, an educated guess suggests that the buying decision will foremost depend on the 'hard facts'. Let us, for the sake of argument, assume for the remainder of the article that this assumption is basically correct.

As seen above, electric vehicles struggle with the recharging issue. Having to chart your long-distance trip like an airline captain must (defining 'waypoints' in advance, that is, stops at one of the still limited number of recharging stations), and to make (possibly several) thirty-(or even more)-minutes-stops for recharging does not sound overly attractive to the potential buyer. And fuel cell vehicles are barely available yet, and so are hydrogen filling stations. There is no reason to live with these deficiencies when he or she can just by an ordinary vehicle at about the same price[41] and fare much better.

Consequently, the environmental bonus has turned out to be a dud. As of 28 February 2017, only ~12,600 applications were filed.[42] The "one-million-vehicles-on-the-road-by-2020"-goal will most likely be missed.[43] And the United States' one-million-goal for 2020 is already a correction of their initial target, which was by

---

[39]Meyer (1995), pp. 63–64; Klodt (1994), pp. 10–14.

[40]*See* Dose (2008), pp. 156–158 for a more general discussion of this policy approach.

[41]Without the environmental bonus, electric vehicles are more expensive.

[42]BAFA (2017), p. 2.

[43]NPE (2016), p. 14.

the year 2015.[44] Consumers do not respond sufficiently to any of the innovations presented to them, and market risk obviously remains great.

Alleviating these concerns would apparently require to fully implement the necessary infrastructure, making recharging/refueling as easily available as for fossil gas. However, this would obviously be a herculean task. Here is where the major difference to other industries comes in:

> [. . .] Germany's 2020 vision insists on a cross-sectoral industry approach that transcends traditional industry boundaries in order to create the systemic, sustainable electromobility solutions required to meet the country's ambitious targets. Intrinsic to ordinary vehicle drivers buying into electromobility is the presence of a complete, systemic electric mobility solution. By this is meant a holistic approach to electromobility; covering everything from the vehicle itself through to a charging network, traffic management system and smart grid power supply.[45]

To put it another way, providing full-fledged infrastructure for any of these systems would require a coordinated effort, and it would be ruinously expensive for a single or for just a few business enterprise(s).

What we are dealing with here is indivisibility as a reason of market failure. The technique of marginal analysis implies that properly adapting to prevalent market conditions presupposes divisibility of investment into small units. In the case of electric transportation, however, an all-or-nothing-approach seems inevitable. Without full-fledged infrastructure in place, there can be no relevant consumer demand. This alters risk perception. If a consortium of business enterprises were to make the effort of providing full infrastructure, but consumers later prefer a competing technology or simply continue to buy conventional vehicles, the loss might be too great to bear.

Battery swap provides an unfortunate example. The technology seems fit to account for what has just been described as the major obstacle for marketability. If Tesla's ninety-second-swap were to become an industry standard,[46] electric vehicles would even surpass refueling speed of conventional vehicles significantly. It would make electric driving extremely attractive. The driver does not even have to leave the vehicle for the automated swapping process. This very promising technology was heralded by the start-up company "Better Place", with major pilot projects in Israel and Denmark. Both countries were supplied with a nationwide net of swapping stations. However, consumer response was lukewarm (for example, the stations only worked with just one specific electric vehicle) and the company went bankrupt.[47]

---

[44]http://www.reuters.com/article/us-autos-electric-moniz-idUSKCN0UZ2MK [accessed 1 March 2017].

[45]GTAI (2015/16), p. 19.

[46]The failure of Tesla's pilot project is most likely owed to the fact that recharging at Tesla stations is for free, while there was a charge for the battery swap. Also, the battery swap required making an appointment in advance. Given these unfortunate circumstances, the failure is not surprising and, in my opinion, does not suggest consumer resentment in general.

[47]http://www.jpost.com/Business/Business-News/Death-of-Better-Place-Electric-car-co-to-dissolve-314380; http://www.nytimes.com/2013/05/27/business/global/israeli-electric-car-company-files-for-liquidation.html?_r=0 [accessed 2 March 2017].

To conclude, market risk, indivisibility and project size coalesce to precipitate market failure.[48] The Federal Government itself aptly describes this as a chicken-and-egg-dilemma.[49]

3.2 *Dubiousness of State Intervention to Account for the Market Failure in Question*

So further state intervention may be in order after all. Given the nature of the market failure in question, effective intervention can only come in the form of a definitive choice *before* all the technological issues are fully settled. To put it another way, the government picks one system, pushes nationwide implementation of the corresponding infrastructure and focuses on electric vehicles with the respective propulsion system. Additionally, to foreclose the combustion engine alternative, vehicles of that sort could be banned, as recently suggested by the German Green Party for the year 2030.[50] Similarly, the German Bundesrat, in a non-binding statement, calls for further incentives to make electric vehicles more attractive, or, respectively, ordinary vehicles unattractive enough so as to ensure that no applications for ordinary vehicles would still be filed beyond 2029.[51] Despite the Government officially still following a multi-technology avenue, the aforementioned 300-million-"measure to support the installation and upgrade of electric charging infrastructure across Germany" could be interpreted as a step into that direction.

While accounting for the reason of market failure as discussed, overall economic soundness of such a course of action is far from being clear. Resembling classic top-down regulation-based governance, it is likely to misidentify the economically most efficient solution,[52] hence create some market failure itself. Justifiability seems to be a matter of lesser evil and therefore depend on the empirical specifics.

---

[48]*See* Meyer (1995), pp. 68–70 and Gerjets (1982), pp. 64–65 for a general analysis of the connection between uncertainty, indivisibility and project size.

[49]Reply of the Federal Government to an inquiry from Parliamentary Representatives (Green Party), Bundestagsdrucksache [Federal Parliament Doc.] 18/11295 (23 February 2017), p. 5 (reply to question no. 20), available at http://dipbt.bundestag.de/dip21/btd/18/112/1811295.pdf [accessed 23 February 2017].

[50]Decision "Energiewende retten, Verkehrswende einleiten" ["Save the Energy Revolution, Start a Transportation Revolution"] of the Green Party's 40th Federal Assembly, November 2016, at p. 6, available at https://www.gruene.de/fileadmin/user_upload/Dokumente/BDK_2016_Muenster/EV-01_Energiewende_retten__Verkehrswende_einleiten.pdf [accessed 3 March 2017].

[51]Deutscher Bundesrat [Federal Counsel = the Upper House of Parliament, representing the German Federal States in federal legislation], Bundesratsdrucksache [Federal Counsel Doc.] 387/16 (Beschluss) (23 September 2016), at p. 4 (no. 4), available at http://www.bundesrat.de/drs.html?id=387-16%28B%29. Unfortunately, a common misinterpretation of the statement has been that the Counsel would suggest a *legal* ban. However, this is clearly not the case.

[52]*Cf.* OECD (2008), pp. 38–42.

That means it may only much later turn out that an *inefficient* choice was made. This future generation will then be stuck with the bad system for a long time because of the existing—and, for the time being, practically irreversible—nationwide infrastructure and the diffusion of matching electric vehicles. If we consider the amount spent for the whole system as a (partial) measure of total willingness-to-pay for climate protection, then the money wasted on inefficiency could otherwise be used for additional climate protection measures (if future generations so desire).

So again, we are stricken with a situation in which our efforts to keep options for future generations open (clean air, no detrimental climate change, putting crude oil to better use[53]) could, at the same time, narrow their options. How should we proceed?

4 Proposal: Time as the Relevant Currency of Sustainability

If we do nothing, the chicken-and-egg-dilemma might remain unsolved and relevant diffusion of electric transportation be delayed 'till the cows come home'. Carbon dioxide emissions would continue at the present or an even increased level with all the climatic ramifications. Future generations would suffer from them for a very long time. Some research suggests that "the climate change that takes place due to increases in carbon dioxide concentration is largely irreversible for 1,000 years after emissions stop".[54] Conversely, we could condemn them to a pointless waste of economic resources.

In addition, it should be noted that future generations might be unhappy even with an *efficient* system of electric transportation. As discussed above, there is no objective standard of rational preferences in economics. Economic rationality is always relative to the chosen objectives (providing positive utility). An action is rational when it best serves to optimise allocation and thus to maximise utility. Future generations may find individual traffic undesirable altogether no matter what system, or value climate protection less, or prefer some other path that has the electric transportation system appear as a waste of resources.

The uncertainty as to these questions seems to prompt precaution. Some initial disambiguation is in order.

4.1 Precautionary Approach: Disambiguations

First, Davidson suggested a precautionary approach that requires us to preliminarily treat climate change 'as if' it were a wrongful harm to future generations.[55] The

[53]Crude oil is not only the notorious raw material for plastics, but also for pharmaceuticals.

[54]Solomon et al. (2009), p. 1704.

[55]Davidson (2008).

rationale behind this is that moral philosophy is still wrestling with demonstrating that a moral duty to pursue intergenerational justice exists.[56]

Second, the 'precautionary principle' has—notoriously—long been implemented in the European Union with respect to all kinds of alleged risks. The problem with it is that it is paradoxical. It calls for precaution because of scientific uncertainty. However, just because of that uncertainty, it is unclear what will do greater damage: The alleged risk (if no precautionary action is taken) or the precautionary action itself (imposing possibly unwarranted duties; diminishing social welfare by hindering technological innovation).[57] Unfortunately, the European Union is further deviating from a science-based course to precaution,[58] despite continued *pro forma* judicial rejection of precaution based on merely hypothetical risks.[59]

4.2 Prima Facie Obligation to Temporally Minimise De Facto Bindingness of Present-Day Policy Choices

Instead, I suggest that *prima facie*, precaution as to future generations' freedom to choose should largely do away with any notion of damage. As discussed throughout this article, we should not purport to know future preferences. This holds particularly true, I believe, when we are talking about centuries ahead, or even more. We just need to look back about 50 years to realise how much societal attitudes and thus preferences can change over a relatively small (only *intra*generational!) period. Therefore, it does not seem in order to 'weigh' future disutility suffered from a diminishment of options inflicted by present-day decision-making. We should not try to foretell whether future generations feel more uncomfortable with continued climate change, or with an inefficient or undesired electric transportation system.

What remains as a relevant point of reference is time itself. Present generation's choice of which of the available policy actions—all inevitably diminishing future options—to pursue should depend on the length of time future generations will *de facto* be bound by this choice.[60]

The *prima-facie*-reservation accounts for immediate and severe adverse effects (esp. human life, health) of policy choices. Those should certainly be avoided

[56]*See* Wolf (2005) for an overview; see also Williamson (2015).

[57]Meyer (2015), p. 75.

[58]Meyer (2015).

[59]Case T-13/99, Pfitzer Animal Health v. Council, 2002 E.C.R. II-3305, para. 143 et seq. *See also* Case C-269/13 P, Acino AG v. Comm'n, 2014, para. 57 (http://curia.europa.eu); Case C-192/01, Comm'n v. Denmark, 2003 E.C.R. I-9693, para. 49; Case C-236/01, Monsanto Agricoltura Italia SpA et al. v. Presidenza del Consiglio dei Ministri et al., 2003 E.C.R. I-8105, para. 106; Case T-70/99, Alpharma v. Council, 2002 E.C.R. II-3495, Rn. 156.

[60]Kolmar and Stolte (1996) for a different resolution of the dilemma.

independent of time considerations. However, such choices are quite unlikely and will often already be covered by existing regulation (penal law in particular[61]).

In the case of electric transportation, the contribution of carbon dioxide to climate change, transportation's share of total anthropogenic carbon dioxide emissions,[62] and atmospheric lifetime are key factors in determining the length of time future generations will be exposed to climate change precipitated today. (It should be noted that even if scientific climate models were able to precisely extrapolate the climate in hundreds of years from now based on present data—wishful thinking, evidently—, there would still remain a significant amount of uncertainty. We do not know what kind of future technologies to counter the effects of carbon dioxide emissions might exist, and whether future generations will bring those technologies to bear.)

Likewise, an estimation would have to be made how much time it would take to dismantle an electric transportation system future generations disapprove of.

Even if the aforementioned 1000-year-persistence of climate change effects were only a very rough estimate, it seems likely that as a result, policy action to establish a specific electric transportation system *now* will turn out to be preferable.

5 Conclusion

Both legal and economic considerations strongly suggest that present-day policymakers should refrain from inferring any assumptions as to future generations' preferences when pursuing intergenerational sustainability.

The idea of democratic self-determination discredits present generation's presuming to know what is best for the future. And economics, by principle, abstains from any objective assessment of the value of human choices.

Consequently, a legitimate policy goal can only be to keep options open for future generations—at least when "fundamental anthropological attributes" are concerned. However, keeping options open often requires active action (fighting climate change, for instance). Actions taken may, inevitably, diminish future options elsewhere.

Taking ignorance of future preferences seriously leads the way out of this decision-making deadlock. The length of time future generations will *de facto* be bound by a present-day decision should be the crucial factor in the policy choice to be made.

---

[61]Often used for illustration is a time bomb to be set to go off in a distant future. This amounts to attempted murder. The illustration is commonly attributed to Feinberg (1986), p. 154. *See* Jodoin (2010) for the role of criminal law in intergenerational justice.

[62]In the United States, e.g., transportation accounted for 28% of total *anthropogenic* greenhouse gas emissions in 2006, https://climate.dot.gov/about/transportations-role/overview.html [accessed 3 March 2017].

References

Appel I (2005) Staatliche Zukunfts- und Entwicklungsvorsorge. Zum Wandel der Dogmatik des Öffentlichen Rechts am Beispiel des Konzepts der nachhaltigen Entwicklung im Umweltrecht. Mohr Siebeck, Tübingen

Barry BM (1977) Justice between generations. In: Hacker PMS, Raz J (eds) Law, morality, and society. Essays in honour of H. L. A. Hart. Clarendon Press, Oxford, pp 268–284

Beaucamp G (2002) Das Konzept der zukunftsfähigen Entwicklung im Recht. Untersuchungen zur völkerrechtlichen, europarechtlichen, verfassungsrechtlichen und verwaltungsrechtlichen Relevanz eines neuen politischen Leitbildes. Mohr Siebeck, Tübingen

Berger R (2015) E-mobility index Q3 2015. https://www.rolandberger.com/publications/publication_pdf/roland_berger_e_mobility_index_q3_2015_20150911.pdf

Birnbacher D (2008) Langzeitverantwortung – das Problem der Motivation. In: Gethmann CF, Mittelstraß J (eds) Langzeitverantwortung. Ethik. Technik. Ökologie. Wissenschaftliche Buchgesellschaft, Darmstadt, pp 26–39

Bundesamt für Wirtschaft und Ausfuhrkontrolle [Federal Office for Economic Affairs and Export Control] (cite: *BAFA*) (2017) Elektromobilität (Umweltbonus). Zwischenbilanz zum Antragstand vom 28 Februar 2017 [Electric Transportation (Environmental Bonus). Interim Numbers of Applications as of 28 February 2017]. http://www.bafa.de/SharedDocs/Downloads/DE/Energie/emob_zwischenbilanz.pdf?__blob=publicationFile&v=9

Cansier D (2008) Langzeitverantwortung und Diskontierung. In: Gethmann CF, Mittelstraß J (eds) Langzeitverantwortung. Ethik. Technik. Ökologie. Wissenschaftliche Buchgesellschaft, Darmstadt, pp 58–73

Cropper ML, Aydede SK, Portney PR (1992) Rates of time preference for saving lives. Am Econ Rev 82:469–472

d'Arge RC, Schulze WD, Brookshire DS (1982) Carbon dioxide and intergenerational choice. Am Econ Rev 72:251–256

Davidson MD (2008) Wrongful harm to future generations: the case of climate change. Environ Values 17:471–488

Deutsche Gesellschaft für Internationale Zusammenarbeit GmbH [German Company for International Cooperation (state-owned)] (cite: *GIZ GmbH*) (2016) Electromobility. Overview, examples, approaches. Sustainable Urban Transport Technical Document #15. http://www.sutp.org/files/contents/documents/resources/B_Technical-Documents/GIZ_SUTP_TD15_E-Mobility.pdf

Dogerlioglu-Demir K, Koçaş C (2015) Seemingly incidental anchoring: the effect of incidental environmental anchors on consumers' willingness to pay. Mark Lett 26:607–618

Dose N (2008) Problemorientierte staatliche Steuerung. Ansatz für ein reflektiertes Policy-Design. Nomos Verlagsgesellschaft, Baden-Baden

Feinberg J (1986) Wrongful life and the counterfactual element in harming. Soc Philos Policy 4:145–178

Felser G (2010) Wahrnehmung von Preisen und Kosten aus psychologischer Sicht. In: Meyer S, Fischer MG (eds) Gesundheit und Wirtschaftswachstum – Recht, Ökonomie und Ethik als Innovationsmotoren für die Medizin. Springer, Berlin, pp 193–204

Frederick S (2003) Measuring intergenerational time preference: are future lives valued less? J Risk Uncertain 26:39–53

Gerjets J (1982) Forschungspolitik in der Bundesrepublik Deutschland. Cologne (no publisher)

German Federal Government (2009) National electromobility development plan. http://www.bmub.bund.de/fileadmin/bmu-import/files/pdfs/allgemein/application/pdf/nep_09_bmu_en_bf.pdf

Germany Trade & Invest (cite: *GTAI*) [The Economic Development Agency of the Federal Republic of Germany] (2015/16) Electromobility in Germany: Vision 2020 and Beyond. https://www.gtai.de/GTAI/Content/EN/Invest/_SharedDocs/Downloads/GTAI/Brochures/Industries/electromobility-in-germany-vision-2020-and-beyond-en.pdf?v=3

Grabka MM, Andersen HH, Henke K-D, Borchardt K (2003) Kapitaldeckung für die GKV? Zur Berechnung der finanziellen Auswirkungen eines Umstiegs vom Umlage- auf das Kapitaldeckungssystem. Schmollers Jahrbuch 123:265–283. Also available at http://econpapers.repec.org/RePEc:zbw:espost:66217

Henderson N, Bateman I (1995) Empirical and public choice evidence for hyperbolic social discount rates and the implications for intergenerational discounting. Environ Resour Econ 5:413–423

Henke KD, Borchardt K (2003) Reform proposals for health-care systems. Capital funding versus pay-as-you-go in health-care financing reconsidered. Center of European Studies (CES) ifo DICE (Database for Institutional Comparisons in Europe) = *CESifo DICE Report 2/2003*: 3–8. Available at http://www.cesifo-group.de/DocDL/dicereport3-03-forum-1.pdf

Jefferson T (1816) Letter to Samuel Kercheval. http://teachingamericanhistory.org/library/document/letter-to-samuel-kercheval/

Jodoin S (2010) Crimes against future generations: implementing intergenerational justice through international criminal law. Intergenerational Justice Rev 10:10–17

Kleiber M (2014) Der grundrechtliche Schutz künftiger Generationen. Mohr Siebeck, Tübingen

Klodt H (1994) Grundlagen der Forschungs- und Technologiepolitik. Institut für Weltwirtschaft, Arbeitspapier Nr. 664. Kiel (no publisher)

Kolmar M, Stolte K (1996) The illusion of intergenerational preference aggregation: limits of individualistic population ethics. Sonderforschungsbereich 178 "Internationalisierung der Wirtschaft", Diskussionsbeiträge, Serie II – Nr. 297

Lind RC (1990) Reassessing the Government's discount rate policy in light of new theory and data in a world economy with a high degree of capital mobility. J Environ Econ Manag 18:8–28

Loewenstein G, Thaler RH (1989) Anomalies: intertemporal choice. J Econ Perspect 3:181–193

Mathis K (2011) Discounting the future? Cost-benefit analysis and sustainability. In: Mathis K (ed) Efficiency, sustainability, and justice to future generations. Springer, Berlin, pp 165–180

Meyer M (1995) Forschungssubventionen aus wettbewerbspolitischer Sicht. Nomos Verlagsgesellschaft, Baden-Baden

Meyer S (2015) "Gefühlsschutz" und hazardbasierte Vorsorge im Unionsrecht als Herausforderung des Rechtsstaatsprinzips. In: Möstl M (ed) Lebensmittelanalytik und Recht, Schriftenreihe zum Lebensmittelrecht, vol 35. Verlag P.C.O, Bayreuth, pp 63–107

Mückl S (2007) "Auch in Verantwortung für die künftigen Generationen". "Generationengerechtigkeit" und Verfassungsrecht. In: Depenheuer O, Heintzen M, Jestaedt M, Axer P (eds) Staat im Wort. Festschrift für Josef Isensee. C. F. Müller, Heidelberg, pp 183–204

Nationale Organisation Wasserstoff- und Brennstoffzellentechnologie [National Organisation Hydrogen and Fuel Cell Technology] (cite: *NOW GmbH*) (2011) Umsetzungsbericht zum Förderprogramm "Elektromobilität in Modellregionen" des BMVBS. Stand Mai 2011 [Implementation Report for the Grant Program "Electric Transportation and Pilot Regions" of the Federal Ministry of Transport and Digital Infrastructure as of May 2011]. http://www.bmvi.de/SharedDocs/DE/Anlage/VerkehrUndMobilitaet/modellregionen-elektromobilitaet-umsetzungsbericht-mai-2011.pdf?__blob=publicationFile

Nationale Plattform Elektromobilität [German National Platform for Electric Mobility (coordinating platform founded on the initiative of the Federal Government)] (cite: *NPE*) (2016) Wegweiser Elektromobilität. Handlungsempfehlungen der Nationalen Plattform Elektromobilität [Guide to Electric Transportation. Recommendations for Action from the National Platform for Electric Mobility]. http://nationale-plattform-elektromobilitaet.de/fileadmin/user_upload/Redaktion/Wegweiser_Elektromobilitaet_2016_web_bf.pdf

OECD (2008) Environmental policy, technological innovation and patents. OECD, Paris

Parfit D (1984) Reasons and persons. Clarendon Press, Oxford

Roemer J, Suzumura K (eds) (2007) Intergenerational equity and sustainability

Solomon S et al (2009) Irreversible climate change due to carbon dioxide emissions. Proc Natl Acad Sci U S A 106:1704–1709

Williamson D (2015) What can I hope about the Earth's future climate? Affective resources for overcoming intergenerational distance, Kantian and otherwise. Moral Philos Polit 2:57–82

Wolf C (2005) Intergenerational justice. In: Frey RG, Wellman CH (eds) A companion to applied ethics. Blackwell Publishing Ltd, Hoboken, pp 279–294

Stephan Meyer Berlin. Professor of Public Law at the University of Applied Sciences Wildau and Supernumerary Professor of Public Law at the University of Erfurt. D-15745 Wildau, Hochschulring 1, Tel. + 49 (0) 3375 508 232. stephan.meyer@th-wildau.de. Fields of Interest: Public Law (Law and Risk, Legal Governance and Welfare Economics, Philosophy of Law, Legal Theory).

Part III
Regulatory Innovation

Creating Social Norms Through Media, Cascades and Cognitive Anchors: Judicial Activism and the Quality of Energy Law from the Perspective of Behavioural Law and Economics

Mariusz J. Golecki and Jarosław Bełdowski

Abstract This chapter is devoted to the topic of judicial activism (or lack thereof) and the quality of energy law from a behavioural law and economics point of view. It complements our previous research by showing that a third branch of government (judiciary) is not immune to impact from social norms, cascades and cognitive anchors created by media (Golecki and Bełdowski, Environmental law and economics, 471–486, 2017). We start with three basic assumptions of the quality of judicial decisions and the latter's overview from the perspective of law and economics. We then move to the impact of heuristics and biases on adjudication, as well as listing some cascades in energy law. The German nuclear energy policy is discussed in order to note its sudden shift after the Fukushima catastrophe. Subsequently, the legislative reaction is further described to grasp the fallacy of German constitutional ruling on the matter. We suggest that the case of the German nuclear phase-out strengthens our previous findings concerning the sensitivity of judges towards availability of cascades. The conclusions are drawn at the end of the paper.

1 Three Basic Assumptions of the Quality of Judicial Decisions

The quality of judicial decisions appears to be one of the most salient topics in contemporary jurisprudence. The point of departure for the proposed analysis requires the acceptance of three basic assumptions. Firstly, it is assumed that the process of adjudication could potentially be analysed as a complex decision-making process, which is to be evaluated against a normative benchmark in the form of any

M. J. Golecki (✉)
Department of Legal Theory and Philosophy of Law, Faculty of Law and Administration, University of Łódź, Łódź, Poland

J. Bełdowski
International Comparative Studies Department, Warsaw School of Economics, Warsaw, Poland

K. Mathis, B. R. Huber (eds.), *Energy Law and Economics*, Economic Analysis of Law in European Legal Scholarship 5, https://doi.org/10.1007/978-3-319-74636-4_10

normative decision-oriented model of application of law adopted within a particular jurisdiction.[1] In such a process one may distinguish between different types of justifications for any decision pertaining to application of law. Those justifications are in general based on (referring to the concept of rationality adopted and applied in judicial discourse) one of three types of rational arguments: deductive, consequentialist, and arguments from coherence and consistency.[2]

Secondly, the scope of those decisions may vary within any legal system, in the sense that the adopted normative decision-oriented models differ in axiological and justificatory elements, allowing different forms of valid legal reasoning.[3] The model of the judicial decision-making process turns out to be a relatively adequate reconstruction based on the generalisation of judicial and administrative aspects of judicial processes. One of the most important differences between different normative models of adjudication rests upon the strict or flexible division between application of law by a court and the judicial law-making. This border, even if not always clear, seems to refer to the constitutional setting, such as the content of separation of powers and the legitimacy of judge made law.

Thirdly, both in legal theory and in practical legal discourse it is generally assumed that the judicial decision-making process should be evaluated against two benchmarks: rationality and accuracy of rulings.[4] Both aspects seem to be controversial, but generally it is accepted that rationality of judicial decisions is strongly connected to the equivalence between justification and preferences of decision-makers.[5] We will argue that instead of the predictive rational choice theory, the model of adjudication should rather be based on the more explanatory approach offered by the theory of bounded rationality.[6] This theory considers that human cognitive abilities are not unlimited and therefore human agents, including judges and officials, have limited computational skills and memory.[7]

The main research question thus pertains to the conditions under which judge made law could expand and judges supplement legislation in their effort to fill gaps

---

[1]Cf. Posner (2008), pp. 19–56.

[2]This approach assumes that judicial decisions should be based on reason, however, practical reasonability is limited and decisions can in fact be based on irrational motives or emotions. This position has been explained by MacCormick, who suggested that: "*any mode of evaluative argument must involve, depend on, or presuppose, some ultimate premises which are not themselves provable, demonstrable or confirmable in terms of further or ulterior reasons, yet on the other hand, that our adherence to ultimate principles in the evaluative and normative spheres is not derived by reasoning . . . does not show that our adherence to such principles is other than a manifestation of our rational nature*", MacCormick (1978), p. 265.

[3]Posner (2008).

[4]Vermeule (2006), pp. 3–4. In particular, he identifies two concurring institutional aspects: institutional capacities and systemic effects.

[5]Cf. Fix-Fierro (2003), Hadfield (2008).

[6]This moderate approach has been suggested by Simon in 1991 and applied to the model of adjudication by Vermeule (2006).

[7]Cf. Guthrie et al. (2000), Vermeule (2006) and Gigerenzer (2007).

or amending existing law, based on the assumption that the quality of law is to be maximised, while keeping in mind the fact that judges cognitive capacities are strictly constrained. This problem is especially important in energy law, where judges must act under social pressure and where the technical information and the capacity to evaluate alternative solutions is based on technical expertise and analytical skills.

2 Quality of Judicial Law-Making from the Perspective of Law and Economics

The difference between judge made law and statutory law played an important, if not crucial role for the founders of the law and economics movement.[8] R. Coase demonstrated that a comparative analysis of precedents and statutes, presented for the first time in *The Federal Communications Commission* and developed further in *The Problem of Social Cost,* should play an important role for transaction cost economics.[9] At the same time he stressed that the object of his interest was simply to explain some of the economic aspects of how the legal system functions, rather than to engage in a legal debate or the discussion taking part in legal scholarship, in particular in jurisprudence.[10] Nevertheless, a number of his observations made primarily in the first chapter of his book titled *The Firm, the Market and the Law* show evidently, that he did indeed try to elaborate his idea of the theory of law based on the assumption that the transaction costs have an impact on the construction of the legal system, its formation and its application.[11]

The observations offered in *The Problem of Social Cost* are concentrated on both judicial incentives and courts' institutional structure. The comparison between courts and state legislatures led to the normative proposition according to which the law-making activity of the courts should be increased at the expense of the legislature and statutory law. The legislative bias and the vulnerability of lawmakers to the impact of interest groups and lobbies may well be identified as the constant object of Coase's criticism. The Coasean intuition on the quality of judge made law created a point of departure for the economic model encapsulating the propositions elaborated on by different authors belonging to the so-called Chicago School of Law and Economics. Following the assumption articulated by R. Posner, some authors offered significant arguments in favour of the efficiency of the common law

[8]Posner (1980, 2008), Calabresi (1982) and Tullock (1997).

[9]Coase (1988), pp. 10–16.

[10]Later Coase repeatedly distanced himself from this thesis, according to which the object of his study was the theory of law, emphasising rather the only economic aspects of his studies (Kitch 1983, p. 192).

[11]Coase (1988), pp. 8–30.

hypothesis.[12] According to this theory, the evolution of judge made law may be explained as the maximisation of the allocative efficiency as the real goal of judge made law. These observations resulted with economic model of law-making process proposed by I. Ehrlich and R. Posner. The model is based on the three assumptions:

- The process of law-making is bound to incur different costs;
- The increase of the precision of legal rules requires incurring higher expenditure by the legislature[13];
- Identification of the types of costs associated with the establishment of the rule of law with a certain degree of precision remains critical.[14]

The function of the cost of law-making activity, as viewed by I. Ehrlich and R. Posner, consists of the following elements: Firstly, the costs of law-making by the legislature, such as information costs, these costs depend on the degree of uniformity (homogeneity) in the subject area of the regulation, and hence increase when they apply to different types of behaviour or different areas of legal entities' activity. Secondly, the costs of the establishment of the rule including the costs of formulation of the rule in linguistic form (provision) and the cost of taking a political decision by the legislature. Thirdly, increasing the precision of the legal rules leads to increased cost of law-making, resulting from the excessive scope of application of the standards with regards to orders and prohibitions (over-inclusiveness). This observation led R. Posner to conceptualise the notion of wealth maximisation as a result of the creation of law by judges. Posner observes that judges do not in general have the capacity to make decisions regarding a preferable distribution of resources. This inability of judges to set out referential distributive schemes results from both the particular safeguards and procedural constraints, such as different facets of judicial independence and neutrality, and the adversarial nature of litigation in general.[15] What remains as a potential option within their capacity to act is simply efficiency maximisation.[16]

However, this explanation lacks the description of the institutional mechanism leading to the efficiency of judge made law. In this context, the more advanced concepts have been developed.[17] As it has been observed by Ponzetto and Fernandez, on the one hand Posner is right when he stresses the relative efficiency of judge made law, because pure statute law is in fact never desirable. On the other hand, when social change is considered, the traditional doctrine of formally binding precedent based on *stare decisis* as adopted in the common law systems seems to

[12]Mercuro and Medema (1997), p. 61.

[13]This follows from the previously adopted assumptions, according to which the degree of precision is proportional to the incurred cost of adoption of a given legal rule.

[14]Ehrlich and Posner (1974), pp. 257–260.

[15]Posner (1980), pp. 487–490.

[16]Posner (1993).

[17]Gennaioli and Schleifer (2007), pp. 43–68; Ponzetto and Fernandez (2008), pp. 382–384.

result in a considerable degree of inflexibility and rigidity.[18] As Ponzetto and Fernandez suggest, legislation seems to be preferable to judge made law under the condition of radical, fast social change, when the incremental way of building judge made law loses its attraction and becomes inefficient compared to the pure statutory law.

Finally, it has been suggested by them that the comparison should be limited to pure judge made law and mixed statutory law, with some elements of judge made law in a dynamic setting. There the mixed system turns out to be better than pure statutory law, while the problem with the mixed system consists of the fact that statutory law and legislative amendments enable legislatures to adapt some suboptimal laws to reflect the preferences of special-interest groups that influence it, rather than that of the society as a whole. Finally, it seems that the more frequent the social change, the more likely that a mixed system will be efficiency enhancing.[19] Generally it could be suggested pursuant to this theory that the more intense legislative change leads to relaxed precedent, since courts must have additional ability to interpret or adopt the enacted rule.[20]

3 The Impact of Heuristics and Biases on Adjudication

It is generally assumed that a judicial decision-making process is deliberative, i.e. it is a rational process of a conscious character, controlled, free based on rational criteria and rules and supported by rational argumentation.[21] Although this model could be regarded as the adequate requirement reflected by the rational features of judicial reasoning it does not however consider the characteristic features of the cognitive apparatus of judges as limited human beings.[22] Addressing the limitations of human cognition the proponents of the theory of bounded rationality in cognitive psychology and behavioural law and economics stress the influence of unconscious, automatic processes, of associational character, that would be intuitive upon the

[18]Hirsch (2005).

[19]Ponzetto and Fernandez (2008), pp. 405–406; Hadfield (2010).

[20]In this context the opposite solution, namely the application of judge made law in case of rapid social change is at least partly applicable, as proposed by Calabresi, who states that: "*There is an alternate way of dealing with the problem of legal obsolescence: granting to courts the authority to determine whether a statute is obsolete, whether in one way or another it should be consciously reviewed. At times this doctrine would approach granting to courts authority to treat statutes as if they were no more and no less than part of the common law. At other times it would be used to enable courts to encourage, or even to induce, legislative reconsideration of the statute*", Calabresi (1982), p. 2. It is obvious that this kind of radical change depending on technological changes, natural disasters or other rapid and unexpected events may become especially frequent within the field of energy law.

[21]MacCormick (1978) and Alexy (1989).

[22]Simon (1991), Vermeule (2006) and Rachlinski (2007–2008).

process of decision-making performed by judges. Nevertheless, it seems that the attempts that are formulated within those movements aimed at explaining the indeterminacy of decisions in the application of law are unsatisfactory. The indeterminacy of decisions means that their content depends not only on the legal rules or legal reasons, but also on other elements of unconscious character: intuition and emotions. Those explanatory attempts failed primarily because of their purely speculative character. They were not verified empirically or the proposed verification was incorrect and proved unsatisfactory within the light of later achievements in the field of cognitive psychology or cognitive sciences. It appears that the only exception to this state of affairs is behavioural economic analysis of law, which is just a modification of classical economics to consider the limits of cognition (bounded rationality) and to examine the consequences of the so-called duality of cognitive processes (DPT).

The concept of bounded rationality has been introduced in cognitive psychology by H. Simon, and later on successfully applied in economics and legal theory.[23] Following classical behavioural law and economics literature, it should be observed that agents often consider their cognitive limitations, attempting to minimise the costs of decision-making process and at the same time trying to diminish the rate of errors.[24]

This state of affairs leads to wide usage of mental shortcuts and rules of thumb in some specific contexts. The problem remains however, given the assumption that in some cases, because of these tools, human behaviour differs in systematic ways from that predicted by the standard economic model, namely the rational choice theory, and it should be emphasised, that this strategy may result in predictable mistakes.[25] The departures from the standard model are generally divided into two categories: judgment and decision-making.[26] Both judgments and decisions demonstrate systematic departures from the rational choice model. This finding refers both to legal and non-legal contexts. It has been observed that judges are prone to both types of departures from the standard rational choice model.[27] This phenomenon is partly explained by the way in which actors apply the so-called rules of thumb.[28] In the context of applying law, those rules of thumb are very often based on the availability heuristics, where the frequency of some event is estimated by judges based on how easy it is to recall other instances of this type. Thus, some fundamental theoretical explanations of the characteristics, origin, and the nature of cognitive process are to be applied as a defeasible hypothesis. One such theory is associated with dual process theory. In line with the model of dual process theory (DPT), intuitive processes in the form of heuristics and cognitive inclinations may be explained by

[23]Kahneman and Tversky (1979), Guthrie et al. (2000) and Sunstein and Vermeule (2003).

[24]Jolls et al. (1998).

[25]Kahneman et al. (1982).

[26]Jolls et al. (1998).

[27]Kahneman (2003).

[28]Kahneman and Tversky (1979).

the acceptance of a hypothesis of a complex character of cognitive process where, alongside conscious (deliberative) activities, there are also unconscious (intuitive) activities. The functional complexity is being analysed within DPT concerning evolutionary psychology, as well as experimental cognitive psychology. According to this theory the delimitation of both systems: intuitive PT1 and deliberative PT2 is of a purely functional character, yet still their activities may correspond to an action of relevant parts of the human brain.[29] Moreover, it is stressed that intuitive processes are connected with emotions.[30]

4 From Heuristics to Cascades: Emotions and Social Norms Creation in Judge Made Law

The DPT urges theoreticians to take the position of scepticism towards the commonly accepted assumptions concerning the deliberative character of decision-making processes within the field of the application of law.[31] According to some dual-process theories, a clear distinction between intuition and deliberation is possible. Intuitive processes, on the one hand, are described as unconscious, automatic, fast, parallel, effortless, and having a high capacity. Deliberate decisions on the other hand, are thought to be accessible to conscious awareness, slow, sequential, effortful, rule-governed and having a limited capacity.[32] Heuristic of availability consists on estimation of a given action as more probable where this situation is more easily recalled rather than typical and relevant from the statistical point of view.[33] A particular type of availability is delusion of hindsight bias, which is connected to the process of ascription of greater probability to situations, which are already known to have happened, although their original probability (*ex ante*) was minimal. Heuristic of representation consists in associating the objects with the well-known prototype (exemplary, prototypical categorisation) instead of comparing the object to the conditions encapsulated in a rule, which establishes a given category. This type of categorisation differs from theoretical categorisation, which is based on the rule where the object is categorised because of the description of its necessary features.[34]

The problem of the influence of emotions upon reasoning has been addressed many times in literature. It has been suggested that emotional responses are connected with the operation of the experiential system (System 1). In one of the most interesting and comprehensive studies on the impact of affect upon decisions

[29]Bennett and Broe (2010).

[30]Damasio (1994).

[31]Cf. Peer and Gamliel (2014).

[32]Kahneman (2003).

[33]Kahneman and Tversky (1979).

[34]Kahneman (2011) and Golecki et al. (2016).

related to the System 1 intuitive process. The crucial role of intuition in the decision-making process brings emotion into the process itself and therewith enables emotions to influence the final, allegedly rational, decision. Additionally, it is obvious that emotional responses are not only important, but sometimes are a necessary condition for reaching any reasonable (System 2 shaped) conclusion. Accordingly, A. J. Wistrich, et al. observed that the presence of emotions does not pose a serious danger for the rule of law if the emotions are accurately detected and properly controlled on procedural and institutional level.[39] The excessive reliance on them may of course lead to erroneous judgements and create a serious threat for the judicial system. Given the fact, that emotions or affective responses are an aspect of System 1 intuitive processing, it should be observed that emotional responses, like other System 1 responses, are not always wrong, but they should be carefully observed, monitored and controlled. Especially in situations where they are likely to lead to systemic errors or founding judicial decisions on criteria which are explicitly prohibited. In line with the IOM, the potential ways in which the operations of System 1, such as emotional impulses or intuitions, lead to systemic errors of undue influence upon judicial decisions can be generally classified. Those situations and criteria constitute a list of judicial vices, which might be treated as opposite of judicial virtues. As somewhat opposed to the concept of judicial virtue, the modern IOM model based on the insights of the DPT theory seems to be unable to constitute a catalogue of those positive interactions of reason and emotion. However, it can offer a list of potential judicial vices in respect to the uncontrolled, unobservable entanglement between reason and emotion. The list of such vices based on the unacceptable influence upon emotions includes the affect heuristic and the motivated cognition.[40] The affect heuristic pertains to the situation in which emotions appear rapidly and automatically, excluding the possibility of control over System 1 by System 2. This heuristic has been described by D. Kahneman in the following way: "*the affect heuristic is an instance of substitution, in which the answer to an easy question (How do I feel about it?) serves as an answer to a much harder question (What do I think about it?)*".[41]

Motivated cognition refers to a process of accepting an intuitive preference as the most logical option, excluding counter arguments or other possible reasons to such an extent that the decision makers even under the deliberate process reach the same conclusion. This phenomenon has been described and explained by Z. Kunda. She suggests that the so called motivated cognition leads to such a high preference for a particular option, that it "*triggers the operation of cognitive processes that lead to the desired conclusions*" (so that) "*goals enhance the accessibility of those knowledge structures – memories, beliefs, and rules – that are consistent with the desired conclusions*".[42] This mechanism may also play an important role within the context

[39] Wistrich et al. (2015).

[40] Kahneman et al. (1982) and Kunda (1990).

[41] Kahneman (2011), p. 139.

[42] Kunda (1990), p. 493.

of judicial behaviour. As A. J. Wistrich et al. observed when referring to application of law by judges:

> emotions influence how people perceive others, what they remember about others, and how they process information about others. Emotions guide 'people's attitudes, beliefs, and inferential strategies'. Therefore individuals affected by this bias may even perceive people they like, as having positive qualities and people they do not like, as possessing negative ones. Consequently, even deliberative reasoning can be influenced by intuitive, emotional reactions.[43]

This analysis leads to a question of whether and eventually how the judicial vices in forms of emotion-based heuristics could be eliminated from the judicial process.

This problem has been convincingly discussed by T. Maroney, who emphasises that it is possible and necessary to embody the sphere of emotions into the institutional framework of the judiciary.[44] The affect heuristic is the only reservation to the plausibility of this proposition. If the emotional response creates bias in some situations, it remains outside the scope of control of System 2, because it simply creates a cognitive illusion.[45] It should be stressed that the motivated cognition leads to preference for a particular option inducing such an operation of cognitive processes, which eventually leads to the one solution based on emotional response and only justified on intellectual basis. This solution is later on *ex* post justified on an intellectual basis with reference to rational arguments. Moreover, the possibility of overcoming the effects of motivated reasoning is outside the scope of the acting agent, since—as any illusion—it affects the behaviour in an unconscious way. Therefore, the agent is not able to counteract or overcome the consequences of illusory reasoning. That effect may be additionally strengthened by further feedbacks from outside, whereby the benchmark of a judgement is effectively pushed to the extreme position where no deliberation based on balancing pros and cons is possible. Thus, affect heuristic may under some conditions build foundations for irrational considerations and lead to poor decisions.

5 From the Love Canal to the Fukushima Case and Beyond: Towards Cascades in Energy Law

The impact of emotions upon the decision-making process has been studied in special regard to legislative and judicial decisions. The influence of heuristics of availability and affect could be analysed in particular cases where the legislative or judicial decision pertains to controversial issues such as environmental policy or energy law. In both cases, emotions could play an important role shaping the public

[43]Wistrich et al. (2015), p. 863.

[44]Maroney (2011).

[45]Maroney claims that even judicial anger could effectively be channelled through the virtue of righteousness. Maroney (2012).

discourse and leading to suboptimal decisions. Moreover, the influence of emotions upon the decision-making process may not only induce misguided decisions, but even create the whole "availability cascades" consisting of decisions and comments mutually strengthening one emotion-driven message based on dubious assumptions. As Kahneman explains,

> the availability cascade is a self-sustaining chain of events, which may start from media reports of a relatively minor event and lead up to public panic and large scale government action. On some occasions, a media story about risk catches the attention of a segment of the public, which becomes aroused and worried. This emotional reaction becomes a story in itself, prompting additional coverage in the media, which in turn produce greater concern and involvement.[46]

It is indisputable that the availability cascades shape public opinion and seriously influence or even guide the discourse leading to a decision-making process within a framework of democratic representatives. The question remains to what extent the process of spreading irrational arguments and building the cascades influences not only public opinion but also the opinion of experts. One of the most well-known examples of these phenomena concerns the regulatory decisions in the U.S. where the problem of contaminated land led to imposition of strict liability on the broad category of subjects without proper rational justification. The case known as the Love Canal case started with headlines of the local newspaper *The Niagara Gazette* predicting in 1976 an environmental disaster because the canal (connecting the upper and lower of Niagara rivers) had turned into a municipal and industrial chemical dumpsite in the 1920s.[47] The disaster was triggered by a record of rainfall leading to the release of poisonous waste around its neighbourhood.[48] The reaction by the both the state and federal level was to relocate over 800 families and to introduce episodic legislation.[49]

The whole framework of the Superfund has been criticised as inefficient and overregulated and the legislation was found to be based on availability heuristic.[50] Anchoring and adjusting heuristics are visible within the process of non-reflexive acceptance of a given number and subsequent adjustment of the quantity, according to the process of receiving further, more detailed information. All these processes may, to some extent, influence judges and jurors.[51] This is especially important

[46]Kahneman (2011), p. 142. It seems that this mechanism could also be applied to some controversial judgments and the problem of populist adjudication or judicial populism.

[47]Pollak and Russell (1976).

[48]New York State Department of Health. "Love Canal: Public Health Time Bomb; A Special Report to the Governor and Legislature." Albany, N.Y. 1978.

[49]Cf. Golecki and Bełdowski (2017).

[50]It has been observed that "(a)vailability provides a convincing explanation of Superfund's existence and its endurance. The behavioural account of Superfund is that the availability of "Love Canal" as a symbol for the problem of abandoned hazardous waste dumps greatly intensified public concern, to the point where a legislative response became nearly inevitable, no matter what the actual facts might be." Jolls et al. (1998), pp. 1520–1521.

[51]Jolls et al. (1998) and Golecki (2015).

given the fact that the heuristics of representativeness and availability are often associated with emotional responses or particular effects. In their refined study of the Love Canal affair, Kuran and Sunstein (1999) suggested that the whole process of unfolding the Love Canal cascade was primarily based on some unreasonable fears spread throughout the public by newspapers. Accordingly, they blame the politicians and the legislators for adopting exaggerated means such as the special legislature on toxic waste and the Superfund. The CERLA legislation is hence criticised as an exuberant policy decision taken by non-experts.

However, there is a second part to the story. The question arises regarding the immunity of judges and other non-democratically elected experts who—at least theoretically—should make reasoned and well-balanced and well-informed decisions, adequate to the level of their expertise. It seems that judges at least in some cases are not immune to cascades. Moreover, they sometimes may play an active role as agents of cascades. It is possible that courts must consider public opinion, especially in those cases in which they adjudicate on risk and must consider some potentially devastating jeopardy.

Going back to the Love Canal affair, one must admit that judge made law pertaining to liability for environmental damage has also been affected by the availability effect. The *Love Canal* disaster led to judicial proceedings too, but it was the judgment in *United States v. Fleet Factors* (901 F.2d 1550 11th Cir. 1990), which paved the way for the extension of tort liability for contamination on to lenders such as banks and other financial institutions providing capital to the potentially insolvent owners or operators. This decision set out the new standard, which left many questions unanswered and stretched the basis of liability for lenders, regarded by some scholars as unfair. The phenomenon of availability cascades influencing judicial decisions may of course be applied to other judicial decisions.[52]

[52]The obvious candidate here would be e.g. the U.S. Supreme Court's decision in *Board of Trade of Chicago v. Christie Grain & Stock Co.*, 198 U.S. 236 (1905), where the case has provided the Supreme Court with an excellent opportunity to clear and restate the judge-made legal regulation, to review and possibly overrule the state-based statutory limitations of speculation. Moreover, the Supreme Court could have possibly aim at altering the whole regulatory framework to set out a new legal distinction between legal and illegal forms of speculation. The court opted for a third solution, drawing a new distinction between gambling and financial insurance, understood as an uncertainty based economic activity. The solution was found strange and built upon the particular case against speculation as dangerous moral problem. The whole line of anti-speculative judgments in the U.S. could be explained by the availability cascade and lobbying of the financial brokers. Cf. Golecki (2012).

6 Nuclear Energy in Germany, Fukushima Cascade and Federal Constitutional Court Ruling

The nuclear energy policy emerged in 1956 with the formation of the Ministry of Atomic Affairs in Federal Republic of Germany and the further enactment of the Atomic Energy Act (Atomgesetz) coming into force in 1960.[53] Its development was relatively smooth in the beginning with support of leading German corporations such as Siemens, AEG and ThussenKrupp. The first commercial nuclear power plant started its operations in 1969 in Obrigheim. However, another attempt to build a nuclear power plant in Wyhl was blocked in 1975 by anti-nuclear activists. The latter were absorbed politically by *Die Grüne Party* (the Green Party), which was established in 1980 and gained its first seats in the Federal Parliament in 1983. For the first time in history, the Greens formed a coalition government with the Social Democrats from 1998 up to 2005. In 2000 the German Government announced its plan to close all nuclear power plants by 2022. This was executed by means of the Phase-Out Amendment Act of 2002. Consequently, two power plants in Stade and Obrigheim were closed in 2003 and 2005 respectively and renewable energy subsidies were introduced. After the elections in 2009 the new government formed by the Christian Democrats and the Liberals changed its energy policy, but nuclear energy was emphasised to be a "bridging technology" and new residual electricity volumes were allocated in the Eleventh Act Amending the Atomgesetz in 2010 (11th Amendment).

In general, the average life of each nuclear power plant in Germany was extended for another 12 years. Nevertheless, in reaction to the tsunami on 11 March 2011 and the meltdown of three reactor cores in Japan, the German legislature decided to introduce statutorily fixed end dates for the operational lifetimes of the domestic power plants in the Thirteenth Act Amending the Atomgesetz in 2011 (13th Amendment). Consequently, the prolongation from the 11th Amendment was struck down and the nuclear energy suppliers of three of Germany's four largest suppliers and one operating nuclear power plant operating company brought constitutional complaints to the Federal Constitutional Tribunal (Bundesverfassungsgericht, BvR).

The complaint concentrated on the acceleration of the phase-out of the use of nuclear energy in 2011 without challenging the Phase-Out Amendment Act of 2002. The BvR held that the decision to phase-out the use of nuclear energy cannot be regarded as expropriation of property rights, but it also held that the right to property embedded in Article 14 of the Basic Law had been violated by fixing end dates for the operational lifetimes of nuclear power plants in Germany. The former was ruled out based on the argument that the public authorities did not acquire nuclear power plants—an essential part of the definition of expropriation in the opinion of the BvR. However, the right to property has been encroached on various grounds although some of the actions were regarded as proportional. Nevertheless, the ones, which

[53] Jahn and Karolczuk (2012).

shifted the balance towards unconstitutionality, were for example the too short adjustment period between the 11th and 13th amendments; no transitional periods; no compensation clauses or other settlement provisions. On this occasion, the BvR dusted off the concept of "frustrated investment", which protects legitimate expectations within the stability of a legal situation as a basis of investments in property and its use. The BvR admits that it is not extended to the general regulatory framework, which can be changed and to which market players are obliged to adhere to it. But the 13th Amendment has not provided any channels for nuclear power plants companies to adjust. In the opinion of BvR, the Phase-Out Amendment Act of 2002 established a legitimate expectation, which is worth protecting. The residual electricity volumes were denied to be converted from nuclear energy to others used by the same corporation. In the opinion of the BvR such an approach has not been justified. This situation could have been avoided by "*means of a different staggering of the end dates for the nuclear power plants*".[54] The most intriguing part of the BvR's reasoning is best encapsulated in a press release issued after the ruling:

> It is also not objectionable that the legislature was reacting to the events in Fukushima even though no new finding as to dangers could be derived from them. To what extent a change in political values or increased public concerns or fears can also sustain measures that – like the acceleration of the nuclear phase-out – significantly interfere with the fundamental rights of the persons concerned and what weight is to be attributed to them cannot be generally established. In any event, the evaluation of a high-risk technology that is particularly dependent on political assessment and the public acceptance of the risks of damage may also ascribe a weight to events that only change the public's awareness of the risks without bring to light new dangers.[55]

It is interesting to note how the situation at the time may have had an impact on the BvR ruling. Wittneben compared the political reaction to the Fukushima disaster in Germany with the reaction in UK (which was minimal). Her findings can be summarised as follows:

- The German Government was facing two major regional elections a few weeks after the disaster—they were forced to act decisively,
- German media spent more time covering the Fukushima disaster—in the UK the main topic was British military involvement in Libya,
- Germans have more faith in renewable energy—German companies are technological leaders,
- Germans are more afraid of nuclear energy—they were affected by the Chernobyl disaster and were also likely to be a field of a nuclear conflict during the Cold War

[54]It is noteworthy that some judgments of the BvR have already been criticised on the bases of lack of empirical knowledge and misinterpretation of statistical data. Cf. Petersen (2013).

[55]The Thirteenth Amendment to the Atomic Energy Act Is for the Most Part Compatible with the Basic Law, Press Release No. 88/2016 of 6 December 2016, https://www.bundesverfassungsgericht.de/SharedDocs/Pressemitteilungen/EN/2016/bvg16-088.html [accessed 29 August 2017].

- For some historic and cultural reasons Germans feel cultural proximity to Japan—they were more concerned with the events taking place in Japan.[56]

Accordingly, it could rightly be pointed out that the whole Nuclear Phase-Out case coincides with the structure and the nature of cascade. The BvR has been involved in the cascade, finding that the legislature has the full capacity of being affected by the Fukushima case, even if the case seems to be entirely irrelevant from a statistical and technical point of view.

7 Conclusion

The growth of judicial activism and the empowerment of courts in cases such as the judgment of the BvR on the Phase-Out Amendment Act of 2002 demonstrates a clear need for revision of present models of adjudication. Firstly, it is not entirely true that judges remain neutral and independent, insulated from public emotions. The opposite seems to be true. Courts—as any other institution taking part in an adjudication and law-making process—are not entirely immune to availability cascades and may well take decisions framed by media span and availability cascades. In general, it is important that judges are often forced to perform their tasks under veil of ignorance but they are of course exposed to affects, heuristics, biases and manipulations gives sufficient ground for review of dominant concept of judicial rationality and impartiality. The claim put forward in this paper is a modest one. We urge that an analysis of the judicial rationality from the perspective of dual process theory takes place. This should allow the encapsulation of heuristics and biases with the wider model of adjudication and judge made law. Moreover, the proposed interdisciplinary approach may contribute to the introduction of the institutional and procedural changes that would consider the complex nature of the cognitive processes, as well as their limits in the context of law application. Especially in such areas as environmental law and energy law. Meanwhile it seems that a new, more naturalistic and less normative approach to judicial activism and courts, in general, plays an increasing role in this area of investigation within jurisprudence. Those theories also attempt to explain the cultural, political and economic causes of a given phenomenon, namely the constant and discernible growth of judicial activism and courts understood, both as legal institutions and as social institutions.

Acknowledgments The paper has been prepared within the framework of the research project 2015/17/HS5/00495 financed by the National Science Centre, Poland.

[56]Wittneben (2012).

References

Alexy R (1989) A theory of legal argumentation. The theory of rational discourse as theory of legal justification. Oxford University Press, Oxford

Bennett H, Broe GA (2010) Judicial decision-making and neurobiology: the role of emotion and the ventromedial cortex in deliberation and reasoning. Am J Forensic Sci 42:11–18

Calabresi G (1982) A common law for the age of statutes. Harvard University Press, Cambridge

Coase RH (1988) The firm, the market, and the law. University of Chicago Press, Chicago

Damasio A (1994) Decartes' error: emotion, reason, and the human brain. Avon, New York

Ehrlich I, Posner RA (1974) An economic analysis of legal rulemaking. J Leg Stud 3:257–286

Fix-Fierro H (2003) Courts, justice and efficiency. A socio-legal study of economic rationality in adjudication. Hart Publishing, Oxford

Gennaioli N, Schleifer A (2007) The evolution of common law. J Polit Econ 115:43–68

Gigerenzer G (2007) Gut feelings: the intelligence of the unconscious. New York

Golecki MJ (2012) Evolutionary theories of derivatives regulation. Aestimatio IEB Int J Financ 4:152–167

Golecki MJ (2015) New York Times v. Sullivan in European context. The optimal liability for libel from the perspective of behavioural law and economics. In: Mathis K (ed) European perspectives on behavioural law and economics. Springer, Cham, pp 243–267

Golecki MJ, Bełdowski J (2017) Between Love Canal and Rada di Augusta: the optimal liability for environmental damages in American and European law from the perspective of behavioural law and economics. In: Mathis K, Huber BR (eds) Environmental law and economics. Springer, Cham, pp 471–486

Golecki MJ, Romanowicz M, Wojciechowski J (2016) Nudging in tax law? Eyetracking research on limits of efficacy of legal definitions. In: Mathis K, Tor A (eds) Nudging-possibilities, limitations and applications in European law and economics. Springer, Cham, pp 289–313

Guthrie C, Rachlinski JJ, Wistrich AJ (2000) Inside the judicial mind. Cornell Law Rev 86:777–892

Guthrie C, Rachlinski JJ, Wistrich AJ (2007) Blinking on the bench: how judges decide cases. Cornell Law Rev 93:1–43

Hadfield G (2008) The levers of legal design: institutional determinants of the quality of law. J Comp Econ 36:43–73

Hadfield G (2010) The dynamic quality of law: judicial incentives, legal human capital and the adaptation of law. J Econ Behav Organ 79:80–94

Hirsch AJ (2005) Evolutionary theories of common law efficiency: reasons for (cognitive) skepticism. Fla State Univ Law Rev 32:425–441

Jahn D, Karolczuk S (2012) German exceptionalism: the end of nuclear energy in Germany! Environ Polit 21:159–164

Jolls C, Sunstein CR, Thaler R (1998) A behavioral approach to law and economics. Stanford Law Rev 50:1471–1550

Kahneman D (2003) A perspective on judgment and choice. Mapping bounded rationality. Am Psychol 58:697–720

Kahneman D (2011) Thinking, fast and slow. Macmillan, London

Kahneman D, Tversky A (1979) Prospect theory: an analysis of decision under risk. Econometrica 47:263–293

Kahneman D, Slovic P, Tversky A (1982) Judgment under uncertainty: heuristics and biases. New York

Kitch EW (1983) The fire of truth: a remembrance of law and economics at Chicago, 1932–1970. J Law Econ 26:163–234

Kunda Z (1990) The case for motivated reasoning. Psychol Bull 108:480–498

Kuran T, Sunstein CR (1999) Availability cascades and risk regulation. Stanford Law Rev 51:683–768

MacCormick N (1978) Legal reasoning and legal theory. Oxford University Press, Oxford

Maroney TA (2011) Emotional regulation and judicial behavior. Calif Law Rev 99:1485–1555

Maroney TA (2012) Angry judges. Vanderbilt Law Rev 65:1207–1286
Mercuro N, Medema SG (1997) Economics and the law. From Posner to post-modernism. Princeton University Press, Princeton
Peer E, Gamliel E (2014) Heuristics and biases in judicial decisions. Court Rev 4:114–118
Petersen N (2013) Avoiding the common-wisdom fallacy: the role of social sciences in constitutional adjudication. Int J Const Law 11:293–318
Pollak D, Russell D (1976) Dangerous chemicals found leaking from Hooker Dump. Niagara Gazette, 2 November 1976
Ponzetto G, Fernandez P (2008) Case law versus statute law: an evolutionary perspective. J Leg Stud 37:379–430
Posner RA (1980) The ethical and political basis of the efficiency norm in common law adjudication. Hofstra Law Rev 8:487–490
Posner RA (1993) What do judges maximize? (The same thing everybody else does). Supreme Court Econ Rev 3:1–41
Posner RA (2008) How judges think. The University of Chicago Press, Cambridge
Rachlinski J (2007–2008) Heuristics, biases and philosophy. Tulsa Law Rev 43:865–883
Simon HA (1991) Bounded rationality and organizational learning. Organ Sci 2:125–134
Slovic P, Finucane M, Peters E, MacGregor DG (2002) The affect heuristic. In: Gilovich T, Griffin D, Kahneman D (eds) The psychology of intuitive judgment: heuristics and biases. New York, Cambridge University Press, pp 217–229
Sunstein CR, Vermeule A (2003) Interpretation and institutions. Mich Law Rev 2:885–951
Tullock G (1997) The case against the common law. Durham
Vermeule A (2006) Judging under uncertainty. An institutional theory of legal interpretation. Harvard University Press, Cambridge
Wistrich AJ, Rachlinski JJ, Guthrie C (2015) Heart versus head: do judges follow the law or follow their feelings? Texas Law Rev 93:855–923
Wittneben BBF (2012) The impact of the Fukushima nuclear accident on European energy policy. Environ Sci Pol 15:1–3

Mariusz J. Golecki Łódź and Warsaw. Professor at the University of Lodz, Department of Legal Theory and Philosophy of Law, Director of the Laboratory for Cognitive Research in Law, University of Lodz, Faculty of Law and Administration, ul. Kopcinskiego 8/12, 90-232 Łódź, Poland mjgolecki76@gmail.com. Fields of Interest: Economic Analysis of Law, Behavioural Law and Economics, Legal Philosophy and Legal Theory, Theory of the EU law, Comparative Law.

Jarosław Bełdowski Warsaw. Assistant Professor at International Comparative Studies Department at Warsaw School of Economics. 02-554 Warsaw, Al. Niepodleglosci 162, Tel. +48 22 564 93 45. jbeldowski@yahoo.com. Fields of Interest: New Institutional Economics, Economic Analysis of Law, Contract Law, Comparative Law, Judicial Studies.

Capacity Mechanisms: An Intervention Needed in Failing Markets?

Markus Schreiber

Abstract The author discusses capacity mechanisms from a European and Swiss perspective. Such mechanisms may serve as a potential remedy for perceived problems in the energy market. These potential problems pertain to the security of electricity supply in a changing market environment, which has a new focus on renewable energy. The author examines whether these potential problems constitute market failures and provides an overview of the most relevant capacity mechanisms in the current discussion. In addition, the paper analyses the European legal framework regarding capacity mechanisms as state aid and draws conclusions for Switzerland. In this context, it discusses problems that arise when economic terms such as "market failure" are used as a legal standard.

1 Introduction

The energy sector appears particularly suitable for the analysis of the interrelation between law and economics: In continental Europe, there is still some hesitation to apply an economic analysis of law in areas other than legislation. Continental judges do not normally revert to economic arguments in their assessment of cases. However, some argue that economic arguments may be valid where economic efficiency is the purpose of the law.[1] In Energy law, statutes often explicitly stipulate the need of an efficient and secure energy supply.[2] Switzerland even has a corresponding constitutional provision that, *inter alia*, calls for an "economical" energy supply.[3]

[1]Eidenmüller (2015), pp. 452 et seqq.

[2]For Switzerland, see Article 1 Energy Supply Act, SR 734.7.

[3]Article 89(1) Federal Constitution, SR 101.

M. Schreiber (✉)
Faculty of Law, University of Lucerne, Lucerne, Switzerland
e-mail: markus.schreiber@unilu.ch

K. Mathis, B. R. Huber (eds.), *Energy Law and Economics*, Economic Analysis of Law in European Legal Scholarship 5, https://doi.org/10.1007/978-3-319-74636-4_11

The focus of this paper will be the security of the electricity supply. With new energy policies emphasizing fluctuating renewable energy sources, there is some debate as to whether the security of the electricity supply might be in danger in the future. The paper will first discuss potential problems that may arise in the electricity market. Then, it will discuss so-called capacity mechanisms, which have been proposed to address these potential problems. Finally, it will assess the legal framework for such mechanisms in Europe and discuss possible implications for Switzerland.

2 The "Missing Money" Problem

2.1 The Lack of Incentives for New Flexible Generating Capacity

Electricity is a good with very special physical characteristics.[4] One of these is that for our electricity grids and the items that use electricity (such as household appliances etc.) to work, both the production and consumption of electricity have to be even.[5] The tolerance for fluctuations in the grid is very low: the European Association of Transmissions Systems Operators (ENTSO-E) requires the use of all available options to restore the grid's normal condition as soon as the frequency differs from the standard 50 Hz by only 0.2 Hz.[6]

Currently, conventional and nuclear power plants supply electricity for the base load in times of minimal demand.[7] This makes economic sense, since such power plants offer very low generation costs, but are comparatively slow to adjust their production.[8] In 2015, nuclear power was responsible for 33.5% of Switzerland's domestic electricity production.[9] In addition to the base-load power plants, fast-responding power plants with relatively high generation costs such as gas power plants supply extra capacity in times of peak load, when there is high demand.[10] In Switzerland, hydropower plants are crucial in this role, since they can convert the potential energy of the water, which is stored in the reservoir, into electric energy

[4]Cf. Jacobs (2015), pp. 894 et seqq.

[5]Verband Schweizerischer Elektrizitätsunternehmen (VSE) (2016a), p. 1; Hewicker et al. (2013), p. 35.

[6]*ENTSO-E*, Operations Handbook, Policy 1: Load-Frequency Control and Performance, A-D2.5.

[7]Regarding the role of nuclear power plants in Switzerland cf. Hewicker et al. (2013), p. 36.

[8]Cf. Hewicker et al. (2013), p. 36; Sailer (2012), p. 792.

[9]BFE, Elektrizitätsstatistik (2015), p. 13.

[10]Hewicker et al. (2013), p. 36; Sailer (2012), p. 792.

within an extremely short time.[11] In 2015, hydropower made up 59.9% of Switzerland's domestic electricity production.[12]

Traditionally, electricity producers are remunerated only for the electricity they produce, i.e. per Mega-Watt hour (MWh). This is referred to as an "energy-only" market.[13] In "peak load" situations with high electricity demand, the prices in the wholesale market are based entirely on the marginal utility for the buyers.[14] This leads to rather high scarcity prices.[15] In the "old world" of energy markets described above, this system provides sufficient incentives to install new generating capacity.[16]

However, with the ongoing transition to (new)[17] renewable energy sources, the energy-only market in the EU and Switzerland could potentially lead to a "missing money problem"[18]: electricity demand is rather inelastic, which can lead to a gap in generating capacity in times of peak load.[19] In addition, most consumers have contracts that guarantee the supply of electricity regardless of the current market environment.[20] Renewable energy sources also create an additional demand in backup generating capacity because of their intermittent production characteristics.[21] Some argue that currently, the returns on electricity production are not high enough to incentivize an adequate level of flexible generating capacity.[22] Flexible technologies such as gas turbines may only be needed a few days each year, which may not be enough to generate sufficient profits.[23] Other studies conclude that the high "peak

[11]Hewicker et al. (2013), pp. 39 et seq.; cf. the technology's description at Sailer (2012), pp. 786 et seq.

[12]BFE, Elektrizitätsstatistik (2015), p. 13.

[13]The term is used here in the same way as by Perner and Riechmann (2015), p. 59, who use it for any system which "rewards wholesale power mainly through a per MWh-charge", notwithstanding the possibility of contracts relating to, *inter alia*, back-up capacity. Regarding this "implicit" remuneration of capacity, see also r2b research to business energy consulting (2014), pp. 2, 18, 44 and 31 regarding balancing energy.

[14]r2b research to business energy consulting (2014), pp. 20, 24 et seq.

[15]Avenir Suisse (2013), p. 19.

[16]Cf. Perner and Riechmann (2015), p. 62.

[17]Switzerland uses the term "new renewable energies" to differentiate between rather new energy sources (wind, solar, biomass etc.) and the long-established hydropower.

[18]Gonzalez-Diaz (2015), pp. 3 et seqq.

[19]Gonzalez-Diaz (2015), p. 3. This is exacerbated by the fact that electricity cannot easily be stored, Keppler (2017), p. 568. See also r2b research to business energy consulting (2014), pp. 11 et seq.

[20]r2b research to business energy consulting (2014), pp. 2, 22 with fn. 33; KEMA Consulting GmbH (2013), p. 35.

[21]Gonzalez-Diaz (2015), pp. 3, 6; Keppler (2017), p. 563.

[22]Cf. Gonzalez-Diaz (2015), pp. 3, 4. Cf. Elberg et al. (2012), p. 45: "significant challenges" in the energy-only market.

[23]Elberg et al. (2012), p. 70; Büro für Energiewirtschaft und technische Planung GmbH (BET) (2011), p. 28; Bundesverband Erneuerbare Energie (BEE) et al. (2012), p. 11; Keppler (2017), p. 563.

load" prices[24] on the few days of scarcity lead to sufficient returns for conventional power plants.[25]

Additional problems arise when electricity prices are capped.[26] The German Electricity Market Act (*Strommarktgesetz*) explicitly stipulates that electricity prices are not to be capped by regulatory means.[27] However, the German renewable energy subsidies affect the market price drastically. Swiss subsidies, e.g. the feed-in tariff at cost (*Kostendeckende Einspeisevergütung*), potentially have similar effects.

This problem is exacerbated by the fact that renewable energy sources have very low marginal costs of energy production.[28] This may lead to a price level in the energy-only market of zero or close to zero.[29] In recent years, electricity prices in the wholesale markets have sometimes even been negative, so that market participants were paid to take on the surplus electricity.[30] Gas power plants and other flexible technologies, which often have relatively high marginal costs, are therefore pushed out of the market, with current plants being mothballed and new investments halted.[31] In addition, low certificate prices in the EU emissions trading scheme make coal power plants more competitive than cleaner and more flexible gas power plants.[32] The Europe-wide cross-border electricity trade also places power plants across the continent into competition with foreign plants. Some authors argue that the resulting market consolidation, which forces the least-competitive plants out of the market, may lead to a situation in which countries no longer have the domestic generating capacity that they would consider desirable.[33]

Because of the potential[34] "missing money" problem, several countries have implemented or are discussing some form of capacity remuneration.[35] This leads to the question of whether such interventions by the legislator would be justified.

---

[24]See Nicolosi (2012), pp. 8 et seq. Cf. the critical assessment by Keppler (2017), pp. 565 et seq.

[25]r2b research to business energy consulting (2014), pp. 20, 29, 60 et seq.; Frontier Economics and consentec (2014), p. 58.

[26]Gonzalez-Diaz (2015), pp. 3, 4; Keppler (2017), p. 563.

[27]By adding a § 1a subsection 1 to the Energiewirtschaftsgesetz, BGBl. 2016 I 1786.

[28]Gonzalez-Diaz (2015), pp. 3, 5; Keppler (2017), p. 563. For a more detailed discussion of the so-called merit order effect, see Sect. 2.2.1.

[29]Gonzalez-Diaz (2015), pp. 3, 5.

[30]Sia Partners (2013); Cludius et al. (2014), pp. 304 et seq.

[31]Gonzalez-Diaz (2015), pp. 3, 5; Perner and Riechmann (2015), p. 60; Elberg et al. (2012), p. 46; Keppler (2017), p. 563.

[32]Clò (2011), pp. 78 et seq.; Perner and Riechmann (2015), p. 63.

[33]Perner and Riechmann (2015), pp. 59 et seq.

[34]As shown above, economists debate the energy-only market's ability to provide sufficient incentives for backup generating. As a lawyer, the author is not qualified to comment on this dispute. The ongoing debate shows that there are at least some question marks concerning an energy-only market, which already justifies a closer look at potential capacity mechanisms. See Elberg et al. (2012), p. 45.

[35]Perner and Riechmann (2015), p. 59.

From an economic standpoint, this would be the case if the "missing money" problem could be qualified as a market failure.[36]

2.2 *Qualification as a Market Failure*

In this section, the root causes of the potential "missing money" problem will be analysed further. Legal interventions into the energy-only market (i.e. an amendment of such markets with capacity markets) may seem justified if these causes qualified as market failure.

2.2.1 Commercial Risks

There are some factors that influence the profitability of flexible generating capacity and result from a changing market environment. For example, the liberalisation of EU electricity markets has made some existing overcapacities become apparent when exposed to competition.[37] The currently lower price level will therefore lead to a market consolidation.[38]

Another example is the lower industrial production after the 2008 economic crisis. This led to lower CO_2-certificate prices, which affects the competitiveness of cleaner gas plants.[39] Additionally, the lower industrial production also reduced demand for electricity, resulting in lower electricity prices. Such market developments should be considered a natural part of the commercial risks of all market participants, not constituting market failure or justifying interventions into the market.[40]

A further development is the technological innovation in the renewable energy sector. This innovation influences the so-called "merit order" (Fig. 1). The merit order describes the sequence in which different types of power plants enter the market.[41] When there is low electricity demand, only the power plants with the lowest marginal costs of production (the base load plants such as nuclear plants) will

---

[36]Cf. Perner and Riechmann (2015), p. 60, who argue that in the absence of "systematic market failures", any intervention in the markets would be "unfounded". See also Breyer (1979), pp. 553 et seq.; r2b research to business energy consulting (2014), p. 3. For a general discussion of the legitimisation of interventions into the energy market through the assumption of market failures, see Eekhoff and Jänsch (2016). A more liberal acceptance of regulatory interventions specifically for the case of security of electricity supply can be found at Eekhoff and Vossler (2016), pp. 8 et seq.

[37]Perner and Riechmann (2015), p. 63; r2b research to business energy consulting (2014), p. 15.

[38]r2b research to business energy consulting (2014), p. 15.

[39]See fn. 32 supra.

[40]Perner and Riechmann (2015), p. 63; r2b research to business energy consulting (2014), p. 15.

[41]r2b research to business energy consulting (2014), p. 24.

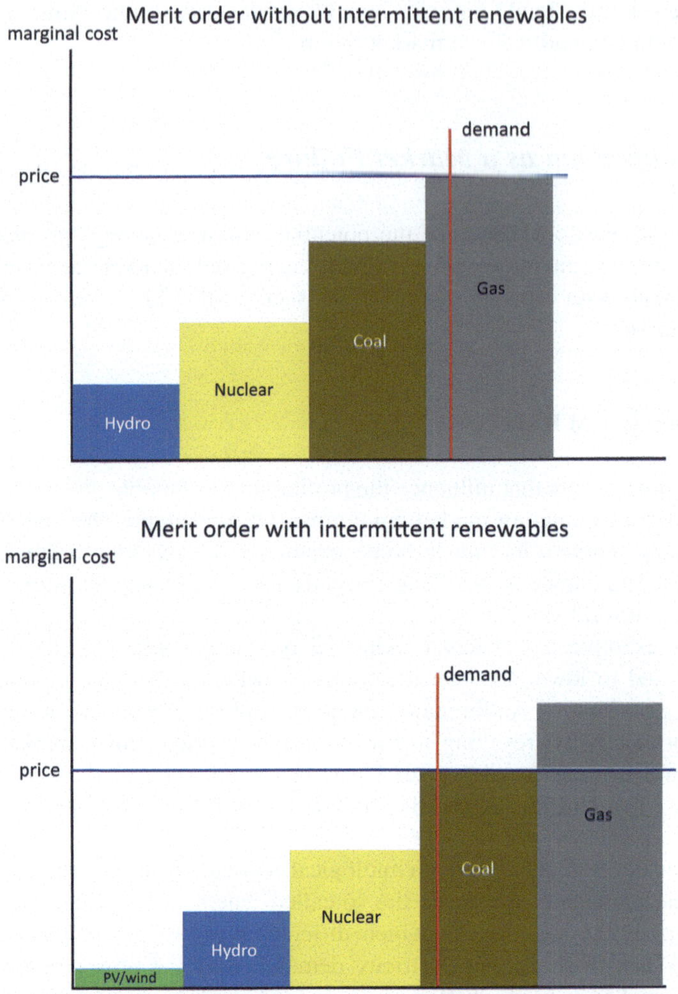

Fig. 1 The merit order effect. Source: own work using information from Sia Partners (2013)

produce electricity. With rising demand, other plants with higher marginal costs will enter the market. Finally, in times of peak demand, flexible plants with high marginal costs such as gas turbine plants will start producing electricity. Renewable energy sources have very low marginal costs of production,[42] since their operating costs are low and they do not need fuel, but mostly use free resources such as wind and solar energy. Feed-in-tariffs and other subsidies further lower costs. Solar energy production is often highest during the hours of the day when demand is also high. This means that in a time when expensive peak-load plants would normally start

[42]Nicolosi (2012), p. 10; Gonzalez-Diaz (2015), pp. 3, 5; Cludius et al. (2014), p. 303.

producing, solar energy lowers the electricity prices and shifts the merit order in the direction of the cheaper-producing plants.[43] The results are significantly lower electricity prices than would have been the case without the renewable energy production.[44] This so-called "merit order effect" has severe implications for the profitability of conventional (especially gas) power plants.[45]

To the extent that this phenomenon derives from technological innovation of renewables alone, it is considered a general commercial risk and not a market failure.[46] The legal environment, which often favours renewable energies over conventional forms of electricity production, however, also influences the merit order effect, may be considered a case of regulatory failure and will be discussed in the following section.

2.2.2 Government Interventions

Government interventions into the electricity markets severely affect market outcomes and involve both legislative, as well as regulatory action. An example are the subsidies for electricity from renewable energy sources, such as the Swiss feed-in tariffs. These subsidies and the corresponding increase in renewable capacity further reduce the wholesale electricity prices, which makes it tougher for conventional, flexible power plants to compete.[47] However, it should be noted that many countries also have massively subsidized conventional and nuclear power plants.[48] Laws that force grid operators to feed-in electricity from renewable sources with priority over all conventional producers also amplify the merit order effect described under Sect. 2.2.1 supra.[49] Such laws also exist in Switzerland.[50]

A second example of a government intervention that affects the profitability of flexible power plants are emissions trading schemes. While these are intended to reduce carbon-intensive electricity production, their design often leads to an initial spike in new conventional generating capacity: when emissions certificates are initially allocated free of charge, this creates strong incentives for new installations

[43]Nicolosi (2012), p. 10; Sensfuß et al. (2008), p. 3087; r2b research to business energy consulting (2014), p. 155; Cludius et al. (2014), p. 303; Keppler (2017), p. 563; Meyer and Gore (2015), p. 10.

[44]For a detailed analysis, see Sensfuß et al. (2008) and Cludius et al. (2014).

[45]For the effects on the types of power plants in the market, see Nicolosi (2012), p. 11 fig. 3.3; Sensfuß et al. (2008), pp. 3091 et seqq.

[46]For a general discussion of technical factors that necessitate capacity mechanisms, see Hawker et al. (2017), pp. 54 et seq.

[47]Perner and Riechmann (2015), p. 63. See Sect. 2.2.1 supra for a discussion of the merit order effect and the implications of subsidies for the low marginal costs of renewable energy sources.

[48]Coady et al. (2017), pp. 15 et seqq.; Badcock and Lenzen (2010), pp. 5043 et seqq.

[49]Sia Partners (2013). Such laws are, however, defended by Bundesverband Erneuerbare Energie (BEE) et al. (2012), pp. 17 et seq.

[50]Article 7a subsection 1 Energy Act, SR 730.0.

to be preponed, leading to a sudden overcapacity and thus lowering electricity prices.[51]

Finally, the issue of regulatory price caps has already been addressed above. For flexible power plants to be cost-efficient, the market must allow for sufficiently high scarcity (peak load) prices.[52] If laws set a price cap, such high peak load prices can no longer be reached, thus endangering the profitability of flexible power plants.[53] The effects of a price cap strongly depend on its exact level. While price caps set at the marginal costs of flexible power plants or lower will have the most dramatic effects, even higher price caps can cause inefficiencies.[54]

Such government interventions can severely affect the efficiency of wholesale electricity markets.[55] However, they should not be considered market failures, but may rather be seen as regulatory failures. The term "regulatory failure", as well as the broader term "government failure", are not as well-defined as the term market failure.[56] One author defines government failure in the context of regulation as "substantial imperfection in government performance".[57] Irrespective of whether the regulatory interventions described above match a definition of regulatory or government failure, they do not represent cases of market failure.[58] However, one might ask whether such potential regulatory failures may also justify additional regulatory interventions.

2.2.3 The Free Rider Problem

A free rider problem exists where a good or service benefits market participants who do not have to pay for it. This leads to an undersupply of that good or service.[59] The free rider problem often relates to public goods. These are goods that fulfil two criteria: Their consumption is non-rival, i.e. my consumption of the good does not

[51] Perner and Riechmann (2015), p. 63.

[52] r2b research to business energy consulting (2014), p. 38.

[53] r2b research to business energy consulting (2014), p. 38.

[54] r2b research to business energy consulting (2014), pp. 38 et seqq.

[55] For a more general discussion of political factors which influence electricity markets, see Hawker et al. (2017), p. 55.

[56] Orbach (2013), p. 46. Cf. Breyer (1979), pp. 586 et seq., who does not provide a specific definition of regulatory failure but instead lists criteria to help identify failing regulatory regimes. Fritsch (2014), p. 371 uses the categories of "political failure" (*Politikversagen*) and "bureaucratic failure" (*Bürokratieversagen*). Reasons for regulatory failure are explained by Hettich (2014), pp. 209 et seq.

[57] Orbach (2013), p. 56.

[58] Cf., however, Perner and Riechmann (2015), p. 67, who list the threat of regulatory interventions under market failures.

[59] Buchanan (1999), p. 83.

restrict the consumption by others,[60] and the good is non-exclusive, meaning that nobody can effectively be prevented from consuming the good.[61]

The generating capacity provided by power plants contributes to the security of a country's energy supply. Everyone, including owners of renewable energy plants, benefit from this effect. However, electricity consumers and generators do not equally share the costs of installing the additional capacity. Since the power plant's owner is only paid for electricity that is produced, the additional (potential) capacity and its effect on energy supply security are not remunerated. For this reason, the possible missing money problem can be characterized as a free rider problem.

However, it seems questionable whether the security of supply provided by the power plant owner is really a public good.[62] An increase in energy consumption would lower the capacity available to everyone else. Some authors thus argue that energy supply security is not "non-rival".[63] A good that is non-exclusive, but fails to meet the requirement of non-rivalry is known as a common-pool resource or common good.[64] Free rider problems affect common goods, as well as public goods.[65]

Still, as shown above in Sect. 2, there is no consensus among economists on whether there is a market failure in the energy-only market. This also extends to the free rider argument: electric utilities typically charge large (especially industrial) electricity consumers not only based on their consumption. Instead, such consumers face additional demand charges, which reflect the consumers' peak demand.[66] Thus, some argue that these demand charges reflect the respective consumer's demand for backup capacity so that at least this portion of the market does not "free ride".[67] The same authors further argue that there is no market failure even for the rest of the market, which does not pay demand charges. Since electricity tariffs consider the

[60] This was first formulated by Samuelson (1954), p. 387, who referred to public goods as "collective consumption goods".

[61] r2b research to business energy consulting (2014), p. 33. For an application of public goods theory to global problems such as climate change, see Nordhaus (1999).

[62] Elberg et al. (2012), p. 56, refer to security of supply as a public good. Perner and Riechmann (2015), p. 65 argue that the provision of capacity at least "has characteristics of a public good". Also see European Commission (2016a), p. 38 ("has certain features of a public good"). enervis et al. (2013), p. 40 refer to security of supply as a public good but acknowledge that it might rather be a common good in fn. 20. Also cf. Nicolosi (2012), pp. 2 et seq. and the detailed discussion at Keppler (2017), pp. 566 et seqq.

[63] r2b research to business energy consulting (2014), p. 34. Also cf. enervis et al. (2013), p. 40 fn. 20.

[64] Ostrom et al. (1999), p. 278; "Allmende-Gut" in German, see r2b research to business energy consulting (2014), pp. 34 et seq.

[65] Cf. Ostrom et al. (1999), p. 279.

[66] See Hledik and Greenstein (2016) for current plans to extend such demand charges to residential consumers.

[67] r2b research to business energy consulting (2014), p. 35, according to whom security of supply is a private good for the market segment of large consumers.

average load profile of the different consumer groups,[68] they hold that at least an indirect attribution of costs is possible, thus eliminating the free rider problem. In the future, with the introduction of Smart Metering technology, all consumers may face demand charges. Switzerland plans to allow demand charges for all consumers in the revised Energy Supply Regulation.[69] This would eliminate a large part of the free rider problem.[70]

The free rider problem, if it exists in energy-only markets, constitutes a market failure, since it leads to an under-provision of the common good (in this case, the security of supply or, more specifically, the necessary generating capacity).[71] It may therefore legitimize a response by the legislator.[72] This problem is different from the mere market risk of having to invest in expensive infrastructure during a time of low electricity prices.[73]

2.2.4 Summary of Results

The potential "missing money" problem derives from several developments in the electricity market. Some of them, such as the technological innovation in the renewable energy sector or the reduction of overcapacities in the generating market, constitute commercial risks that do not legitimize government interventions. Such government interventions themselves cause distortions in the market. Examples of this are subsidies for renewable electricity and price caps. It is questionable whether such interventions legitimize further regulatory or legislative action. Finally, the potential "missing money" problem has characteristics of a free rider problem. This is because security of supply may be regarded as a public or common good. However, economists debate both the existence of the problem itself, as well as the characterisation of security of supply as a public or common good.

As a result, there is currently no consensus among economists as to the existence of market failure in the energy-only market.

---

[68]For Switzerland, see Article 6 subsection 3 Electricity Supply Act (StromVG), SR 734.7.

[69]Article 18 of the draft Regulation. See Federal Department of the Environment, Transport, Energy and Communications (2017), p. 13.

[70]European Commission, decision C (2014) 5083 final, p. 34 table 1. Also cf. Keppler (2017), p. 570.

[71]Cf. Coffee (1984), p. 725 for public goods.

[72]A somewhat more cautious assessment ("could potentially justify") can be found at Perner and Riechmann (2015), p. 66. Cf. the critical opinion by Pasour (1981).

[73]See Sect. 2.2.1 supra; Perner and Riechmann (2015), pp. 66 et seq.

3 Possible Capacity Mechanisms

Studies have proposed many different capacity mechanisms to address the potential missing money problem. This paper uses the term "capacity mechanisms" to refer to any mechanism that remunerates the provision of capacity in addition to or outside of the energy-only market.[74] It is not possible to discuss the entire variety of possible mechanisms in this paper. An inquiry by the European Commission identified 35 different capacity mechanisms in the EU alone.[75] Instead, the following section attempts to group the most often discussed mechanisms together based on their main characteristics. The most important differences are whether the reserve capacity also participates in the regular energy-only market and whether a central agency contracts the capacity or individual market participants make this decision.[76] In addition to the number of different mechanisms, the nomenclature is quite inconsistent across different publications.[77] In this paper, the following categories and terms are used (Fig. 2).

3.1 Strategic Reserve

The strategic reserve creates a certain amount of backup capacity, which supplements the regular generating capacity in times of need. A central agency, for example a transmission systems operator (TSO) or regulatory agency,[78] determines the required capacity, e.g. for the next few years.[79] The central agency then contracts that capacity from qualifying[80] generators, e.g. from the bidder with the lowest price during an auction.[81] This capacity is then taken out of the general (energy-only) market and only sold on the market when a trigger criterion is met.[82] Such a trigger could be, for example, a certain price level in the energy-only market.[83] The

[74]Cf. Bundesverband Erneuerbare Energie (BEE) et al. (2012), pp. 27 et seq. Also see r2b research to business energy consulting (2014), p. 1.

[75]European Commission (2016b), p. 9. For a thorough discussion, see European Commission (2016a), pp. 50 et seqq.

[76]Cf. Perner and Riechmann (2015), p. 69.

[77]Cf., for example, the terms used by Hawker et al. (2017), p. 53.

[78]See Büro für Energiewirtschaft und technische Planung GmbH (BET) (2011), pp. 47 et seq.

[79]Gonzalez-Diaz (2015), p. 10; Elberg et al. (2012), pp. 49 et seq.

[80]E.g. in terms of reliability of the generating capacity or the time it takes to provide the contracted capacity, Frontier Economics and consentec (2014), p. 35.

[81]Cf. Gonzalez-Diaz (2015), p. 10; Elberg et al. (2012), p. 50.

[82]Gonzalez-Diaz (2015), p. 10; Frontier Economics and consentec (2014), p. 34; Elberg et al. (2012), p. 47; Bundesverband Erneuerbare Energie (BEE) et al. (2012), p. 33; also cf. r2b research to business energy consulting (2014), p. 87.

[83]Gonzalez-Diaz (2015), p. 11; Frontier Economics and consentec (2014), pp. 34 et seq.; Elberg et al. (2012), p. 48.

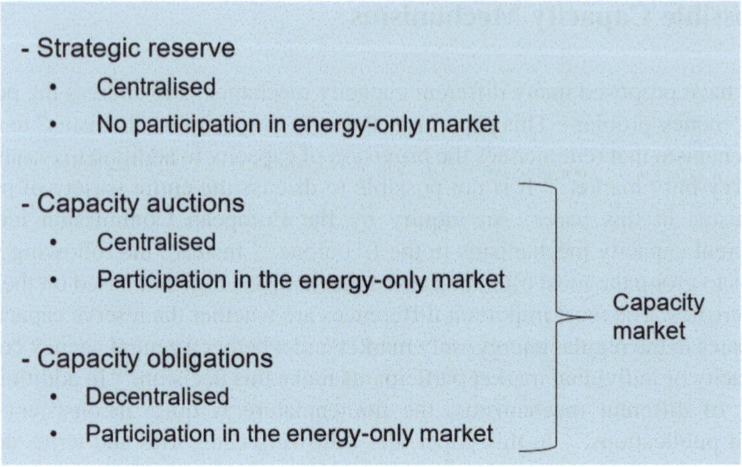

Fig. 2 Capacity auction and capacity obligation schemes are often called "capacity markets". The broader term "capacity mechanisms" also includes strategic reserves in addition to the other two categories. These capacity mechanisms can theoretically apply both to existing and newly built power plants, depending on the specific scheme (Gonzalez-Diaz 2015, p. 7; Frontier Economics and consentec 2014, p. 31)

generators that are part of the strategic reserve then offer their electricity at the trigger price level.[84]

According to this design, the strategic reserve is a measure of last resort to prevent an interruption of electricity supply in rare cases of exceptional demand.[85] Should the generators not deliver the contracted capacity despite the trigger event, a penalty would have to be paid by the respective power plant owner.[86] Some authors suggest that a penalty could be awarded before a trigger event arises, if the capacity is not held ready.[87] This might be useful in the case of newly built power plants, where an additional penalty could already set in once construction of the plant is not accomplished in due time.

The central agency may contract the capacity several years in advance, and proposed contract durations range from one to twenty years.[88] Some authors suggest that the contract duration should be long for newly built power plants and shorter for existing plants.[89] The contracted capacity is often rather small compared to the

[84]Elberg et al. (2012), p. 48.

[85]Frontier Economics and consentec (2014), p. 34; r2b research to business energy consulting (2014), p. 87.

[86]Frontier Economics and consentec (2014), p. 35; Elberg et al. (2012), p. 51.

[87]Elberg et al. (2012), p. 51.

[88]Frontier Economics and consentec (2014), p. 35; Elberg et al. (2012), p. 50; Büro für Energiewirtschaft und technische Planung GmbH (BET) (2011), p. 43.

[89]Elberg et al. (2012), p. 50.

aggregate peak demand of the respective country.[90] The central agency usually refinances its capacity purchase through levies, for example a surcharge on the grid fees.[91]

Often, old power plants will be best suited for the strategic reserve.[92] Strategic reserve mechanisms may also allow demand response (DR) systems to participate in the auctions.[93] Demand response relates to a concept where electricity consumers are paid for their willingness to reduce their consumption in times of peak load.[94] In that case, they would not offer generating capacity, but a reduction in demand.

Since generators in the strategic reserve have to offer their electricity at the trigger price, the strategic reserve mechanism creates an implicit price cap in the wholesale market.[95] The higher the trigger price, the more generating capacity will be traded in the energy-only market.[96] Low trigger prices, in contrast, will force energy sources with relatively high marginal costs out of the market.[97] High trigger prices may lead to a situation where the market price is higher than the marginal cost of the last available generator, but lower than the trigger price, leading to a lack of capacity.[98] For these reasons, finding the right trigger price is crucial,[99] but may be difficult. Another problem with strategic reserves is determining the necessary reserve capacity.[100] Also, political pressure because of rising electricity prices could lead to an inefficiently low trigger price.[101] This may create a situation where less capacity is offered in the energy-only market.[102]

Strategic reserves are used in Sweden and Finland, who mostly rely on hydropower and need the reserves in case of a particularly dry year.[103] Since Switzerland

---

[90]Frontier Economics and consentec (2014), p. 34 provide an example of 5 GW reserve capacity compared to the German peak load of approximately 80 GW. See also Elberg et al. (2012), p. 54.

[91]Frontier Economics and consentec (2014), p. 36; r2b research to business energy consulting (2014), p. 87; Elberg et al. (2012), p. 51.

[92]Gonzalez-Diaz (2015), p. 11. Also see European Commission (2016a), p. 58: "Reserves are typically not designed to attract new generation capacity".

[93]Cf. Elberg et al. (2012), p. 50. These are also often referred to as demand side management (DSM) or demand side response (DSR).

[94]For a discussion of demand response see Jacobs (2015), pp. 896 et seqq. and the response by Huber (2015), pp. 89 et seq. "Demand response" may also simply refer to pricing schemes where consumers are charged a higher price in times of high demand, see Jacobs (2015), p. 897. The broader term "demand side management" often includes programs aimed at improving the consumers' energy efficiency in addition to a demand response mechanism.

[95]Elberg et al. (2012), p. 49.

[96]Elberg et al. (2012), p. 49.

[97]Elberg et al. (2012), p. 49. Also see Meyer and Gore (2015), p. 11.

[98]Elberg et al. (2012), p. 51.

[99]Meyer and Gore (2015), p. 11.

[100]Elberg et al. (2012), pp. 54 et seq.

[101]Elberg et al. (2012), p. 55.

[102]Elberg et al. (2012), p. 55. Also see Meyer and Gore (2015), p. 11.

[103]Gonzalez-Diaz (2015), p. 11.

also relies heavily on hydropower, the practical experiences in the aforementioned countries may help Swiss decision makers. Currently, it seems as if both Sweden and Finland may abolish their strategic reserves in the future.[104]

3.2 Capacity Auctions (Capacity Markets)

Capacity auctions are like strategic reserves in that a central agency sets the required capacity and then auctions it off to the lowest bidder.[105] The agency's transactions are also financed through some form of levy on the consumer's electricity prices.[106] Again, depending on the mechanism, demand response systems may participate in the auctions.[107] However, there are significant differences to a strategic reserve:

Most importantly, the contracted capacity is not excluded from the general (energy-only) market.[108] Instead, the additional capacity remuneration is to be used for the construction and/or operation of the plant, which then sells the electricity normally.[109] Thus, capacity auctions create a true, separate market for capacity as reflected in the term "capacity markets".

Some of the proposed capacity auction mechanisms only apply to newly built power plants[110]; others may also apply to existing plants.[111] Some authors suggest splitting the two capacity markets into one for existing and one for newly built power plants.[112] The European Commission prefers a single market for old and new plants to increase competition.[113]

One potential negative side effect of capacity auctions is that the additional electricity offered on the market may lower overall electricity prices even more.[114] This can lead to the so-called "waterbed effect", where generators gain additional revenue in the capacity market but lose a similar amount of money in the energy-

---

[104]Naas-Bibow and Ramstad Wenger (2015), p. 332. Originally, Sweden was going to abolish its strategic reserve from 2019/2020 on, but has now extended the scheme through 2025, European Commission (2016a), p. 58.

[105]Gonzalez-Diaz (2015), p. 13; r2b research to business energy consulting (2014), p. 87; Elberg et al. (2012), pp. 56 and 57 et seq. for the specifics of a so-called "descending clock auction".

[106]r2b research to business energy consulting (2014), p. 87; Elberg et al. (2012), p. 62; Büro für Energiewirtschaft und technische Planung GmbH (BET) (2011), p. 49.

[107]Elberg et al. (2012), p. 64.

[108]r2b research to business energy consulting (2014), p. 87.

[109]Gonzalez-Diaz (2015), p. 13; r2b research to business energy consulting (2014), p. 87.

[110]Gonzalez-Diaz (2015), p. 13.

[111]Cf. r2b research to business energy consulting (2014), p. 87; Elberg et al. (2012), pp. 58, 66 et seq.

[112]Öko-Institut et al. (2012).

[113]European Commission (2016b), p. 13.

[114]Cf. Gonzalez-Diaz (2015), p. 13.

only market.[115] Another negative consequence might be an incentive for investors who would have built a power plant in any case to wait for the additional remuneration from the capacity mechanism, thus generating windfall profits.[116]

There are some practical experiences with capacity auctions. For example, the European Commission has approved a capacity auction mechanism in the United Kingdom, a decision that is currently being challenged in court.[117]

3.3 Capacity Obligations

Capacity obligations are decentralized capacity mechanisms.[118] Instead of tasking a central institution (such as the transmission systems operator or the regulatory agency) with the acquisition of reserve capacity, the capacity obligation extends to a large group of market participants. For example, energy supply companies could be required to contract a certain amount of reserve capacity, e.g. in relation to their peak demand.[119] Depending on the specific design, this scheme could include "capacity certificates",[120] which may be traded in a secondary market. A potential penalty system could demand that any electricity purchase is "covered" by a corresponding amount of capacity certificates,[121] or that electric utilities must possess enough certificates to cover their customers' aggregate peak demand.[122] The price of such certificates would be paid in addition to the electricity price itself, thereby providing power plant owners with an additional income source.[123] The capacity providers would themselves be penalized if they could not deliver the contracted capacity, either irrespective of the market situation or in a time of "scarcity", which could be defined e.g. as a time in which the wholesale electricity price exceeds a certain threshold.[124] Therefore, the capacity obligation scheme

[115]Perner and Riechmann (2015), p. 70.

[116]Cf. Gonzalez-Diaz (2015), p. 13.

[117]European Commission, decision C(2014) 5083 final. See the summary at OJ 2014 C 348/1. The pending court case has the case number T-793/14, see OJ 2015 C 81/21. Regarding the commission decision, see Gonzalez-Diaz (2015), p. 13; Hancher (2015), pp. 177 et seqq. as well as the discussion in Sect. 5.1.

[118]Frontier Economics and consentec (2014), pp. 36 et seq. exclusively use the term "decentralized, comprehensive mechanism". The term "capacity obligations" is used by Avenir Suisse (2013), pp. 40 et seq.

[119]Avenir Suisse (2013), p. 40.

[120]Frontier Economics and consentec (2014), p. 36.

[121]r2b research to business energy consulting (2014), p. 88.

[122]Cf. European Commission (2016a), p. 66 for the mechanism that France is currently implementing.

[123]r2b research to business energy consulting (2014), p. 88.

[124]Frontier Economics and consentec (2014), p. 37; r2b research to business energy consulting (2014), p. 88 with fn. 119.

includes potential penalties for both sides, the market participant who contracts the capacity, as well as the supplier of that capacity.[125]

While this mechanism is "decentralized" in the sense that market participants contract the energy instead of a central agency,[126] the trade for capacity could also take place in a centralized market place, e.g. an exchange.[127] This would, in theory, have the benefit of increasing liquidity and competition in the market and should lower prices and transactions costs.[128] Electricity consumers could also participate in these markets, offering a reduction of their consumption when needed.[129] Market participants could trade capacity both in the short and in the long term, depending on the exact characteristics of the mechanism.[130]

An advantage of this mechanism is the incentives it creates for electricity utilities to lower the peak load consumption of their customers, for example through real-time tariffs.[131] The capacity market should also lead to sufficient funds for investors in new generating capacity when there is not enough capacity in the market.[132] However, controlling whether all parties involved have fulfilled their obligations could demand great regulatory efforts.[133] These controls might require a central "regulator", either an actual regulatory agency or, for example, a transmission systems operator.[134] This counteracts some of the benefits of a decentralized system.

Some practical experiences with decentralized mechanisms exist, e.g. on the east coast of the United States.[135] In Europe, France is currently implementing a decentralized capacity obligation scheme.[136]

---

[125] See European Commission (2016a), p. 66 for France.

[126] Frontier Economics and consentec (2014), p. 36; r2b research to business energy consulting (2014), pp. 87 et seq.

[127] Avenir Suisse (2013), p. 41.

[128] Cf. Avenir Suisse (2013), p. 41.

[129] Avenir Suisse (2013), p. 41. Large consumers, such as industrial cold storage facilities, would seem the most likely candidates for this.

[130] Cf. Avenir Suisse (2013), pp. 41 et seq. This could also be left entirely to the involved parties, see Frontier Economics and consentec (2014), p. 38.

[131] Avenir Suisse (2013), p. 41.

[132] Avenir Suisse (2013), p. 41.

[133] Avenir Suisse (2013), p. 41.

[134] Cf. Frontier Economics and consentec (2014), p. 36. For the latter, see Avenir Suisse (2013), p. 41.

[135] Gonzalez-Diaz (2015), p. 14.

[136] European Commission (2016a), p. 65.

4 Potential Alternatives to Capacity Mechanisms

Several alternative options may reduce the need for capacity mechanisms. For example, the discussion in Sect. 3.1 above has introduced demand response mechanisms. These could reduce the needed production in times of peak demand.[137] As shown above, the price inelasticity in electricity markets is one of the reasons for the potential "missing money" problem. Better integration of price signals on the demand side could therefore help lessen this problem.[138] New "Smart metering" technologies that allow real-time pricing are going to be essential for this.[139] However, demand response's potential for demand reduction may not be high enough to eliminate the need for capacity mechanisms in the short-to-medium term.[140]

The larger the (physical) electricity market is, the easier it is to balance demand and supply since high and low demand and supply in different areas of the market offset each other.[141] In a sufficiently large physical market, the negative effects of volatile production from renewable energies are markedly lower.[142] For this reason, increasing the cross-border (interconnector) transmission capacities would help reduce the need for capacity mechanisms.[143] Increased cross-border flows would also increase the liquidity in the market, which results in better price signals for generators.[144]

Storage technologies are another option to reduce the need for capacity mechanisms. By storing excess electricity and converting the stored energy back to electricity in times of peak demand, storage can integrate volatile renewable production and reduce the need for peak-load power plants.[145] Currently, most large-

[137]Gonzalez-Diaz (2015), p. 8; r2b research to business energy consulting (2014), pp. 49 et seq.; Büro für Energiewirtschaft und technische Planung GmbH (BET) (2011), p. 32; Bundesverband Erneuerbare Energie (BEE) et al. (2012), pp. 39 et seq.

[138]Cf. r2b research to business energy consulting (2014), pp. 50 et seqq.; Avenir Suisse (2013), p. 58.

[139]Perner and Riechmann (2015), p. 68; Avenir Suisse (2013), pp. 58 et seq.

[140]Gonzalez-Diaz (2015), p. 10.

[141]r2b research to business energy consulting (2014), p. 46.

[142]r2b research to business energy consulting (2014), pp. 46 et seqq.

[143]According to r2b research to business energy consulting (2014), pp. 48 et seq., the planned investments in the trans-European grid should suffice to achieve this goal. Cf. the sceptical assessment by Büro für Energiewirtschaft und technische Planung GmbH (BET) (2011), pp. 33 et seq.

[144]Perner and Riechmann (2015), p. 68.

[145]Regarding storage options as an alternative to capacity mechanisms, cf. the critical assessment by Büro für Energiewirtschaft und technische Planung GmbH (BET) (2011), pp. 31 et seq.; also see Bundesverband Erneuerbare Energie (BEE) et al. (2012), pp. 37 et seqq.

scale storage technologies are still in a developmental stage.[146] In the future, storage facilities could even participate in capacity mechanisms, if the latter is needed.[147]

As a rather extreme measure, some have even called for (additional)[148] subsidies for conventional or nuclear power plants.[149] In Switzerland, politicians and electric utilities have demanded subsidies for nuclear, hydropower and conventional plants to make up for lower electricity prices because of foreign renewable energy subsidy schemes.[150] However, such subsidies for conventional plants could incentivize an overproduction by base-load power plants.[151] This could further lower electricity prices and even exacerbate the "missing money" problem for flexible peak-load plants.[152]

As the discussion shows, several options may serve as an alternative to capacity mechanisms. Due to the potential design flaws and inefficiencies of capacity mechanisms, some authors suggest that Governments should exploit these alternatives before considering capacity mechanisms.[153]

5 Situation in the European Union and in Switzerland

5.1 Legal Restrictions Under EU State Aid Law

5.1.1 The State Aid Frame Work for Capacity Mechanisms

In 2015, the European Commission launched an inquiry into capacity mechanisms to assess whether these constitute state aid, whether they are needed in EU electricity markets and how they should be designed to avoid distortions of the market. The Commission published its final report in November 2016.[154] The report concludes that capacity mechanisms "in principle" constitute state aid under EU competition

[146] KEMA Consulting GmbH (2013), pp. 79 et seq.

[147] Frontier Economics and consentec (2014), p. 37.

[148] See fn. 48 supra.

[149] See the discussion at Avenir Suisse (2013), pp. 33 et seq.

[150] Christoph Blocher, interview in the newspaper Tagesanzeiger, 15 December 2016, available at www.tagesanzeiger.ch/schweiz/standard/es-bleibt-nur-die-subventionierung/story/17521878; Markus Häfliger, Stromlobby fordert Not-Subventionen für Wasserkraft, Tagesanzeiger, 19 April 2017, available at www.tagesanzeiger.ch/schweiz/standard/stromlobby-fordert-notsubventionen-fuer-wasserkraft/story/23086774.

[151] Avenir Suisse (2013), p. 34.

[152] Avenir Suisse (2013), p. 34.

[153] Perner and Riechmann (2015), pp. 76 et seq.

[154] European Commission (2016b).

law.[155] Regarding the current situation in European electricity markets, the report finds a high level of supply security, with a tendency towards overcapacities.[156] However, the report also concedes that the situation varies between Member States, and that new energy policies in countries such as Germany may change this situation in the near future.[157] The Commission points to the inability of electricity markets to establish sufficiently high scarcity prices and to many consumers' inability to reduce their demand in times of peak load.[158]

As an answer to a potential lack of capacity in energy-only markets, the Commission report favours market reforms, such as a removal of price caps or the facilitation of demand response, over the introduction of capacity mechanisms.[159] However, the Commission also discusses the criteria under which it will evaluate capacity mechanisms based on the Guidelines on State aid for environmental protection and energy.[160] The Guidelines communicate the Commission's approach to the evaluation of state aid under Article 107(3)(c) of the Treaty on the Functioning of the European Union (TFEU).

5.1.2 Market Failure as a Requirement for Government Intervention

The first test that the Commission applies to capacity mechanisms is whether it is actually needed to address "a well-defined problem of security of supply that the market cannot solve by itself".[161] The Member State in question must provide evidence for this need, and include an identification of market failures, as well as a quantification of the expected capacity gap.[162] The Commission is less likely to accept capacity mechanisms the more regulatory interventions by the Member State have distorted electricity markets.[163]

---

[155] European Commission (2016b), p. 2. For a thorough discussion of the state aid problem, see Hancher (2015), who comes to the same conclusion, id. at pp. 170 et seq. Further, see Hawker et al. (2017), p. 56.

[156] European Commission (2016b), p. 3.

[157] European Commission (2016b), pp. 3 et seq. For a detailed discussion, see European Commission (2016a), pp. 10 et seqq.

[158] European Commission (2016b), pp. 4 et seq.

[159] European Commission (2016b), pp. 5 et seqq. Regarding the different options, see European Commission (2016a), pp. 40 et seqq.

[160] European Commission, Communication from the Commission, Guidelines on State aid for environmental protection and energy 2014–2020, OJ 2014 C 200/1. The Guidelines discuss capacity mechanisms in section 3.9.

[161] European Commission (2016b), p. 7. Note that in its report, the Commission omits the step of assessing whether the measure serves a well-defined objective of common interest, cf. Guidelines (fn. 153), section 3.2.1. Ensuring security of electricity supply should be regarded as such an objective.

[162] European Commission (2016b), p. 7. See the Guidelines (fn. 153), section 3.9.2.

[163] This is especially true for price caps, see Hancher (2015), p. 173.

As shown in Sect. 2, there is considerable debate among economists as to whether the "missing money" problem constitutes a market failure. Since the European Commission has explicitly stipulated the requirement of a market failure in the Guidelines on state aid in the energy sector, an economic assessment now has legal implications. This is an especially illustrative example of the interrelation between law and economics in the energy sector. The question now is how the European Commission can test the legal requirement of a market failure if economists disagree on its existence. A similar question arises for the judges should a decision by the Commission be challenged in the European courts.[164] It would seem inequitable for the courts to be able to rely on one economic opinion while dismissing others, especially since most judges in Europe have no economic training. The underlying issue of how lawyers may apply legal standards that use economic criteria seems to warrant further academic attention, not just in the field of energy law.[165] If the existence of a market failure is a legal prong, how can lawyers (e.g., judges dealing with the issue) establish whether this criterion is fulfilled? Since the concept of market failure allows for many different lines of argument, traditional expert opinions may not provide sufficient support to courts and would only show one narrow side of the discussion. Is the existence of a market failure even a "fact", which could be introduced as evidence?[166]

Traditionally, European courts have granted the Commission a wide margin of discretion in its state aid decisions, especially concerning economic questions.[167] The courts only assess whether the Commission has followed the procedural rules, whether the reasoning is logically consistent, whether the facts have been properly determined, and whether there are no obvious mistakes or abuses of power in using the Commission's discretion.[168]

Regarding the Commission and its specialized Directorate-Generals, there is certainly more economic expertise among the staff than among most courts, which justifies a certain judicial restraint. However, there has always been debate on whether the democratic legitimation of the Commission is comparable to that of the Member States' governments.[169] Also, the principle of subsidiarity (Article 5 (3) TEU) requires that legislative decisions are made at the lowest possible level, i.e. at the national rather than the supranational level, unless a national measure would be insufficient. Granting Member States a margin of discretion vis-à-vis

[164]For a recent state aid decision on the energy sector that was challenged by a Member State, see General Court, case T-47/15, ECLI:EU:T:2016:281—Germany/Commission.

[165]For the similar problem of econometric evidence in EU competition law, see Lianos and Genakos (2012).

[166]Cf. the discussion at Lianos and Genakos (2012), pp. 82 et seqq. for econometrics, which pose similar questions.

[167]Kühling (2012), N 108 et seqq.

[168]Kühling (2012), N 109.

[169]Regarding the Commission's increased democratic legitimation since the Treaty of Lisbon, see Ruffert (2016), N 56 et seq. For a discussion of the situation before the Treaty of Lisbon, see Majone (1998).

supranational institutions supports this principle.[170] Therefore, it can be argued that the Commission should grant the Member States a similar margin of discretion in determining a market failure. The Commission should only assess whether the Member State has applied accepted economics methods in determining the market failure. In cases where economists disagree on the existence of a market failure, the Commission should not strike down state aid mechanisms simply by following a different economic opinion than the Member State.

5.1.3 The Commission's Approach in the UK State Aid Case

The Commission's decision on the UK's capacity auction scheme seems to be consistent with this proposal. First, the Commission describes the UK's submission concerning the existence of a market failure.[171] It names two market failures identified by the British Government and interestingly uses the indicative mode, making it seem as if the Commission views the UK's submission as a given fact: "The first market failure is that reliability is a public good. [...] The second market failure is the 'missing money' problem."[172] Referring to the "missing money" problem, the Commission states that it "has been identified and described in academic literature and affects energy-only markets".[173] Later, however, the Commission uses language which suggests that the Commission nevertheless distinguishes between the UK's submission and its own assessment, starting several sentences with the words "The UK submits that..."[174]

In its assessment of the UK capacity mechanism, the Commission holds that the UK has used appropriate methodology in establishing a potential future lack of capacity: "[T]he UK has put in place a methodology to identify the generation adequacy concern. The modelling work undertaken by the UK shows that the enduring reliability adequacy standard [...] may reach critical levels as of 2018/2019."[175] However, instead of assessing whether there is also a market failure in the UK's electricity market, the Commission then simply relies on the British Government's submission: "[...] [A]s described in recitals (83) to (86), the UK has identified two market failures that prevent the market from bringing the necessary capacity to meet the established generation adequacy standard."[176] The Commission then discusses how the UK capacity mechanism addresses the characteristics of reliability as a public good and the "missing money problem".[177]

---

[170]Fabbrini (2015), pp. 7 et seqq.

[171]European Commission, decision C (2014) 5083 final, pp. 20 et seq.

[172]European Commission, decision C (2014) 5083 final, p. 20.

[173]European Commission, decision C (2014) 5083 final, p. 20.

[174]European Commission, decision C (2014) 5083 final, p. 21, marg. no. 86 et seq.

[175]European Commission, decision C (2014) 5083 final, pp. 31 et seq.

[176]European Commission, decision C (2014) 5083 final, p. 34.

[177]European Commission, decision C (2014) 5083 final, p. 34 table 1.

This approach by the Commission seems to grant the Member States a considerable margin of discretion. If the Member State uses economic models to show a potential future lack of capacity, the Commission seems to accept this submission without a detailed assessment of its own. In addition, the Commission seems to hold the view that the "missing money problem" has been sufficiently established in the academic literature and that security of supply, at least in the current market without smart metering technologies and real-time pricing, has characteristics of a public good.

5.1.4 Further Requirements Under EU State Aid Law

If the Member State manages to prove the need for an intervention because of market failure, the Commission will then assess the mechanism based on the principles of appropriateness and proportionality, its incentive effects and negative effects on competition and trade.[178] In this context, the Commission has stated a preference for technology-neutral, market-wide mechanisms that include the largest possible number of potential capacity providers.[179] The Commission further advises that market-wide capacity mechanisms should be open to cross-border participation.[180]

5.2 *Implications of EU State Aid Law for Swiss Energy Regulation*

While Switzerland is not a Member State of the EU, Swiss legislation in the energy sector often considers EU law.[181] One reason for this is the planned bilateral agreement on the energy market, which has been put on hold after the Swiss popular vote on immigration restrictions,[182] but is still an option for the future.[183] The Swiss legislator thus has an incentive to avoid implementing laws that would violate a possible future energy agreement with the EU.

Right now, since Switzerland is not an EU Member State, EU competition law does not bind the Swiss legislator. In case the EU and Switzerland agree on a

[178]Regarding these principles, see the Guidelines (fn. 153), section 3.1. Also see the contribution by Régis Lanneau in this volume for a general discussion of EU state aid principles.

[179]European Commission (2016b), p. 13 et seq. Also cf. the Guidelines (fn. 153), sections 3.9.3. and 3.9.6.

[180]European Commission (2016b), p. 16. Also see the Guidelines (fn. 153), section 3.9.6. See Hawker et al. (2017), pp. 56 et seq. on the effects of cross-border participation. For a discussion of a possible regulatory framework for such cross-border participation, see Mastropietro et al. (2015).

[181]See, for example, BBl 2013 7561, pp. 7584 et seq.

[182]AS 2014 1391.

[183]For a thorough discussion, see Hettich et al. (2015).

bilateral agreement on the energy sector, this agreement would likely introduce EU state aid rules to the Swiss energy industry.[184] Should the Commission's Guidelines on State aid for environmental protection and energy apply to such an Agreement, the Swiss legislator may have to prove that a market failure exists, but should be granted a considerable margin of discretion in making this assessment.

Currently, the Swiss energy-only market features a high level of security of supply compared to other European countries.[185] For this reason, there is no present need for capacity mechanisms in Switzerland.[186] If this situation changed in the future, the question would arise whether the legislator should introduce capacity mechanisms.

If the European neighbour states implement capacity mechanisms, the Swiss legislator may have to react.[187] Since European capacity mechanisms would lower the prices in the (energy-only) wholesale electricity markets, the profitability of Swiss power plants could be called into question.[188] A participation of Swiss power plants in European capacity mechanisms may be possible, at least in the case of a bilateral agreement on energy. However, this would force Swiss power plants to hold their capacity ready for scarcity situations in the neighbouring countries, thus possibly endangering Swiss supply security.[189] Therefore, a Swiss capacity mechanism may become the better option.

In a remarkable move, the Swiss Federal Office of Energy, the Swiss federal energy regulator ElCom and the largest associations of electric utilities have issued a position paper on a German green book for a future energy market design.[190] Because of the potential effects on the Swiss electricity market, the position paper recommends that Germany should not introduce capacity mechanisms.[191] In the new "Electricity Market Act", Germany has decided against capacity markets but has introduced a strategic reserve.[192]

If the European neighbour states abstain from introducing capacity mechanisms, a unilateral introduction of capacity mechanisms in Switzerland does not seem preferable.[193] Due to the small size of the Swiss electricity market, cross-border

[184] For example, the Bilateral Agreement on Air Transport (SR 0.748.127.192.68) has introduced state aid rules modeled after Article 107 TFEU in Articles 13, 14 of the Agreement. See Hoffet et al. (2015), p. 2.

[185] ElCom (2016), p. 14.

[186] Avenir Suisse (2013), p. 51.

[187] See Meyer and Gore (2015), pp. 12 et seqq.; Hawker et al. (2017), pp. 55 et seq. on cross-border effects of capacity mechanisms.

[188] Avenir Suisse (2013), pp. 52 et seq.

[189] Avenir Suisse (2013), p. 53.

[190] Swiss Federal Office for Energy (SFOE) et al. (2015).

[191] Swiss Federal Office for Energy (SFOE) et al. (2015), p. 5.

[192] §§ 13e et seqq. Energy Industry Act (EnWG) as amended by the Electricity Market Act, BGBl. 2016 I 1786.

[193] In general, unilaterally implemented capacity mechanisms tend to have negative (cross-border) effects, see Meyer and Gore (2015), pp. 12 et seqq. Also cf. Hawker et al. (2017), pp. 55 et seq.

trade may have a larger impact on the profitability of Swiss power plants than a Swiss capacity mechanism might have.[194] The largest association of Swiss electric utilities has spoken out against the introduction of Swiss capacity mechanisms, but believes that Swiss producers should be allowed to participate in foreign capacity mechanisms.[195] From an economic standpoint, a Europe-wide single capacity mechanism may be preferable, but the current EU strategy seems to focus on national mechanisms only.[196] In a recent Swiss parliamentary debate on energy policy, politicians from two different parties have brought up the issue of capacity mechanisms, which shows that the topic is still on the agenda.[197]

Instead of introducing capacity mechanisms, the Swiss legislator may prefer to pursue options to improve the energy-only market's design. For example, according to one study, a full liberalisation of the Swiss electricity market could improve price signals for electricity consumers.[198] However, discussions with regional Swiss energy utilities show that there is often a fear of not being able to compete with larger corporations in a fully liberalized market. The political chances of a full market liberalisation, which was originally envisioned as part of the Energy Strategy 2050,[199] are currently unclear.

6 Conclusion

The discussion has shown that there is currently no consensus among economists as to whether electricity markets suffer from market failures that may soon threaten security of supply. This disagreement is especially relevant since EU state aid regulation, which may become more important for Switzerland in the future, requires proof of a market failure for Member States to implement capacity mechanisms. The paper suggests that states should have a margin of discretion in determining whether a market failure exists and how to address it. This seems to be consistent with the European Commission's approach to the United Kingdom's capacity auction scheme. Switzerland currently enjoys a high level of energy supply security. However, legislation in European neighbour states may affect the Swiss electricity market as well, which may necessitate Swiss capacity mechanisms in the future.

Acknowledgement The author thanks Jan Broulik from Tilburg University, Netherlands, James W. Coleman from Southern Methodist University, TX, Bruce R. Huber from the University of Notre Dame, IN and Régis Lanneau from Université Paris Nanterre, France, for helpful remarks.

---

[194] Cf. Avenir Suisse (2013), p. 53.

[195] Verband Schweizerischer Elektrizitätsunternehmen (VSE) (2016b), p. 3.

[196] Hawker et al. (2017), pp. 57 et seq.

[197] AB 2017 N 284 et seqq., opinions by Bastien Girod, Peter Schilliger and Christian Wasserfallen.

[198] Avenir Suisse (2013), pp. 59 et seq.

[199] BBl 2013 7561, p. 7583.

The author is part of the research project SCCER CREST (www.sccer-crest.ch), which is funded by The Swiss Innovation Agency (Innosuisse).

References

Avenir Suisse (2013) Keine Energiewende im Alleingang. Wie die Schweiz mit Ökostrom und Kapazitätsmärkten umgehen soll. Diskussionspapier. Zurich

Badcock J, Lenzen M (2010) Subsidies for electricity-generating technologies: a review. Energy Policy 38:5038–5047

Breyer S (1979) Analyzing regulatory failure. Mismatches, less restrictive alternatives, and reform. Harv Law Rev 92(3):547–609

Buchanan JM (1999) The demand and supply of public goods. Liberty Fund, Indianapolis

Bundesverband Erneuerbare Energie (BEE), Greenpeace Energy and IZES Institut für ZukunftsEnergieSysteme (2012) Kompassstudie Marktdesign. Leitideen für ein Design eines Stromsystems mit hohem Anteil fluktuierender erneuerbarer Energien. Bochum

Büro für Energiewirtschaft und technische Planung GmbH (BET) (2011) Kapazitätsmarkt. Rahmenbedingungen, Notwendigkeit und Eckpunkte einer Ausgestaltung. Studie im Auftrag des Bundesverbands Neuer Energieanbieter e.V. (bne), Aachen

Clò S (2011) European emissions trading in practice. An economic analysis. Edward Elgar Publishing, Cheltenham, UK

Cludius J, Hermann H, Matthes F, Graichen V (2014) The merit order effect of wind and photovoltaic electricity generation in Germany 2008–2016. Estimation and distributional implications. Energy Econ 44:302–313

Coady D, Sears IPL, Shang B (2017) How large are global fossil fuel subsidies? World Dev 91:11–27

Coffee JC (1984) Market failure and the economic case for a mandatory disclosure system. Va Law Rev 70:717–753

Eekhoff J, Jänsch J (2016) Marktversagen und Regulierung in Strom- und Gasmärkten. In: Baur JF, Salje P, Schmidt-Preuss M (eds) Regulierung in der Energiewirtschaft. Ein Praxishandbuch. Carl Heymanns Verlag, Cologne, pp 13–22

Eekhoff J, Vossler C (2016) Regulierung als Grundstein wettbewerblicher Ordnungspolitik. In: Baur JF, Salje P, Schmidt-Preuss M (eds) Regulierung in der Energiewirtschaft. Ein Praxishandbuch. Carl Heymanns Verlag, Cologne, pp 3–12

Eidenmüller H (2015) Effizienz als Rechtsprinzip. Möglichkeiten und Grenzen der ökonomischen Analyse des Rechts. Mohr Siebeck, Tübingen

Elberg C, Growitsch C, Höffler F, Richter J (2012) Untersuchungen zu einem zukunftsfähigen Strommarktdesign. Endbericht im Auftrag des Bundesministeriums für Wirtschaft und Technologie (BMWi). Energiewirtschaftliches Institut an der Universität zu Köln (EWI), Cologne

ElCom (2016) Stromversorgungsqualität 2015. Bericht der ElCom, Berne

enervis, BET and Verband Kommunaler Unternehmen (VKU) (2013) Ein zukunftsfähiges Energiemarktdesign für Deutschland. Langfassung. Berlin

European Commission (2016a) Commission Staff Working Document Accompanying the document Report from the Commission. Final Report of the Sector Inquiry on Capacity Mechanisms, SWD(2016) 385 final. Brussels

European Commission (2016b) Report from the Commission. Final Report of the Sector Inquiry on Capacity Mechanisms, COM(2016) 752 final. Brussels

Fabbrini F (2015) The margin of appreciation and the principle of subsidiarity: a comparison. iCourts Working Paper Series No. 15, 2015. Copenhagen

Federal Department of the Environment, Transport, Energy and Communications (2017) Erstes Massnahmenpaket zur Energiestrategie 2050. Teilrevision der Stromversorgungsverordnung. Erläuternder Bericht. Berne. Available at https://www.admin.ch/ch/d/gg/pc/documents/2833/1_Bericht-StromVV_de.pdf

Fritsch M (2014) Marktversagen und Wirtschaftspolitik. Mikroökonomische Grundlagen staatlichen Handelns. Vahlens, Munich

Frontier Economics; consentec (2014) Folgenabschätzung Kapazitätsmechanismen (Impact Assessment). Ein Bericht für das Bundesministerium für Wirtschaft und Energie (BMWi). Brussels, Cologne, London, Madrid

Gonzalez-Diaz FE (2015) EU policy on capacity mechanisms. In: Hancher L, de Hauteclocque A, Sadowska M (eds) Capacity mechanisms in the EU energy market. Law, policy, and economics. Oxford University Press, Oxford, pp 3–31

Hancher L (2015) Capacity mechanisms and state aid control. A European solution to the "Missing Money" problem? In: Hancher L, de Hauteclocque A, Sadowska M (eds) Capacity mechanisms in the EU energy market. Law, policy, and economics. Oxford University Press, Oxford, pp 157–181

Hawker G, Bell K, Gill S (2017) Electricity security in the European Union – the conflict between national capacity mechanisms and the single market. Energy Res Soc Sci 24:51–58

Hettich P (2014) Kooperative Risikovorsorge. Regulierte Selbstregulierung im Recht der operationellen und technischen Risiken. Schulthess, Zurich

Hettich P, Walther S, Tschudin SS (2015) Schweiz ohne Stromabkommen. Zurich

Hewicker C, Raadschelders J, Werner O, Ebert M, Engelhardt C, Mennel T, Verhaegh N (2013) Energiespeicher in der Schweiz. Bedarf, Wirtschaftlichkeit und Rahmenbedingungen im Kontext der Energiestrategie 2050. Schlussbericht. Study for the Swiss Federal Office of Energy, Berne

Hledik R, Greenstein G (2016) The distributional impacts of residential demand charges. Electr J 29 (6):33–41

Hoffet F, Dietrich M, Brei G, Girard A (2015) State Aid 2015 Switzerland. Available at: http://www.eversheds-sutherland.com/documents/global/switzerland/Publications/GCRCH_State_Aid_2015.pdf

Huber BR (2015) Demand response and market power. Iowa Law Rev Bull 100:87–96

Jacobs SB (2015) Bypassing federalism and the administrative law of negawatts. Iowa Law Rev 100:885–945

KEMA Consulting GmbH (2013) Energiespeicher in der Schweiz. Bedarf, Wirtschaftlichkeit und Rahmenbedingungen im Kontext der Energiestrategie 2050. Schlussbericht. Study for the Swiss Federal Office for Energy, Berne

Keppler JH (2017) Rationales for capacity remuneration mechanisms: security of supply externalities and asymmetric investment incentives. Energy Policy 105:562–570

Kühling J (2012) Art. 107 AEUV (TFEU). In: Streinz R (ed) EUV/AEUV. Vertrag über die Europäische Union und Vertrag über die Arbeitsweise der Europäischen Union. C.H.Beck, Munich

Lianos I, Genakos C (2012) Econometric evidence in EU competition law: an empirical and theoretical analysis. CLES Research Paper series 06/12. London

Majone G (1998) Europe's "Democratic Deficit". The question of standards. Eur Law J 4:5–28

Mastropietro P, Rodilla P, Batlle C (2015) National capacity mechanisms in the European internal energy market: opening the doors to neighbours. Energy Policy 82:38–47

Meyer R, Gore O (2015) Cross-border effects of capacity mechanisms: do uncoordinated market design changes contradict the goals of the European market integration? Energy Econ 51:9–20

Naas-Bibow J, Ramstad Wenger C (2015) Norway. In: Hancher L, de Hauteclocque A, Sadowska M (eds) Capacity mechanisms in the EU energy market. Law, policy, and economics. Oxford University Press, Oxford, pp 321–334

Nicolosi M (2012) Notwendigkeit von Kapazitätsmechanismen. Endbericht. Ecofys Institute

Nordhaus WD (1999) Global public goods and the problem of global warming. In: Annual lecture of the 3rd Toulouse conference of environment and resource economics. Toulouse

Öko-Institut; LBD Beratungsgesellschaft; Raue LLP (2012) Fokussierte Kapazitätsmärkte. Ein neues Marktdesign für den Übergang zu einem neuen Energiesystem. Study for the Umweltstiftung WWF Deutschland, Berlin

Orbach B (2013) What is government failure? Yale J Regul Online 30:44–56

Ostrom E, Burger J, Field CB, Norgaard RB, Policansky D (1999) Revisiting the commons. Local lessons, global challenges. Science 284:278–282

Pasour EC (1981) The free rider as a basis for government intervention. J Libertarian Stud 5:453–464

Perner J, Riechmann C (2015) Energy market design with capacity mechanisms. In: Hancher L, de Hauteclocque A, Sadowska M (eds) Capacity mechanisms in the EU energy market. Law, policy, and economics. Oxford University Press, Oxford, pp 59–78

r2b research to business energy consulting (2014) Arbeitspaket Funktionsfähigkeit EOM & Impact-Analyse Kapazitätsmechanismen. Endbericht Leitstudie Strommarkt im Auftrag des Bundesministeriums für Wirtschaft und Energie, Cologne

Ruffert M (2016) Art. 17 EUV (TEU). In: Calliess C, Ruffert M (eds) EUV/AEUV. Das Verfassungsrecht der Europäischen Union mit Europäischer Grundrechtecharta. Kommentar. C.H.Beck, Munich

Sailer F (2012) Das Recht der Energiespeicherung am Beispiel von Elektrizität. In: Müller T (ed) 20 Jahre Recht der Erneuerbaren Energien. Nomos, Baden-Baden, pp 777–811

Samuelson PA (1954) The pure theory of public expenditure. Rev Econ Stat 36:387–389

Sensfuß F, Ragwitz M, Genoese M (2008) The merit-order effect. A detailed analysis of the price effect of renewable electricity generation on spot market prices in Germany. Energy Policy 36:3086–3094

Sia Partners (2013) Power at a negative price. An insidious effect of a market model promoting renewables. Brussels. Available online at http://energy.sia-partners.com/power-negative-price-insidious-effect-market-model-promoting-renewables

Swiss Federal Office for Energy (SFOE); ElCom; swisselectric; swissgrid; Verband Schweizerischer Elektrizitätsunternehmen (VSE) (2015) Stellungnahme zum Diskussionspapier "Ein Strommarkt für die Energiewende" des Bundesministeriums für Wirtschaft und Energie (Grünbuch). Gemeinsame Position des Bundesamtes für Energie (BFE), der Eidgenössischen Elektrizitätskommission (ElCom), der Organisation der grossen schweizerischen Stromverbundunternehmen swisselectric, des Schweizer Übertragungsnetzbetreibers Swissgrid und des Verbandes Schweizerischer Elektrizitätsunternehmen (VSE), Berne

Verband Schweizerischer Elektrizitätsunternehmen (VSE) (2016a) Beiträge der Erzeugungstechnologien zur Stromversorgung und Stabilität des elektrischen Systems. Aarau

Verband Schweizerischer Elektrizitätsunternehmen (VSE) (2016b) VSE-Stellungnahme Revision StromVG - Schlussbericht Marktdesign. Aarau

Markus Schreiber Lucerne. Research Assistant and Ph.D. student at the Chair for European Law, International Law, Public Law and Comparative Public Law, University of Lucerne. CH-6002 Lucerne, Frohburgstrasse 3, P.O. Box 4466, Tel. + 41 41 229 59 47; Fax + 41 41 229 53 97. markus.schreiber@unilu.ch. Fields of Interest: Energy Law, Public Law (Constitutional Law, Administrative Law), European Law, Comparative Law.

Energy Labels: Nudging Policy to Avoid Trade Implications?

Rolf H. Weber

Abstract Labelling schemes have increasingly emerged as a valuable tool for improving environmental sustainability. Energy labels attempt at steering consumers' behaviour and producers' manufacturing patterns; this kind of steering can be induced by a corresponding nudging policy. Labels have the advantage of being the least trade restrictive measure although conflicts with WTO law are not excluded. Therefore, this contribution sheds light on the use of energy labels in the context of WTO law with a particular focus on public procurement procedures, since energy labels have become an important element therein ("green procurement").

1 Introduction

Since Ronald Coase's seminal essay more than half a century ago, the thereby resulting discipline of "law and economics" commends market-based instruments as the best means to avoid pollution of the environment and to achieve energy efficiency.[1] However, on the basis of the Coase theorem the realisation of environmental sustainability through improved energy efficiency is confronted with the difficulty in negotiating adequate solutions because of the geographic scope of externalities. Therefore, labelling schemes are gaining increased attention as a prominent example of an efficient environmental stewardship, for example labels related to energy consumption of electronic devices.

Finding the right measures to achieve energy efficiency is not an easy task for governments, given the various (often contradictory) interests involved in the legislation process and the plethora of possible instruments available. Since a single "ideal" instrument is not available, political bodies tend to resort to a mix between

[1]See Weber (2017), pp. 355–365.

R. H. Weber (✉)
Faculty of Law, University of Zurich, Zurich, Switzerland
e-mail: rolf.weber@rwi.uzh.ch

K. Mathis, B. R. Huber (eds.), *Energy Law and Economics*, Economic Analysis of Law in European Legal Scholarship 5, https://doi.org/10.1007/978-3-319-74636-4_12

regulatory restrictions ("command-and-control regulations") and marked-based instruments.[2]

Energy labels enable producers or retailers to easily transmit relevant information about the environmental performance of their products to the consumers who in turn are granted the opportunity to base their purchasing decision on this information. Energy labels belong to the policy tools attempting to promote sustainable trade; these so-called "trade-related environmental measures" are intended to incentivise the import or export of products that meet certain environmental standards. Contrary to other trade-related policies like import bans, energy labels are usually perceived to be the least restrictive policy alternative since they operate along the lines of the dynamics of the free market; insofar, they are different from other more rigid regulatory restrictions like taxes.[3]

Nevertheless, energy labels are not unproblematic in view of the prevailing rules of international trade law. Therefore, this contribution, based on the developed characteristics of labels and nudging policies, sheds particular light—through the lenses of the relations between energy efficiency and sustainability—on the use of energy labels in the context of WTO law with a particular focus on public procurement procedures; these processes appear quite suitable for having applied principles of a "green economy".

2 Characteristics of Energy Labels and Nudging Policy

So far, a generally accepted definition of the term "energy label" is not available[4]; since this policy tool is not yet fully established, a precise notion of the term is difficult to develop. Energy labels usually encompass all labels containing information about the ecological quality of a product (related to production and performance), thereby promoting an environmental goal.[5] Energy labels aim at steering the behaviour of consumers and producers likewise: consumers, on the one hand, should be made aware of the environmental performance of a product and thus be encouraged to make a conscious purchasing decision. This behaviour, on the other hand, is expected to have the additional effect of incentivising manufacturers to produce their goods in the most environmentally responsible way possible.[6]

---

[2]For a comprehensive overview of the different regulatory tools for climate change mitigation see Weber (2017), pp. 365 et seq.

[3]See also Joshi (2004), pp. 70 et seqq.

[4]In everyday language, the word label is used to cover a broad spectrum of tags, containing information like brand names, origins of products or their size; to be more distinctive, legal scholars often refer to the term labelling schemes.

[5]Banerjeea and Salomon (2003), p. 109.

[6]Appleton (1991), p. 9.

2.1 Characteristics of Energy Labels

(a) Compulsoriness: A key feature of energy labels consists in the question of their compulsoriness. Energy labels can be affixed to the product voluntarily or contain information considered so relevant for the consumer that the law imposes its declaration:

(i) *Voluntary energy labels* leave it at the producer's discretion to decide which information should be displayed on the product. Thereby, it is assumed that consumers can be guided by market-driven nudging policies: if there is sufficient consumer demand for a "green" product, an energy label will provide a marketing advantage.[7] In this regard, voluntary labels work like brands and can be considered as a form of advertising.[8] Typically, the government does not regulate voluntary labels.[9] However, in many countries, some labels for example official "Bio" labels for organic food, are regulated by law. Other widespread labels like "FSC" (Forest Stewardship Council) for sustainably produced wood or "Max Havelaar" are marketed based on private certification mechanisms.

(ii) *Mandatory energy labels* generally require a product to be labelled displaying certain environment-related characteristics.[10] These characteristics may refer to the production, use, or disposal of the product at issue. Since such a labelling requirement restricts the economic freedom of the producer and the retailer it must be based on a sufficient legal foundation and is usually stated in a specific law. A prominent example of rules providing for governmentally imposed mandatory energy labels can be seen in the "Energy Labelling Directive"[11] from the EU, which aims at increasing consumers' awareness of the energy use of electronic goods by means of declaration at the point of sale.

Initially, most energy labels were voluntary. These days regulators tend to implement more and more legal requirements in respect to product information. Consequently, the market-based approach of environmental sustainability moves into the direction of the command-and-control approach.

(b) Explicitness: A further characteristic of energy labels concerns their explicitness. Energy labels can also be differentiated regarding the design and degree of informative details displayed. Some energy labels indicate the overall performance of a product, often operating based on a classic color-coded scheme. Thus, they allow for a direct comparison between different products in a category. Other energy labels have gained the status of a well-known brand (e.g. the above mentioned Bio and FSC labels); these labels operate based on consumers' trust and recognition

[7] Appleton (1991), p. 8.

[8] Appleton (1991), p. 146.

[9] Appleton (1991), p. 9.

[10] Appleton (1991), p. 10.

[11] European Parliament and the European Council (2010).

value instead of written information. Recently, so-called carbon footprint labels mirroring the greenhouse gas emissions have attracted increased attention.[12]

(c) Standardisation: The third source of differentiation addresses the requirement of how the information on the label is displayed. Some labels are designed as specific declaration obligations, containing clear legal rules on what must be declared and how to declare it. This is typically the case with the mentioned EU energy-related labels but also with harmful materials (e.g. poisonous chemicals) or with nutritional values in foodstuffs.

In rare cases, the rules underlying a label are even standardised on an international level. An example thereof is the CITES certification scheme regulating the trade of products of animals and plants in danger from extinction, introduced by the Convention on International Trade in Endangered Species of Wild Fauna and Flora.[13] However, other labels leave the decision about design and application to the discretion of the producer. In these cases, the label may be certified by private bodies (or not at all).

2.2 Nudging Policies and Efficiency of Labels

(a) Nudging Policies: A nudge, in the original understanding of Thaler and Sunstein, is any aspect of the choice architecture that alters people's behaviour in a predictable way without forbidding any options or significantly changing their economic incentives; to count as a mere nudge, the intervention must be easy and cheap to avoid.[14] Such a policy instrument does not force addressees (consumers) to comply with certain labels but to consider them in their behaviour. The nudging policy is often discussed based on the example of a product ban vs. a product warning.[15]

If nudges lead to a certain behaviour through voluntary incentives, difficult legal weighing processes of colliding interests can be avoided. For example, nudges that provide information or make certain information more salient by way of labels do not cause any further problems in respect of compliance with international trade law.

The efficiency of the nudging depends on the possible circumstantial assumptions of human behaviour. Contrary to the one-dimensional concept of the homo oeconomicus (Thomas Hobbes) the nudging approach should encompass further human motives. Transparent information is a key factor for influencing the diverse motives; labels are well suited as an important tool for improved information. But more difficult issues than those posed by informational nudges might occur on a sub-conscious or an emotional level since theses nudges can be manipulative and

[12]See e.g. Carbon Trust (2012) and The Economist (2011).

[13]For more information see www.cites.org.

[14]Thaler and Sunstein (2008).

[15]Baisch (2016), pp. 217 and 224.

irreconcilable.[16] Indeed, if nudges aim at changing preferences, attention must be paid to the risk of interference with the freedom of the individual "to do as one pleases".[17]

(b) Efficiency: A more policy-oriented than law-determined topic concerns the efficiency of energy labels. It is obvious that only transparent, scientifically reliable and consistent energy labels can be effective in supporting consumers' choice.[18] In view of the large number of labels that currently flood the market, contentions about their efficiency are expressed and phrases such as "means of green-washing" circulate; in addition, scholars have diagnosed a "confusing variety of competing labels".[19] The willingness of consumers to invest time and effort to evaluate each individual energy label because of the overload of information might decrease and thereby lower their value. In such situations, the nudging effects are evanishing.

Not surprisingly, studies have shown that the strongest determinant of whether energy labels have an impact on the production and purchasing behaviour is the degree of regulation or the level of compulsoriness. The highest degree of efficiency may be evidenced in cases of governmentally imposed energy labels since this situation would provide for high credibility of labels, typically cover a broad range of products and thus lower information costs for consumers.[20] A further factor is the dissemination of the respective energy labels: a widespread use leads to economies of scale and consequently lowers the costs for producers.

3 Implications of Energy Labels on International Trade Law

3.1 Tacking Stock of Legal Challenges

Trade and environment are closely correlated: the production, transportation, consumption and disposal of goods are a main source of greenhouse gas emissions and therefore have a significant impact on the environment. The relevance of conducting trade in a sustainable manner is further reinforced by the steadily, growing volume of products traded around the world.

Sustainability goals are well acknowledged within international trade law: in particular, the Agreement Establishing the World Trade Organization (WTO Agreement) expressly states that the expansion of trade must be carried out, "in accordance with *the objective of sustainable development*, seeking both to *protect and preserve*

[16]Schweizer (2016), pp. 93, 99 and 100; van Aaken (2015), pp. 13 et seq.

[17]Schweizer (2016), p. 101; van Aaken (2015), p. 10.

[18]European Food Sustainable Consumption and Production Roundtable: Guiding Principles, available at: www.food-scp.eu/files/Guiding-Principles.pdf [accessed 5 October 2017].

[19]Howse (2014), p. 593.

[20]Howse (2014), p. 595.

the environment" (emphasis added).[21] This objective of environmental protection is further reflected throughout the various provisions of the covered agreements and was repeatedly reiterated by jurisprudence.

However, although the Appellate Body clearly stated that it is the WTO Member States' sovereign right to adopt environmental measures,[22] the scope of this sovereign competence remains controversial in practice. Even if the so-called "trade and environment disputes" have been increasing throughout recent years,[23] the WTO dispute settlement organs have so far not provided clear guidance to determine the limits for domestic environmental measures.

This legal insecurity is also reflected in the controversy surrounding energy labels: on the one hand, energy labels are regularly praised as a preferred policy measure for being the least trade restrictive environmental measure. On the other hand, however, labelling schemes have increasingly become subject of trade disputes, showing that their compatibility with WTO law remains still uncertain. The relevance of reducing this legal uncertainty is further reinforced by the fact that energy labels are becoming a widespread instrument. While most developed countries have used some kind of energy efficiency labelling scheme for years, a growing number of emerging economies and developing countries like South Africa, Argentina, Sri Lanka or Ghana are now resorting to these measures.[24] Another factor adding to the picture of legal uncertainty is the growing tendency of mandatory environmental labelling schemes, abandoning the previous practice of voluntary labelling schemes.[25]

3.2 *Process and Production Methods: Technical Regulations*

Since energy labels usually refer to environmental conditions in the manufacturing processes, the question arises whether such "process and production methods" (PPM) are compatible with WTO law. PPM that are visible as a physical characteristic of the end-product (so-called "incorporated PPM") are allowed to be used under WTO law. However, in case of so-called "non-product PPM" considerable doubt exists whether they are in line with WTO law.[26] This legal uncertainty is of relevance in the context of energy labels since their purpose consists in the objective of informing the consumers about (invisible) production characteristics (for example

[21]See first recital of the Preamble of the Agreement Establishing the World Trade Organization.

[22]WTO (1998), para. 185.

[23]WTO (1998, 2012a, 2013).

[24]See WTO and UNEP (2009), para. 121.

[25]Academic contributions on labels partly date back decades and cover only the then prevailing practice of voluntary labelling schemes, thus not reflecting present realities of mandatory labels.

[26]See Charnovitz (2002), pp. 59–110; Potts (2008), pp. 8 et seqq.

air contamination, consumption of energy/natural resources, greenhouse gas emissions).

The Agreement on Technical Barriers to Trade (TBT) applies to technical regulations. At least mandatory energy labels are to be considered technical regulations since they usually reflect product characteristics or PPM. Therefore, energy labels need to comply with the two fundamental principles of the TBT Agreement, namely the non-discrimination obligation and the proportionality principle, as set forth in Article 2 of the TBT Agreement. As a consequence, mandatory energy labels that accord foreign products a "treatment no less favourable" to "like products" from within its borders, as well as labels that are more trade-restrictive than necessary to fulfill a legitimate objective, will most likely be found in violation of the TBT Agreement.[27]

3.3 *Non-discrimination Under the GATT*

Whether energy labels do comply with the two basic principles of the General Agreement on Tariffs and Trade (GATT), namely the national treatment principle and the most favoured nation principle, is still subject to debate and decisions rendered by the dispute settlement bodies of the WTO. The following principles need to be addressed:

3.3.1 National Treatment Obligation

Under Article III:4 GATT, three criteria are subject to evaluation: Firstly, whether the contested measure is a 'law, regulation or requirement'; secondly, whether the foreign and the domestic product at issue are 'like', and thirdly, whether the measure accords 'less favourable treatment' to foreign products as compared to domestic ones. Since mandatory eco-labels are usually 'formal legal instruments'[28] with a legal basis in domestic law, the first criteria is generally met.

In a second step, a complaining party must demonstrate that the eco-label under question leads to discriminations of 'like' foreign and domestic products allegedly discriminated against. Here again, the question of PPM comes into play. Generally, the question of likeness is assessed based on the four criteria, consistently recognised by WTO jurisprudence, namely physical characteristics (properties, nature, and quality), end uses in a given market, consumers' tastes, as well as habits and tariff classifications.[29] Apart from consumer's taste, only one of the four criteria refers to

[27]See WTO (2012b), para. 342.

[28]See e.g. WTO (2012b, c), para. 7.815.

[29]WTO (1996a), para. 20; with reference to WTO (2011), para. 18; reiterated by WTO (2000a), para. 8.130 and para. 8.132.

PPM. Therefore, PPM can only be a decisive criterion in the likeness test, when the responding party can make a *prima facie* case for strong consumer preference. In the case of the EUTR, the EU must establish that its citizens' have a strong preference for timber products made out of sustainably harvested wood. Only then illegally logged timber and sustainable timber will be found to be 'unlike' and thus not subject to the non-discrimination obligation in Article III:4 GATT. However, traditional WTO jurisprudence suggests that non-product-related PPM cannot be considered in the assessment of likeness.[30]

The third criterion, 'less favourable treatment' is less disputed. An eco-label provides less favourable treatment when it modifies the conditions of competition in the relevant market to the detriment of imported products,[31] both *de jure* and *de facto*.[32] As clarified within the context of labels in the case of *US – COOL*, an eco-label must be proven to have a negative 'effect on the competitive opportunities in the market' to be found in violation of national treatment obligation of the GATT.[33]

3.3.2 MFN Obligation

The MFN obligation in Article I:1 GATT also covers 'laws, regulations or requirements referring'[34] and 'like products', however, as a third criterion, it prohibits the granting of any 'advantage, favour or immunity that is not accorded immediately and unconditionally' to another WTO Member State.

As clarified by prior jurisdiction, the term 'advantage' can be interpreted broadly as encompassing any advantage that creates more favourable import opportunities or affects the commercial relationship between products of different origins.[35] Analogous to the national treatment obligation, the MFN clause also covers *de jure*, as well as *de facto* discrimination.[36]

3.3.3 Quantitative Restrictions

Should an eco-label be found to fall outside the scope of both the TBT Agreement, as well as the non-discrimination obligations of the GATT, it could still be challenged

[30]First stated in GATT (1991), para. 5.14.

[31]The benchmark standard of equal competitive opportunities was first established by the GATT (1989); subsequently followed in WTO jurisprudence, see e.g. WTO (1996b), pp. 16–17.

[32]WTO (1997), para. 223.

[33]WTO (1997), para. 270.

[34]The term customs duties and charges also referred to in Article I:1 GATT is not relevant for eco-labels and does not need to be discussed in this context.

[35]WTO (2000b), para. 84.

[36]See e.g. WTO (1997), para. 232; WTO (2014), para. 7.600.

under the subsidiary applicable Article XI GATT, which forbids WTO Members to enact prohibitions or restrictions of imports or exports.

The wording of Article XI:1 GATT is very broad in scope. It refers not only to quotas and import or export licenses, but also to 'other measures'. As clarified by the Panel in *Japan – Semiconductors* it encompasses not only laws or regulations, but also "administrative structures".[37] In *Argentina – Hides and Leather* the Panel established that Article XI GATT undoubtedly extends to a *de-facto* discrimination.[38] Accordingly, Article XI GATT forbids Member States to impose any kind of limitations on imports or exports.[39] Therefore, however, it is worth noting that Article XI GATT (like Articles I and III GATT) protects the competitive opportunities of exports, not mere numbers of trade flows.[40] A complaining party basing its claim on a violation of Article XI GATT must thus prove that the responding party's eco-label negatively affects its competitive opportunities.

4 Energy Labels in Public Procurement Law

In view of the fact that the legal compliance of energy labels with the general WTO law is not easy to establish, energy labels have gained increasing importance in the field of public procurement.[41]

4.1 Green Procurement

In recent years, public procurement has been characterised by a development commonly termed "green procurement", referring to the policy of considering environmental criteria when awarding public procurement contracts.[42] From an environmental perspective, this development is a significant paradigm shift. Traditionally, public procurement legislators and practitioners gave weight to economic criteria predominantly and thereby ignored the significant implications public purchases may have on the environment.

Against this background, energy labels have become an increasingly important instrument in the public procurement process. Generally, as outlined hereinafter,

[37]GATT (1988), para. 117.

[38]WTO (2001), para. 11.17.

[39]WTO (1999); as upheld by Appellate Body Report WT/DS90/ABR, para 5.128.

[40]WTO (2001), para. 11.20.

[41]The term "public procurement" (or "government procurement") refers to the act of a public body buying the goods or services necessary to carry out public functions on the market place.

[42]For further discussions on this topic see e.g. Arrowsmith and Kunzlik (2009); Sjåfell and Wiesbrock (2016); Corvaglia (2016), p. 607.

there are two methods available to procurement authorities when defining the requirements of the subject matter of the procurement contract, i.e. when establishing the criteria, on which the awarding decision will be based.

4.2 Methods for Defining the Requirements

(i) *Technical specifications* are mandatory requirements referring to the subject matter of the procurement contract; they are laid down as preconditions for the participation in the procurement process. Non-compliance with technical requirements leads to the exclusion from the procurement process. Procurers awarding a transportation contract may, for example, require that the vehicles to be procured are equipped with a particulate filter to reduce greenhouse gas emissions. Offers with cars not meeting this technical specification will thus not be considered for selection.

(ii) *Award criteria* are the voluntary requirements of the good or service to be procured. Procuring entities grant tenderers complying with award criteria a competitive advantage, through allocating them additional points in the evaluation process. The sum of all awarding criteria will ultimately be decisive for the evaluation of the best offer and the awarding of the contract. Within the scope of award criteria, procuring entities could, for instance, establish that tenderers providing for electricity from renewable energy sources receive additional points, as compared to offers envisaging energies from fossil fuel sources.

Energy labels can be included in the procurement process, through reference within the context of these two instruments. Advantages include the fact that energy labels provide for predefined standards, elaborated by the scientific experts in this field. Thus, they usually profit from broad dissemination and acknowledgement. Consequently, energy labels may make it easier for procurers to concisely define the important ecological criteria. From a tenderers perspective, the inclusion of energy labels may be beneficial by lowering the transaction costs of information acquisition.[43] This, in turn, may lead to the streamlining of the procurement process and, furthermore, foster the awareness-raising and standard-setting capacity of green procurement.

4.3 General Procurement Agreement (GPA)

However, although procuring entities generally have broad discretion when defining the requirements of the contract, they still must adhere to a number of legal

[43] Howse (2014), p. 593.

obligations when setting criteria based on energy labels. Therefore, the legal foundations can typically be found in domestic laws, since public procurement is typically regulated on a national level. Nevertheless, some WTO Member States have committed themselves to multilaterally negotiated rules trough signing the Government Procurement Agreement (GPA),[44] a plurilateral agreement setting forth principles of non-discrimination, transparency and economic efficiency.

The 2012 revision of the GPA has reinforced the stance that green procurement is a legitimate concern; the revised rules explicitly allow for the inclusion and consideration of criteria referring to "the conservation of the natural resource" (Article X:6 GPA regarding technical specifications[45]) and "environmental characteristics" (Article X:9 GPA in the case of award criteria). Although this new wording can be rated as a positive signal for the use of energy labels, procurers need to consider other legal obligations as set forth in the GPA. Despite the fact that the agreement itself does not explicitly mention labels, the legal limits of the inclusion of energy labels in the procurement process imposed by international trade law may derive indirectly from the pertinent provisions of the GPA.

Article X GPA sets' forth the general rule that technical specifications should not amount to unnecessary obstacles to international trade (Article X:1 GPA). It further contains the formal requirement to define the ethical specifications "in terms of performance and functional requirements" and not merely based on "descriptive characteristics", and, if possible, to base them on international standards (Article X:2 (b) GPA). In cases where a functional definition is not possible, procurers will be required to indicate that equivalent offers will also be considered, despite deviations from the technical specifications (Article X:3 GPA). Article X:4 GPA clearly specifies that procuring authorities shall not prescribe technical specifications solely referring to trademarks, patents, copyrights, designs, origins, producers or suppliers. Exceptions are only granted if there is no other sufficiently precise or intelligible way to describe the requirements of the contracts.

It follows from these provisions that procurers cannot base their technical specifications exclusively on energy labels. Although these labels are indicative to describe the requirements of the contract, they should not be the only reference value, since this would be too specific and leaves too little room for competition. Consequently, if energy labels are laid down as a condition for the procurement contract, they must indicate that equivalent goods or services (that "demonstrably fulfill the requirements of the procurement") will also be considered for evaluation (Article X:2 and Article X:4 GPA).

Similar conditions can be considered applicable to award criteria. Although the GPA does not contain equivalent provisions concerning award criteria

[44]Although the GPA is a plurilateral agreement and as such only binding to its 47 Member States, it is nevertheless of significant implication, having led to fundamental changes and broad harmonisation of the procurement systems.

[45]The term "technical specifications" refers to the mandatory requirements that tenderers must meet to be considered in the procurement process.

(or "evaluation criteria" in WTO terminology), tenderers are also bound by the principles of non-discrimination and necessity as set forth in the GPA. However, since award criteria are voluntary criteria and thus impose a lower degree of legal obligations on the tenderers, courts might interpret these requirements less strictly than it would be in the case of technical specifications.

4.4 EU Court Practice

Some legal guidance can also be found in recent European Union (EU) case law. In a ruling that is usually referred to as the "Max Havelaar Case", the Court of Justice of the European Union (CJEU) assessed the compatibility of a tender for the supply and management of coffee machines with the applicable EU law. In the case at issue, the procurer, the Dutch province of Noord Holland, inserted technical specifications and award criteria referring to the fairtrade label "Max Havelaar"[46] and the energy label "EK0".[47] Although the procuring entity explicitly indicated that alternative labels will also be considered, the CJEU still found that the Max Havelaar label was not a suitable reference for technical specifications, since its scope was too broad, encompassing not only product specific requirements, but rather "the conditions of the contract performance".[48] In respect to the implementation of labels within the context of award criteria, the CJEU decided that the Dutch authority had not used its discretion in accordance with EU law. It was found to have failed to meet the three criteria established by the court, namely (i) a clear nexus between the award criteria, i.e. the label at issue, and the subject matter of the contract, (ii) a transparent enumeration of the criteria underlying the label at hand, and (iii) the "or-equivalent-indication" assuring that equivalent offers (not bearing neither the Max Havelaar nor the EK0 label) will also be considered in the evaluation process.[49]

5 Conclusions

Environmental sustainability is a pressing issue but finding the "ideal" instrument for its improvement remains difficult. Increasingly however, energy labels are promoted to realise the globally discussed objectives. Energy labels belonging to the policy

---

[46]CJEU, Case C-368/10, European Commission v. Kingdom of the Netherlands (2012), ECLI:EU:C:2012:284 (Max Havelaar Case).

[47]The Max Havelaar label seeks to promote the interests of local producers in developing countries and maintain "fair" trade conditions.

[48]Max Havelaar Case, above n 46, paras. 73 et seq.

[49]Max Havelaar Case, paras. 84 et seq.

tools, which steer consumers' and producers' behavioural patterns, can serve as a nudge in the market.

International trade law, particularly WTO law, contains some constraints in respect of the use of energy labels in a cross-border context. The non-discrimination principles of WTO law do not allow a preferential treatment of domestic products based on energy labels since such "certifications" could be considered as constituting inacceptable technical regulations.

In contrast, more room to manoeuvre is given under the regulations governing public procurement. As outlined in the contribution, an energy label could be issued as an award criterion and thereby contribute to a "green procurement".

Acknowledgments The support of the previous research assistant MLaw Rika Koch is highly appreciated.

References

Appleton AA (1991) Environmental labelling programmes: international trade law implications. Kluwer Law International, London, The Hague and Boston

Arrowsmith S, Kunzlik P (2009) Social and environmental policies in EC procurement law: new directives and new directions. Cambridge University Press, Cambridge

Baisch R (2016) Nudging: information, choice architecture and beyond. In: Mathis K, Tor A (eds) Nudging – possibilities, limitations and applications in European law and economics. Springer, Cham, Heidelberg, New York, Dordrecht and London, pp 217–246

Banerjeea A, Salomon BD (2003) Eco-labelling for energy efficiency and sustainability: a meta-evaluation of US programs. Energy Policy 31:109–123

Carbon Trust (2012) Carbon footprinting guide: https://www.carbontrust.com/resources/guides/carbon-footprinting-and-reporting/carbon-footprinting

Charnovitz S (2002) The law of environmental "PPMs" in the WTO: debunking the myth of illegality. Yale J Int Law 27:59–110

Corvaglia MA (2016) Public and private standards: ensuring sustainability under the WTO agreement on government procurement. J Int Econ Law 19:607–627

European Parliament and the European Council (2010) Directive 2010/30/EU. On the indication by labelling and standard product information of the consumption of energy and other resources by energy-related products; http://eurlex.europa.eu/LexUriServ/LexUriServ.do?uri=0J:L:2010:153:0001:0012:EN:PDF

GATT (1988) Panel Report. Japan – Trade in Semi-Conductors

GATT (1989) L/6439. Panel in United States Section 337 of the Tariff Act of 1930

GATT (1991) Panel Report. United States – Restrictions on Imports of Tuna (unadopted [US – Tuna I])

Howse R (2014) Consumer labelling on trial at the WTO: misunderstanding the behavioral law and economics of consumer information. In: Reflections on the constitutionalisation of international economic law, Liber Amicorum for Ernst-Ulrich Petersmann. Nijhoff, Leiden

Joshi M (2004) Are eco-labels consistent with World Trade Organization Agreements? J World Trade 69(38):69–92

Potts J (2008) The legality of PPMs under the GATT, challenges and opportunities for sustainable trade policy. International Institute for Sustainable Development (IISD)

Schweizer M (2016) Nudging and the principle of proportionality. In: Mathis K, Tor A (eds) Nudging – possibilities, limitations and applications in European law and economics. Springer, Cham, Heidelberg, New York, Dordrecht and London, pp 93–119
Sjåfell B, Wiesbrock A (eds) (2016) Sustainable public procurement under EU law: new perspectives on the state as stakeholder. Cambridge University Press, Cambridge
Thaler RH, Sunstein CR (2008) Nudge: improving decisions about health, wealth and happiness. Yale University Press, New Haven
The Economist (2011) Following the footprints: http://www.economist.com/node/18750670
van Aaken A (2015) Judge the nudge. In search of the legal limits of paternalistic nudging in the EU. University of St. Gallen Law & Economics Working Papers 3
Weber RH (2017) Emission trading systems: a Coasean answer to climate change? In: Mathis K, Huber BR (eds) Environmental law and economics. Springer, Cham, Heidelberg, New York, Dordrecht and London, pp 355–377
WTO (1996a) WT/DS8/AB/R, WT/DS10/AB/R and WT/DS11/AB/R. Appellate Body Report. Japan – Taxes on Alcoholic Beverages II
WTO (1996b) WT/DS8/AB/R, WT/DS10/AB/R and WT/DS11/AB/R. Panel Report. Japan – Measures Affecting Consumer Photographic Film and Paper
WTO (1997) WT/DS27/AB/R. Appellate Body Report. European Communities – Regime for the Importation, Sale and Distribution of Bananas
WTO (1998) WT/DS68/AB/R. Appellate Body Report. United States – Import Prohibition of Certain Shrimp and Shrimp Products
WTO (1999) WT/DS90/R. Panel Report. India – Quantitative Restriction on Imports of Agricultural, Textile and Industrial Products
WTO (2000a) WT/DS135/AB/R. European Communities – Measures Affecting Asbestos and Asbestos-Containing Products
WTO (2000b) WT/DS139/R, WT/DS142/R. Appellate Body Report. Canada – Certain Measures Affecting the Automotive Industry
WTO (2001) WT/DS121/R and Corr. 1. Panel Report. Argentina – Measures Affecting the Export of Bovine Hides and the Import of Finished Leather
WTO (2011) BISD 18S/97. The Report of the Working Party on Border Tax Adjustments
WTO (2012a) WT/DS394/R, WT/DS395/R and WT/DS398/R. Appellate Body Report. China – Measures Related to the Exportation of Various Raw Materials
WTO (2012b) DS381 (compliance ongoing). Appellate Body Report. United States – Measures Concerning the Importation, Marketing and Sale of Tuna and Tuna Products (US – Tuna II)
WTO (2012c) WT/DS384/AB/R WT/DS386/AB/R. Appellate Body Reports. United States – Certain Country of Origin Labelling (COOL) Requirements
WTO (2013) WT/DS412, 426/AB/R. Appellate Body Reports. Canada – Certain Measures Affecting the Renewable Energy Generation Sector/Canada – Measures Relating to the Feed-in Tariff Program
WTO (2014) WT/DS400/R and Add.1, WT/DS401/R and Add.1. Appellate Body Reports. European Communities – Measures Prohibiting the Importation and Marketing of Seal Products
WTO and UNEP (2009) Trade and climate change. A report by the United Nations Environment Programme and the World Trade Organization

Rolf H. Weber Zurich. Professor em. at the Faculty of Law, University of Zurich (Switzerland), teaching and publishing in international business law, with special topics in competition law, international finance, and trade regulation. He is director of the European Law Institute and the Center for Information Technology, Society, and Law at the University of Zurich. Besides, he is attorney-at-law in Zurich. He can be contacted by e-mail at <rolf.weber@rwi.uzh.ch>.

Consumer Protection in Energy Markets: Selected Insights from Behavioural Law and Economics and Regulatory Practice

Mariusz J. Golecki and Piotr Tereszkiewicz

Abstract This paper discusses how biases and heuristics, e.g. the anchoring effect, affect consumer choices on the energy market. The first part is devoted to analysing the Dyson judgment of the Court of Justice of the European Union, which concerned the EU vacuum cleaner energy label. It is submitted that the Dyson case provides a powerful illustration of how consumers' choices can be affected by anchoring effect. The paper's second part discusses, at a more abstract and theoretical level, in what manner biases and heuristics affect consumer choices. In particular, the paper analyses several strategies of categorisation, which are discernible in consumer decision-making.

1 Introduction

All people consume energy commodities on a daily basis. However, compared to other commodities, energy is invisible, and people therefore do not generally know or realise when they use it a lot. Making people aware of their energy-related behaviour is a huge challenge for regulators and policy-makers. In this regard, regulatory instruments such as energy labels and disclosures could fulfil an important role in alerting consumers to their use of energy. The effectiveness of energy labels and disclosures in conveying the right content depends largely on how they are structured and presented. The objective of this paper is to discuss how certain heuristics and biases may affect consumer choices in the field of energy. More specifically we purport to show how the anchoring effect applied in labels and disclosures shapes consumer choices.

M. J. Golecki (✉)
Department of Legal Theory and Philosophy of Law, Faculty of Law and Administration, University of Łódź, Łódź, Poland

P. Tereszkiewicz
Faculty of Law and Administration, Jagiellonian University of Cracow, Cracow, Poland
e-mail: piotr.tereszkiewicz@uj.edu.pl

K. Mathis, B. R. Huber (eds.), *Energy Law and Economics*, Economic Analysis of Law in European Legal Scholarship 5, https://doi.org/10.1007/978-3-319-74636-4_13

2 Vacuum Cleaner Energy Labelling: An Analysis of the Dyson Ltd vs. European Commission Case

2.1 The Dyson Judgment: Background and Content

It is worthwhile to analyse the recent case Dyson Ltd vs. European Commission, tried by the Court of Justice of the European Union (CJEU).[1] The case concerned EU rules on vacuum cleaner energy labelling. Before we go on to discuss the CJEU decision, it is necessary to provide a short overview of the applicable legal framework. Typical electric mains-operated vacuum cleaners are subject to EU energy labelling and eco-design requirements under the Directive 2010/30/EU of the European Parliament and of the Council of 19 May 2010 on the indication by labelling and standard product information of the consumption of energy and other resources by energy-related products (Directive 2010/30/EU).[2] Directive 2010/30/EU establishes a framework for the harmonisation of national measures on end-user information, particularly by means of labelling and standard product information, on the consumption of energy and where relevant of other essential resources during use, and supplementary information concerning energy-related products, thereby allowing end-users to choose more efficient products (Article 1(1) and (2)). According to Article 5(a) Directive 2010/30/EU, Member States are obliged to ensure that suppliers placing on the market or putting into service products covered by a delegated act, issued to supplement Directive 2010/30/EU, supply a label in accordance with Directive 2010/30/EU and the delegated act.

In order to supplement Directive 2010/30/EU with respect to energy labelling of vacuum cleaners, the Commission adopted Regulation (EU) No 665/2013 of 3 May 2013 (Regulation 665/2013).[3] Article 3 of Regulation 665/2013 provides that each vacuum cleaner should be supplied with a printed label in the format and containing the information set out in Annex II to Regulation 665/2013 (see Fig. 1). The format of the label shall retain as a basis the classification using letters from A to G. The steps of the classification shall correspond to significant energy and cost savings from the end-user perspective. Furthermore, the steps of classification shall deploy a colour scale, which consists of no more than seven different colours from dark green to red.

According to a revision clause of Article 7 of Regulation 665/2013, the European Commission shall review Regulation 665/2013 in light of technological progress no later than 5 years after its entry into force. The review shall, among others, assess whether it is feasible to use measurement methods for annual energy consumption,

[1]Judgment of 11 November 2015 (Case T-544/13), Dyson Ltd. vs. European Commission, ECLI: EU:T:2015:836.

[2]OJ 2010 L 153, p. 1.

[3]Commission Delegated Regulation (EU) No 665/2013 of 3 May 2013 supplementing Directive 2010/30/EU of the European Parliament and of the Council of 19 May 2010 on the indication by labelling and standard product information of the consumption of energy and other resources by energy-related products, OJ 2013 L 192, p. 1.

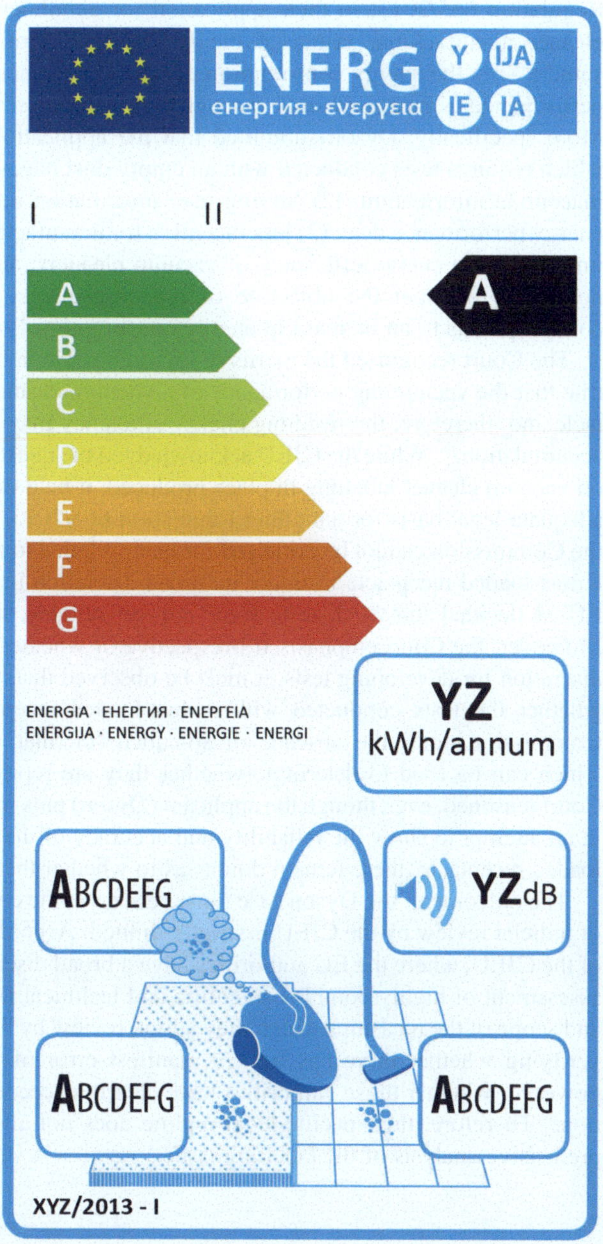

Fig. 1 Sample energy label from the European Commission (Annex II of Regulation 665/2013)

dust pick-up and dust re-emission that are based on a partly loaded rather than an empty receptacle.

The above-mentioned legal framework on energy labelling was contested before the CJEU by a major vacuum cleaner manufacturer who sought annulment of

Regulation 665/2013. In their application for annulment, Dyson, the UK vacuum cleaner manufacturer, criticised the European Commission for misleading consumers as to the energy consumption of vacuum cleaners inasmuch as the cleaning performance is measured only through tests conducted with an empty receptacle. More specifically, Dyson submitted that the application of Regulation 665/2013, which requires tests conducted with an empty dust bag, will lead to: (1) reporting of inaccurate information; (2) 'during use' information not being integrated into the energy performance date; (3) less incentive for manufactures to invest with a view to improving the energy efficiency of vacuum cleaners; and (4) labelling which does not serve to attain the objective of reducing energy consumption and, on the contrary, leads to an increase in energy consumption.[4]

The Court recognised the merits of Dyson's position by acknowledging that "it is true that the vacuuming performance of a vacuum cleaner with a dust-loaded receptacle and, therefore, the resulting energy efficiency may be reduced because of dust accumulation."[5] While the CJEU acknowledged the questionable results that the rules on vacuum cleaner labelling in place produced, it held that this did not constitute an adequate legal basis for annulling Regulation 665/2013. The Court pointed out that the Commission cannot be criticised for having failed to require tests conducted with a dust-loaded receptacle if, under its broad discretion in light of Directive 2010/30/EU, it decided that such tests were not yet reliable, accurate and reproducible.[6] Moreover, the Court emphasised irrespective of whether the Commission has broad discretion for developing tests, it must be observed that, with respect to the question whether the tests conducted with a dust-loaded receptacle are reproducible, the Commission notes the absence of so-called 'circular' tests between laboratories which can be used to determine whether they are reproducible. Consequently, the Court reasoned, even though the applicant (*Dyson*) puts forward numerous arguments in an attempt to show the reliability and accuracy of the test conducted with a dust-loaded receptacle, there remain doubts as to whether that test is reproducible.[7]

The outcome of the Dyson case must be seen in the context of EU law. The scope of judicial review by the CJEU is strictly limited. According to well-settled case-law of the CJEU, where the EU authorities have a broad discretion, in particular as to the assessment of highly complex scientific and technical facts to determine the nature and scope of the measures which they adopt, review by the EU judiciary is limited to verifying whether there has been a manifest error of assessment or a misuse of power, or whether those authorities have clearly exceeded the limits of their discretion.[8] Therefore, this specific legal regime does not allow the CJEU a more comprehensive analysis of the labelling issue.

---

[4]Dyson Judgment, para. 44.

[5]Dyson Judgment, para. 46.

[6]Dyson Judgment, para. 47.

[7]Dyson Judgment, paras. 49–50.

[8]Judgment of 21 July 2011 in Etimine, C-15/10, ECR, EU:C:2011:504, para. 60.

2.2 *The Dyson Judgment and Designing Disclosures*

While the verdict reached by the CJEU is clearly unfavourable to *Dyson*, it appears justified that the court recognises that the EU mandated vacuum cleaner labelling might be questionable. In what follows we would like to analyse the EU vacuum cleaner energy label in light of some insights from the economic analysis of contract law.

To begin with, we draw upon Craswell's illuminating thesis that legal scholarship and, more importantly, regulators, tend to adopt a "quantised" or "particle-based" view of information.[9] From this perspective, all information can be decomposed into its smallest particles or bits. As each bit consists of only a single assertion, then each bit must either be true (accurate) or false (inaccurate). Furthermore, the quantised view of information assumes that disclosure is a binary (all-or-nothing) trait, as long as it is applied to these smallest possible bits of information. Under this view of information, there is no such thing as greater or lesser degrees of disclosure of any single bit included in the same disclosure (e.g. Energy label).

We consider Craswell's proposition as useful starting point in analysing more specific issues. Most importantly, Craswell's proposition shifts the focus onto the relative effect of disclosure. The fundamental question to ask is how some bits of disclosure interfere with the communication of other bits of disclosure contained in the same piece of information.[10]

It is claimed that some information can be communicated without any interference with other information.[11] While this may be possible, it is also plausible that the degree of interference rises with the amount of bits of information conveyed. Increasing the prominence of a specific bit of disclosure, e.g. the Energy Efficiency label may reduce the attention that consumers pay to other information included in the same disclosure. On the one hand, the most prominent elements of a disclosure act are likely to be most effective at attracting the consumer's attention. On the other hand, such elements of disclosure are bound to interfere with other disclosures and thereby reduce their efficiency.[12] A regulator should examine the actual scope of interference between different bits of disclosure and decide in advance which of the pieces of information disclosed is more important.

---

[9]Craswell (2006), p. 569.

[10]Craswell (2006), p. 583.

[11]For examples where no such effect was established in the context of specific disclosures, see Russo et al. (1981), pp. 124–125; Preston and Richard (1986), pp. 608–609.

[12]Craswell (2006), p. 584.

2.3 Framing and Salience in Labelling

It is increasingly recognised that people can be influenced by how information is presented or 'framed'.[13] Needless to say, the importance of a particular frame depends on the context in which it is applied. With regards to the EU energy vacuum cleaner labels, it is evident that the frontal image of the energy efficiency category features more prominently than other bits of information included in the label. This has important implications for how the total disclosure contained in the label is interpreted. The energy efficiency indicator is arguably perceived as the most important bit of information on the label. It has the potential of diverting the consumer's attention away from other bits of information contained on the label. One could even claim that the EU vacuum cleaner label is 'efficiency indicator-framed'.[14] What is particularly intriguing is that the 'efficiency indicator' competes for the consumer's attention with other similarly important information, such as data regarding e.g. carpet cleaning performance class or the sound power level or the price. For specific classes of consumers (such as senior citizens who might value low level of noise, or residents of apartments with fully carpeted floors), these categories of data may be more important than the efficiency indicator.

Furthermore, the vacuum cleaner label case proves that vivid and salient information can have a stronger impact on behaviour than information that is abstract.[15] Salience makes disclosure more much targeted and its likelihood to affect human behaviour increases. In our view, the 'framing effect' and the 'salience effect' in disclosure can be difficult to distinguish in the face of various disclosure designs. In our example, the disclosure of efficiency indicator is clearly more salient than the other bits of information contained on the vacuum cleaner label. Salience of one bit of information entails the risk that other bits of information are treated as 'shrouded attributes', to which consumers do not pay much attention.[16]

2.4 Modifying Disclosure

In the Dyson case, the applicant's major assertion was that data contained in the energy label should be collected on the basis of tests conducted with a dust-loaded receptacle. Essentially, Dyson contented that energy label did not contain correct data, as these data were collected on the basis of tests of which Dyson claimed that they did not demonstrate energy performance in realistic conditions of use. This claim relates to the data on which an energy label is based rather than the content of the label. Still, the question what data are used in labels is an important issue in the

[13]Tversky and Kahneman (1973), p. 257; Sunstein (2011), p. 1353.

[14]We draw here on the usage by Sunstein (2011), p. 1354.

[15]Sunstein (2011), pp. 1354–1355.

[16]Gabaix and Laibson (2006); Sunstein (2011), p. 1355.

process of designing disclosures. As was decided by the CJEU, the current provisions in place would need modifying so that future labels can be based on test, which are currently considered not reproducible. Irrespective of specific EU labelling rules, which dictated the outcome of the case, it is worthwhile to consider whether Dyson's critique regarding the effects of vacuum cleaner energy labelling could be implemented. What would the modified vacuum cleaner energy label look like? A possible regulatory response would be to insert an additional disclosure that energy tests were performed using an empty dust bag. This would constitute a clear qualification of the statement regarding the energy performance and be a fair description of the data collecting process on which the label is based.

However, this approach would raise two questions. First, it is unclear whether this additional information would have any significant effect on consumers. Examples of introducing footnotes in disclosures or labels by means of an asterisk are well-known from other fields of law, e.g. loan marketing materials where a careful reader learns that an attractive interest rate is contingent on the applicant's creditworthiness. Second, depending on the label format, it is arguable that additional content added to the energy label could reduce its accessibility to consumers. It has been powerfully argued that attempts at simplifying disclosures quite often result in much less relevant content being disclosed.[17] Further, they do not necessarily improve decision-making, which is the case powerfully argued by Ben-Shahar and Schneider. Most importantly, the complexity of many decisions cannot be easily reduced to useful and simple forms on which disclosures are based.[18] The label on vacuum cleaners favours one quality of the appliance (energy-efficiency) over others. Furthermore, the data on which disclosures should be based are not always available, and collecting them can be costly or difficult and fraught with troublesome judgments.[19] The *Dyson-case* provides a good example for the proposition that the content of disclosure can be based on questionable data (tests), which renders the trustworthiness of disclosure questionable. We submit that periodical tests should be carried out so as to collect information on how consumers interpret specific disclosures, such as vacuum cleaner labels, and are affected by them. This would enable a continuous process of improving disclosures as empirical verdicts on their quality and efficiency become available.

[17]Ben-Shahar and Schneider (2013), pp. 121–125.

[18]Ben-Shahar and Schneider (2013), p. 152.

[19]Ben-Shahar and Schneider (2013), p. 152.

3 The Quality of Consumers' Choice and Its Limits: The Impact of Heuristics and Biases on Energy Law

3.1 General Assumptions

The Dyson case shows how difficult it is to design disclosures that will convey correct information and will be easily understood by consumers.[20] Generally it is assumed that consumers and regulators behave in a rational way. However, the concept of rationality seems far from obvious, since there is no single and universally accepted criterion of rationality.[21] In practice courts are simply expected to deliver a coherent and persuasive justification based on the meaning of statutes and precedents. The more detailed concept of rationality of judicial decision-making has been articulated by law and economics scholars, who assume that judges tend to maximise their utility function.[22] This concept is based on the assumption according to which a single judge could in general be characterised by a set of coherent and intransitive preferences. It must be noted that rational choice theory is based upon the assumptions according to which preferences should be characterised by the following features: stability, durability, constancy, persistence. Based on this model, individuals act according to the theory of rational choice, which was presented by von Neumann and Morgenstern in the 1944 book 'Theory of Games and Rational Behaviour'.[23] The notion of rationality of players means that all the actors aim to maximise their functions of utility. Moreover, the concept of rationality is based on the theory of revealed preferences based on the subjective theory of values, which means that moral norms are limited to hypothetical imperatives and should be linked to the actions of a player aiming to maximise their satisfaction. The notion of rationality is thus a purely instrumental concept. It is connected to the effective realisation of aims rather than to an autonomous choice of those aims. According to this theory a given subject has invariable, ordered, and non-transferrable preferences with regards to all possible states of things or actions. Such rationality is not connected to the behaviour of particular individuals but rather is used as a convenient tool for predicting future actions. Therefore, the concept of judicial rationality is predicative rather than descriptive.

The only criterion of rationality used within this notion is connected to the existence of a limited coherence of preferences. Nevertheless, the process of their formation is basically outside the scope of the research of law and economics. The primary aim of the concept of rationality is to introduce some order in existing relations rather than to describe or to explain them. It is assumed that a decision

---

[20] Cf. the contrasting views of Sunstein (2011), pp. 1353–1369; Ben-Shahar and Schneider (2014), pp. 121–137.

[21] Alexy (1989), pp. 212–287; Korobkin and Ulen (2000), pp. 1060–1066; Guthrie et al. (2000); Guthrie et al. (2007); Christine et al. (1998).

[22] Ibidem, pp. 1062–1064.

[23] Von Neumann and Morgenstern (1944).

making process is deliberative, i.e. it is a process of conscious character, controlled, free, sequential and based on criteria and rules. The proponents of the theory of bounded rationality in cognitive psychology and behavioural law and economics stress the influence of unconscious, automatic processes, of associational character, that would be intuitive upon the process of decision-making performed by agents, including consumers.[24]

Nevertheless, it seems that the attempts that are formulated within those movements that aim to explain the indeterminacy of decisions in the application of law are unsatisfactory. The indeterminacy of decisions means that their content depends not only on the legal rules or legal reasons, but also on other elements of unconscious character: intuition, impulses and complexes. Those explanatory attempts failed, because of their purely speculative character. They were not verified empirically or the proposed verification was incorrect and proved unsatisfactory within the light of later achievements in the field of cognitive psychology or cognitive sciences. It seems that the only exception to this state of affairs is behavioural economic analysis of law which is just a modification of classical economics to consider the limits of cognition (bounded rationality) and to examine the consequences of the so-called duality of cognitive processes described within the framework of dual process theory (DPT).[25]

The concept of bounded rationality has been introduced in cognitive psychology, and has later on been successfully applied in economics and legal theory. The theory of bounded rationality, at least to some extent, supplements traditional rational choice theory. It considers that human cognitive abilities are not unlimited and therefore human agents including judges and officials have limited computational skills and memory.[26]

We assume that legal theory may sensibly respond to cognitive failures in more or less the same way as classical economics responded to the problem of market failure, and subsequently to the problem of bounded rationality. Firstly, following classical behavioural law and economics literature, it should be observed that agents often consider their cognitive limitations, attempting to minimise the costs of a decision-making process and at the same time trying to diminish the rate of errors. This state of affairs leads to wide usage of mental shortcuts and rules of thumb in some specific contexts. However, given the assumption that in some cases, because of these tools, human behaviour differs in systematic ways from the predicted standard economic model using rational choice theory, the problem of predictability remains. The departures from the standard model are generally divided into two categories: judgment and decision-making.[27] It is widely accepted in the psychological literature that judgments are based on rules of thumb leading to systematic departures from models of rational predictions, whereas actual decisions usually violate the

---

[24]Korobkin and Ulen (2000), pp. 1075–1102; Kahneman (2003), pp. 697–700.

[25]Kahneman (2011), pp. 20–24.

[26]Gigerenzer (2007).

[27]Sunstein (2000); Guthrie et al. (2000); Guthrie et al. (2007); Sunstein and Thaler (2009); Tereszkiewicz (2016).

assumptions of expected utility theory, as it has been described within the framework of the prospect theory.[28]

Both judgments and decisions demonstrate systematic departures from the rational choice model. This finding refers both to legal and non-legal contexts. It has been observed that agents are generally prone to both types of departures from the standard rational choice model. This phenomenon is partly explained by the way in which actors apply the so-called rules of thumb. In the context of applying the law, those rules of thumb are very often based on the so called availability heuristics, where the frequency of some event is estimated by judges on the basis how easy it is to recall other instances of this type.

However, it does not necessarily mean that legal theory should uncritically adopt the findings proposed by cognitive psychology or behavioural law and economics. It seems that the complexity of cognitive processes requires a more independent approach, based on the implementation of the results of empirical studies. Such studies should be conducted also in a strictly legal context, including some experiments designed to verify the theoretical propositions applied to the application of law.

Thus, some fundamental theoretical explanations of the characteristics, origin and the nature of cognitive processes must be applied as a defeasible hypothesis. One of these theories is associated with dual process theory. According to the model of dual process theory (DPT), intuitive processes in the form of heuristics and cognitive inclinations may be explained with the acceptance of a hypothesis of a complex character of cognitive process where, alongside conscious (deliberative) activities, there are also unconscious (intuitive) activities. The functional complexity is being analysed within DPT concerning evolutionary psychology, as well as experimental cognitive psychology. According to the second thesis, the delimitation of both systems: intuitive S1 and deliberative S2 is of a purely functional character, yet their activities may correspond to an action of relevant parts of the human brain.[29] Moreover, it is stressed that intuitive processes are connected with emotions.

The DPT urges theoreticians to take the position of scepticism towards the commonly accepted assumptions concerning the deliberative character of decision-making processes within the field of the application of law. According to some versions of the dual-process theory a clear distinction between intuition and deliberation is possible. Intuitive processes, on the one hand, are described as unconscious, automatic, fast, parallel, effortless, and having a high capacity. Deliberate decisions on the other hand, are thought to be accessible to conscious awareness, slow, sequential, effortful, rule-governed and having a limited capacity. The strong separation thesis has been postulated by Sloman, in which he claims that intuition

[28]Kahneman and Tversky (1979), pp. 263–293; Guttel and Harel (2008), pp. 467–499; Kahneman (2011), pp. 278–288.

[29]Ibidem, pp. 3–38.

and deliberation are completely distinct and separable processes, since they are: "two systems, two algorithms that are designed to achieve different computational goals".[30]

On the other hand, some theories proposed a very weak or even a "no separation" thesis. For example, the so called integrative model of automatic and deliberate decision making is based on the assumption that every decision is based on an automatic process. It has been observed that many cognitive operations are in general based on automatic and unconscious processes, which could in many cases be supervised by other, deliberative and conscious processes, controlling the output of the former intuition-based cognitive operations. The two processes seem not only very closely connected, but in fact they seem integrated in one model, containing the operations of both intuition and deliberation.[31]

Generally, the role of intuition seems twofold: on the one side, it is a condition, if not a necessary condition, for initiating a decision-making process. The significance of intuition is increasing within the situation of information deficit, shortening of the time horizon and activities performed within uncertainty. Hence, one may accept, following Posner argument, that intuition is increasing the effectiveness of decision-making processes (also within the meaning of economics, allocative effectiveness which is connected to the economic costs of decision making and law application).[32]

In behavioural law and economics literature, it has been pointed out that heuristics and biases lead to systemic problems and inadequacies strongly influencing consumer's choice.[33]

Secondly, it seems that ignorance about the complex character of cognitive processes leads to the adoption of very rigorous requirements by the bodies dealing with the application of law. Such an attitude results in allocative ineffectiveness as the standards are based on the assumption of a purely deliberative and rational character of decision-making processes. Moreover, within the prescribed conditions it is not possible to achieve an institutional point of equilibrium as the participants of a legal discourse still accept the unrealistic assumption concerning the uniquely deliberative character of those decisions that concern the application of law.

The influence of intuitive processes on the application of law is visible within heuristics, which are gradually recognised, classified and explained within the context of duration of cognitive processes, as well as regarding the consequences of their effect on the process of the application of law. Processes of this type consist of the following heuristics: anchoring and adjusting, availability, representativeness. It should generally be assumed that the catalogue of heuristics is not a finite list.

---

[30]Sloman (2002), pp. 379 et seq.

[31]Glöckner and Betsch (2008), pp. 215–228.

[32]Posner explains that: "People are not omniscient, but incompletely informed decisions are rational when the costs of acquiring more information exceed the likely benefits in being able to make a better decision. A fully informed decision in such circumstances-the sort of thing a person makes who cannot prioritize his tasks-would be irrational", Posner (1992), p. 19.

[33]Korobkin and Ulen (2000), pp. 1070–1074.

A crucial prerequisite in favour of this hypothesis may be the proposition introduced by Sunstein to broaden the catalogue of the identified heuristics to include some other heuristics, which can fundamentally modify the process of law application. Such a result may occur when certain intuitively appropriate rules are applied unconsciously. These unconscious rules are regarded by Sunstein as moral, such as: "do unto others as you would have done unto you", "treason should be severely punished", "action is more conducive to damage than omission". It seems obvious that the heuristics may influence the decisions concerning the acceptance of particular legal consequences within the process of law application (e.g. the amount of fee, compensation).[34]

Going back to the influence of heuristics upon the decision-making process, it should be emphasised that anchoring and adjusting can be observed within the process of non-reflexive acceptance of a given number and subsequent adjustment of the quantity according to the process of receiving further and more detailed information.

Heuristics of availability are linked to the process of estimation of a given action as more probable in the context where this situation is more available as a hypothetical imagination than as a memory. A particular type of availability is a delusion of hindsight bias, which is means that a greater probability to situations which are already known to have happened are perceived, even though their original probability (ex ante) was minimal. Heuristics of representativeness is visible within the process of categorisation of objects concerning their similarity to the prototype (exemplary, prototypical categorisation). This type of categorisation differs from theoretical categorisation, based on the rule where the object is categorised because of the description of its necessary features. Anchoring and adjusting heuristics are visible within the process of non-reflexive acceptance of a given number and subsequent adjustment of the quantity according to the process of receiving of further, more detailed information. All these processes may, to some extent, influence judges and consumers.

Given the fact that different energy law regimes apply either standards or rules, the impact of this finding may be helpful in the context of specific problems concerning the nature of retroactivity, the character of verification and the quality of judge made law.

The applicability of rules and standards could be referred to the heuristic of representation. Representation matters especially in cases where agents must refer to typical situations to categorise objects and other situations. Different modes of categorisation may result in different decisions. The process of categorisation attracted attention of many scholars in cognitive sciences; especially cognitive linguistics, neuropsychology and cognitive psychology. Two general views on the essential characteristics of this process have been presented so far. Some scholars claim that categorisation has a unified structure and thus could be embraced in a

[34] Sunstein (2005), pp. 531–573.

single model.[35] The other view is based on the opposite assumption, namely the belief that categorisation is not only complex but also hybrid—in different situations subjects categorise objects according to different patterns explained by different categorisation strategies. This approach could be described in the hybrid categorisation model (HCM). The difference between these two approaches seems relevant for the understanding of the psychological characteristics of categorisation, and it pertains to such areas of cognitive psychology as the theory of learning, processing or decision-making. It seems that the distinction between the two approaches is even more important for legal theory, and more precisely for the descriptive theory of legal interpretation and adjudication. In a series of experiments it has been proven that the HCM holds in cases of legal interpretation and it can thus be applied as explanatory device when the representative examples supersede application of legal rules.

According to the HCM the process of categorisation is understood as a kind of decision-making process pertaining to the relationship between a given object (On) and a general category (Cn). Generally, an item could be classified as belonging to the category or not. A review of the literature on concepts and categorisation suggests four different models of categorisation (categorisation strategies). In deciding whether the object On belongs to a particular category Cn, the categorisation may be based on following strategies.

3.2 Determination Whether the Test Object Matches with a Rule Which Defines a Given Category

The rule on the category A (Cat A) sets out some conditions for category membership such as C1, C2, C3. Those conditions should conform to the characteristic of the objects. The process of identification thus concentrates on decoding procedure. Some basic characteristics of an object should be reviewed and checked for the presence of features F1, F2, F3, corresponding to the conditions encoded in a given rule. Some of these features of the object and conditions contained in rule may by negative, some may be positive. In case of a given positive condition where a positive match is detected, the correct decision should reflect the fact that O does belong to Cat A. In case of a given negative condition if positive match is detected, the correct decision should reflect the fact that O does not belong to Cat A. This strategy is commonly described as a rule-based strategy.

Accordingly, the agent who applies a rule-based categorisation strategy to produce a categorisation decision should engage in three step process, namely:

[35]Evans J (2008).

(a) Selectively assessing each feature (F1, F2, F3) of the object O (e.g. dimensions-F1, color-F2, location F3) corresponding with the conditions embedded in a rule (C1, C2, C3).
(b) Determining whether for each assessed characteristic (feature) the perceptual information coincides with the value endorsed in rule and contained within its conditions (e.g. 'is this item big enough').
(c) Blending and confronting the outcomes of the second stage to determine the type of categorisation involved in decision-making process.

3.3 Determination of the Similarity of the Test Object O to a Memorised Exemplars E1, E2 of a Given Category Cat. A

In this case the categorisation procedure is based on a serious of automatic computations of similarity between the object O1 and the exemplary representations of some objects (exemplars) E1, E2, E3 belonging to the category Cat. A. The exemplary based categorisation strategy operates in a following manner, made of a two step procedure:

(a) retrieving stored exemplars similar to the tested object;
(b) selecting the category whose retrieved exemplars are on some measure most similar to the test object.[36]

It is assumed that the exemplars are stored in long-term memory (LTM) and the computations are performed with the engagement of working memory (WM). The categorisation decision is thus based on a process of retrieving the most similar exemplars belonging to the category, where it is assumed that the exemplars had been previously identified as belonging to the category. The whole process is thus based on the retrieval of memorised objects, the comparison of the objects and the identification of the most similar one.

3.4 Determination of the Similarity Between a Given Object O and the Prototype of a Given Category (Prot. A)

In this case, it is assumed that the categorisation strategy is based on the comparison between the prototype and the object. The correspondence between the prototype and the radial metaphor based on a given prototype and the object is especially discernible in some theories of categorisation referred to in law. Sometimes it is claimed that many legal concepts are just prototypes and the linguistic categorisation

[36]Estes (1994).

in law is strongly connected to the way prototypes are shaped by both; language habits and legal discourse.[37] Other studies underline the presence of prototypes in legal language, especially in legal definitions. However, it could be said that no adequate and satisfactory functional model of this categorisation strategy has been offered so far. Many different theories of prototypes coexist and compete in cognitive linguistics. Since the theory has not produce a clear–cut model of this categorisation strategy it is impossible to design an experiment based approach to its operation and verification of the characteristics of the prototype-based categorisation strategy.

3.5 *Theory Based Categorisation*

A very similar story may be offered about the fourth categorisation strategy, namely the theory based categorisation. It has been claimed that the categorisation strategy may well be based on determination on whether the features of the test object are best explained by the so-called 'theory' that underlies the category. This categorisation strategy is similar to the rule-based categorisation in some respect.[38] However, there is an essential difference between the two. Whereas the content of the rule seems observable and determinable, the content of a given theory is not. The rule is so to speak 'publically accessible' whereas the category-shaping or supporting theory is not, being a merely 'private' explanation for the existence of a given category. Thus, even if the concept of the theory based strategy of categorisation seems intellectually attractive, the underlying theory is underdeveloped.

Accordingly, it seems that the model of decision-making should reflect the functional description of rule based categorisation. Rule based categorisation has been investigated from the perspective of its functional meaning and the connections between different cognitive processes.[39] The main differences between rule-based and other categorisation strategies include five basic characteristics:

(a) Analytic vs. holistic processing: whereas rule application involves selective attention to and apprehension of the critical attributes (conditions with respect to the rule and features in respect to the test object), other categorisation strategies do not induce any of these processes, relying exclusively on the retrieval of the stored exemplars. Concurringly the rule application is always based on selection belonging to the analytic process, whereas other types of non-rule based strategies are rather holistic considering the whole object rather than selecting particular characteristics and discriminating against specific features—conditions contained within a category—creating rule.

---

[37]Golecki et al. (2016), pp. 290–294.

[38]Nosofsky (1986), pp. 39–57; Nosofsky et al. (1994), pp. 53–79.

[39]Smith and Sloman (1994), pp. 377–386; Smith et al. (1998), pp. 167–196.

(b) Differential vs. equal weighting of attributes: the rule application procedure involves attending to some special attributes indicated by the rule. Additionally this procedure attaches different weights to different attributes, whereas non-rule based strategy does not refer to any selective attention during the most important exemplar-retrieval stage. Thus the non-rule based strategy procedure may give the same weight to all attributes.
(c) Instantiation of abstract conditions vs. matching concrete information: the conditions endorsed by the rule are more abstract than the representation of the test object. Hence, the rule application strategy is based on the assumption that the categoriser determines whether the information in the tested object meets the conditions of the rule. In contrast, in many cases of exemplar similarity the representations of both exemplar and test objects are assumed at the same level of specificity.
(d) High loads on working memory vs. low loads on working memory: working memory is usually more actively involved in rule application. This may result from two apparently different reasons. Firstly, the rule could be a new one or a complex one. In both cases the agent (the categoriser) needs to refer to the working memory to understand and to apply the rule, especially if the rule contains numerous conditions, both positive and negative ones. From the purely functional perspective both situations must lead to a considerable load on working memory, whereas the retrieval of exemplars from long-term memory usually induces a relatively small load on working memory.
(e) Serial vs. parallel processing: the distinction between rule-following and non-rule based strategy concerns the absence or presence of some serial processing. It appears that serial processing may be linked rather to the rule application than to retrieval and selecting processes, since the rule contains multiple conditions, which may require multiple acts of selective attention and serial operations which finally lead to strategic or controlled processing rather than automatic processing. The rule based categorisation strategy seems to be based on conscious and complex information processing, whereas the non-rule based strategy potentially embraces intuitive and subconscious processing. The heuristics of availability and representativeness could thus been addressed and potentially controlled within the procedural framework of the adjudication. Moreover, the concept of justification of judgement a result of application of legal rules reflects the assumptions on which the HCM is based. The HCM proves that the process of legal interpretation can be controlled after all and the divergences from the rule based categorisation even if it occurs. In fact this should not influence the final decision, which should still be reasonably explained and justified along with the rule based categorisation rather than any other alternative, because no other alternative enables the decision maker to justify the decisions in reasonable way, i.e. by reference to the rule-object relationship.

Within the context of *Dyson-case* it could be suggested that consumers are not able to categorise according to the model of the rule based categorisation. Given the fact that the essential data are not available or might be misleading (this is the issue raised by Dyson), the only strategy the consumer has must be based on intuitive choice resulting from a general impression rather than rigorous analysis of data. In other words even if the consumers wanted to spend time and effort on searching for relevant information and processing data, it seems impossible to adopt this strategy. Moreover, it should be considered that consumers are much more inclined towards the exemplar based or prototype based categorisation, which rests upon the anchoring effect when dealing with energy labels. The anchor, in the form of a label, serves as the most important condition, which shapes potential consumers' choice because of the veil of ignorance regarding the actual energy consumption. As shown above in the Dyson case, the energy vacuum cleaner label draw consumers' attention prominently to only one feature of the device out of several features which could be regarded as relevant by different consumers. This made the process of choosing the right device for specific classes of consumers arguably more difficult.

4 Conclusion

The Dyson case provides support for the proposition that many disclosure types of energy consumption are imperfect and entail risk of misleading its recipients. As was the case with tests performed on an empty vacuum cleaner dust bag, limits as to the availability of reliable methods of testing may significantly impact on the content of disclosures (labels) enacted. The alternative to a 'smart' disclosure of results obtained in a perhaps questionable manner, in some cases might be a more complex disclosure that fails at conveying its content to the average consumer. Architects of disclosures, such as legislators and regulators, are confronted with difficult choices involving considerations as to what values must be given priority, as was shown in the Dyson case. We do not purport to provide any universal guidance in this respect. Choices on the content and format of disclosures (labelling) must be made with due regard to all values and risks at stake in any given case. Where regulations in place value the energy efficiency of household appliances higher than other characteristics (e.g. level of noise), 'targeted' labels appear as justified means to achieving the aim of reducing the energy consumption by the greatest possible number of consumers. Moreover, when such labels appear on most typical household appliances (vacuum cleaners, washing machines, dishwashers, refrigerators and tumble dryers), it is very likely that consumers' choices will be influenced and thus channelled towards the goals endorsed by legislators. The process of influencing consumer choices regarding the energy consumption by targeted labels should be regarded as a long-term challenge, which may yield results after several years. At the same time, we submit that empirical tests of disclosures and labels on representative samples of consumers at pre-enactment stage may go a long way toward mitigating risks that disclosures will involve certain misleading communications, which might disadvantage specific sections of consumers. Further, the framework of disclosure should consider the functional characteristics of categorisation, as has been discussed in this contribution. More generally, the increasingly consolidated scholarship of behavioural law and economics should form the basis upon which a critical assessment of legislation mandating disclosures and labelling will rest.

Acknowledgments The paper has been prepared within the framework of the research project 2015/17/HS5/00495 financed by the National Science Centre, Poland.

References

Alexy R (1989) A theory of legal argumentation. The theory of rational discourse as theory of legal justification. Oxford University Press, Oxford

Ben-Shahar O, Schneider CE (2014) More than you wanted to know. The failure of mandated disclosure. Princeton University Press, Princeton

Christine J, Sunstein Cass R, Thaler R (1998) A behavioral approach to law and economics. Stanford Law Rev 50:1471–1546

Craswell R (2006) Taking information seriously: misrepresentation and nondisclosure in contract law and elsewhere. Va Law Rev 92:565–632

Estes WK (1994) Classification and cognition. Oxford University Press, New York

Evans J (2008) Dual-processing accounts of reasoning, judgment, and social cognition. Annu Rev Psychol 59:255–278

Gabaix X, Laibson D (2006) Shrouded attributes, consumer myopia, and information suppression in competitive markets. Q J Econ 121:505–540

Gigerenzer G (2007) Gut feelings: the intelligence of the unconscious. New York

Glöckner A, Betsch T (2008) Modeling option and strategy choices with connectionist networks: towards an integrative model of automatic and deliberate decision making. Judgm Decis Mak 3:215–228

Golecki MJ, Romanowicz M, Wojciechowski J (2016) Nudging in tax law? Eyetracking research on limits of efficacy of legal definitions. In: Mathis K, Tor A (eds) Nudging – possibilities, limitations and applications in European law and economics. Springer, Cham, pp 289–313

Guthrie C, Rachlinski JJ, Wistrich AJ (2000) Inside the judicial mind. Cornell Law Rev 86:777–892

Guthrie C, Rachlinski JJ, Wistrich AJ (2007) Blinking on the bench: how judges decide cases. Cornell Law Rev 93:1–43

Guttel E, Harel A (2008) Uncertainty revisited: legal prediction and legal postdiction. Mich Law Rev 107:467–499

Kahneman D (2003) A perspective on judgment and choice. Mapping bounded rationality. Am Psychol 58:697–720

Kahneman D (2011) Thinking, fast and slow. Macmillan, London

Kahneman D, Tversky A (1979) Prospect theory: an analysis of decision under risk. Econometrica 47:263–293

Korobkin RB, Ulen TS (2000) Law and behavioral science: removing the rationality assumption from law and economics. Calif Law Rev 88:1051–1144

Nosofsky RM (1986) Attention, similarity, and the identification-categorization relationship. J Exp Psychol Gen 115:39–57

Nosofsky RM, Palmeri TJ, McKinley SC (1994) Rule-plus-exception model of classification learning. Psychol Rev 101:53–79

Posner R (1992) Economic analysis of law, 4th edn. Little Brown and Co., New York

Preston IL, Richard JI (1986) Consumer miscomprehension as a challenge to FTC prosecutions of deceptive advertising. J Marshall Law Rev 19:605–635

Russo E, Metcalf BL, Stephens D (1981) Identifying misleading advertising. J Consum Res 8:119–131

Sloman SA (2002) Two systems of reasoning. In: Gilovich T, Griffin D, Kahneman D (eds) Heuristics and biases: the psychology of intuitive judgment. Cambridge University Press, New York, pp 379–396
Smith EE, Sloman SA (1994) Similarity- versus rule-based categorization. Mem Cogn 22:377–386
Smith EE, Patalano AL, Jonides J (1998) Alternative strategies of categorization. Mem Cogn 65:167–196
Sunstein CR (ed) (2000) Behavioral law and economics. Cambridge University Press, Cambridge
Sunstein CR (2005) Moral heuristics. Behav Brain Sci 28:531–573
Sunstein CR (2011) Empirically informed regulation. Univ Chicago Law Rev 28:1349–1429
Sunstein CR, Thaler R (2009) Nudge: improving decisions about health, wealth, and happiness. Penguin, London
Tereszkiewicz P (2016) Neutral third-party counselling as nudge toward safer financial products? The case of risky mortgage loan contracts. In: Mathis K, Tor A (eds) Nudging – possibilities, limitations and applications in European law and economics. Springer, Cham, pp 169–196
Tversky A, Kahneman D (1973) Availability: a heuristic for judging frequency and probability. Cogn Psychol 5(2):207–232
von Neumann J, Morgenstern O (1944) The theory of games and economic behavior. Princeton University Press, Princeton

Mariusz J. Golecki Łódź and Warsaw. Dr.habil.iur. LL.M. (Cantab). Professor at the University of Lodz, Department of Legal Theory and Philosophy of Law, Director of the Laboratory for Cognitive Research in Law, University of Lodz, Faculty of Law and Administration, ul. Kopcinskiego 8/12, 90-232 Łódź, Poland mjgolecki76@gmail.com. Fields of Interest: Economic Analysis of Law, Behavioural Law and Economics, Legal Philosophy and Legal Theory, Theory of the EU law, Comparative Law.

Piotr Tereszkiewicz Kraków. Dr.habil.iur. M.Jur. (Oxon). Reader in Private Law at the Jagiellonian University of Cracow. PL-31-007 Kraków, Olszewskiego 2, Tel. + 48 (0)12 663 13 85; Fax + 48 (0)12 422 98 12. piotr.tereszkiewicz@uj.edu.pl. Fields of Interest: Private and Commercial Law (Law of Obligations, Consumer Law, Financial Services), Comparative Law, Economic Analysis of Law, Legal Philosophy and Legal Theory.

Part IV
State Aid

The Trade and Environment Debate on the Regulation of Energy Subsidies in the WTO: What Kept Fossil Fuel Subsidies Off the Radar Screen?

Henok Birhanu Asmelash

Abstract The multilateral rules on subsidies have come under intense scrutiny in the wake of rising trade disputes over renewable energy subsidies. The sudden surge in the number of trade disputes and countervailing duty actions against renewable energy support programs has raised concerns that the multilateral subsidy rules may stand in the way of global efforts to promote the development and deployment of renewable energy sources. This paper shares these concerns, but argues that they are only one side of the environmental concerns that arise from the regulation of energy subsidies in the multilateral trading system. Energy subsidies play a dual role from a sustainable energy transition perspective. While renewable energy subsidies tend to help accelerate the transition, fossil fuel subsidies do exactly the opposite. If the multilateral subsidy rules are to help accelerate but not hinder the transition, then they should not only allow governments to subsidise renewables but also discourage them from subsidising fossil fuels. However, the regulation (or lack of) of fossil fuel subsidies in the multilateral trading system receives relatively little attention in the scholarly, policy and judicial debate on trade and environment. This paper attempts to answer why the fossil fuel subsidy issue receives scant scholarly attention.

1 Introduction

The subsidy rules embodied in the Agreement on Subsidies and Countervailing Measures (SCM Agreement) have been in existence for more than two decades, but their environmental implications have come under intense scrutiny following the proliferation of trade disputes and countervailing duty actions against renewable energy subsidies.[1] Renewable energy subsidies have been the subject of eight formal

[1]Agreement on Subsidies and Countervailing Measures, General Agreement on Tariffs and Trade 1994, 15 April 1994, Marrakesh Agreement Establishing the World Trade Organization, Annex 1A (SCM Agreement).

H. B. Asmelash (✉)
Max Planck Institute Luxembourg for Procedural Law, Luxembourg, Luxembourg
e-mail: henok.asmelash@mpi.lu

K. Mathis, B. R. Huber (eds.), *Energy Law and Economics*, Economic Analysis of Law in European Legal Scholarship 5, https://doi.org/10.1007/978-3-319-74636-4_14

trade disputes and several countervailing duty actions during the last 6 years.[2] This has raised concerns that the multilateral subsidy rules may constrain governments from supporting the development and deployment of renewable energy sources. Underlying these concerns is the recognition that renewable energy sources play a critical role in reducing greenhouse gas emissions and that subsidies are essential to help improve the economic competitiveness of renewable energy sources vis-à-vis their conventional counterparts.

These concerns have brought the regulation of energy subsidies to the forefront of the long-standing debate on the interaction between international trade rules and environmental protection measures (the so-called 'trade and environment' debate in the World Trade Organization (WTO)). Two issues are at stake in this debate. One is whether there is sufficient 'green policy space' for governments to support the development and deployment of renewable energy sources under the SCM Agreement. The Appellate Body tried its best to dispel such concerns in *Canada – Renewable Energy and Canada – Feed-in Tariff Program*,[3] but it was not able to prevent them from giving rise to widespread calls for the 'greening' of the SCM Agreement.[4] The second and often overlooked issue concerns the subsidisation of fossil fuels. Fossil fuel subsidies are several times higher than renewable energy subsidies.[5] Numerous empirical studies have also shown that they are both environmentally harmful and economically inefficient. It is now widely—and rightly—recognised that fossil fuel subsidies drain government budgets, distort markets, encourage wasteful consumption, impede investment in clean energy sources and undermine efforts to deal with the threat of climate change.[6] This realisation has led to calls for and efforts to phase out fossil fuel subsidies.[7] However, fossil fuel subsidies remain prevalent around the world and unchallenged before the WTO.

Much of the academic and policy debate on fossil fuel subsidy reform also takes place outside the WTO and often in isolation from the trade and environment debate concerning the regulation of renewable energy subsidies. This raises two major questions. The first is why little attention is paid to fossil fuel subsidy reform within the wide-ranging debate on trade and environment. The second, and more theoretical question, is why the renewable energy and fossil fuel subsidy issues are often treated

[2]The WTO disputes over renewable energy subsidies are: *Canada-Renewable Energy*; *Canada-FIT*; *China Wind Power Equipment*; *US- Countervailing Measures* (China); *India-Solar Cells*; *EU – Biodiesel*; *EU-Renewable Energy Generation Sector*; and *US-Renewable Energy*. For the list of countervailing measures against renewable energy subsidies from 2008 to 2012, see UNCTAD (2014).

[3]WTO (2013).

[4]See, e.g., Cosbey and Mavroidis (2014), p. 11; Rubini (2012), p. 525; Shadikhodjaev (2015), p. 479; Simmons (2014), p. 422.

[5]The latest estimate from the International Energy Agency (IEA) puts fossil fuel conception subsidies at USD 347 and renewable energy subsidies at USD 167. See IEA (2016).

[6]See G-20 Leaders' Statement: The Pittsburgh Summit, September 24–25, 2009 (Pittsburgh Agreement).

[7]See Asmelash (2016).

in isolation from one another. These questions are of particular importance given the fact that both the subsidisation of renewable energy sources and the phasing out of fossil fuel subsidies share the same ultimate objective –reducing the heavy reliance on fossil fuels.

Fossil fuels have been the dominant source of energy ever since the industrial revolution. They currently comprise over 80% of the global energy supply. Their dominance in the global energy mix is a serious cause for climate change concerns. Meeting the internationally agreed goal of limiting global average temperature increase to no more than 2 °C requires the majority of the world's proven fossil fuel reserves to remain underground.[8] This, in turn, requires an urgent transition towards a clean and sustainable energy future.

While there is ample evidence that this much-sought transition is underway, it is not proceeding at a pace that meets the 2 °C target. Energy transition policies are essential to help accelerate the transition. They need to at least level the playing field between fossil fuels and renewable energy to make the transition happen in due time. From the perspective of sustainable energy transition, the lack of action against fossil fuel subsidies in the WTO should cause as much concern as the surge in the number of challenges against renewable energy subsidies.

It is against this backdrop that I set out to discuss the key issues surrounding the regulation of energy subsidies (both fossil fuel and renewable energy subsidies) in the multilateral trading system and explore the possible reasons behind the limited attention given to fossil fuel subsidies in the trade and environment debate. The trade rules and environment debate takes place in three domains: academic, policy and judicial. The disparity of attention given to fossil fuel and renewable energy subsidies is common to all the three domains. In a previous publication, I discussed why fossil fuel subsidies remain unchallenged before the dispute settlement system while renewable energy subsidies face a spate of legal challenges.[9] I will shift my focus in this paper to the academic debate and explore why fossil fuel subsidies failed to attract as much attention as renewable energy subsidies in the literature on trade and environment. This will be achieved by examining the trade and environment literature and the specific issues that have been dealt therein over the years. The fact that the academic debate on the subject historically covers a broader range of issues than the policy and judicial debate makes this enquiry all the more interesting.

I begin with a general but brief overview of the trade and environment debate in the multilateral trading system. My intent here is not to recount the whole debate but to highlight its nature and evolution with particular emphasis on the trade-related environmental measures that have been the subject of debate and discussion. I will then discuss the trade and environment issues related to the regulation of energy subsidies. I will first lay out the renewable energy subsidy and fossil fuel subsidy issues at stake and how they are addressed in the trade and environment debate on the regulation of energy subsidies. This will be followed by a discussion on the

[8] See IEA (2012), p. 25; McGlade and Ekins (2015), p. 187.

[9] See Asmelash (2015), p. 261.

possible reasons behind the relative absence of fossil fuel subsidies from the debate. The possible reasons discussed here include the misconception about the regulation of energy in the multilateral trading system, the lack of trade disputes over fossil fuel subsidies, and the very nature of the trade and environment debate. I will finish the paper with some concluding remarks.

2 The Trade and Environment Debate

The interaction between trade and environment is one of the most intensely debated issues in the multilateral trading system. At the heart of this debate are concerns as to whether international trade rules constrain governments from taking action to protect the environment, on the one hand, and whether environmental protection can be used as a disguised restriction on international trade, on the other. These concerns first appeared on the international trade agenda in the 1970s, but they were mostly fuelled by the two GATT disputes concerning US import ban on Mexican tuna.[10]

In *US-Tuna I & US-Tuna II*, Mexico and then the European Communities (EC) challenged the US import ban on tuna caught using nets which resulted in the excessive incidental killing of dolphins.[11] The GATT Panels in both cases found that the import ban was GATT-inconsistent and could not be justified under GATT Article XX exceptions.[12] Neither of the panel rulings was formally adopted, but they 'provoked a furious reaction and led many environmentalists to believe that [the multilateral trading system] was dedicatedly and irrevocably biased in favour of free trade'.[13] Environmentalists used these rulings as 'a call to arms' and began denouncing the multilateral trading system as 'GATTzilla'—a monster determined to destroy the environment.[14] Their main concern at the time was the impact of multilateral trade rules in constraining the ability of governments to take unilateral measures to protect the environment.

GATT Contracting Parties attempted to alleviate these concerns by introducing 'environmental provisions' to the various agreements concluded at the end of the Uruguay Round (1986–1994).[15] The most symbolic of these is the preambular recognition of sustainable development that protects and preserves the environment

[10]See Kulovesi (2011), p. 85 (noting that 'the origins of the contemporary debate on trade and the environment can be traced to the two GATT reports in the Tuna-Dolphin dispute').

[11]GATT (1991, 1994).

[12]On the *US-Tuna* Panel rulings, see Thaggert (1994); Kingsbury (1994), p. 1.

[13]See Kulovesi (2011), p. 87; Joseph (1994).

[14]See Esty (1994), p. 35.

[15]See, e.g., General Agreement on Tariffs and Trade 1994, 15 April 1994, Marrakesh Agreement Establishing the World Trade Organization, Annex 1A (GATT 1994), Article XX; Agreement on Trade-related Aspects of Intellectual Property Rights, 15 April 1994, Marrakesh Agreement Establishing the World Trade Organization, Annex 1C (TRIPS), Article 17; Agreement on Technical Barriers to Trade, General Agreement on Tariffs and Trade 1994, 15 April 1994, Marrakesh

as one of the overarching objectives of the WTO.[16] The introduction of environmental provisions and the establishment of the WTO Committee on Trade and Environment (CTE) with an expanded mandate to ensure the mutual supportiveness of trade and environment[17] has undoubtedly made environment part of the mandate of the multilateral trading system.[18] However, the trade and environment debate continued to evolve with new judicial and treaty-making activity.[19] Since environmental issues were brought to the Uruguay Round only in the final stages, they were not fully addressed. It was partly in recognition of this unfinished business that trade and environment issues were placed on the agenda of the Doha Round when it was launched in 2001.

In the judicial arena, Brazil and Venezuela filed the first trade and environment dispute under the WTO era shortly after its establishment in 1995. In *US-Gasoline*, they challenged the US Clean Air Act governing reformulated gasoline and its baseline establishment methods.[20] Both the Panel and the Appellate Body found that the measure was inconsistent with GATT Article III:4, and was not justifiable under GATT Article XX. The Appellate Body agreed with the US that the measure was indeed related to the 'conservation of exhaustible natural resources' within the meaning of GATT Article XX(g), but found the measures to be inconsistent with the 'unjustifiable discrimination' or 'disguised restriction on international trade' requirements of the chapeau (the chapeau test).[21]

US-Gasoline was shortly followed by perhaps the most important trade and environment dispute in the history of the multilateral trading system—*US-Shrimp*.[22] In this dispute, the Appellate Body found that the US ban on shrimp caught by using technologies that may adversely affect sea turtles was provisionally justified under GATT Article XX(g). It relied on the Convention on International Trade in Endangered Species (CITES) to establish that sea turtles are exhaustible natural resources and hence WTO Members are entitled to take otherwise WTO-inconsistent measures to protect them. The original US ban was nevertheless deemed WTO-inconsistent as it failed to pass the chapeau test of GATT Article XX.

The US subsequently removed the discriminatory aspect of the shrimp ban and engaged in negotiations towards an international agreement for the conservation of sea turtles. The combination of these two factors convinced both the Panel and the

Agreement Establishing the World Trade Organization, Annex 1A (TBT Agreement), Article 2.2; SCM Agreement (n 1), Article 8.

[16]See Marrakesh Agreement Establishing the World Trade Organization, opened for signature 15 April 1994 (entered into force 1 January 1995), para.1 of the preamble.

[17]The Marrakesh Ministerial Decision on Trade and Environment, MTN/TNC/45(MIN), adopted 15 April 1994.

[18]See Charnovitz (2007a), p. 19 ('one can hardly doubt that environment is now part of the WTO's mandate').

[19]See Pauwelyn (2004); Charnovitz (2007b), p. 685.

[20]WTO (1996).

[21]WTO (1996), pp. 22 & 29.

[22]WTO (1998).

Appellate Body to conclude (during the compliance proceedings) that the ban is fully justified under GATT Article XX(g).[23]

This was a landmark ruling that represented an important development from the environment perspective.[24] But it has not settled the 'highly emotive' debate on trade and the environment. These classical trade and environment disputes, in fact, have led the debate to focus primarily on two issues: the WTO-consistency of unilateral trade bans and other environmentally motivated trade measures targeting processes and production methods (PPMs); and the relationship between WTO Agreements and Multilateral Environmental Agreements (MEAs).[25] The second issue stemmed particularly from *US-Gasoline* and *US-Shrimp* in which the Appellate Body famously held that WTO Agreements are not to be read in clinical isolation from public international law and subsequently used MEAs to establish whether sea turtles are exhaustible natural resources.[26] However, the Appellate Body left the question whether trade bans imposed pursuant to MEAs are automatically WTO-consistent (i.e. without the need to go through the two-tiered test of GATT Article XX) open.

While these issues continued to dominate the debate other issues emerged with the adoption of the Kyoto Protocol to the United Nations Framework Convention on Climate Change (UNFCCC).[27] Competitiveness concerns in countries that undertook quantified emission limitation and reduction commitments under the Protocol (Annex I Parties) brought environmental Border Carbon Adjustments (BCAs) and their WTO-consistency to the spotlight.[28] Imposing BCAs on imports from non-Kyoto Parties (or parties that refuse or fail to implement their commitments) were touted as effective instruments to remedy the loss of competitiveness by domestic industries subject to carbon taxes or emission limits. The Kyoto Protocol did not require any country to impose BCAs. No country has ever imposed BCAs.[29] Nevertheless, their WTO-consistency became (and continues to be) one of the key issues in the academic debate on trade and environment.[30] It is only in the last few years that the debate expanded beyond its traditional focus on BCAs, PPM-based trade bans, and the relationship between MEAs and WTO Agreements.

---

[23]WTO (2001), Article 215.

[24]See Kulovesi (2011), p. 101.

[25]Kulovesi (2014), p. 55.

[26]*US-Gasoline* (n 21), at 17; *US-Shrimp* (n 23).

[27]See Kyoto Protocol to the United Nations Framework Convention on Climate Change (adopted 11 December 1997, entered into force 16 February 2005) 2303 UNTS 148 (Kyoto Protocol).

[28]See Pauwelyn (2013); Kulovesi (2014), pp. 72 et seq.

[29]There was some talk about introducing BCAs in the EU after the establishment of the EU Emission Trading Scheme (ETS), but it has never gained serious political backing. See Pauwelyn (2013); Kulovesi (2014), p. 75.

[30]As Kulovesi pointed out, the trade and environment conflict represented by the WTO-consistency of trade-related environmental measures such as BCAs is more imagined than real. See Kulovesi (2014).

Subsidies and the multilateral trade rules regulating them were hardly the subjects of the trade and environment debate before 2010. Perhaps the only major exception in this regard is the discussion ignited by Nobel Laureate Joseph Stiglitz in the aftermath of the Kyoto Protocol. As part of his proposal to exert pressure on the US to join the Kyoto Protocol, he suggested that the EU and other Annex I Parties to the Kyoto Protocol should impose countervailing duties on US exports.[31]The gist of his argument was that not charging a carbon tax on energy-intensive industries constitutes a countervailable subsidy. Stiglitz offered little or no explanation as to how the failure to join the Protocol constitutes a subsidy under the SCM Agreement. WTO Scholars quickly dismissed his argument. In their response, Mavroidis and Bhagwati argued that the US inaction or failure to ratify the Kyoto Protocol meets neither the financial contribution nor the benefit requirements of the SCM Agreement.[32]

Another related context in which the regulation of subsidies in the multilateral trading system was raised in the trade and environment debate was in relation to the allocation of free emission allowances. There were some discussions about whether free emission allowances constitute countervailable subsidies under the SCM Agreement.[33] But these discussions are often held as part of the broader discussion about the WTO-consistency of ETSs. However, besides these two instances, the regulation of subsidies hardly featured in the trade and environment debate. This is evident from the apparent lack of academic interest (until recently) in the expiry of the environmental exceptions set out under Article 8 of the SCM Agreement. As we will see below in more detail, it took 5 years for the expiry of Article 8 to attract substantial scholarly attention.

3 The SCM Agreement Under Environmental Scrutiny

The SCM Agreement has been invoked in 114 cases since its entry into force in 1995.[34] However, it is only in the last 6 years that it has come under intense environmental scrutiny.[35] Much of this scrutiny was triggered by the sudden surge in the number of trade disputes and countervailing duty actions against renewable energy subsidies. The emergence of the so-called 'subsidies war' at the start of this decade has brought the regulation of energy subsidies from relative obscurity to prominence in the debate on trade and environment within the multilateral trading

[31]See Stiglitz (2006).

[32]Bhagwati and Mavroidis (2007), p. 299.

[33]See Jegou and Rubini (2011).

[34]WTO (2017).

[35]Only a handful of scholars commented on the environmental implications of the SCM Agreement before 2010. The most notable among these are: Howse and Eliason (2009); Howse (2006), p. 500; Green (2006), p. 377; Bigdeli (2009); Bigdeli (2008), p. 78; Ayala and Gallagher (2009), p. 131.

system. Before delving into the substantive issues shaping the debate, introducing some basic features of the SCM Agreement is apropos.

Under the SCM Agreement, a 'subsidy' exists only where government or any other public body makes a financial contribution that confers a benefit on the recipient.[36] However, only sector- or industry-specific subsidies fall under the ambit of the agreement.[37] Specific subsidies are either prohibited or actionable. Prohibited subsidies are those that are contingent upon export performance or on the use of domestic over imported goods.[38] All other subsidies qualify as actionable subsidies provided that they are specific and cause adverse effects to the interests of other Members.[39]

As noted earlier, the SCM Agreement originally had a third category of 'non-actionable' or 'green' subsidies. This category was introduced for a provisional period of 5 years to provide a 'safe harbour' for environmental, regional and research and development subsidies.[40] The operation of this category was supposed to be reviewed with a view to determining its extension.[41] No agreement was reached at the time, and the category of non-actionable subsidies expired at the end of 1999. This has left the SCM Agreement without any clear mechanism that distinguishes environmentally beneficial subsidies from environmentally harmful ones.

3.1 The Renewable Energy Subsidy Issue

The feed-in tariff program adopted by the Canadian province of Ontario is the first and most prominent environmental subsidy scheme that has ever been challenged at the WTO.[42] Japan and then the European Union claimed that the local-content requirements attached to Ontario's feed-in tariff program were inconsistent with the non-discrimination principles of the Agreement on Trade-Related Investment Measures (TRIMS) and the GATT, and that the feed-in tariff program constitutes a prohibited subsidy under the SCM Agreement. The Appellate Body upheld the Panel's finding that the local content requirements were indeed inconsistent with TRIMS Article 2.1 and GATT Article III:4. Canada's decision not to invoke GATT Article XX (either directly or by virtue of TRIMS Article 3 and 2.1) kept this part of the Appellate Body's finding largely free of 'trade and environment' controversy.[43] What raised controversial trade and environment issues was the finding on whether

[36] SCM Agreement, Article 1.1.
[37] SCM Agreement, Article 1.2 and 2.
[38] SCM Agreement, Article 3.
[39] SCM Agreement, Article 5.
[40] SCM Agreement, Article 8.
[41] SCM Agreement, Article 31.
[42] Canada-Renewable Energy/FIT (n 3).
[43] Bigdeli (2016), p. 121.

Ontario's feed-in tariff program constituted a prohibited subsidy under the SCM Agreement.

Having agreed with the Panel that the feed-in tariffs constitute a financial contribution (i.e. government purchase of goods), the Appellate Body engaged in an extended analysis of the benefit requirement and ultimately concluded that there were no sufficient factual findings on the record to complete the analysis.[44] In doing so, it has not only dismissed the question but also created a jurisprudence, which makes the identification of market benchmarks for benefit analysis difficult. Its novel approach to benefit benchmark analysis 'increases the burden of proof for a complaining party to make a prima facie case and to establish that the concerned products form a single market and that a benefit is conferred'.[45] This, at least in principle, could discourage challenges to renewable energy support policies under the SCM Agreement.

Yet the Appellate Body received more criticism than praise for its apparent attempt to avoid finding that an environmental support scheme was, in fact, a subsidy.[46] Much of the criticism stems from the fact that its effort tends to hide or defer and not to reveal or resolve the limitations of the existing subsidy rules in accommodating environmental support schemes. Two points are raised to illustrate this. First, it may have become difficult to qualify feed-in tariffs as subsidies, but the door is not firmly shut. Future Panels and the Appellate Body itself may find feed-in tariffs to be subsidies even under the new benefit benchmark analysis. Moreover, the Appellate Body may revise its own jurisprudence. It is interesting to note here that although the United States dropped its claim under the SCM Agreement in *India-Solar Cells* following the Appellate Body's finding in *Canada-Renewable Energy// FIT*, India's consultation request in *US-Renewable Energy* includes claims under the SCM Agreement.[47] Second, the feed-in tariff is not the only form that renewable energy subsidies take. There are many other and different forms of renewable energy subsidies that could easily qualify as a 'subsidy' within the meaning of the SCM Agreement (e.g. grants, loans, loan guarantees, and tax concessions). Given these considerations, the bigger question is not whether feed-in tariffs qualify as a subsidy under the SCM Agreement. It is whether there is a legal shelter for renewable energy subsidies (including feed-in tariffs) that could be found to be a 'subsidy' under the

---

[44]See Canada-Renewable Energy/FIT (n 3), para 5.128 & 5.246.

[45]Weber and Koch (2015), p. 779.

[46]For a polemical criticism, see Rubini (2014), p. 895; Cosbey and Mavroidis (2014); Rubini 2015, p. 211.

[47]See Request for Consultations by the United States, *India – Certain Measures Relating to Solar Cells and Solar Modules (India – Solar Cells), WT/DS456/1, G/L/1023 G/TRIMS/D/35, G/SCM/ D96/1, 11 February 2013*; Request for Consultations by the United States, *India – Certain Measures Relating to Solar Cells and Solar Modules (India – Solar Cells), WT/DS456/1/Add1, G/L/1023/Add1, G/TRIMS/D/35/Add1, G/SCM/D96/1/Add1, 13 February 2014*; Request for Consultation by India, *United States – Certain Measures Relating to the Energy Sector (US-Renewable Energy), WT/DS510/1, G/L/1149, 19 September 2016.*

SCM Agreement. This was perhaps the question that the Appellate Body tried to avoid by engaging with what Cosbey and Mavroidis called 'legal acrobatics.'[48]

The literature on the regulation of renewable energy subsidies often starts from the assumption that subsidies (in the absence of carbon pricing) play a crucial role in promoting the development and deployment of renewable energy and hence deserve legal protection.[49] The inclusion of environmental exceptions in the original text of the SCM Agreement appears to reflect the recognition by WTO Members of the need for such protection. The expiry of Article 8 is said to have disturbed the carefully negotiated balance between providing sufficient policy space for governments to deploy subsidies in pursuit of socially desirable goals while limiting the negative impact of subsidies on trade.[50] This has led some commentators to argue that the general exceptions contained in GATT Article XX could/should apply to the SCM Agreement.[51] The thrust of their argument is that the SCM Agreement is simply a *lex specialis* to the GATT rules on subsidies (Articles VI and XVI) and thus the general exceptions contained therein equally apply to it.

It is, of course, inconsistent to justify more trade distortive measures such as trade bans and import quotas on environmental grounds and not to do the same for environmental subsidies.[52] But this is a normative argument. A strict legal reading of GATT Article XX suggests that the general exceptions are meant to apply only to the GATT. The architects of the Uruguay Round agreements seem to be aware of this. That is why they added agreement-specific exceptions (i.e. SCM Agreement Article 8) or made explicit reference to GATT Article XX (i.e. TRIMS: Article 2.1 and 3). The Appellate Body has also established in *China-Raw Materials* that GATT Article XX applies to other WTO agreements only to the extent that there is a specific textual basis.[53] No reference to GATT Article XX can be found in the SCM Agreement.

In the absence of specific exceptions for environmental subsidies under the existing legal framework and given the continued increase in the number of trade disputes and countervailing duty actions against renewable energy subsidies, one question that has come to dominate the scholarship on the regulation of energy subsidies is whether legal reform is necessary. Some commentators are of the view that there is adequate green policy space under the SCM Agreement.[54] They argue that not all government support measures constitute a 'subsidy' within the SCM

48See Cosbey and Mavroidis (2014), p. 12.

49See, e.g., Bacchus (2012).

50Shadikhodjaev (2015), p. 499.

51For further discussion on the arguments for and against the application of GATT Article XX to the SCM Agreement, see Rubini (2012).

52See Howse (2008); see also Havel and Sanchez (2014), p. 382.

53On the applicability of GATT Article XX outside the GATT, see Shadikhodjaev (2015), pp. 499–505; Feld and Switzer (2012), p. 16.

54This view broadly echoes the concern (of economists) that exceptions or 'safe harbours' aimed at promoting public goods can be abused and end up sheltering subsidies that are counterproductive to providing public goods. See Sykes (2003), pp. 22–23.

Agreement and that it is up to governments to design their renewable energy support scheme in a manner compatible with the SCM Agreement.[55] They refer to the Appellate Body' finding in *Canada-Renewable Energy/FIT* to illustrate the presence of adequate policy space under the SCM Agreement. However, this is a minority view. Most others see the need for legal reform. They consider the questionable legal status of renewable energy subsidies as a major source of legal uncertainty, which affects the development of much needed renewable energy sources.[56] Renewable energy support programs may not be able to attract as much investment as they would if there is a risk that the program may be challenged before the WTO (and hence withdrawn) or face unilateral countervailing duty actions. Fear of legal challenges may also deter governments from adopting renewable energy support programs, which in the end affects the renewable energy industry.[57] Incoherence is another problem associated with the lack of specific exceptions for environmental subsidies.[58] It is logically incoherent to prevent governments from using subsidies in pursuit of legitimate public policy goals while allowing them to use more trade restrictive measures for the same purpose (e.g. GATT Article XX). Economists that have been questioning the rationales for the multilateral regulation of subsidies in the first place would no doubt find this double standard to be preposterous.[59] Legal scholars that recognise the existence of the double standard are unanimous in their call for reform. The literature on the regulation of renewable energy subsidies is now replete with reform proposals ranging from resurrecting Article 8 of the SCM Agreement and expanding the application of GATT Article XX beyond the GATT to negotiating a sectoral agreement on energy.[60]

I have already said enough to indicate that I share the second view. As much as it is difficult to reform the existing multilateral subsidy rules, there should be no doubt that reliance on the Appellate Body's judicial activism or acrobatics is not a sustainable solution. As Casier and Moerenhout aptly put it, "WTO Members, not the Appellate Body, need to clarify boundaries in renewable energy support."[61]

[55]See Leal-Arcas and Filis (2015), p. 50 ('the policy space appears to be preserved for WTO members to take measures to support environmental goals, including the promotion of renewables'); Grigorova (2015), p. 17.

[56]See, e.g., Rubini (2017); Giupponi (2015), p. 21.

[57]See Charnovitz (2014), p. 73.

[58]Rubini (2017).

[59]Paul Krugman is often quoted for suggesting that the proper policy response to a foreign state's subsidies is 'to send a thank you note to the embassy'. See Sykes (2007), p. 107. For the economic case for and against the multilateral regulation of subsidies, see Sykes (2010), p. 473.

[60]See, e.g., Howse (2013); Rubini (2017); Cosbey and Mavroidis (2014); Cottier (2014), p. 40; Bigdeli (2011), p. 2; Shadikhodjaev (2015); Wu and Salzman (2014), p. 401; Farah and Cima (2014), p. 515.

[61]See Casier and Moerenhout (2013). This should not be seen as a criticism of the dispute settlement mechanism, which is rightly described as the 'crown jewel' of the multilateral trading system. For a recent account of the role played by the dispute settlement mechanism in strengthening the multilateral trading system, see Howse (2016), p. 9.

Alleged judicial law making by the Appellate Body has already drawn much criticism in policy and academic circles.[62] The United States, in particular, have been openly critical of the Appellate Body.[63] And these criticisms are likely to become more intense under the new administration. Why then do we need to add more pressure on the Appellate Body and risk its credibility by expecting it to achieve a task it was not designed to perform? One should also recall that there are several forms of renewable energy subsidies that cannot be saved by judicial interpretation.[64] To simply argue that government should design their renewable energy subsidy programs according to existing subsidy rules is to be insensitive to the political economy of renewable energy subsidies. Environmental protection is the main justification for renewable energy subsidies worldwide. However, environmental benefits are not always apparent or perceived by taxpayers who bear the costs of the subsidies. This meant that governments frequently promise job creation and domestic technological progress to secure political support for renewable energy subsidies.[65] It is these promises that often commit them to adopting discriminatory support measures such as local content requirements.

3.2 The Fossil Fuel Subsidy Issue

The environmental issues that arise from the regulation of energy subsidies in the multilateral trading system are not limited to renewable energy subsidies. Subsidies to the traditional energy sector are subject to the same rules and raise equally important environmental concerns. One major difference between the two is perhaps the fact that the cause for concern about fossil fuel subsidies is the lack of action against them. Another difference is the level of attention they have received in the policy and academic debate on the regulation of energy subsidies in the multilateral trading system. The regulation of fossil fuel subsidies under the SCM Agreement and its environmental implications is often overlooked in the trade and environment debate. However, before turning to why fossil fuel subsidies received less attention than their green counterparts, I will first lay out the key issues associated with the regulation (or lack of) of fossil fuel subsidies.

Global fossil fuel subsidy estimates range from USD 493 to USD 5300 billion, depending on how subsidies are defined and measured.[66] The oft-cited justification

[62]See, e.g., Greenwald (2003), p. 113; Cartland et al. (2012), p. 979.

[63]This was evident in the recent reappointment controversy. See Shaffer (2016).

[64]The Appellate Body's interpretation will not save renewable energy subsidies such as capital grants, government loans at preferential rates and loan guarantees for technologies that produce electricity from renewable energy sources (e.g. solar energy and wind power) from legal challenges under the SCM Agreement.

[65]See Lewis (2014), p. 10; Sugathan (2013), p. 23.

[66]See IEA (2015) and Coady et al. (2015).

for these subsidies is the provision of access to modern energy services for poor households. However, empirical studies have consistently shown that such subsidies hardly benefit the poor. Instead, they drain public funds away from pro-poor public services such as education and health care, encourage wasteful energy consumption (by high-income households), and undermine the competitiveness of renewable energy sources by artificially lowering fossil fuel prices.[67] The economic literature on fossil fuel subsidies has long established the economic and environmental benefits of reforming such subsidies. In 1992, the World Bank estimated that removing fossil fuel subsidies worldwide (then estimated at USD 230 billion) would reduce global carbon dioxide emissions by 9% and lead to a global welfare gain of USD 33 billion.[68] This has not changed today—only increased. The latest estimate from International Monetary Fund (IMF) indicates that eliminating fossil fuel subsidies would reduce global carbon dioxide emissions by more than 20% and raise global economic welfare by USD 1.8 trillion. This has led to widespread calls for and efforts to phase out fossil fuel subsidies both at national and international levels.

The issue of fossil fuel subsidy reform first appeared on the international environmental agenda during the Kyoto Protocol negotiations in the 1990s.[69] These negotiations resulted in the inclusion of Article 2.1(a)(v) to the final text of the Protocol, calling for the "progressive phasing out of market imperfections and fiscal incentives that run counter to the objective of the Convention, including, inter alia, subsidies in all greenhouse gas emitting sectors."[70] Several intergovernmental agreements have also been concluded since then, both at the regional and international level to phase out fossil fuel subsidies.[71] The most important among these is the 2009 G20 Agreement to phase out (over the medium term) inefficient fossil fuel subsidies and the 2016 G7 pledge to eliminate inefficient fossil fuel subsidies by 2025.[72]

However, fossil fuel subsidies remain prevalent worldwide despite all these intergovernmental efforts. To attempt to explain why these efforts failed to induce fossil fuel subsidy reform would lead me beyond the scope this paper.[73] What is important here is to note that all these intergovernmental efforts and initiatives took place outside the multilateral trading system. This was recognised by none other than the former WTO Director-General, Pascal Lamy. Speaking at a workshop organised

[67]See Burniaux and Chateau (2014), Clements et al. (2013), Coady et al. (2017), Larsen and Shah (1992) and Schwanitz et al. (2014).

[68]Larsen and Shah (1992).

[69]See Depledge (2000), pp. 23–24.

[70]See Kyoto Protocol (n 28).

[71]See Asmelash (2016).

[72]See Pittsbrugh Agreement (n 6); G7 Ise-Shima Leaders' Declaration: G7 Ise-Shima Summit, 26–27 May 2016 (Ise-Shima Agreement).

[73]I have discussed this elsewhere, see Asmelash (2017).

by the Energy Charter Secretariat in the last year of his term in office, Lamy lamented that:

> [T]he on-going political debate on reforming fossil fuel subsidies has largely bypassed the WTO. The surge in world energy prices in recent years has drawn high-level attention to fossil fuel subsidies, including by the G-20. The link between subsidies, consumption of energy and climate change has added a new dimension to the debate. Given that WTO members have decided to tackle the issue of environmentally harmful subsidies in the fisheries sector ... the absence of this topic from the WTO radar screen can be considered as a missed opportunity.[74]

However, what is conspicuously absent from Lamy's speech was the question why fossil fuel subsidies have been absent from the radar screen of the WTO and how to bring them back? Obviously, it is not because WTO Members do not subsidise fossil fuels. Nor is it because WTO rules do not apply to fossil fuel subsidies. The same rules that apply to renewable energy subsidies apply to fossil fuel subsidies. It is also not because WTO Members are not concerned about fossil fuel subsidies. In fact, dual pricing practices in energy producing countries were discussed in the multilateral trading system as early as the 1982 GATT Ministerial Meeting.[75] Such practices were also raised in the WTO accession negotiations of energy producing countries such as Saud Arabia and Russia.[76]

Yet, fossil fuel subsidies have never been challenged in the multilateral trading system. Nor is there any initiative to place fossil fuel subsidy reforms on the WTO negotiating agenda. This is, as Lamy pointed out, despite the fact that WTO Members agreed to negotiate new subsidy rules for environmentally harmful fisheries subsidies some 15 years ago.[77] Are fisheries subsidies more environmentally harmful than fossil fuel subsidies? Would the elimination of fisheries subsidies contribute more to the environment than the removal of fossil fuel subsidies? The lack of legal and policy action to tackle the issue of fossil fuel subsidies in the WTO is perplexing, but what is even more perplexing is the scant attention paid to this lack of action in the academic debate on trade and environment.

In what follows, I will provide possible explanations as to why fossil fuel subsidies received scant attention and how to bring them into the ever-evolving academic debate on trade and the environment.

---

[74]Lamy (2013a).

[75]GATT Ministerial Declaration adopted on 29 November 1982, L/5424, p. 14.

[76]See Milthorp and David (2012).

[77]Doha Ministerial Declaration (20 November 2001) WT/MIN(01)/DEC/1, paras 28 & 31. For a detailed account of the negotiations, see Chen (2010).

4 What Kept Fossil Fuel Subsidies Off the Radar Screen?

A combination of factors may explain why fossil fuel subsidies remain largely off the radar screen of the trade and environment debate in the multilateral trading system. I have already mentioned that this debate takes place in three domains and that fossil fuel subsidies have been off the radar screen of all the three domains. WTO Panels and the Appellate Body only deal with issues that have been brought before them. But no challenge has been brought against fossil fuel subsidies. This is partly because fossil fuel subsidies constitute a weak case under the existing multilateral subsidy rules and countries are unlikely to initiate a formal dispute when they are less likely to win.[78] Another possible explanation is the so-called 'glass-house syndrome'. Most countries subsidise fossil fuels (albeit to varying degrees) and filing a dispute would tantamount to throwing stones from a glass-house. Yet another explanation for the lack of action against fossil fuel subsidies in the multilateral trading system is the lack of pressure from interest groups. Potential victims of foreign fossil fuel subsidies are either disorganised, or they are also fossil fuel subsidy recipients and therefore unlikely to demand their governments to challenge such subsidies legally.[79] Some of these explanations equally apply to the lack of policy discussion on fossil fuel subsidies. Perhaps an additional plausible explanation is that most fossil fuel producing countries were not members of the multilateral trading system until recently. In the absence of key fossil fuel producing countries (e.g. Saudi Arabia (until 2007) and Russia (until 2012), energy issues were left without key stakeholders (or targets of legal and policy measures) in the multilateral trading system (see Sect. 4.1 for more on this). Energy issues were instead addressed in other intergovernmental organisations such as the International Energy Agency (IEA), the Organization of Petroleum Exporting Countries (OPEC) and the Energy Charter Secretariat (ECT).

These explanations may also apply to some extent to the trade and environment scholarship. However, it is important to appreciate the crucial difference between the scholarly debate on the one hand and the judicial and policy debate on the other. One, for example, cannot explain why issues, such as the role—both potential and actual—of the multilateral subsidy rules in the global effort to phase out fossil fuel subsidies and the reasons for, and the implications of, the lack of legal and policy action against fossil fuel subsidies in the multilateral trading system, failed to attract significant scholarly attention through the glasshouse syndrome. In contrast to adjudicators and government officials, academics enjoy a great deal of freedom in the type of issues they chose to engage with.[80]

The Appellate Body is typically constrained by the nature of issues brought before it and more importantly by the provisions of the law. The type of issues

[78]See Asmelash (2015), pp. 279–282 (and the citation therein).

[79]See Asmelash (2015), pp. 282–284.

[80]For a general discussion on the degree of freedom that legal academics enjoy in comparison to judges and lawyers, see Schlag (2014), p. 235; Bianchi (2016), p. 6 et seq.

that governments may choose to address in the multilateral trading system is also constrained by various factors, including their national interests (e.g. glass house syndrome). For example, one cannot expect Saudi Arabia (or any other fossil fuel subsidising country for that matter) to express its concern about the environmental implications of fossil fuel subsidies and propose a ban on fossil fuel subsidies in the multilateral trading system. No such constraints weigh on academics.[81] Why then did the lack of legal and policy action against fossil fuel subsidies in the multilateral trading system receive scant scholarly attention? Below are four possible explanations that (in my opinion) could account for what kept fossil fuel subsidies off the academic radar screen.

4.1 Excluded by the 'Gentlemen's Agreement'?

Part of the reason why the lack of action against fossil fuel subsidies in the multilateral trading system received scant scholarly attention has to do with the widespread misconception about the regulation of energy in the multilateral trading system. There had long been a misconception that the energy sector is not subject to multilateral trade rules.[82] This misconception stems primarily from two sources. The first source of the misconception is the absence of energy-specific multilateral trade rules and the fact that energy issues have not featured prominently in discussions within the multilateral trading system. Although energy products constitute the single largest category of global merchandise exports, trade in energy has largely been kept off the agenda of multilateral trade negotiations. This has led some to suspect that the energy sector is outside the ambit of the multilateral trading system.[83]

However, the lack of energy-related discussions or energy-specific trade rules does not necessarily mean that the general provisions of the various multilateral trade agreements are not applicable to trade in energy. Leaving aside the question whether they are sophisticated enough to address the specificities of the energy sector, existing multilateral trade rules apply to the energy sector.[84] This is particularly evident from the various energy-related disputes that have been filed under the existing multilateral trade rules from *US-Superfund* and *US-Gasoline* to the recent *Canada-Renewable/FIT* and *India-Solar Cells*.

---

[81]In discussing the role of legal academics in responding to judicial activism by the European Court of Justice (ECJ), Anthony Arnul aptly pointed out: 'It is true that academics may be constrained in the work they can do by outside factors, [...] but those considerations are not generally seen as imposing on them any sort of ethical obligation to engage in a particular type of work'. See Arnull (2013), p. 215.

[82]Selivanova (2007).

[83]Selivanova (2010), p. 53.

[84]See, e.g., Marceau (2010), p. 83; Selivanova (2010), p. 53; Lamy (2013b).

What pushed the energy sector to the periphery of multilateral trade negotiations was instead the initial non-participation of important energy-exporting countries in the multilateral trading system.[85] While none of the current members of the Organization of the Petroleum Exporting Countries (OPEC) was among the original Contracting Parties to the GATT, Saudi Arabia and Russia joined the WTO only in 2007 and 2013, respectively.[86] The non-participation of these countries in the early rounds of multilateral trade negotiations provided less incentive for the rest of the membership to specifically address energy issues or negotiate energy-specific multilateral trade rules. This was further exacerbated by the fact that liberalising trade in energy was not a political priority at the time. Energy was cheap and abundant when the first set of multilateral trade negotiations that laid the foundation for the current multilateral trading system were conducted in the late 1940s.[87] It should, therefore, come as no surprise that the energy sector was not specifically addressed.

The second source of the misconception is the alleged existence of a 'gentlemen's agreement' excluding energy issues from the ambit of the multilateral trading system. The low profile of energy issues in the multilateral trading system is occasionally attributed to the existence of this illusive agreement.[88] However, no written evidence of this agreement can be found in the negotiating history of the multilateral trade agreements.[89] Nor is there any other evidence from which to infer its existence.[90] Even a cursory look at one of the numerous instances in which energy-related issues were raised and discussed in the multilateral trading system reveals that the existence of the gentlemen's agreement is more of a myth than reality.

The misconception has been pretty much debunked over the last few years,[91] but it has certainly played a part in detracting attention away from the lack of (legal and policy) action against environmentally harmful fossil fuel subsidies in the multilateral trading system. This is better understood when compared with fisheries subsidies. The environmental harmfulness of fisheries subsidies was recognised about the

[85] Selivanova (2014), p. 275; Desta (2003), p. 523.

[86] The inherent market access bias of the system and the fact that these countries export one product for which market access is not an issue said to have contributed to their reluctance to join the multilateral trading system. See Desta (2003), p. 531 et seq; UNCTAD (2000).

[87] See Lamy (2013b), p. 111; Cottier et al. (2009), p. 1.

[88] See UNCTAD (2000), p. 15.

[89] See Grigorova (2015), (persuasively dispelling the myth of the gentlemen's agreement based on general international law); Marhold (2013), p. 1 (noting that 'the existence, scope and content of the alleged gentlemen's agreement excluding energy is highly debatable. No written form of proof whatsoever of a gentlemen's agreement excluding energy trade from the GATT/WTO forum exists in GATT negotiating history.'), at fn. 2.

[90] Grigorova (2015); Meyer (2016), pp. 144–149 (documenting the instances in which energy issues were raised).

[91] See Selivanova (2010), p. 53 (arguing that it is now commonly accepted that WTO agreements apply equally to energy as to any other product).

same time that the environmental harmfulness of fossil fuel subsidies was recognised. The negative environmental impact of both fossil fuel and fisheries subsidies was well established in the literature in the 1980s.[92] Intergovernmental efforts to address these pervasive subsidies started in the 1990s. However, these efforts took place in different fora. Fossil fuel subsidies were entirely left for the fragmented energy and environmental regimes, while fisheries subsidies were brought to the multilateral trading system. Fisheries subsidies eventually became one of the few environmental-related issues included in the ill-fated Doha round of multilateral trade negotiations.

Their inclusion reflects the common understanding that the existing multilateral subsidy rules are inadequate to discipline environmentally harmful fisheries subsidies. However, it was not questioned (either in the academic or policy circles) whether the same rules could also be adequate to discipline environmentally harmful fossil fuel subsidies. This is surely not because fossil fuel subsidies cause less environmental concerns than fisheries subsidies. Fisheries subsidies are neither more environmentally harmful nor more pervasive than fossil fuel subsidies. The only plausible explanation is the misconception that fossil fuel subsidies were not subject to the multilateral subsidy rules.

4.2 No Dispute, No Debate?

The scholarly debate on trade and environment has the tendency to be driven by case law. This is, of course, not uncommon to international legal scholarship. Case commentary has always been at the heart of traditional legal scholarship. In a recent book where he examined the different theories of international law, Andrea Bianchi observed that international legal scholarship is still preoccupied with traditional legal research: 'The content and scope of rules are frequently discussed, and judicial interpretation is often taken as the ultimate authoritative determination of meaning either to be praised or criticized'.[93] Judicial decisions of international courts and tribunals consistently elicit vivid academic discussions about the nature, object, scope and practical implications of the law in question.

This is especially true for international legal scholarship that focuses on regime interaction. In his critique of the 'court-centric' approach to regime interaction in international legal scholarship, Dunoff argued that: 'Typically, exploration of regime interaction starts – and often stops – with analysis of international court and tribunal decisions'.[94] The trade and environment debate is a perfect example for this. Most of the issues that formed part of the debate are those that have been brought before the

[92]See Schrank (2001), p. 11 et seq; Larsen and Shah (1992) (and the citation therein).

[93]Bianchi (2016), p. 6.

[94]Dunoff (2012), p. 137.

dispute settlement system.[95] The unadopted GATT Panel rulings in *US-Tuna I* and *US-Tuna II* are primarily responsible for bringing the issue of environmentally motivated trade bans and extraterritorial application of environmental measures to the trade and environment debate. The interaction between multilateral trade and environmental agreements came to the forefront of the debate particularly in the wake of the Appellate Body's rulings in *US-Gasoline* and *US-Shrimp*. The treatment of renewable energy subsidies under the SCM Agreement became a topical issue only after *Canada-Renewable Energy/FIT*. The renewable energy subsidy disputes, in particular, have clearly demonstrated the role of legal disputes in shaping the direction and focus of the trade and environment debate. The scant scholarly attention devoted to fossil fuel subsidies can, therefore, be attributed in part to the absence of disputes over fossil fuel subsidies in the multilateral trading system. One dispute over fossil fuel subsidies will inevitably change the situation, but such a dispute is not yet in sight.

4.3 Ask Not What the WTO Can Do for the Environment by a Positive Action, But What It Can Do by Inaction

> To date, most of the all-too-little attention paid thus far to the connection between trade and climate change has focused on how trade rules constrain national actions [...] But WTO rules offer opportunities as well as constraints in the struggle to slow climate change, and these opportunities are currently being missed.[96]

Another key feature of the trade and environment debate is its heavy emphasis on what the multilateral trading system can do for the environment by inaction as compared to what it can do by a positive action. Inaction here refers to multilateral trade rules not preventing governments from adopting trade-restrictive environmental measures. Such inactions typically take the form of environmental exceptions. The various multilateral trade agreements contain environmental exception clauses of one form or another. The scope and application of these clauses has been and continues to be the pivot of the scholarly debate on trade and environment. This overemphasis on environmental exceptions partly reflects the influence of the case law. The justifiability of environmentally motivated trade bans under the environmental exceptions contained in GATT Article XX was the dominant issue in most of the trade and environment disputes.[97] The trade and environment issues that arose from the recent spate of disputes over renewable energy subsidies are not different

[95]See Wu and Salzman (2014), p. 411 (concluding that 'The decisions in these so-called Classic cases were hugely influential, seizing the attention of both the environmental and academic communities, and quite literally creating the field of trade and environment law.'). Perhaps the only major exception in this regard is the discussion over border carbon adjustments.

[96]WEF Ad Hoc Working Group on Trade & Climate Change (2010), p. 13.

[97]See, e.g., *US-Tuna I* (n 12); *US-Tuna II* (n 12); *US-Gasoline* (n 21); *US-Shrimp* (n 23).

either. As explained in the preceding section, the existence or adequacy of environmental exceptions for renewable energy subsidies under the SCM Agreement is the principal focus of the trade and environment debate on the regulation of renewable energy subsidies.

Whether and, if so, how multilateral trade agreements positively contribute to the protection of the environment is a relatively less popular line of inquiry in the trade and environment scholarship. Environmentalists and free trade advocates fiercely disagree on whether free trade harms or benefits the environment. However, despite this disagreement, there is a growing mutual understanding that multilateral trade rules can be used affirmatively to protect the environment.[98] Commonly cited examples include the regulation of trade in dangerous materials, environmentally harmful subsidies, and trade in environmental goods and services. However, these rules (except those relevant to fisheries subsidies and environmental goods and services)[99] receive relatively limited attention.

Part of the reason for the lack of emphasis on such rules stems from the historical roots of the debate. Concerns over the negative impact of free trade on the environment are central to the trade and environment debate. Environmentalists have long argued that free trade is detrimental to the environment to the extent that it enhances industrial production and transportation, improves economic growth (and hence exacerbates the unsustainable use of natural resources), and creates a race-to-the-bottom in environmental standards.[100] The dominance of this view has led to the widespread perception that the multilateral trading system is hostile to the environment.

This, in turn, placed advocates of the multilateral trading system in a defensive position. Their argument in defence of the multilateral trading system often includes reference to the flexibility of multilateral trade rules in accommodating trade-restrictive environmental measures.[101] The frequent resort to the environmental exceptions is perhaps induced by the fact that while the environmental exceptions have already been built into existing multilateral trade agreements, rules that positively contribute to environmental protection were not designed specifically for such purpose (e.g. environmentally harmful subsidies) or they are still under negotiations (e.g. trade in environmental goods and services). Whatever the reason might be, the scant scholarly attention devoted to the lack of action against fossil fuel subsidies echoes the biased focus of the trade and environment debate on what the multilateral trading system can do for the environment by inaction.

[98]See Lamy (2013b), p. 55 et seq.

[99]This is mainly because of their inclusion in the Doha Round of multilateral trade negotiations.

[100]See, in general, Esty (1994).

[101]Esty (1993), p. 32 (noting that 'Much of the discussion to date has focused on possible legal refinements to the GATT to build environmental sensitivity into the international trading system.').

4.4 A Sustainable Development Problem?

Another plausible explanation for the scant attention paid to the fossil fuel subsidy issue in the academic debate on trade and environment relates to the framework underpinning the debate. As the common goal of the trade and environment regimes, sustainable development is the broader framework within which the trade and environment debate currently takes place. The problem with using sustainable development as a frame of reference stems from its vast scope and vagueness. There is no internationally agreed single definition of sustainable development. The absence of a single definition proves that 'sustainable development is a notoriously difficult, slippery and elusive concept to pin down'.[102]

The most widely used definition comes from the Brundtland Report on *Our Common Future*, which for the first time defined sustainable development in 1987 as: 'development that meets the needs of the present generation without compromising the ability of future generations to meet their own needs'.[103] This definition raised more questions than it answered.[104] The vague terminologies such as 'development', 'needs' and 'future generations' have left the concept open to multiple interpretations. Sustainable development has now become an all-embracing concept with three interdependent pillars: economic, social and environmental sustainability.

The underlying assumption behind the concept of sustainable development—at least as used in the context of the multilateral trading system—is that these three pillars are mutually supportive.[105] That is, free trade and free trade agreements promote not only economic development but also social welfare and environmental protection. But mutual supportiveness is only one dimension of the interaction between trade and environment.[106] The other and more problematic dimension of the interaction is represented by tension and conflict between trade and environment. Any conflict between the two entails balancing between trade and environmental objectives. Balancing, as Lydgate pointed out, raises the challenging question of which objective is more important and who is empowered to decide.[107] Balancing has also been more relevant and controversial than mutual supportiveness in dispute settlement. From a sustainable development perspective, the interaction between trade and environment becomes a cause for concern only insofar as environmental protection policies run into conflict with multilateral trade rules. The implication for the trade and environment debate is that the sustainable development represented by

[102]See Williams and Millington (2004), p. 99.

[103]Report of the World Commission on Environment and Development: Our Common Future. Transmitted to the General Assembly as an Annex to document A/42/427—Development and International Co-operation: Environment (4 August 1987) 42nd Session (Brundtland Report).

[104]On the definition of sustainable development, see Sum and Hills (1998), p. 129; Williams and Millington (2004).

[105]Pavoni (2010), p. 649.

[106]Lydgate (2012), p. 621.

[107]Lydgate (2012).

mutual supportiveness receives far less attention than the sustainable development represented by balancing.

The regulation of energy subsidies represents a unique area where multilateral trade rules and environmental protection policies have a potential for both conflict and mutual supportiveness.[108] The two are mutually supportive to the extent that the multilateral trade rules discourage trade distortive and environmentally harmful fossil fuel subsidies. But they may also run into conflict when multilateral trade rules prohibit the subsidisation of renewable energy sources. Looking at the interaction between energy subsidies and multilateral rules on subsidies through the sustainable development conceptual lens puts much more emphasis on the area of conflict than the area of mutual supportiveness.

5 Concluding Remarks

> Reflections on the link between trade and climate change, and on the eventual role of the WTO rulebook on an issue such as fossil-fuel subsidies, must take place. We must prepare ourselves intellectually for the moment when we may be required to act.[109]

Recent trade disputes over renewable energy subsidies have brought the regulation of energy subsidies in the multilateral trading system from obscurity to the spotlight. However, the fossil fuel subsidy dimension of the trade and environment issues that arise from the regulation of energy subsidies receives much less attention than it deserves both in policy and academic circles. Lamy has described the absence of fossil fuel subsidies from the radar screen of the multilateral trading system as a missed opportunity.[110] It is indeed perplexing that fossil fuel subsidies are being discussed outside the multilateral trading system—the only multilateral forum with binding rules applicable to fossil fuel subsidies.

The multilateral trading system also has strong dispute settlement mechanism and well-equipped institutional machinery, which serves as a forum for negotiations and implementation of agreements. The fact that the multilateral trading system has already taken up the issue of environmentally harmful fisheries subsidies makes the lack of action to address fossil fuel subsidies (and the scant scholarly attention to the inaction) all the more perplexing.

Much of the policy and academic debate on fossil fuel subsidies currently takes place in the context of multiple intergovernmental forums, including the G20 and the UNFCCC. The involvement of multiple intergovernmental organisations indicates the crosscutting nature of the issue, but it also underscores the fragmentation of global environmental and energy governance. Intergovernmental efforts to phase out fossil fuel subsidies have neither a single institutional home nor a coordination

[108] See Bigdeli (2008).
[109] Singh (2010).
[110] Lamy (2013a).

mechanism. They are also yet to bear sufficient fruits. Global fossil fuel subsidies remain significantly high despite these widespread efforts. This implies that there is still a vital role for the multilateral trading system. The failure to include fossil fuel subsidies in the Doha Round agenda was perhaps a missed opportunity, but as the ancient proverb goes, 'The best time to plant a tree is twenty years ago. The second-best time is now'.

Previous intergovernmental efforts have laid the groundwork for the multilateral trading system to address fossil fuel subsidies. A growing consensus has emerged in the last few years on the need to phase out environmentally harmful fossil fuel subsidies. The discussion has moved from whether to remove fossil fuel subsidies to when and how best to do so. There is now more information (about the magnitude, taxonomy and impacts of fossil fuel subsidies) available than ever before. International institutions such as the International Energy Agency (IEA), IMF and the Global Subsidies Initiative (GSI) have played a significant role in this regard. The last few years have also seen the formation of an intergovernmental coalition for fossil fuel subsidy reform. The Friends of Fossil Fuel Subsidy Reform (FFFSR), an informal group of eight non-G20 countries, is established to advance intergovernmental efforts to reform fossil fuel subsidies.[111] Similar coalitions have played a vital role in putting sensitive issues on the agenda of the multilateral trading system. For example, the 'Friends of Fish'—a small group of countries concerned by the depletion of global fish stocks because of overfishing—was primarily responsible for the inclusion of harmful fisheries subsidies in the Doha Round agenda.[112] The FFFSR is well positioned to play a similar role.

The stage is almost set for the multilateral trading system to address fossil fuel subsidies. The only missing ingredient is critical reflections on the topic. Numerous open questions remain to be answered. Some of these questions include: Is the multilateral trading system the appropriate venue to deal with fossil fuel subsidies? How can the multilateral trading system contribute to the elimination of fossil fuel subsidies? Are the existing multilateral subsidy rules adequate to discipline fossil fuel subsidies? Is a law reform necessary? What are the legal avenues to do so?

The trade and environment debate on the regulation of energy subsidies has not yet concerned itself with most of these questions. My primary goal in this paper was to offer some explanations for this. Understanding the reasons behind the problem is not solving the problem. But it certainly is an essential step in that direction. To the best of my knowledge, this is the first attempt to explain what kept fossil fuel subsidies off the radar screen of the academic debate on trade and environment. The explanations offered here are not the only possible explanations, but, in my opinion, they are the most important ones. A second step would be to reflect upon possible frameworks within which the above questions could be addressed. Such a framework needs to bring together both the renewable energy and fossil fuel subsidy

[111] The FFSR has already raised the issue of fossil fuel subsidies in the WTO Committee on Trade and Environment (CTE). See WTO (2015, 2016).

[112] See Bigdeli (2008).

dimensions of the regulations of energy subsidies in the multilateral trading system. This is simply because the two issues are two sides of the same coin. Not only do they share the same underlying objectives, but they are also concerned with the same set of rules. Greening the SCM Agreement entails making sure that its rules are both flexible enough (to accommodate renewable energy subsidies) and tight enough (to discipline environmentally harmful fossil fuel subsidies) at the same time.

References

Arnull A (2013) Judicial activism and the European Court of Justice: how should academics respond? In: de Witte B, Muir E, Dawson M (eds) Judicial activism at the European Court of Justice. Edward Elgar Publishing, Cheltenham

Asmelash HB (2015) Energy subsidies and WTO dispute settlement: why only renewable energy subsidies are challenged. J Int Econ Law 18:261–265

Asmelash HB (2016) The G7's pledge to end fossil fuel subsidies by 2025: mere rhetoric or a sign of post-Paris momentum? Eur Soc Int Law 5:7. Reflections 1

Asmelash HB (2017) Falling oil prices and sustainable energy transition: towards a multilateral agreement on fossil-fuel subsidies. In: Arent D et al (eds) The political economy of clean energy transitions. Oxford University Press, Oxford, pp 349–367

Ayala FA, Gallagher KP (2009) Subsidizing sustainable development under the WTO. J World Invest Trade 10:131

Bacchus J (2012) The case for clean subsidies. Harvard Business Review. https://hbr.org/2012/11/the-case-for-clean-subsidies

Bhagwati J, Mavroidis PC (2007) Is action against US exports for failure to sign Kyoto Protocol WTO-legal? World Trade Rev 6:299–310

Bianchi A (2016) International law theories: an inquiry into different ways of thinking. Oxford University Press, Oxford

Bigdeli SZ (2008) Will the "friends of climate" emerge in the WTO? The prospects of applying the "fisheries subsidies" model to energy subsidies. Carbon Clim Law Rev 2:78–88

Bigdeli SZ (2009) Incentives schemes to promote renewables and the WTO law of subsidies. In: Cottier T, Nartova O, Bigdeli S (eds) International trade regulation and the mitigation of climate change. Cambridge University Press, Cambridge, pp 155–192

Bigdeli SZ (2011) Resurrecting the dead? The expired non-actionable subsidies and the lingering question of green space. Manchester J Int Econ Law 8:2–37

Bigdeli SZ (2016) Feed-in-tariffs and the WTO regulation of subsidies—a moment of progressive adjudication in Canada–renewable energy. In: Delimatsis P (ed) Research handbook on climate change and trade law. Edward Elgar Publishing, Cheltenham, pp 119–147

Burniaux J-M, Chateau J (2014) Greenhouse gases mitigation potential and economic efficiency of phasing-out fossil fuel subsidies. Int Econ 140:71–88

Cartland M, Depayre G, Woznowski J (2012) Is something going wrong in the WTO dispute settlement? J World Trade 46:979–1015

Casier L, Moerenhout T (2013) WTO members not the appellate body needs to clarify boundaries in renewable energy support. International Institute for Sustainable Development, Winnipeg

Charnovitz S (2007a) A new WTO paradigm for trade and the environment. Singapore Yearb Int Law 11:15

Charnovitz S (2007b) The WTO's environmental progress. J Int Econ Law 10:685–706

Charnovitz S (2014) Green subsidies and the WTO (World Bank)

Chen C-J (2010) Fisheries subsidies under international law. Springer, Berlin

Clements B, Coady D, Fabrizio S, Gupta S, Alleyne T, Sdralevich C (eds) (2013) Energy subsidy reform: lessons and implications. International Monetary Fund, Washington
Coady D et al (2015) How large are global energy subsidies? IMF Working Paper WP/15/105 (International Monetary Fund)
Coady D, Parry I, Sears L, Shang B (2017) How large are global fossil fuel subsidies? World Dev 91:11–27
Cosbey A, Mavroidis P (2014) A turquoise mess: green subsidies, blue industrial policy and renewable energy: the case for redrafting the subsidies agreement of the WTO. J Int Econ Law 17:1–37
Cottier T (2014) Renewable energy and WTO law: more policy space or enhanced disciplines. Renew Energy Law Policy Rev 5:40–51
Cottier T et al (2009) Energy in WTO law and policy (NCCR Trade Regulation) Working Paper No. 2009/25
Depledge J (2000) Tracing the origins of the Kyoto Protocol: an article by article textual history. (United Nation Framework Convention on Climate Change) Technical Paper FCCC/TP/2000/2
Desta MG (2003) The organization of petroleum exporting countries, the World Trade Organization, and regional trade agreements. J World Trade 37:523–551
Dunoff JL (2012) A new approach to regime interaction. In: Young MA (ed) Regime interaction in international law: facing fragmentation. Cambridge University Press, Cambridge
Esty DC (1993) GATTing the greens: not just greening the GATT. Foreign Aff 72:523–551
Esty DC (1994) Greening the GATT: trade, environment, and the future. Institute for International Economics, Washington
Farah PD, Cima E (2014) World Trade Organization, renewable energy subsidies, and the case of feed-in tariffs: time for reform toward sustainable development. Georgetown Int Environ Law Rev 27:516–537
Feld DS, Switzer S (2012) Whither Article XX? Regulatory autonomy under non-GATT agreements after China—raw materials. Yale J Int Law Online 38:16–30
GATT (1991) DS21/R - 39S/155. Panel report, United States – restrictions on imports of Tuna (US-Tuna I). Circulated 3 September 1991 (not adopted)
GATT (1994) DS29/R. Panel report, United States – restrictions on imports of Tuna (US-Tuna II). Circulated 16 June 1994 (not adopted)
Giupponi BO (2015) Mapping emerging countries' role in renewable energy trade disputes. Transnational Dispute Management 12
Green A (2006) Trade rules and climate change subsidies. World Trade Rev 5:377–414
Greenwald J (2003) WTO dispute settlement: an exercise in trade law legislation? J Int Econ Law 6:113–124
Grigorova J (2015) WTO law and energy resources: the absurdity of a systemic exclusion of the energy sector by a Gentlemen's agreement. Centre for International and Transnational Law
Havel BF, Sanchez GS (2014) The principles and practice of international aviation law. Cambridge University Press, Cambridge
Howse R (2006) World trade law and renewable energy: the case of non-tariff measures. J Eur Environ Plann Law 3:500–518
Howse R (2008) http://worldtradelaw.typepad.com/ielpblog/2008/12/careful-what-you-propose.html
Howse R (2013) Securing policy space for clean energy under the SCM: alternative approaches. In: ICTSD (ed) Clean energy and the trade system group proposals and analysis. International Centre for Trade and Sustainable Development
Howse R (2016) The World Trade Organization 20 years on: global governance by judiciary. Eur J Int Law 27:9–77
Howse R, Eliason A (2009) Countervailing duties and subsidies for climate mitigation. In: Stewart RB, Kingsbury B, Rudyk B (eds) Climate finance: regulatory and funding strategies for climate change and global development. New York University Press, New York

IEA (2012) World Energy Outlook. Organization for Economic Cooperation and Development & International Energy Agency
IEA (2015) World Energy Outlook 2015. Organization for Economic Cooperation and Development & International Energy Agency
IEA, (International Energy Agency) (2016) World energy outlook. IEA, Paris
Jegou I, Rubini L (2011) The allocation of emission allowances free of charge: legal and economic considerations. International Centre for Trade and Sustainable Development. Issue Paper 13
Joseph J (1994) The Tuna-Dolphin controversy in the Eastern Pacific Ocean: biological, economic, and political impacts. Ocean Dev Int Law 25:1–30
Kingsbury B (1994) The Tuna-Dolphin controversy, the World Trade Organization, and the liberal project to reconceptualize international law. Yearb Int Environ Law 5:1–40
Kulovesi K (2011) The WTO dispute settlement system: challenges of the environment, legitimacy and fragmentation. Kluwer Law International, Alphen aan den Rijn
Kulovesi K (2014) Real or imagined controversies? A climate law perspective on the growing links between the international trade and climate change regimes. Trade Law Dev 6:56–92
Lamy P (2013a) Energy policies and the WTO. Workshop on intergovernmental agreements in energy policy, Geneva. https://www.wto.org/english/news_e/sppl_e/sppl279_e.htm
Lamy P (2013b) The Geneva consensus: making trade work for all. Cambridge University Press, Cambridge
Larsen B, Shah A (1992) World fossil fuel subsidies and global carbon emissions. World Bank Policy Research Working Paper WPS 1002
Leal-Arcas R, Filis A (2015) Renewable energy disputes in the World Trade Organization. Oil Gas Energy Law J 15
Lewis J (2014) The rise of renewable energy protectionism: emerging trade conflicts and implications for low carbon development. Global Environ Polit 14:10–29
Lydgate E (2012) Sustainable development in the WTO: from mutual supportiveness to balancing. World Trade Rev 11:621–639
Marceau G (2010) The WTO in the emerging energy governance debate. Global Trade Customs J 5:83–93
Marhold A (2013) The World Trade Organization and energy: fuel for debate. ESIL Reflections 2
McGlade C, Ekins P (2015) The geographical distribution of fossil fuels unused when limiting global warming to 2 °C. Nature 517:187–190
Meyer T (2016) The World Trade Organization's role in global energy governance. In: Van de Graaf T et al (eds) The Palgrave handbook of the international political economy of energy. Palgrave Macmillan UK, Hampshire, pp 139–171
Milthorp P, David C (2012) Energy issues in selected WTO accessions. In: Selivanova J (ed) Regulation of energy in international trade law: WTO, NAFTA, and Energy Charter. Kluwer Law International, Alphen aan den Rijn, pp 259–302
Pauwelyn J (2004) Recent books on trade and environment: GATT phantoms still haunt the WTO. Eur J Int Law 15:575–592
Pauwelyn J (2013) Carbon leakage measures and border tax adjustments under WTO law. In: van Calster G, Prévost D (eds) Research handbook on environment, health and the WTO. Edward Elgar Publishing, Cheltenham, pp 448–506
Pavoni R (2010) Mutual supportiveness as a principle of interpretation and law-making: a watershed for the "WTO-and-competing-regimes" debate? Eur J Int Law 21:649–679
Rubini L (2012) Ain't Wastin' time no more: subsidies for renewable energy. The SCM agreement, policy space, and law reform. J Int Econ Law 15:525–579
Rubini L (2014) The good, the bad, and the ugly. Lessons on methodology in legal analysis from the recent WTO litigation on renewable energy subsidies. J World Trade 48:153–194
Rubini L (2015) The wide and the narrow gate: benchmarking in the SCM agreement after the Canada–renewable energy/FIT ruling. World Trade Rev 14:211–237
Rubini L (2017) ASCM disciplines and recent WTO case law developments: what space for "green" subsidies? In: Cottier T, Espa I (eds) International trade in sustainable electricity:

regulatory challenges in international economic law. Cambridge University Press, Cambridge, pp 1–50
Schlag P (2014) A comment on Thomas Schultz's editorial. J Int Dispute Settlement 5:235–237
Schrank WE (2001) Subsidies for fisheries: a review of concepts. In: FAO (ed) Expert consultation on identifying, assessing and reporting on subsidies in the fishing industry. Food and Agriculture Organization
Schwanitz VJ, Franziska P, Christoph B, Gunnar L (2014) Long-term climate policy implications of phasing out fossil fuel subsidies. Energy Policy 67:882–894
Selivanova Y (2007) The WTO and energy: WTO rules and agreements of relevance to the energy sector. International Centre for Trade and Sustainable Development
Selivanova Y (2010) Managing the patchwork of agreements in trade and investment. In: Goldthau A, Witte JM (eds) Global energy governance: the new rules of the game. Brookings Institution Press, Washington, pp 49–72
Selivanova Y (2014) The WTO agreements and energy. In: Talus K (ed) Research handbook on international energy law. Edward Elgar Publishing, Northampton, pp 257–307
Shadikhodjaev S (2015) Renewable energy and government support: time to "green" the SCM agreement? World Trade Rev 14:479–506
Shaffer G (2016) Will the US undermine the World Trade Organization? The Huffington Post. http://www.huffingtonpost.com/gregory-shaffer/will-the-us-undermine-the_b_10108970.html
Simmons ZS (2014) Subsidizing solar: the case for an environmental goods and services carve-out from the global subsidies regime. UCLA J Environ Law Policy 32:422–484
Singh HV (2010) WTO Deputy Director General. Opening remarks. In: A joint conference on increasing the momentum of fossil-fuel subsidy reform: developments and opportunities, Geneva, October 2010. https://www.wto.org/english/news_e/news10_e/ddg_14oct10_e.htm
Stiglitz JE (2006) Making globalization work. WW Norton & Co., New York
Sugathan M (2013) Winds of change and rays of hope: how can the multilateral trading system facilitate trade in clean energy technologies and services? In: ICTSD (ed) Clean energy and the trade system group proposals and analysis. International Centre for Trade and Sustainable Development 2013
Sum MC, Hills P (1998) Interpreting sustainable development. J Environ Sci 10:129–143
Sykes AO (2003) The economics of WTO rules on subsidies and countervailing measures. Olin Law and Economics Working Paper No. 186. University of Chicago Law School, Chicago
Sykes AO (2007) Trade remedy Laws. In: Guzman AT, Sykes AO, Elgar E (eds) Research handbook in international economic law. Edward Elgar, Northampton, pp 62–102
Sykes AO (2010) The questionable case for subsidies regulation: a comparative perspective. J Legal Anal 2:473–523
Thaggert HL (1994) A closer look at the Tuna-Dolphin case: "like products" and "extrajurisdictionality" in the trade and environment context. In: Cameron J, Geradin D, Demaret P (eds) Trade & the environment: the search for balance. Cameron May Ltd., London, pp 69–95
UNCTAD (2000) UNCTAD/ITCD/TSB/9. Trade agreements, petroleum, and energy policies
UNCTAD (2014) Trade remedies: targeting the renewable energy sector. United Nations Publication
Weber RH, Koch R (2015) International trade law challenges by subsidies for renewable energy. J World Trade 49:757–780
WEF (2010) From collision to vision: climate change and world trade. A discussion paper of the Ad Hoc Working Group on trade and climate change. World Economic Forum
Williams CC, Millington AC (2004) The diverse and contested meanings of sustainable development. Geogr J 170:99–104
WTO (1996) WT/DS2/AB/R. Appellate body report, United States - Standards for reformulated and conventional gasoline (US-Gasoline)
WTO (1998) WT/DSS8/AB/R. Appellate body report, United States-Import prohibition of certain shrimp and shrimp products (US-Shrimp)

WTO (2001) WT/DS58/RW. Panel report, United States - Import prohibition of certain shrimp and shrimp products, recourse to Article 215 of the DSU by Malaysia (US-Shrimp)
WTO (2013) WT/DS412/AB/R & WT/DS426/AB/R. Appellate body reports, Canada. Certain measures affecting the renewable energy generation sector (Canada-Renewable Energy)/Canada - measures relating to the Feed-in tariff program
WTO (2015) Energy efficiency and illegal logging at centre of discussions in environment committee. https://www.wto.org/english/news_e/news15_e/envir_22jun15_e.htm
WTO (2016) WTO members discuss climate change, chemicals and waste management. https://www.wto.org/english/news_e/news16_e/envir_14nov16_e.htm
WTO (2017) Disputes by agreement (as Cited in Request for Consultations). https://www.wto.org/english/tratop_e/dispu_e/dispu_agreements_index_e.htm?id=A20
Wu M, Salzman J (2014) The next generation of trade and environmental conflicts: the rise of green industrial policy. Northwest Univ Law Rev 108:401–474

Henok Birhanu Asmelash Research Fellow, Max Planck Institute Luxembourg for Procedural Law, 4 rue Alphonse Weicker, L-2721 Luxembourg, Tel: (+352) 26 94 88 417, henok.asmelash@mpi.lu. PhD Candidate in International Law and Economics, Bocconi University, Via Roentgen, 20136 Milan, henok.asmelash@mpi.lu.

Promoting Renewable Energies Through State Aid, a Reform is Required

Régis Lanneau

Abstract In this article, I suggest a reconceptualization of state aid to include non-action by a government in a situation in which a clear negative externality exists. Indeed, the current state of state aid regulation, which only focuses on positive action, appears inefficient to incentivize the promotion of sustainable ways to produce energy. This reconceptualization would not require a radical change in positive law, merely a reinterpretation in line with the economic orthodoxy.

1 Introduction

> Not only do fossil-fuel subsidies undermine efforts to mitigate climate change, but they are also costly and distortive.[1]

> The general objective of environmental aid is to increase the level of environmental protection compared to the level that would be achieved in the absence of the aid [...] The primary objective of aid in the energy sector is to ensure a competitive, sustainable and secure energy system in a well-functioning Union energy market.[2]

"The state—the machinery and power of the state—is a potential resource or threat to every industry in the society. With its power to prohibit or compel, to take or give money, the state can and does selectively help or hurt a vast number of industries".[3] The power to give money to achieve some political ends is apprehended and harnessed, in legal terms, through the notions of subsidies (WTO, SCM agreement) or state aids (EU law). Article 107 TFEU is characterizing state aid as "any aid granted by a Member State or through State resources in any form whatsoever which

---

[1]OECD (2015), p. 11.

[2]European Commission (2014a, b), §30.

[3]Stigler (1971), p. 3.

R. Lanneau (✉)
Université de Paris Ouest Nanterre la Défense, Nanterre Cedex, France
e-mail: regis.lanneau@sciencespo.fr

K. Mathis, B. R. Huber (eds.), *Energy Law and Economics*, Economic Analysis of Law in European Legal Scholarship 5, https://doi.org/10.1007/978-3-319-74636-4_15

distorts or threatens to distort competition by favouring certain undertakings or the production of certain goods [. . .], in so far as it affects trade between Member States".[4] Case law is not restricting state aid to narrowly understood subsidies (direct transfer) and includes loans, direct investment, tax reliefs, preferential tariffs, tax remission, free allocation of pollution rights, etc.. . . Moreover, and in a conventional approach to state aid (and subsidies control), it is because state aid potentially has an impact on the competitive position of economic agents (because of a benefit or an advantage they are providing) and creates some trans-frontiers spill-overs (affecting trade between Member States) that these "spendings" are or should be controlled at a supra-national level.[5] State aid is in general considered as incompatible with the internal market of the European Union (EU). Such an incompatibility rests on the idea that, "market-based economy provides the best guarantee for raising living conditions in the EU to the benefit of citizens".[6] Nevertheless, like other state interventions in the economy, state aid (broadly conceived) could also enhance welfare if used to correct market failures (mostly when a positive externality is identified).[7] Support schemes are thus not always considered as incompatible. Article 107(2)[8] and (3)[9] TFEU provides a list of measures, which are or may be

---

[4]In the language of the European Court of Justice, the aid should create (1) a selective (2) advantage (3) affecting competition between Member States (4) using states resources and be attributable to the State. These criteria are slightly different from the wording of Article 107 TFEU.

[5]For details regarding the economic analysis of state aids, see Spector (2009); Röller et al. (2008); Neven and Verouden (2008); Collie (2000) and Dewatripont and Seabright (2006).

[6]European Commission (2005).

[7]This logic is recognized by the European Commission: "*State aid measures can sometimes be effective tools for achieving objectives of common interest. They can correct market failures, thereby improving the functioning of markets and enhancing European competitiveness*" (European Commission 2005, pt. 10). The Lispsey-Lancaster theorem is clearly not considered by such a statement. It also added, more mysteriously from an economic point of view: "*They can also help promote* e.g. *social and regional cohesion, sustainable development and cultural diversity, irrespective of the correction of market failures*".

[8]"2. The following shall be compatible with the internal market:

(a) aid having a social character, granted to individual consumers, provided that such aid is granted without discrimination related to the origin of the products concerned;
(b) aid to make good the damage caused by natural disasters or exceptional occurrences;
(c) aid granted to the economy of certain areas of the Federal Republic of Germany affected by the division of Germany, in so far as such aid is required in order to compensate for the economic disadvantages caused by that division. Five years after the entry into force of the Treaty of Lisbon, the Council, acting on a proposal from the Commission, may adopt a decision repealing this point".

[9]"3. The following may be considered to be compatible with the internal market:

(a) aid to promote the economic development of areas where the standard of living is abnormally low or where there is serious underemployment, and of the regions referred to in Article 349, in view of their structural, economic and social situation;
(b) aid to promote the execution of an important project of common European interest or to remedy a serious disturbance in the economy of a Member State;

compatible with the internal market.[10] These provisions are sufficiently broad to leave considerable scope for interpretation to the European Court of Justice and the European Commission.

State support (including aid) in the energy sector is targeted and debated especially since the beginning of the twenty-first century. Targeted because according to the OECD, state support for the production and consumption of fossil fuels in OECD countries amounted to about 55–90 billion USD every year during the period of 2005–2011.[11] This figure is just an estimate and does not focus particularly on the energy sector or European countries, but the OECD includes most of the European countries and fossil fuels are a type of energy and are used to produce energy. Such state support is not without questioning the efficiency of the enforcement of Article 107 TFEU. Moreover, this support seems incompatible with the 2020 climate targets of the European Commission to reduce greenhouse gas emissions by at least 20% compared with 1990 levels, increase the share of renewable energy in final consumption to 20% and move towards a 20% increase in energy efficiency[12] and more generally with the required need to create a low carbon economy to ensure sustainable development. It is true, that, in 2014, EU greenhouse gas emission were down by 22.9% compared to the 1990 levels and that the share of renewable energy consumption reached 16%. It is also true that energy industries contributed to a reduction of the equivalent of 413 million tons of CO_2 equivalent between 1990 and 2014 through the development of renewable energy. However, the energy sector is still responsible for 28.2% of the EU emission in 2014. Besides, if this transition is, in part, the result of state support for promoting renewable energy sources, it does not mean that these support schemes are necessarily cost efficient. Debated, because energy policies are sensitive by nature—for both consumers (e.g. because it affects prices) and producers (because they should adapt to new models and realities)—and are raising geopolitical (e.g. energy independence and security of energy supplies), social (e.g. sufficiently cheap access to energy for poor households), strategic (e.g. how to ensure a change in the energy mix without hampering economic growth) and of course environmental questions.

Controlling state aid could then be considered as crucial for limiting the emergence of inefficient support schemes and the transition towards a low carbon economy. Support for renewable energies is not mentioned by this article but could be (and has been) linked with Article 107(3)(c) TFEU regarding "*aid to facilitate the development of certain economic activities or of certain economic*

(c) aid to facilitate the development of certain economic activities or of certain economic areas, where such aid does not adversely affect trading conditions to an extent contrary to the common interest;
(d) aid to promote culture and heritage conservation where such aid does not affect trading conditions and competition in the Union to an extent that is contrary to the common interest;
(e) such other categories of aid as may be specified by decision of the Council on a proposal from the Commission".

[10]Some specific regulations for coal exist.

[11]OECD (2013), p. 3.

[12]European Commission (2008a), pp. 2–4.

areas, where such aid does not adversely affect trading conditions to an extent contrary to the common interest".[13] This formulation of course requires some specifications. Thus, "*in order to familiarise Member States and firms with the criteria that it will apply in deciding whether or not aid measures planned by the Member States are compatible with the common market*" (European Commission 2001) and to help them design measures that minimize distortion of the EU internal market while contributing to European common goals, the European Commission issued guidelines on state aid for environmental protection in 1994,[14] 2001,[15] 2008[16] and 2014[17] upon which it relies. These guidelines especially encourage Member States to support renewable energies and, since 2008, also include detailed rules regarding the energy sector. They were accompanied by the General block exemption Regulation (GBER)[18] that is now aligned with the guidelines provisions so that it also includes energy issues. Both documents are based on (often explicit and sometimes faulty) economic reasoning and, for the 2014s version, are trying to curb market distortions created by previous regulations.

It will not be possible, in this paper, to analyze and critically assess in detail all the specific rules included in these guidelines (254 paragraphs) and GBER (56 articles; even if not all of them deal with energy and renewable energies). Instead, I will use a law and economics approach to inquire into the efficiency of state aid control of the energy sector. If it becomes apparent that the guidelines and GBER are indeed incentivizing states to promote renewable energies in what could appear as cost effective ways (Sect. 2 below), the conceptualization of state aid must be made broader to achieve cost efficient supports by Member States (Sect. 3 below). This result will simply derive from a basic economic approach of state intervention: if internalizing positive externalities is the primary reason for allowing support, non-actions towards negative externalities could also be considered a support scheme.

---

[13]It is interesting to note that this article does not explicitly mention negative externalities and does not adopt an economic conceptualization.

[14]European Commission (1994), Community guidelines on State aid for environmental protection, 10 March 1994, 94/C 72/03.

[15]European Commission (2001), Community guidelines on State aid for environmental protection, 3 February 2001, 2001/C 37/03.

[16]European Commission (2008b), Community guidelines on State aid for environmental protection, 1 April 2008, 2008/C 82/01. Hereafter EG 2008.

[17]European Commission (2014a). Guidelines on State aid for environmental protection and energy 2014–2020, 28 June 2014, 2014/C 200/01. Hereafter EG 2014.

[18]For the last version of the GBER, see Commission Regulation n° 651/2014 of 17 June 2014 declaring certain categories of aid compatible with the internal market in application of Articles 107 and 108 of the Treaty.

2 Incentivizing Renewable Energies in Cost Effective Ways

From an economic point of view state direct support is required only in the presence of a positive externality.[19] Indeed, in such a situation, decisions of private agents will not be optimal since the private benefits do not reflect the social benefits. Upon the European Commission's recognition of this fact,[20] it then went on, in 2005 and 2008, to further consider that aid could also promote sustainable development "irrespective of the correction of market failures".[21] This statement, which does not appear directly in the 2014 guidelines, is quite puzzling from an economic point of view. Indeed, it is because markets are not considered to sufficiently promote sustainable development—which is also not univocal[22]—that a support is required, hence there must be a positive externality that is not internalized, a benefit that is not sufficiently considered under the current operation of the markets. Of course, this "sufficiently" depends, in part on a conceptualization of markets and their functioning, which cannot be perfectly scientific. As Dalhman remarked:

> What is involved is a value judgment: if you believe that markets internalize everything, you will believe that externalities do not exists; on the other hand, if you believe that markets do not internalize side effects, you will believe in the persistence of externalities as deviations from an attainable optimum. This is not science; it is metaphysics: value judgments and political goals will enter into the determination of whether externalities occur in our world.[23]

In such a situation where governments retain a certain freedom of interpretation, positive externalities are just a guide (or a narrative) for justifying state intervention.[24] The best, which could be achieved is, thus, to make sure that this guide remains a compass through the procedural constraints it creates, hoping that it will reduce the freedom of governments to act. This is precisely the purpose of the guidelines and GBER. However, it is essential to understand this economic confusion[25] to fully understand the evolution of European Commission's documents.

The purpose of this section will not be to demonstrate the rise of sound economic reasoning by identifying the differences between the successive version of the documents, or to reveal an evolution in the economic theory exploited by the Commission,

[19]It is indeed doubtful that a support is required to lower transaction costs (to facilitate coordination or reduce information asymmetries) or in the case of a negative externality. Regulation is probably a more efficient tool to increase welfare.

[20]European Commission, Less and better targeted state aid: a roadmap for state aid reform 2005–2009, 7 June 2005, COM(2005) 107 final, pt. 10.

[21]How then could it be considered as efficient?

[22]The concept of sustainable development is indeed debated in economics. Analyses are distinguishing between strong and weak sustainability. If the concept were univocal, such statement could make sense since it is not possible to produce "too much" but the diversity of its interpretation creates shadows.

[23]Dalhman (1979), p. 60.

[24]But the benchmark to appreciate when a positive externality occurs should be specified.

[25]Confusion to the extent that going beyond of what is required is not technically a positive externality.

but to inquire into the economic structure of the last documents published and still in force: the 2014 guidelines (Sect. 2.1) and the 2014 GBER (Sect. 2.2).

2.1 *The Economic Structure of the 2014 Guidelines*

The 2008 guidelines stated that

> The primary objective of state aid control in the field of environmental protection is to ensure that state aid measures will result in a higher level of environmental protection than would occur without the aid and to ensure that the positive effects of the aid outweigh its negative effects in terms of distortions of competition, taking account of the polluter pays principle (hereafter 'PPP') established by Article 174 of the EC Treaty.[26]

The 2014 guidelines are more pragmatic. Referring to the communication "Energy 2020 – A strategy for competitive, sustainable and secure energy",[27] the purpose of the revision is explicitly

> based on strengthening the internal market, promoting more effectiveness in public spending through a better contribution of state aid to the objectives of common interest, greater scrutiny on the incentive effect, on limiting the aid to the minimum necessary, and on avoiding the potential negative effects of the aid on competition and trade.[28]

If the general principles for assessing the compatibility of aid remains similar between the different versions of the guidelines and rests, apparently on a strong consequentialist and economic approach (Sect. 2.1.1), then the specific dispositions for aid for the production of electricity from renewable energy sources[29] highlight some evolution towards a more economic approach (Sect. 2.1.2).

2.1.1 General Compatibility Provisions

Since at least 2005, the European Commission has been considering that "appreciating the compatibility of state aid is fundamentally about balancing the negative effects of aid on competition with its positive effects in terms of common interest".[30] This trade-off logic perfectly matches the economic rationale provided that a

---

[26]EG 2008, pt. 6.

[27]European Commission (2010), § 8.

[28]EG 2014, pt. 12.

[29]The guidelines are identifying more environmental and energy measures than just the promotion of renewable energies. For example, it mentioned among a number of other measures, (1) aid for energy from renewable sources, (2) energy efficiency measures, including cogeneration and district heating and district cooling, or (3) aid for resource efficiency and in particular aid to waste management Of course, these measures can be compatible if and only if they also satisfy the compatibility provisions.

[30]European Commission (2005), pts. 10 and 11.

baseline defining the market, as well as the conditions under which it functions optimally, is stipulated to assess the negative effects on competition.

This general principle, while still valid, has been broken down into seven conditions, which aid needs to fulfil to be considered compatible with the EU internal market:

1. Contribution to a well-defined objective of common interest: in the present case, an increased level of environmental protection compared to the level that would be achieved in the absence of the aid. It could also ensure a "competitive, sustainable and secure" EU internal energy market.
2. Need for a state intervention: the aid must correct a (residual) market failure.
3. Appropriateness of the aid measure: the aid should constitute the less distortive instrument to achieve the objective of common interest.
4. Incentive effect: the aid must encourage beneficiaries to change their behavior.
5. Proportionality of the aid: the aid should be limited to the minimum required to achieve the objective of common interest. This of course requires counterfactual reasoning.
6. Avoidance of undue negative effects on competition and trade: "*the negative effects of the aid measure in terms of distortions of competition and impact on trade between Member States must be limited and outweighed by the positive effects in terms of contribution to the objective of common interest*".[31]
7. Transparency: governments should publish information about the aid they are providing.

If this list is sufficient to demonstrate an (aspired) economic underlying logic in the reasoning of the Commission—it explicitly mentions market failures or incentives—few comments are required to fully understand that these principles could have been better structured and should have been further supplemented with theoretical considerations.

First, the Commission is asking states to carry out real impact assessment analyses, which is not surprising. Indeed, the OECD suggests that this practice is likely to improve the quality of decision-making,[32] and almost all OECD countries have such programs.[33] However, these programs have many differences, such as the variations in the definition of the type of regulation and intervention submitted to regulatory impact assessment. The Commission is thus simply enlarging the requirement for a regulatory impact assessment to the field of state aid—especially when the national requirement for a regulatory impact assessment does not cover all aspects of support measures or when the control of such impact assessment is lacking. The purpose of this assessment is to force Member States to gather (dynamic dimension) and provide (positive dimension) information regarding the expected consequences of the aid.

---

[31]EG 2014, pt. 88.

[32]Deighton-Smith et al. (2016), p. 9.

[33]See for example the webpage dedicated to RIA, http://www.oecd.org/gov/regulatory-policy/ria.htm [accessed 27 August 2017].

Second, from an economic point of view, it is possible to reduce the number of criteria from 7 to 3 or 4. This of course derives from the classical three step approach existing in the field of regulatory impact assessment: (1) explaining the problem, (2) inquiring into regulatory options, (3) quantifying direct and indirect benefits and costs of each option which should lead to the identification of the best regulatory option. Quite often (4) transparency is also mentioned as a tool to ensure a better accountability of decision makers.

Indeed, the list provided by the Commission is not without redundancies. The incentive effect criterion seems to be included within the previous criterion: a measure cannot be appropriate if it does not lead to change in behavior. Similarly, the proportionality of the aid necessarily includes the undue negative effects on competition and trade: hampering competition and trade are obvious negative effects for the Commission, which believes in the efficiency of the market system. Moreover, "undue" means not proportionate to the achievement of the goal. It is difficult to understand why an appropriate aid would lead to bad consequences regarding competition and trade.[34] If the former redundancy could not be rationalized, the second could just stress the logic of the protection of the internal market. It is also possible to consider that the need for a state intervention is included in the third criterion: an aid cannot be appropriate if state intervention is not required. Even worse, regarding the need for state support, the Commission is using the economic logic of market failures, mentioning negative externalities. It is difficult to imagine a situation in which a negative externality could be reduced through state support, especially considering the declared adhesion to the polluter pays principle.[35] Similarly, asymmetric information and coordination cannot be efficiently reduced through state support. It is then quite difficult to figure out the purpose of this criterion in the case of the intervention considered by the guidelines. The Commission is not introducing any concepts regarding transaction costs and administrative costs; if it is true that its purpose is to ensure that the internal market is functioning properly, such omission is problematic since considering externalities without a consideration for transaction costs is negating the progress initiated by Coase.

The list provided by the Commission could then be restructured. The first criterion is about the problem at stake. In the case of the guidelines, it is "*to increase the level of environmental protection compared to the level that would be achieved*

---

[34]It would be the exactly the opposite, *infra*.

[35]The Commission is considering that this situation would happen to "*to counterbalance the effects of negative externalities, where it is not possible to identify the polluter and make it pay for repairing the environmental damage it has caused*" (EG 2008, pt. 53). It remains difficult to identify an occurrence of this type of situation, *infra*. See also Article 191 (2) TFEU: "Union policy on the environment shall aim at a high level of protection taking into account the diversity of situations in the various regions of the Union. It shall be based on the precautionary principle and on the principles that preventive action should be taken, that environmental damage should as a priority be rectified at source and that the polluter should pay.

In this context, harmonisation measures answering environmental protection requirements shall include, where appropriate, a safeguard clause allowing Member States to take provisional measures, for non-economic environmental reasons, subject to a procedure of inspection by the Union".

in the absence of the aid".[36] Criteria 2, 3 and 4 are merely stating that the state should prove that using an "aid" makes sense compared to other regulatory options: there is a positive externality,[37] which would require financial support from the state to be internalized. Criteria 5 and 6 are then assessing the relevance of the aid details (e.g. its amount and conditionality). It is interesting to note that if the purpose of the aid is indeed to internalize a positive externality, it is difficult to understand why it would hamper competition.[38] The seventh criteria is facilitating control—hence reducing the administrative costs associated with the control of state aid—and accountability (hence watchfulness of decision makers, which should lead to fewer contentious support schemes).

Third, the Commission is not mandating the use of any methodology to model the impact assessment of the aid, it merely mentions the need to "demonstrate" that the aid is compatible. However, this requires an ex ante assessment, which cannot be provided without using models. The risk would then be for Member States to choose the model, which "fits" with their political position and then "sell" the result to the Commission. For instance, using neoclassical rationality or prospect theory will clearly not lead to the same policy implications. Adding a requirement regarding the justification and coherence of the models, which are used to realize such assessments, including their weaknesses and uncertainties, would probably be an improvement. Nevertheless, it is true that the transparency requirement could trigger a debating phase, during which the model used to justify the aid will be tested and improved. Computing methods—if they are used to assess the proportionality—should also be developed and "judged"; so should the conception of the "relevant" market to assess these competitive distortions. A demonstration cannot rest on a merely chosen but not carefully considered narrative. The purpose of specifying the methodology is not to reach perfect scientific proof—which is impossible in the realm of things that could be other than they are[39]—but both to facilitate reflexivity reflection (from the policymakers) and judgement (by the Commission).

Fourth and linked with the previous point, the Commission is offering a narrative but the margin of interpretation remains wide. The guidelines constitute the "grammar" that Member States should use to present their support measures to the

[36]European Commission (2005), pt. 30.

[37]The problem of definition of what is a positive externality will be developed further in the third section of this paper.

[38]At pt. 98, the Commission is writing: "*If the aid is proportionate and limited to the extra investment costs, the negative impact of the aid is in principle softened. However, even where aid is necessary and proportionate, aid may result in a change in behaviour of the beneficiaries which distorts competition. A profit seeking undertaking will normally only increase the level of environmental protection beyond mandatory requirements if it considers that this will result, at least marginally in some sort of advantage for the undertaking*". It is difficult to understand exactly why in such a situation it would hamper competition. From an economic point of view, internalizing an externality will increase competition, not stifled it. The Commission then took the example of decontaminating a site when the "author" of the pollution cannot be identified.

[39]This difference is made especially by Aristotle, who distinguished between two (among three) types or reason: praxis and episteme.

Commission. From an economic point of view, the purpose is of course to lower transaction costs by specifying a language.

2.1.2 The Case of Aid for the Production of Electricity from Renewable Energy Sources

The guidelines state that they will "*ensure the transition to a cost-effective delivery through market based mechanisms*",[40] implying its predecessors were mostly concentrating on reaching the EU environmental targets, while being more flexible regarding the qualification of state aid. Therewith, the guidelines are trying to introduce more market discipline.

Two main problems resulted from the aid schemes allowed before 2014. First, the common practice among Member States was to use feed-in tariffs,[41] meaning the certainty that during a certain period, electricity produced by renewable energy sources will be bought at a specific price; the logic followed by the Commission was that of the infant industry[42] (since the technology was not considered to be mature).[43] This mechanism, of course, distorts competition since market signals are blurred and the future change in electricity price and technologies does not have to be considered when investments are made. Besides, the market discipline would not push agents to innovate and thus lower their prices (which would benefit consumers). This mechanism could also lead economic agents to divert investment away from the investment necessary to meet pick demand (if the grid is not fed through an auction system),[44] since the technologies of electricity production from renewable energy sources are not adapted (yet) to meet this kind of challenge.[45] It is of course possible for a Member State to compensate the cost of a public service obligation if it is of general economic interest to "aid" this (capacity) investment[46] as long as it is clear that such investments are required to ensure the stability of the distribution of energy to consumers.

---

[40]EG 2014, pt. 107.

[41]See for example https://www.pv-magazine.com/features/solar-incentives-and-fits/feed-in-tariffs-in-europe/ [accessed 20 March 2017]. After it the situation in France in 2014 was in regard to size and incentive and for a term of 20 years as follow: Rooftop: <36 kW = €0.1440/kWh, 36–100 kW = €0.1368/kWh, 100 kW–12 MW = €0.0612/kWh; Building Integrated Photovoltaic: <9 kW = €0.2539/kWh, 9 kW–12 MW = €0.0612/kWh; Ground-mounted: 0–12 MW = €0.0612/kWh.

[42]See for example, on the logic of the protection of infant industry, Melitz (2005).

[43]The maturity logic is used in European Commission 2014, for example §110.

[44]For some details, see Decker (2014), pp. 223–235.

[45]It takes time and it is costly to increase the capacity of production, which will depend on the energies which are captured. For example, without sun or wind, sun power or wind power is simply not possible to create. These technologies are not yet sufficient to ensure the stability of the grid.

[46]To ensure the stability of the electric grid, it should be possible to increase the amount of electricity generated on a regular basis. Most of the time, gas plants are used for that. See also Decker (2014).

The second problem was related to market fragmentation within the EU internal market. This was because of the attention being focused more on the production of electricity using renewable energy than considering cost effectiveness of the measures: the price of the megawatt per hour varies from less than € 5 million (Romania) to more than 20 million Euro (in Spain).[47] Moreover, the total production of electricity from renewable energy sources varied widely between Member States and, except for Portugal, generation is roughly following the feed-in tariff. The risk of maintaining such a situation is that it allows for subsidy shopping (and a race to subsidies), especially when we consider that the Commission is pushing towards a "European" grid and an integrated electricity market (which is not yet a reality).[48]

The whole purpose of the 2014 guidelines regarding electricity produced from renewable resources is to create a market discipline. First, "*it is important that beneficiaries sell their electricity directly in the market and are subject to market obligations*".[49] Beginning in 2016, feed-in tariffs should gradually (since the guidelines have no effect on already approved schemes)[50] be replaced by feed-in premiums (an aid in addition to the market price). Indeed, it is now mandatory for producers to sell their production service on the market. This would push economic agents to optimize their structure and how they function according to the market price (assuming a liquid intraday market exists and is operational). Still following the logic of the (criticized)[51] "infant industry" the Commission is allowing small installations (below 3 MW for wind and 500 kW for other sources) and "demonstration projects"[52] to be exempt. Second and beginning in 2017, granting aid should follow "*a competitive bidding process on the basis of clear, transparent and non-discriminatory criteria*".[53] This mechanism is supposed to lower the amount of aid granted and to ensure that only cost-efficient producers will be subsidized, assuming of course that competitive bidding is working as it is supposed to work. The Commission is then allowing Member States to avoid this bidding process when it can be demonstrated that it will lead to over support (because of strategic bidding) or will result "in low project realisation rates". If these two situations are theoretically possible and sometimes real (at least for the first one), the "low project realization rate" could be avoided by specifying the conditions under which the aid will be granted; ex ante proof that aid will be granted following such specified conditions will of course remain extremely difficult. Strategic bidding will also be

---

[47]CEER (2013). See also CEER (2015).

[48]European Commission (2016a), pp. 2–5 for example.

[49]EG 2014, pt. 124.

[50]§ 247 EG 2014: "The Commission will apply these Guidelines to all notified aid measures in respect of which it is called upon to take a decision after their applicability, even where the projects were notified prior to that date. However, individual aid granted under approved aid schemes and notified to the Commission pursuant to an obligation to notify such aid individually will be assessed under the Guidelines that apply to the approved aid scheme on which the individual aid is based."

[51]For example, Easterly (2001).

[52]EG 2014, pt. 125.

[53]EG 2014, pt. 126.

reduced since the bidding should be opened to producers from other Member States, which is a further requirement stemming from the logic of the single market. Nevertheless, Member States can demonstrate that only "one or a very limited number of projects or sites could be eligible"[54] to be exempt from the bidding. Once again, small installations are exempt from this process.

Parallel to these specific measures, the Commission is also allowing support through the mechanism of green certificates. When the conditions to obtain green certificates are carefully defined,[55] they should help producers of "green" electricity in the short run while incentivize producers from conventional (fossil fuel) energy to adapt their production processes. Since the market determines the price of the certificates, they should then exert a continues pressure to adapt and innovate. If green certificates are too easy to obtain, or granted for a "long" period of time, this mechanism could lose its power.

It is difficult to argue that the Commission is not inspired by mainstream economic theory both through the vocabulary it is using and the logic it is following (sometimes quite strangely). However, the administrative costs are not addressed. They are indirectly considered in the GBER.

2.2 *The Economic Logic of the 2014 General Block Exemption Regulation*

An aid is prohibited if, and only if, it is considered as incompatible with the internal market. The scheme (or the revision) considered should be notified to the European Commission which could authorized it or not; if the Commission does not respond within a certain period of time,[56] the scheme is deemed compatible. If not notified, the scheme is considered in principle as unlawful but can be authorized ex-post. However, in that case no implicit approval is possible.[57] This mechanism is

---

[54]EG 2014, pt. 126.

[55]The Commission will especially pay attention to the fact that "(1) is essential to ensure the viability of the renewable energy sources concerned; (2) does not, for the scheme in the aggregate, result in overcompensation over time and across technologies, or in overcompensation for individual less deployed technologies in so far as differentiated levels of certificates per unit of output are introduced; and (3) does not dissuade renew able energy producers from becoming more competitive". Of course, these criteria are still abstract but the Commission is not ready to renounce its control power.

[56]Two months in general to take a decision or launch an "in depth investigation" (Council Regulation 659/1999, laying down detailed rules for the application of Article 93 of the EC Treaty, 22 March 1999, modified by Council Regulation 734/2013, amending Regulation (EC) No 659/1999 laying down detailed rules for the application of Article 93 of the EC Treaty, 31 July 2013).

[57]Council Regulation 659/1999, laying down detailed rules for the application of Article 93 of the EC Treaty, 22 March 1999, modified by Council Regulation 734/2013, amending Regulation (EC) No 659/1999 laying down detailed rules for the application of Article 93 of the EC Treaty, 31 July 2013.

supposed to incentivize Member States to notify the Commission of their aid schemes. Furthermore, the implicit authorization is a way to lower administrative costs. Of course, these administrative costs will vary with the number of schemes that the Commission must consider. The purpose of the GBER is to lower the administrative costs created by this system (Sect. 2.2.1). For electricity produced from renewable energies, the GBER also provides some interesting specific provisions (Sect. 2.2.2).

The GBER should of course be considered and interpreted in combination with the guidelines. However, they cannot be considered as a single document considering the scope of the GBER, which is far broader than the guidelines since it covers more than mere environmental aid and aid in the domain of energy.

2.2.1 The Economic Logic of Exemption

The GBER is part of the State Aid Modernization agenda. The economic logic of exemption is easy to understand. When some categories of aid are considered unproblematic, they can be exempted from notification. Indeed, considering the probability that these aids would be considered illegal and/or the limited distortions of trade and competition, the procedure of notification would create more costs (administrative costs) than benefits (deriving from the reduction of distortions of trade and competition). Moreover, exempting these aids will allow the Commission to focus on schemes with a more significant potential for distortions. It could then act faster and in a more informed way. The GBER is merely specifying the conditions under which some considered measures could be exempt from notification. However, one must be aware that the purpose of the Commission is not to avoid states from wasting their resources but only to waste their resources when this waste could distort trade and competition within the internal market.[58]

Not surprisingly, the Commission introduced a notification threshold, as a first layer to identify which aid schemes cannot be exempt. This logic is simple: the greater the limitation on the amount of aid, the less likely it is to have the potential to distort trade and competition. No less than 29 thresholds are introduced in Article 4 of the GBER distinguishing aid areas and beneficiaries, period of time, cluster or infrastructures. For energy infrastructures, the aid cannot be exempt if it represents more than 50 million Euros "per undertaking, per investment project" but the threshold for broadband infrastructures is 70 million Euros "per project" and the one for research infrastructures 20 million Euro "per infrastructure". These differences could be explained by the potential distortion of competition and trade the aid could produce in a specific domain considering its function and its structure. Compared to the former version of the GBER these thresholds have been raised and new categories included, notably aid for energy infrastructures.

[58]Spector (2009), p. 178.

The figures are of course arbitrary in that there is objectively no way to say that the aid should be limited to 45, 55 or 75 Euro to be certain that the benefits (the reduction of administrative costs) will be lower than the costs (the granting of distortive aids). This is another example of the inherent limits of rules compared to standards[59] or the way the law is addressing problems (and its binary legal or illegal categorization). It would also be expected that Member States will prefer to grant aid just below the threshold to avoid notification and remain free to respond to the demand from pressure groups.

These thresholds are even less ideal when considering that the aid will not only consist in a direct monetary transfer (in which case it would be easy to assess the aid amount) but in other and more indirect forms. For example, when the state is warranting (directly or indirectly through specific rules regarding state own enterprises for example) a loan made by some economic agents, or is just communicating its will to intervene in favor of a specific enterprise, the aid could be difficult to evaluate in its amount. This could create some legal uncertainties for aids granted around the threshold level and therefore contention is to be expected.

Nevertheless, Article 5 of the GBER introduces the principle that to benefit from its regulation, it should be "*possible to calculate precisely the gross grant equivalent of the aid ex ante without any need to undertake a risk assessment*". What will be considered as a precise calculation remains unclear. The Commission thus decided to specify criteria by which the type of aids that will be considered as transparent. Among there are: the grants and interest rate subsidies, the "loans, where the gross grant equivalent has been calculated based on the reference rate prevailing at the time of the grant", the "aids in form of tax advantages, where the measure provides for a cap ensuring that the applicable threshold is not exceeded". By providing this list, the Commission is incentivizing Member States to choose these modalities.

Being exempted from the scheme should also have an incentivizing effect: the market conditions should not be considered as sufficient to incentivize undertakings to adopt the measure targeted by the state.[60] It is doubtful that the Commission will consider the change in behavior introduced by the mere possibility of obtaining an aid, which could lead economic agents in a market to wait for a state scheme. The bidding process to grant the aid is certainly a way to lower this risk and explain the special treatment it is receiving in the eyes of the Commission. Once again, the Commission is providing a list of aids, which will be considered as having an incentive effect and specify the conditions that should be met for each type of aid. For example, "*aid shall be considered to have an incentive effect if the beneficiary has submitted a written application for the aid to the member state concerned before work on the project or activity starts*" as long as this application is containing a given amount of information. Tax advantages will also be considered as incentivizing as long as "*(a) the measure establishes a right to aid in accordance with objective criteria and without further exercise of discretion by the Member States; and (b) the*

[59]Kaplow (1992).

[60]Article 6 GBER.

measure has been adopted and is in force before work on the aided project or activity has started, except in the case of fiscal successor schemes, where the activity was already covered by the previous schemes in the form of tax advantages".

It is not the purpose of this paper to analyse in detail the conditions under which the GBER will apply. It is sufficient to mention that the logic followed by the Commission is consequentialist and is broadly speaking making economic sense. Of course, aids for energy must comply with this GBER to be exempted from the notification procedure. Moreover, it seems that the Commission is going beyond the mere preservation of competition and trade. By mentioning the conditions under which the aid should be granted on top of the threshold logic, it is also trying to lower the possibility for states to engage in wasteful interventions.[61] Of course, it is not because an aid is not following the GBER that it is automatically considered as illegal. All the other criteria of state aids must also be met: advantage—which could lead to distortion of competition and trade—selectivity, state resources. But the GBER is also trying to incentivize Member States to structure aids around the "good practices" it implicitly presents. However, most of these conditions are "interpreted" by Member States when they design their support schemes and only through complaints will these interpretations be restricted in their possibilities.

2.2.2 The Case of Aids for Renewable Energy Sources

As with any other areas of aids, the GBER is setting a threshold under which the exemption could apply and distinguishes between investment aids and operating aids. For the former, the threshold is 15 million Euros.[62] For the latter the threshold varies: 15 million Euros per undertaking, per project for the promotion of energy from renewable sources in small scale installations and 150 million Euros per year when the aid is granted based on a competitive bidding process,[63] which is clear, transparent and non-discriminatory. The use of the market system to grant the aid is indeed supposed to lower the risk of overcompensation of undertakings and, should make it easier for Member States to reach their own environmental targets. Indeed, if the efficiency of these targets could be questioned, the competitive bidding should lower the probability that they are fulfilled in a non cost-efficient way.

Below these thresholds, some specific rules apply to obtaining an exemption. The aid intensity for investment aid for the promotion of energy from renewable resources is limited in principle up to 45% of the eligible costs which are the "*extra investment costs necessary to promote the production of energy from renewable sources*"[64]; conversely, the eligible costs are the ones which are considered as having an incentivizing effect in the sense of the Commission. The GBER identifies

[61] Spector (2009), pp. 178 and 181.

[62] Article 4(s) GBER.

[63] Article 4(v) GBER.

[64] Article 41(6) GBER.

three different methods to compute these costs, but largely leaves the choice to the Member States; the third method, which is imprecise, only allows an intensity of 30%.[65] It is nevertheless possible to reach an aid intensity of 100% when the aid is granted through a bidding process, which is supposed to promote cost efficient installations. The promotion of the bidding process is certainly a way to make sure that Member States are not "giving" aid to national champions even if their investments are not cost efficient. Of course, it is possible for Member States to lower the intensity of these aids, but it is to be expected, considering the likelihood of rent-seeking, that the intensity will always be closer to its maximum. In any case, the exemption is only possible for new installations.

Regarding operating aid, the rule is simple: the bidding process cannot be limited to specific technologies.[66] Of course, if, this procedure leads to sub-optimal results, something that must be demonstrated by Member States, they could restrict the bidding process to specific technologies. The Commission provides five possible reasons to do so, this list is non-exhaustive: "*(i) longer-term potential of a given new and innovative technology; or (ii) the need to achieve diversification; or (iii) network constraints and grid stability; or (iv) system (integration) costs; or (v) the need to avoid distortions on the raw material markets from biomass support*".[67] If these conditions make sense, the possibility to prove the "longer-term potential" or the "need to achieve diversification" is prone to a vast array of interpretations. The question of grid stability is difficult to understand when considering the current technologies but it is probably trying to anticipate new technologies, which could replace gas plants (often operated to meet peak demand).

As also specified by the Guidelines, this type of aid should be granted through feed-in premiums and the bidding process is not required for small installations (1 MW for all renewable resources except wind, 6 MW for wind). Even smaller installations (500 kW for all renewable sources except wind and 3 MW for wind) could still benefit from feed-in tariffs. For these installations, the risk of competitive or trade distortion is negligible. This does not mean that supporting these

[65] Article 41 GBER: "*The eligible costs shall be the extra investment costs necessary to promote the production of energy from renewable sources. They shall be determined as follows:*

(a) *where the costs of investing in the production of energy from renewable sources can be identified in the total investment cost as a separate investment, for instance as a readily identifiable add-on component to a pre-existing facility, this renewable energy-related cost shall constitute the eligible costs;*
(b) *where the costs of investing in the production of energy from renewable sources can be identified by reference to a similar, less environmentally friendly investment that would have been credibly carried out without the aid, this difference between the costs of both investments identifies the renewable energy-related cost and constitutes the eligible costs;*
(c) *for certain small installations where a less environmentally friendly investment cannot be established as plants of a limited size do not exist, the total investment costs to achieve a higher level of environmental protection shall constitute the eligible costs*".

[66] Article 42 GBER.

[67] Article 42 GBER.

installations cannot sometimes be wasteful. It will simply not be addressed through the mechanism of state aids but through national procedures.

This brief presentation of the guidelines and the GBER stresses the fact that the Commission developed a set of very detailed rules to ensure legal certainty and to guide Member States when they are designing support schemes. Moreover, it is certain that the reasoning of the Commission draws largely from economic reasoning and wording so that for an economist, the harnessing of state aid through the rules of the guidelines and the GBER makes perfect sense.

3 Expanding the Conceptualization of State Aid

The problem with the Commission's (detailed) approach is that it is only focusing on "positive" action by Member States; only "active" support designs are considered. If the purpose of the Commission is indeed to lead the way towards a new energy mix of renewable energy and decarbonized (e.g. nuclear) energies, it is probably necessary to expand the conceptualization of state aids to address the question of negative externalities directly (Sect. 3.1). Indeed, even if the Commission mentions the rationale of negative externalities to justify support schemes, it is probably not taking the problem to its heart. Doing so would certainly be of greater benefit. This expanded approach to state aid would, of course, push the Commission to address states aid in a completely different way, but, and this should be noted, it could still use the tools it has already developed. Nevertheless, this approach would have to face difficult, but not impossible, policy making challenges (Sect. 3.2).

3.1 State Aid and Negative Externalities

In the current conceptualization of state aid, negative externalities are considered by the Commission in a very specific way. In the 2008 guidelines, it says

> Full implementation of the PPP would thus lead to correction of the market failure. The PPP [polluter pays principle][68] can be implemented either by setting mandatory environmental standards or by market-based instruments. Some of the market-based instruments may involve the granting of State aid to all or some of the undertakings which are subject to them.[69]

---

[68]From an economic point of view, the PPP (polluter pays principle) is creating a property right to be "free" from pollution; while doing so, Coasian bargaining could theoretically be possible.

[69]EG 2008, pt. 8. Moreover, as the first quotation of this paper stressed, it seems that the benchmark to evaluate if there are externalities lies in the standards set by the European Commission which is a very peculiar way to address externality questions.

Negative externalities are thus a way to justify some support for the industries, which are "subject" to them, a qualification that remains unclear. A few examples of such a situation exist in the different versions of the guidelines. Regarding aid for energy savings, the Commission considers that "*This type of aid addresses the market failure linked to negative externalities by creating individual incentives to attain environmental targets for energy saving and for the reduction of greenhouse gas emissions*".[70] The same holds true for aid regarding renewable energies,[71] early adaptation to future Community standards,[72] contaminated sites,[73] relocation,[74] cogeneration and aid for public heating,[75] or carbon capture and storage[76] but these are the only occurrences mentioned and the reasoning provided by the Commission is not always rigorous. Granting below market price pollution permits is also considered as an indirect way to deal with negative externalities.[77] It thus seems that the Commission is only trying to cure the consequences rather than cure the origin of the problem. The reconceptualization of state aid will go one step further and address the origin of the negative externality. Such a reconceptualization would make sense from an economic point of view (Sect. 3.1.1). The question of its implementation will then be addressed (Sect. 3.1.2).

3.1.1 The Economic Rationale

The economic rationale of the Commission is known: if the social costs are higher than the private costs, then economic agents will be incentivized to produce "too much". It is thus required to force them to internalize the negative externality they are creating. Or, in the wording of the 2008 guidelines:

> The most common market failure in the field of environmental protection is related to negative externalities. Undertakings acting in their own interest have no incentive to take the negative externalities arising from production into account either when they decide on a particular production technology or when they decide on the production level. In other words, the production costs that are borne by the undertaking are lower than the costs borne by society. Therefore undertakings have no incentive to reduce their level of pollution or to take individual measures to protect the environment.[78]

Of course, this conceptualization does not consider the problem of transaction costs (hence property rights), administrative costs and government failures so that

[70] EG 2008, pt. 47; EG 2014, pt. 142.
[71] EG 2008, pt. 47.
[72] EG 2008, pt. 45.
[73] EG 2008, pt. 53.
[74] EG 2008, pt. 54; EG 2014, pt. 237.
[75] EG 2008, pt. 51.
[76] EG 2014, pt. 162.
[77] EG 2008, pt. 55.
[78] EG 2008, pt. 20; see also EG 2014.

the reasoning is not perfectly rigorous from an economic point of view,[79] but it cannot be denied that the Commission is aware of the problem. If the Commission is contemplating the possibility to use market based instruments like pollution permits or more traditional command and control regulations, it seems not to understand the power that State aid has as a tool to achieve the same ends. This is even more surprising since it also recognizes that "*if the PPP were fully implemented, further government intervention would not be necessary to ensure a market-efficient outcome*".[80] Why then try to only cure the consequences and not the source of the problem?

From an economic point of view, the divergence between social costs and private costs is because, in part, of the absence of well-defined property rights. The PPP could be considered as a rule to make sure that some of the externalities produced, when they do not concern a huge number of people, could be internalized through Coasian bargaining or tort law. If transaction costs are too high to ensure an efficient outcome, a government intervention could make sense.

This is where the Commission's logic could be pushed one step further.[81] For an economist, only the consequences matter. From a theoretical point of view it is the same regardless of whether there is a positive action or a simple abstention. The purpose is to try to minimize the net costs or to maximize the net benefits. If we are thus considering that the economic optimum should constitute the benchmark through which state intervention will be assessed, the result is obvious: the fact that the government is not doing anything in presence of a well-known negative externality could be considered as a state aid. Indeed, the consequence of this situation is to distort the signal sent by the market price (the true cost should be the social cost and not the private cost), which would create a competitive advantage to some energy producers over others.

If we believe that the Pigouvian tax or the auction of pollution permits (instead of grandfathering)[82] are options to solve such a situation, then the state is using its public resources to create a competitive advantage. Even worse, the consequences of the pollution—increase in the costs of morbidity, mortality, effects on the maintenance of buildings and landmarks, effects on tourism, etc.—are borne by the entire economy and therefore to reduce the consequences of the problem (hospitalization, maintenance, etc.) tax payer's money is required.

Not only would such a conceptualization address the problem at its roots but it would also reduce the amount of support required for the development of green energies. In regards to dirty energies, it is true that they are not always competitive because the benchmark is the distorted price signal from the energy market. Feed-in

[79]The cost of intervention is not explicitly considered by the Commission when addressing the question of the compatibility of a state aid with the internal market.

[80]EG 2008, pt. 24.

[81]This logic could also apply to the concept of subsidies under WTO; see for example Esty (1994), for example, pp. 66–67.

[82]Which is also a mechanism to help old and often dirtier plans to the detriment of new comers.

premiums could then be required as they produce a "positive" externality compared to such a benchmark. However, a strict adhesion to the PPP would lead to the consideration that these technologies are simply not creating externalities regarding pollution; in a "normal" situation, they should not need any support, but the normal situation would occur if and only if polluters were paying for their pollution (or the consequences of their pollution). Moreover, instead of taxing producers of negative externalities (which would lead to some budget inputs), the solution is to help producers, which are using "green" energies (which is leading to budget outputs). The compensation of these producers should then be made adequate to avoid new distortions. The information required to do so would not be costlier to obtain than the information needed to design a system to force polluters to internalize the costs of their pollution. Indeed, it is compared to the welfare loss of the negative externality that the amount of the positive externality should be considered.

Wouldn't it thus make sense to curb the distortion by forcing the producers to internalize their externalities?

It is certain that the amount of aid will be reduced because the standard will be to tax pollution or create pollution permits and not to subsidize different industries. Furthermore, it is clear that the price of energy could increase but the resulting tax amount could be used to lower some other taxes (especially on employment)[83] or to subsidize a certain amount of consumption by (poor) citizens. Moreover, another way to promote energy saving is by creating a demand for energy savings. But such a demand will critically depend on the price of energy. If the price is fully internalizing the social costs, it would lead economic agents to adapt more quickly to greener technology and to change their behavior regarding energy saving. Just stating that it is a "gesture for the planet" is blatantly inefficient if this preference is not also internalized. It would also stimulate innovation to meet the preference for consumers (for a cheaper price), which will lead to more sustainability of European economies. It would even reduce the time and costs of designing support schemes, which should be adapted to the evolution of technologies and understanding of issues; policymakers could then focus on more important regulations or on identifying sources of negative externalities not yet internalized. Linked to this benefit, under this conceptualization, the incentive to lobby the government or the regulator (regarding the amount and the conditions to obtain the subsidy) will be reduced. It will also create more legal certainty especially if the price of carbon is set.[84] Finally, it will encourage the collection of data on the real costs of externalities and not merely on how to "show" that we are "engaged" in an energy transition.

This picture might seem a little idealistic because the problems related to implementation were not discussed here. However, as the next subdivision will show, this next step would not be too difficult to complete.

[83]This is the so called "double benefit" of a tax: it is incentivizing to internalize externality and it is creating a surplus that it is possible to use to create even more welfare.

[84]The problem will then be to determine this level. Should we consider national or international costs?

3.1.2 A Difficult Implementation?

This new conceptualization of state aid will lead to two main questions. First, does it fit with the "legal" framework of a state aid as understood by the ECJ or the Commission? Second, how is it possible to assess the costs of the externalities that a Member State is trying to internalize?

Regarding the first problem, it is certain that the procedure of notification of state aid must be reconsidered. Only positive action can be notified; a non-action is more difficult to identify. Nevertheless, the purpose of the notification is related to the possible consequences of the action; and not all support schemes are notified to the Commission. Moreover, under the guidelines, the state should prove that the intervention is required and the best way to solve a problem, which means that if a taxation of a polluter is more efficient, it should be privileged. Furthermore, there are reasons to believe that it is indeed the case. By striking down most schemes under the justification that a tax or a pollution permit would be more efficient, the Commission could incentivize states to change their approach to the problem.

Under this new conceptualization, most of the work will be decentralized and use the court system instead of the Commission. This decentralization has interesting features: with state aid, the need of a support is decided by the state (which could then privilege some industries over others); with the reconceptualization, the aid is decided on the "material" consequences of perceived negative externalities (there will be an obligation to act). By adopting a conceptualization under which a non-intervention is considered as a state aid when the externality is well-known (and since the point of time when it is well-known), it will not only create a sufficient level of legal certainty (notably because the existence of a negative externality does not depend on the state in which we are living), but it will incentivize the development of studies regarding these externalities and their pricing. Major problems would then be logically solved, provided a period of time is offered to governments to adapt their regulations.

Regarding the legal criteria of state aid, no major changes are required except that the field will be more integrated into competition law than considered as a separate and specific body of rules. To be qualified as a state aid, the support scheme should be (1) selective, (2) create an advantage, which (3) has the potential to distort competition and trade and (4) use state resources.

The selectivity criterion is probably the most complex[85] with regards to EU law, despite an apparently clear principle favoring certain undertakings or the production of certain goods. The purpose of this criterion is to distinguish between general (economic policy) measures and selective ones. The ECJ is looking at the consequences of the "intervention" and not only on its wording.[86] The non-intervention

[85]See for example, European Commission (2016b).

[86]Judgment of the Court of Justice of 29 June 1999, DMTransport, C-256/97, para. 27; Judgment of the General Court of 6 March 2002, Territorio Histórico de Álava—Diputación Foral de Álava et aL. v Commission, Joined Cases T-127/99, T-129/99 and T-148/99, para. 149.

when a clear negative externality exists will of course treat industries, which are using polluting processes differently compared with industries, which are investing in "green" technologies. From a competition point of view, the selectivity principle means that the actors producing a similar good (e.g. electricity) are not facing the charges that they would normally have to bear. The problem would then be to define the "charges that they would normally have to bear", which means that we need a baseline (or a "system of reference") since it is because of derogations that selectivity will be considered. If the system of reference is to be constituted by the social benefits and the social costs (given by a certain technology), then by not taking actions to force undertakings to internalize the externalities they are producing, the state is treating undertakings in "similar" situations differently.

The fact that an advantage is created when the state is not forcing an undertaking to internalize a negative externality is quite easy to demonstrate since it is mitigating the charges of some undertakings more than the charges of others although they are producing the same good (electricity). Of course, from this point of view, the state should also pay compensation when there is a "clear" positive externality to some action.

The potential to distort competition and trade is obvious in the energy sector at least when the intervention is reaching a certain magnitude. Considering that electricity is an example of a perfectly homogeneous good, the method of production will be chosen according to the private costs and benefits. If the state is not forcing to internalize externalities, "green" energy producers from other Member States will be relatively less competitive, which will reduce the amount of trade between the countries. Of course, if this reconceptualization is adopted, it will have the effect of forcing all Member States to adopt internalization strategies, and ideally make them the same strategies (otherwise there will be a distortion between undertakings of different countries).

Regarding the use of state resources, it is possible to draw on the idea of forgoing on the collection of state resources.[87] Since the state could have auctioned the right to pollute or tax the pollution (in a case where there is a clear negative externality), it is forgoing the collection of state resources. This assumes of course that there is no common good and that the state (when transaction costs are positive), or individual (s) (when transaction costs are near zero) have a right to a "clean" environment. But

[87]ECJ, Commission vs Kingdom of the Netherlands, C-279/08P: "*With regard to the first branch of the first plea, alleging the lack of an advantage financed through State resources, the General Court holds that the measure in question is not based on emission allowances allocated directly by the State. However, the possibility of trading those allowances confers on them a value on the market, which can be sold by the undertakings at any time. In addition, by purchasing emission allowances, the undertakings avoid a fine. The emission allowances, which are assimilated to intangible assets, were put at the disposal of the undertakings concerned free of charge, whereas they could have been sold or put up for auction. The Kingdom of the Netherlands has thus foregone the collection of State resources. Consequently, the measure in question constituted an advantage granted to the undertakings concerned through State resources*".

this derives implicitly from the PPP. Refusing to act to lower the magnitude of an externality would not be compatible with the PPP.

Of course, recognizing that there is an aid, means that it is required to "evaluate" it to address the question of restitution. It is certainly true that an exact assessment of the magnitude of the welfare loss created by a negative externality is not easy and impossible most of the time. This would require having an estimate of the marginal damage created by pollution and to have a precise idea of the level of pollution created during the production process.

Nevertheless, the purpose of the restitution is simply to incentivize economic agents to act as they should. Assessing exactly the magnitude of the "aid" because of a non-intervention is not thus the problem; suffice it to have a rough approximation; and the Court was not afraid, in the past to address the question of the existence of a state aid even if its magnitude would have been difficult to assess.

Moreover, in the case of pollution, if we have an idea of the shape of the curve of marginal abatement costs and the marginal damage created by the pollution, it would be possible to minimize the welfare loss created by an appropriate measure by selecting taxes when the slope of the curve of the marginal damage is lower (in absolute value) than the marginal abatement costs, and pollution permits in other cases. However, if the state is grossly overestimating or underestimating a situation, then it is probably better for them not to act either negatively or positively. It would then be required to ask the states to justify their calculation when they are intervening and to open this calculation method to discussion. It is also to be expected that such a reconceptualization will stimulate studies about appropriate calculation methods.

It thus seems that the reconceptualization advocated here would not require an incredible change regarding the present regulation, simply a change in the baseline to assess if the measure is selective. Of course, this solution will contribute to increasing the cost of energy in the short run, which will be politically unwise before the end of an office term. However, it should be kept in mind that there is no such thing as a free lunch. Someone will end up paying for the negative externalities at some point, be it the present or the future generation. In any case, a solution is fully relevant if and only if the conditions for its political adoption are present which is not necessarily the case.

3.2 State Aids, Negative Externalities and Policy Making

The reconceptualization of state aid will lead to at least two policy challenges. First, it will be necessary that such reconceptualization could be implemented (Sect. 3.2.1). Second, in a globalized environment, this reconceptualization could have a tremendous impact on the competitiveness of European enterprises (Sect. 3.2.2). However, these difficulties should not be over-estimated.

3.2.1 Implementing the Reconceptualization

Implementing such a new conceptualization will not be easy. First, compared to the status quo, the reconceptualization will lower, at least in the short run, the competitiveness of "polluting" companies and it is to be expected that therefore, lobbying actions will be undertaken. Indeed, for polluting industries, this reconceptualization will increase their production costs without increasing their benefits; they will of course prefer the logic of support schemes, which will not modify their cost structure. Second, for "green" industries, if the benefits are obvious in term of relative competitiveness, their costs will remain the same or be lowered (through the reduction of support scheme or the reduction of the magnitude of the support or the reduction of the demand linked to the increase in price) because of this reconceptualization. Third, citizens will face an increase in the price of energy, which is normally not something they are enjoying. It might thus seem, at first glance, that the political conditions are not fulfilled for such a move, especially if this move is implemented through a modification of the treaties (in which case unanimity is required).

Nevertheless, one must consider the benefits of such a reconceptualization with regards to the improvement of health, pollution relating diseases or even life expectancy. These benefits are certainly not perceived or very indirectly by most citizens but they are real. Moreover, this system will drastically reduce the number of support schemes[88] (since the need for a support scheme will be reduced to "real" positive externalities) and the amount of medical expenditure (especially if there is some form of social security system), maintenance of buildings, etc. At the same time state resources (through taxes or auctions regarding pollution permits) will increase. Therefore, it could logically be followed that there will be tax cuts for an amount at least equivalent (while still keeping the benefits of the improvement of the environment). Furthermore, considering that some taxes are more distortive than others (taxes regarding employment for example) some extra benefits are also to be expected. Conversely, it seems difficult to deny, at least in a closed economy, that the reconceptualization will lead to more benefits than costs.

Of course, there will be some redistributive effects since the relative position of citizens and enterprises will not be the same before and after the implementation of this reconceptualization. But it will incentivize them to change their behavior and adapt their production processes which is one of the purpose of the reconceptualization; by strictly abiding by a polluter pays principle, everybody must pay for the "true" cost of their activities, which should incentivize them to adopt optimal behavior from the point of view of the society.

Rent-seeking will not be eliminated under this reconceptualization but will logically be lowered. Indeed, the amount of money, which could be derived from a certain support scheme will be reduced since the baseline will now be the economic

[88]The amount of "support" offered by the state remains largely unknown; but it represents at least 50 billion in OECD countries just for fossil fuels industries.

optimum. Moreover, if rent seeking will occur regarding the design of the tax or pollution permits schemes,[89] the margins of discretion are reduced, hence the amount of money which could be obtained through these actions.

Through education it might be possible to achieve a broad consensus on the need of such reconceptualization but it will probably take a lot of time to achieve such consensus for results that are still unpredictable now. Nevertheless, as we have shown in the previous section, the ECJ has all the legal instruments to operate such a move—only a new interpretation is required. The only prerequisite to ensure that the reconceptualization will be effective would be to broaden the possibility to file a complaint in front of ECJ or the Commission, something that should remain relatively easy. Nevertheless, if positive support schemes can be challenged in front of a court, negative support schemes should also be subject to court action. If the Commission is also using its power to strike down almost all support schemes presented by Member States because some other actions could have been employed to achieve the same end (taxing pollution or creating pollution permits), the condition for the reconceptualization would be gathered. Of course, this process will only be gradual but it is far from impossible to implement this reconceptualization.

3.2.2 The International Level and the Problem of Competitiveness

If the ECJ and the Commission are abiding by this new conceptualization, the first problem, which will be mentioned, will be the relative competitiveness of European enterprises vis-à-vis non-European enterprises. Indeed, all things being equal, they will face higher costs. Few solutions could then be considered.

First, it would be possible to develop a tax system, which "compensates" for the amount of the "eco-taxation" created so that the relative competitiveness of the enterprise would remain the same. If, for example, the compensation is achieved through lowering corporate taxes, or employment taxes, it is possible, at least theoretically, to balance out these costs and benefits to achieve the same level of competitiveness. Of course, because of the one size fits all logic of a tax code (and the rent-seeking associated with it to obtain privilege or exemptions) this solution might be difficult to implement perfectly and distributional effects are to be expected. It is required to mention, at this point, that the Commission is indeed considering such a situation.

In the 2014 Guidelines, it states that

> Member States can grant the aid in the form of a reduction of the tax rate or as a fixed annual compensation amount (tax refund), or as a combination of the two. The advantage of the tax refund approach is that undertakings remain exposed to the price signal, which the environmental tax gives. Where used, the amount of the tax refund should be calculated on the basis of historical data, i.e. the level of production, and the consumption or pollution observed for the undertaking in a given base year. The level of the tax refund must not go beyond the Union minimum tax amount that would result for the base year.[90]

---

[89]Rent seeking should be higher for taxes than for pollution permits.

[90]EG 2014, pt. 174.

This statement is particularly interesting since it recognizes that it would not distort the price signal (which is the purpose of the reconceptualization) and that the competitiveness problem could be lowered through tax compensation.

To be legal, the Commission is specifying that it "*will consider that tax reductions do not undermine the general objective pursued and contribute at least indirectly to an increased level of environmental protection, if a Member State demonstrates that (i) the reductions are well targeted to undertakings being mostly affected by a higher tax and (ii) that a higher tax rate is generally applicable than would be the case without the exemption*".[91] More especially and not surprisingly, it indicates that

> The Commission will consider the aid to be necessary if the following cumulative conditions are met: (a) the choice of beneficiaries is based on objective and transparent criteria, and the aid is granted in principle in the same way for all competitors in the same sector if they are in a similar factual situation; (b) the environmental tax without the reduction leads to a substantial increase in production costs calculated as a proportion of the gross value added for each sector or category of individual beneficiaries; and (c) the substantial increase in production costs could not be passed on to customers without leading to significant sales reductions.[92]

What is even more striking is that the Commission is stating rules regarding tax exemptions: undertakings should pay at least 20% of the national tax or it should commit to achieve environmental protection objective "*which have the same effects as if beneficiaries pay at least 20% of the national tax*".[93] This threshold is of course arbitrary and the possibility to commit to achieve the environmental protection objective is relevant if and only if the state cannot use these 20% more efficiently for environmental protection. There is no need to develop this possibility in detail, suffice it to say that the commission already developed some tools to address these problems. Of course, the efficiency of this system could be questioned in its details but not in its principle.

Second, it would also be possible to tax the products coming from outside the EU if the production process is considered as generating a clear negative externality. This is the logic of the "environmental dumping" and environmental countervailing tariffs. The difficulty of this solution would be to identify when a situation of environmental dumping exists and to assess its magnitude. This could also have consequences regarding developing countries, which do not always have the possibility to use "green" technologies. But if the pollution emitted by these countries is "clearly" affecting other countries, it remains unclear if such measures would create some inefficiencies. In the current state of WTO regulations, indirect subsidies through lax environmental regulations are not considered yet as allowing countervailing measures despite many provisions, which could be interpreted to allow such measures. Indeed, if Article 1.1(ii)[94] and (iii)[95] on the agreement on

[91]EG 2014, pt. 170.

[92]EG 2014, pt. 177.

[93]EG 2014, pt. 178.

[94]A subsidy shall be deemed to exist if: "government revenue that is otherwise due is foregone or not collected".

[95]A subsidy shall be deemed to exist if: "a government provides goods or services other than general infrastructure, or purchases goods".

subsidies and countervailing measures could be interpreted in a way to consider that lax environmental regulation constitute subsidies (the use of the environment is allowed for free and the government is forgoing taxes which it could have collected), then Article 6.7(f) is not considering that the "failure to conform to standards and other regulatory requirements in the importing country" can justify countervailing measures.

4 Conclusion

In this article, I suggest a reconceptualization of state aid to include non-action by a government in a situation in which a clear negative externality exists. Indeed, the current state of state aid regulations, which only focuses on positive action, appears inefficient to incentivize the promotion of energy production using sustainable resources. This reconceptualization would not require a radical change in positive law, merely a reinterpretation in line with the economic orthodoxy. If it is doubtful that this reconceptualization will arise out of a Member State demand, then the ECJ could easily, through a reinterpretation of the positive law ensure that the welfare increase provided by such reconceptualization will materialize.

References

CEER (Council of European Energy Regulators) (2013) Status review of renewable and energy efficiency support schemes in Europe. C12-SDE-33-03

CEER (Council of European Energy Regulators) (2015) Status review of renewable and energy efficiency support schemes in Europe in 2012 and 2013. C14-SDE-44-03

Collie DR (2000) State aid in the European Union: the prohibition of subsidies in an integrated market. Int J Ind Organ 18:867–884

Dalhman CJ (1979) The problem of externality. J Law Econ 22(1):141–162

Decker C (2014) Modern economic regulation. Cambridge University Press, Cambridge

Deighton-Smith R, Erbacci A, Kauffmann C (2016) Promoting inclusive growth through better regulation, the role of regulatory impact assessment. OECD regulatory policy working papers, No. 3. OECD, Paris. https://doi.org/10.1787/5jm3tqwqp1vj-en

Dewatripont M, Seabright P (2006) Wasteful public spending and state aid control. J Eur Econ Assoc 4(2/3):513–522

Easterly W (2001) The lost decades: developing countries' stagnation in spite of policy reform 1980–1998. J Econ Growth 6(2):135–157

Esty DC (1994) Greening the GATT: trade, environment and the future. Institute for International Economics, Washington, DC

European Commission (1994) Community guidelines on State aid for environmental protection, 10 March 1994, 94/C 72/03

European Commission (2001) Community guidelines on State aid for environmental protection, 3 February 2001, 2001/C 37/03

European Commission (2005) Less and better targeted state aid: a roadmap for state aid reform 2005–2009, 7 June 2005, COM(2005) 107 final

European Commission (2008a) Communication from the Commission to the European Parliament, the Council, the European Economic and Social Committee and the Committee of the Regions - 20 20 by 2020 – Europe's climate change opportunity, COM/2008/0030 final
European Commission (2008b) Community guidelines on State aid for environmental protection, 1 April 2008, 2008/C 82/01. Hereafter EG 2008
European Commission (2010) Energy 2020, a strategy for competitive, sustainable and secured energy. Brussels, European Union
European Commission (2014a) Guidelines on State aid for environmental protection and energy 2014–2020, 28 June 2014, 2014/C 200/01. Hereafter EG 2014
European Commission (2014b) Competition policy brief. New State aid rules for a competitive aviation industry. http://ec.europa.eu/competition/publications/cpb/2014/002_en.pdf
European Commission (2016a) Regulation of the European Parliament and the Council on the internal market of electricity. 30 November 2016. COM(2016) 861 final
European Commission (2016b) Commission Notice on the notion of State aid as referred to in Article 107(1) of the Treaty on the Functioning of the European Union, 2016, 2016/C 262/01
Kaplow L (1992) Rules versus standards: an economic analysis. Duke Law J 42:557–629
Melitz M (2005) When and how should infant industries be protected? J Int Econ 66:177–196
Neven D, Verouden V (2008) Towards a more refined economic approach in state aid control (Chap. 4). In: Mederer W, Pesaresi N, Van Hoof M (eds) EU competition law. Claeys and Casteels, Deventer
OECD (2013) Inventory of estimated budgetary support and tax expenditures for fossil fuels 2013. OECD, Paris
OECD (2015) OECD companion to the inventory of support measures for fossil fuel 2015. OECD, Paris
Röller L-H, Friederiszick HW, Verouden V (2008) European state aid control: an economic framework. In: Bucirossi P (ed) Handbook of antitrust economics. The MIT Press, Cambridge
Spector D (2009) State aids: economic analysis and practice in the European Union. In: Vives X (ed) Competition policy in the EU. Oxford University Press, Oxford
Stigler GJ (1971) The theory of economic regulation. Bell J Econ 2:3–21

Régis Lanneau Paris. Associate Professor in Public Law at the University of Paris Nanterre, 200 avenue de la république, 92001 Nanterre, Bureau F410. regis.lanneau@sciencespo.fr. Fields of Interest; Public law, law and economics, regulation, legal philosophy and legal theory.

State Measures in Support of Sustainable Mobility Infrastructure: The Case of Estonia, the Netherlands, and Norway

Ana Trías

Abstract This paper explores the legal instruments Member States can use to accomplish supranational targets to encourage the development of infrastructure for the refuelling and recharging of clean and efficient vehicles for road transportation. The case study examines in depth the concrete legal measures taken by Estonia, the Netherlands and Norway, which are particularly successful in the electrification of road transport, and analyses the supranational assessment of these strategies under state aid law.

1 Introduction

1.1 Research Question and Methodology

The European Union (EU) has developed a number of policies aimed at increasing the sustainability of transportation, particularly in residential areas. To fulfil EU and national goals, Member States may make use of a wide range of legal instruments to encourage the development of infrastructure for the charging of clean and efficient vehicles (CEV) for road transportation. This paper studies the concrete legal measures taken by the three countries in Europe that have achieved the highest rate of electrification of road transport. The geographical scope of the empirical case study is hence limited to Estonia, the Netherlands and Norway.

Estonia was the first country in the world to put in place a nationwide fast-charging network for plug-in electric vehicles (PEV).[1] The Dutch light-duty PEV fleet is the

[1]Estonian World (20 February 2013) Estonia becomes the first in the world to open a nationwide electric vehicle fast-charging network. http://estonianworld.com/technology/estonia-becomes-the-first-in-the-world-to-open-a-nationwide-electric-vehicle-fast-charging-network [accessed 29 May 2017]; Reuters (20 February 2013) Estonia goes electric with new car charger network. http://www.reuters.com/article/us-estonia-environment-cars-idUSBRE91J1EM20130220 [accessed 29 May 2017]; Forbes (20 February 2013) Estonia Launches Nationwide Electric Vehicle Fast-Charging

A. Trías (✉)
Center for European Integration Studies, University of Bonn, Bonn, Germany

K. Mathis, B. R. Huber (eds.), *Energy Law and Economics*, Economic Analysis of Law in European Legal Scholarship 5, https://doi.org/10.1007/978-3-319-74636-4_16

largest fleet in Europe, the world's fourth largest overall and the second largest per capita after Norway.[2] Norway, a non-EU country that is part of the European Free Trade Association (EFTA), has also been highly successful with its CEV program. It has the largest per capita fleet in the world and the highest CEV to conventionally fueled car ratio.[3] It can therefore be said that Estonia is the most successful jurisdiction in terms of relative coverage and Norway and the Netherlands in terms of relative uptake.

It may be argued that smaller countries with no significant geographic obstacles, like high mountains and islands, are more likely to achieve nation-wide coverage. To see if the size of the territory plays a key role in determining how to support CEV and more particularly PEV, the study encompasses two rather flat countries with comparable size (Estonia and the Netherlands) and a larger one featuring geographical obstacles as fjords and islands (Norway).

Similarly, it is conceivable that a country with high gross domestic product (GDP) and population will be in a good position to finance network infrastructures via state aids and tariffs. Meanwhile, a Member State with fewer budgetary resources may have access to EU cohesion funds, and a country with few inhabitants might find it difficult to finance extensive infrastructure through (affordable) tariffs.[4] To see if this thesis holds, the three countries chosen differ in terms of demographics and nominal GDP. Norway is the largest, richest country in terms of GDP of the three under scrutiny, and places second in population. While it is unable to access EU funds, its financing choices are relevant to this study as they put forward a successful strategy for the electrification of road transport. Netherlands is the most populous and dense country. It ranks second amongst the three in terms of total and per capita GDP and last in size. With a slightly larger territory than the Netherlands, Estonia has the lowest total and per capita GDP, as well as a less, more geographically scattered population.

1.2 Scope and Definitions

This case study assesses the development of infrastructure to road CEV, including heavy- (buses and trucks)[5] and light-duty vehicles (cars and vans), as well as two-

---

Network. http:/www.forbes.com/sites/justingerdes/2013/02/26/estonia-launches-nationwide-electric-vehicle-fast-charging-network/#2610e3782610 [accessed 29 May 2017].

[2]Hybridcars (16 January 2014) Top 6 Plug-In Vehicle Adopting Countries—2013. http://www.hybridcars.com/top-6-plug-in-car-adopting-countries [accessed 29 May 2017].

[3]Hybridcars (16 January 2014) Top 6 Plug-In Vehicle Adopting Countries—2013. http://www.hybridcars.com/top-6-plug-in-car-adopting-countries [accessed 29 May 2017].

[4]It should be noted that GDP is not a totally accurate or reliable indicator in the energy and climate policy sectors, since it does not account for depreciation of assets and depletion of natural resources. Nevertheless, it helps determine the availability of funds to rollout networks, as well as Member States' access to cohesion funds.

[5]Vehicles of categories M2, M3 and N2, N3 as defined in Directive 2007/46/EC of the European Parliament and of the Council of 5 September 2007 establishing a framework for the approval of

and three-wheelers and quadricycles.[6] For this study, CEV are defined as vehicles relying primarily on an alternative fuel. In turn, Article 2(1) of the EU Directive on the deployment of alternative fuels recharging and refuelling infrastructure (the Alternative Fuels Directive) [4] conceptualises 'alternative fuels' as

> fuels or power sources which serve, at least partly, as a substitute for fossil oil sources in the energy supply to transport and which have the potential to contribute to its decarbonisation and enhance the environmental performance of the transport sector. They include, inter alia: electricity, hydrogen, biofuels as defined in point (i) of Article 2 of Directive 2009/28/EC, synthetic and paraffinic fuels, natural gas, including biomethane, in gaseous form (compressed natural gas (CNG)) and liquefied form (liquefied natural gas (LNG)), and liquefied petroleum gas (LPG).[7]

The EU Communication laying out a comprehensive European alternative fuels strategy for the long-term substitution of oil as energy source in all modes of transport (the Alternative Fuels Communication), identifies electricity, hydrogen, biofuels, natural gas, and LPG as currently the principal alternative fuels with a potential for long-term oil substitution. Among these fuels, electricity is the cleanest and easiest to produce and the only capable of powering CEV that do not emit harmful substances. Therefore, focus will be put on this particular alternative fuel from this point on.

Like postal networks and petrol stations, infrastructure for the provision of alternative fuels is not a primary network but an overlay to transport and, in the case of electricity, also to energy infrastructure. Each alternative fuel requires the modification of the primary network on which it relies.[8] Networks that supply electricity to road CEV can be more or less centralised, depending on the technology they use.

Most common are plug-in charging stations, classifiable by the rate at which they refill batteries. From lower to higher performance, current technologies are: alternative current (AC) Level 1 and 2, and direct, hereafter current (DC). An additional

---

motor vehicles and their trailers, and of systems, components and separate technical units intended for such vehicles.

[6]Vehicles of categories M1 and N1 as defined in Directive in Directive 2007/46/EC of the European Parliament and of the Council of 5 September 2007 establishing a framework for the approval of motor vehicles and their trailers, and of systems, components and separate technical units intended for such vehicles; Vehicles of category L as defined in Vehicles of category L as defined in Directive 2002/24/EC of the European Parliament and of the Council of 18 March 2002 relating to the type-approval of two or three-wheel motor vehicles and repealing Council Directive 92/61/ EEC.

[7]Directive 2014/94/EU of the European Parliament and of the Council of 22 October 2014 on the Deployment of Alternative Fuels Infrastructure.

[8]The only exception is biofuel blended into a conventional fuel at a level compatible with traditional vehicles (less than 7% for biodiesel and less than 10% for bioethanol); Cf. European Free Trade Association Surveillance Authority, Decision of 16 September 2015 raising no objections to the programme for alternative fuels infrastructure (Norway), 336/1 5/COL, 6 [31]. The impact of overlaying charging networks on the design and capacity of current road transport and energy infrastructure systems will not be studied here.

standard (SAE J3068) is currently being developed for higher rates of AC charging.[9] Each plug-in charging standard requires a different plug. Currently, most vehicles enable charging through AC level 1 and 2 systems, while DC refuelling is only possible for high-end CEV. Conversely, road EEV in lower price ranges are limited to plug-in AC level 1 and 2 chargers.

Wireless systems are based on electric induction. Not yet available to the general public, they are being tested in pilot projects (e.g. in Korea and the United Kingdom). These technologies are more convenient than plug-in charging, as they allow refuelling on the move. If a communication function is embedded into the charging system, battery power stored in parked cars can be put back into the grid at times of high demand (and marked as a credit on the customer's bill).[10] This smart feature transforms parked cars into flexibility sources, thereby decreasing the need to invest in smart grid reinforcements.

Plug-in systems will be studied in more depth, because they currently are the only commercially available technology capable of electrifying transport. For this study, the term plug-in infrastructure is defined broadly as comprising all types of electric vehicle supply equipment (EVSE) that uses a cord, regardless of the standard used and location chosen.

Authorities designing strategies in support of PEV normally consider the level of competition possible to avoid overcompensation and crowding out. In turn, competition is influenced by the extent up to which the duplicability of the infrastructure is economically viable. Duplicability of PEV charging infrastructure is influenced by objective and subjective factors. Duplication seems economically feasible in densely populated areas, particularly in countries where PEV are being adopted. Additionally, customer behaviour allows the distinction of three main segments:

1. Overnight charging through poles stations at home or close to the home;
2. Charging during the day in strategic places (as workplaces, hospitals and schools) or close to them;
3. Charging on the road at petrol stations or public parking spaces by highways and roads.

Competition for the market is possible in each of these segments. For example, a tender could be held for the installation of charging stations alongside roads. Segments could also be combined in one PEV programme. For instance, one and the same tender may result with the entrustment of a firm with the installation of charging stations alongside roads and in public places.

Competition on the market is also feasible. Among others, business owners that want to offer charging services to attract customers and Residential PEV owners who

[9]Alternative Fuels Data Center of the US Department of Energy, Developing Infrastructure to Charge Plug-In Electric Vehicles. http://www.afdc.energy.gov/fuels/electricity_infrastructure.html [accessed 12 June 2017].

[10]The Engineer (2010) Unplugged: inductive charging on the road. http://www.theengineer.co.uk/unplugged-inductive-charging-on-the-road [accessed 6 April 2017].

install a home station can compare offers by PEV infrastructure firms. Once the infrastructure is in place, competition will exist within each segment and, up to a more limited extent, between segments. For instance, a person may choose to charge at the workplace instead of at home based on price incentives.

PEV are considered a downstream market because their functioning/uptake is only possible once charging networks are deployed. Meanwhile, smart grids, roads and electricity are all considered upstream markets, since they enable the construction and operation of the charging grid. Each market has a differentiated value chain. For example, markets for PEV include inputs, manufacturing and sales. Similarly, roads and smart grids can be owned, constructed, managed and used by different players. Electricity markets can also be categorised as wholesale or retail, and specific tariffs may be set to support the uptake of PEV.

2 Legal Framework for State Intervention in Support of CEV

2.1 EU Policy Goals

Network infrastructures require grids that allow adopters of CEV to operate their units fully, but their development is costly and associated with a number of challenges.[11] Economic issues of building a CEV charging/refuelling network include the high cost of rollout, fluctuations in electricity prices and low usage in case of slow uptake of the type of CEV propelled by the specific type of fuel supplied by the network in place. In many jurisdictions, there is legal uncertainty surrounding investments by firms that hold of special or exclusive rights in the sector. Efforts to ensure interoperability and adequate technical standards are still necessary. This, in turn, is hindered by rapid technological change and policymakers' hesitations regarding which standard to choose, which are typical of a highly dynamic market. Hence, it is unlikely that the market will ensure the politically desired level of investment in the short to medium term. The problem is more severe regarding

[11]This is not only the case of PEV; the EU experience with carbon capture and storage (CCS) also exemplifies the need for state intervention. CCS "consists of the capture of carbon dioxide (CO2) from industrial installations, its transport to a storage site and its injection into a suitable underground geo- logical formation for the purposes of permanent storage." After Directive 2009 in support of CCS entered into force, the Commission issued a Communication summarising the state of CCS development in 2013. In this document, the Commission identifies barriers for CCS development, including the lack of adequate transport infrastructure. Similarly, experts point out that "A strategic and pan-European approach should be taken to developing Europe's CO2 transport infrastructure, both pipelines and ships, which should be on a par with critical developments in Europe's electricity grid and natural gas pipeline networks in respect of policy attention, EU support and enabling mechanisms" (EASAC 2013). Without state intervention in support of a CCS network, the technology has not developed as expected.

investment in unprofitable locations (e.g. rural areas) and certain (more innovative) technologies.[12]

Since market failure to provide for refuelling infrastructure is a fundamental barrier to the development of alternative fuels in the transport sector,[13] EU institutions have worked on a policy framework aimed at enhancing environmental protection in the transport sector.

2.1.1 Europe 2020 and Horizon 2020

The so-called 'Europe 2020 Strategy' focuses on increasing competitiveness and energy security through a more efficient use of energy and other resources.[14] It is complemented by the 'Horizon 2020 Regulation' establishing a research and development (R&D) framework.[15] Article 19 of this Regulation is the legal basis for the European Green Vehicles Initiative (EGVI), a public-private partnership between the Commission and the private sector aimed i.e., at improving energy efficiency in the transport sector by 50% from 2010 to 2030, including a raise of 80% in the efficiency of urban vehicles.

2.1.2 The Renewables Strategy

Directive 2009/28/EC sets binding targets for Member States, including a market share target of 10% of renewables in transport fuels by 2020.[16] According to the current Commission Proposal for a Renewables Directive, the target of a 27% share for renewable energy by 2030 is an EU-wide one only, not binding at the national level.[17] Achieving the agreed 2030 framework objectives would require a contribution of 14–16% renewable energy in transport.[18]

According to Article 15(4), Member States shall ensure that competent authorities develop provisions for the integration and deployment of renewable energy when planning, developing or upgrading alternative fuel networks. Article 25 establishes an EU-level obligation for fuel suppliers to provide a certain share (6.8% in 2030) of

[12]EFTA Surveillance Authority Decision No 77595 of 16 September 2015 raising no objections to the programme for alternative fuels infrastructure (Norway).

[13]European Commission (2013c).

[14]European Commission (2010a).

[15]Regulation (EU) No 1291/2013 of the European Parliament and of the Council of 11 December 2013 establishing Horizon 2020—the Framework Programme for Research and Innovation (2014–2020) and repealing Decision No 1982/2006/EC.

[16]Directive 2009/28/EC of the European Parliament and of the Council of 23 April 2009 on the promotion of the use of energy from renewable sources and amending and subsequently repealing Directives 2001/77/EC and 2003/30/EC.

[17]European Commission (2016c).

[18]Hancher (2016).

low-emission and renewable fuels. Additionally, the proposal cites the conclusions of the Electricity Regulatory Forum held last June 2016, emphasising the need for a strong carbon signal and encouraging the development of new rules on support schemes for renewables.

2.1.3 The CEV Strategy

The Communication on ‘A European strategy on clean and energy efficient vehicles’ set out medium- to long-term actions in support of light and heavy duty CEV for road transportation, thereby complementing the EGVI.[19] Action points enshrined in the Communication include the revision of consumer incentives and taxation rules, as well as further standardisation and policy coordination between Member States to support CEV and refuelling infrastructure.

The Commission concretised some of these goals in its ‘Roadmap to a Single European Transport Area’,[20] a White Paper calling for a reduction in the dependence of transport on oil and a 60% decrease in greenhouse gas emissions from transport by 2050 (as measured against the 1990 levels). Targets should be achieved i.e., through the development of a sustainable alternative fuels strategy and infrastructure, set out in the ‘Clean Power for Transport Package’. Aimed at developing a single market for alternative fuels for transport in Europe, the Package is comprised of the following instruments:

- Alternative Fuels Communication;
- Alternative Fuels Directive;
- Accompanying Impact Assessment;[21]
- Staff Working Document setting out the needs in terms of market conditions, regulations, codes and standards for a broad market uptake of LNG in the shipping sector.[22]

2.1.4 The Alternative Fuels Directive

Adopted in 2014, the Alternative Fuels Directive acknowledges the need for state intervention to overcome the so-called chicken and egg problem.[23]This is a market failure whereby the lack of charging infrastructure hinders the uptake of electric vehicles and the lack of vehicles hinders the rollout of the charging infrastructure.[24]

---

[19]European Commission (2010b).

[20]European Commission (2011).

[21]European Commission (2013c).

[22]European Commission (2013b).

[23]Directive 2014/94/EU of the European Parliament and of the Council of 22 October 2014 on the Deployment of Alternative Fuels Infrastructure.

[24]Commission Decision C(2015) 5572 final of 11 August 2015 on State Aid SA.38769 (2015/N), The Green Deal for Publicly Accessible Charging Infrastructure Scheme (The Netherlands).

The Directive sets policy goals for Member States to achieve, rather than prescribing means to these ends.[25] Article 3 calls upon Member States to adopt a national policy framework for the development of the market as regards alternative fuels in the transport sector and the deployment of the relevant infrastructure. Support measures for alternative fuels infrastructure shall be implemented in compliance with state aid rules and EU environmental- and climate-protection legislation in force, as mandated by Article 2(5) and 2(6), respectively.

Article 4 targets the supply of electricity for transport. Pursuant to Article 4(1), Member States shall ensure, by means of their national policy frameworks, that an appropriate number of recharging points accessible to the public are put in place by 31 December 2020. The aim is to enable electric vehicles to circulate at least in densely populated areas, and, where appropriate, within networks determined by the Member States. Additionally, Member States shall encourage the deployment of recharging points not accessible to the public, in accordance with Article 4(3). Article 4(4) states that power recharging points for electric vehicles, excluding wireless or inductive units, must comply with certain technical standards. Article 4 (13) mandates the EU to pursue further standardisation in several fields, including that of wireless charging technologies.

Article 4(8) regulates the choice of electricity supplier. The version of this provision initially proposed by the Commission gave consumers the right to contract electricity simultaneously with several suppliers to separate electricity supply for CEV charging from other consumption purposes.[26] The draft text did not specify whether consumers could contract electricity for their CEV directly from the supplier or only through the operator of a charging station. The position of the European Parliament at first reading clarifies this issue: Member States must ensure that operators of recharging points can choose suppliers freely; a similar right is not envisaged for consumers. The adopted version of Article 4(8) does not allow offers from electricity suppliers to reach consumers. As a corollary, the number of suppliers able to sell electricity at a charging station is limited to one, i.e., the firm chosen by the manager of the refuelling point.[27] Pursuant to Article 4(9), all recharging points accessible to the public shall also allow CEV users to recharge on an ad hoc basis. Articles 4(7)(10)(11) broadly regulate, respectively, smart metering, non-discrimination by distribution system operators (DSOs) and retail prices.

Besides setting mandatory targets for the development of charging infrastructure for electricity, the Alternative Fuels Directive mandates the deployment of natural gas refuelling infrastructure in all Member States. Article 6 includes obligations to rollout infrastructure for the supply of liquefied and compressed natural gas (LNG and CNG, respectively). The term 'natural gas' is often a designation for methane,

[25]Directive 2014/94/EU of the European Parliament and of the Council of 22 October 2014 on the Deployment of Alternative Fuels Infrastructure.

[26]European Commission (2013a).

[27]This modification was not included in: European Economic and Social Committee (2013b) or Committee of the Regions (2013).

the second leading greenhouse gas after carbon dioxide. In cases where the term denotes another hydrocarbon fuel, methane is still emitted during the production and transport of such gas, as well as coal and oil.[28] Methane's effect on global warming may account for a whopping third of the climate warming from well-mixed greenhouse gases between the 1750s and today.[29]

The preference for electricity and natural gas among a wide range of alternative fuels seems somewhat at odds with the principle of technological neutrality enshrined in Recital 22 of the Alternative Fuels Directive. Additionally, Recital 8 specifies that standards and legislation should not give preference to any particular type of technology.[30] According to Recital 25,

> [e]lectro-mobility is a fast developing area. Current recharging interface technologies include cable connectors, but future interface technologies such as wireless charging or battery swapping need to be considered as well. Legislation needs to ensure that technological innovation is facilitated.

The European Economic and Social Committee stressed this inconsistency in the EU legislative approach. In particular, it noted that

> the development of the national policy framework for clean fuels and their infrastructure, which Member States are to create under the proposal, should include all those energy sources, such as biofuels, that are seen as important in the communication.[31]

2.1.5 European Strategy for Low-Emission Mobility

The 2016 Commission Communication on a "European Strategy for Low-Emission Mobility" aims at increasing the efficiency of the transport system, the amount of low-emission alternative energy for transport and the number of low- and zero emission vehicles.[32] Regarding infrastructure development, the Communication underscores the importance of reaching the targets set by the Alternative Fuels Directive, interoperability and standardisation.

2.1.6 European Strategy on Cooperative Intelligent Transport Systems

The 2016 Commission Communication on "A European strategy on Cooperative Intelligent Transport Systems, a milestone towards cooperative, connected and automated

[28]United States Environmental Protection Agency (EPA). Overview of Greenhouse Gases. https://www.epa.gov/ghgemissions/overview-greenhouse-gases [accessed 2 December 2016].

[29]United States National Aeronautics and Space Administration (NASA). Methane's Impacts on Climate Change May Be Twice Previous Estimates. https://www.nasa.gov/vision/earth/lookingatearth/methane.html [accessed 2 December 2016].

[30]These provisions were introduced in: European Parliament (2013), p. 6, para. 8.

[31]European Economic and Social Committee (2013b).

[32]European Commission (2017).

mobility" focuses on information and communications technology (ICT) services to enable the transition towards Cooperative Intelligent Transport Systems.[33] This Communication emphasises the need to mix and match technologies, which presupposes a high level of interoperability and standardisation at all levels—including the infrastructure.

2.1.7 Proposed Electricity Directive

Recital 27 of the current Commission proposal for a new Electricity Directive states that the new market rules should create favourable conditions for electric vehicles of all kinds, and promote the "deployment of publicly accessible and private recharging points for electric vehicles and ensure the efficient integration of vehicle charging into system operation." Recital 42 specifies that DSOs must cost-efficiently integrate recharging infrastructure for electric vehicles. Chapter IV includes, the tasks of the integration of electrical vehicles and data management, and Article 32(2) provides that network development plans shall encompass infrastructure elements necessary to connect recharging points for electric vehicles.

2.1.8 EU Funds

Efforts to increase sustainability and energy efficiency in the transportation sector and more specifically in road transportation qualify for a number of EU funding programmes. Cohesion instruments such as The European Regional Development Fund (ERDF) and the Cohesion Fund (CF) focus on less developed regions, as well as on priority areas. Therefore, some of them are open to Estonia but not to the Netherlands (as the CF for the 2014–2020 period).[34] Other funds are generally available to all Member States. These include loans and guarantees from the European Investment Bank (EIB), specific funds like the Joint European Support for Sustainable Investment in City Areas (JESSICA) and broader schemes like the Connecting Europe Facility (CEF).[35] Whether a programme entails a cohesion

---

[33] European Commission (2016b).

[34] Information available at www.ec.europa.eu/regional_policy/en/funding/cohesion-fund/—last retrieved 13 June 2016. Other cohesion instruments for sustainable and urban mobility include the European Structural and Investment Funds (ESIF), the Joint Assistance to Support Projects in European Regions (JASPERS), the territorial and regional cooperation programs INTERREG and URBACT III and the plan for innovative actions in sustainable urban development. Information available on the website of the European Local Transport Information Service (http://www.eltis.org/resources/eu-funding—last retrieved 19 June 2016).

[35] Information available on the website of the European Local Transport Information Service (www.eltis.org/resources/eu-funding—last retrieved 19 June 2016). Other EU funds applicable to sustainable mobility include those of the European Energy Efficiency Fund, the European Fund for Strategic Investments (EFSI), the Programme for the Environment and Climate Action (LIFE), the Horizon 2020 initiative and the Fuel Cell and Hydrogen Joint Undertaking for H2 mobility related projects. Some of these funds (as EFSI) are joint initiatives of the Commission and the EIB.

element depends on its specific design. For example, a substantial portion of the CEF budget (i.e., 11.305 billion Euros for the period 2014–2020) is available only for projects in Member States eligible under the CF.

2.2 *Legal Instruments of Member States*

In addition to EU funds for the development of new technologies and innovation for the decarbonisation of transportation,[36] Member States have a number of legal instruments available to them to develop PEV infrastructure and fulfil the requirements of the Alternative Fuels Directive. These include:

1. Imposition, removal or modification of unilateral regulation;
2. Imposition, removal or modification of taxation;
3. Consensual constraints;
4. Public benefits;
5. Public sector management;
6. Information.[37]

2.2.1 Regulation

Regulation can be used in different forms and for various purposes. Three main types of regulation can be distinguished: prohibitions, command-and-control obligations and incentives.

Regulatory prohibitions may preclude holders of special or exclusive rights in energy markets, such as electricity network operators from participating in the market for CEV charging infrastructure. The reasoning behind this is that network operators could use monopoly profits and synergies to build charging poles, and use the limited duplicability of this infrastructure to expand their monopoly power. In jurisdictions where regulation does not prohibit holders of special or exclusive rights from entering competitive markets, it may subject their activity to specific conditions such as legal or ownership unbundling.

Regulation can also include command-and-control rules requiring, for instance, that operators of electricity grids or petrol stations install charging/refuelling stations for one or more types of CEV.

Finally, regulation can set incentives for the development of CEV infrastructure. For example, tariff regulation may allow cost recovery for grid financing or focus on

[36]Regulation (EU) No 1316/2013 of the European Parliament and of the Council of 11 December 2013 establishing the Connecting Europe Facility, amending Regulation (EU) No 913/2010 and repealing Regulations (EC) No 680/2007 and (EC) No 67/2010, p. 129; see also European Parliament (2014), p. 10, para. 16.

[37]Daintith (1987).

keeping electricity charging prices as low as possible to make electric CEV use more attractive and counter disincentives such as longer refuelling periods compared to petrol-propelled vehicles. Additionally, regulation may set non-financial incentives for end-customers, allowing them i.e., to use bus lanes or park in restricted areas.[38]

2.2.2 Taxation

Taxation may be relaxed to incentivise the development of CEV related markets, for example by exempting buyers of CEV from one or more taxes applicable to the purchase of vehicles propelled by fossil fuels. Taxes may also be raised to rollout charging networks.

2.2.3 Consensual Constraints

Consensual constraints entail the control of an activity through agreements between the undertakings carrying it out and the state. Notably, Member States can grant special or exclusive rights to develop charging infrastructure. Article 2(3) of the Directive coordinating the procurement procedures of entities operating in the water, energy, transport and postal services sectors (the 'Utilities Directive') defines special or exclusive rights as

> rights granted by a competent authority of a Member State by way of any legislative, regulatory or administrative provision the effect of which is to limit the exercise of activities [. . .] to one or more entities, and which substantially affects the ability of other entities to carry out such activity.[39]

As laid-out in Article 106(2) TFEU, special or exclusive rights may have the character of a revenue-producing monopoly (when applied to profitable activities) or entail the entrustment with the operation of services of general economic interest (SGEI) (when granted for unprofitable projects). The latter category entails State funding while the former does not, because there is no profitability gap that needs covering.

According to its Article 5(1), the Utilities Directive applies to transport by railway, automated systems, tramway, trolley bus, bus or cable. As transport by car is neither listed nor a harmonised sector, it could be argued that the Directive and its limitations to the Member States' ability to grant special or exclusive rights do not apply. However, according to Article 3(3), the Directive is applicable to the development or operation of fixed networks intended to provide a service to the public in

[38]Cf. i.e., EFTA Surveillance Authority Decision No 76339 of 21 April 2015 on the State aid measures in favour of electric vehicles (Norway).

[39]Directive 2004/17/EC of the European Parliament and of the Council of 31 March 2004 coordinating the procurement procedures of entities operating in the water, energy, transport and postal services sectors.

connection with the production, transport or distribution of electricity and to the supply of electricity to such networks. Therefore, Member States may grant special or exclusive rights for the development of PEV charging infrastructure under the conditions imposed Utilities Directive. Additionally, these rights should not infringe fundamental freedoms or Article 102 TFEU.

2.2.4 Public Sector Management

Public sector management may be linked to special and exclusive rights or not. For example, the state may grant a legal monopoly to a public undertaking or manage an infrastructure it built under the Market Economy Investor Principle (MEIP). This principle applies to prima facie profitable projects, since it requires that "a public authority invests in an enterprise on terms and in conditions which would be acceptable to a private investor operating under normal market economy conditions."[40]

2.2.5 Information

Information can be provided by Member States to accelerate the rollout of PEV infrastructure. For example, aggregated data on demographics, traffic flows and other factors that impact the business case for infrastructure developers may be provided to them by public authorities under due consideration of privacy law.

2.3 State Aid Control

Some of the instruments for state intervention listed above are more likely to have budgetary implications than others, like a relaxation or removal of taxation and the granting of public benefits. All measures conferring a selective economic advantage to one or more undertakings through state resources amount to state aids. The Commission has given guidance on its assessment of the presence of state aid to infrastructure development under Article 107(1) TFEU in its Notice on the Notion of Aid (NOA), and issued guidelines explaining the conditions under which it will approve a state aid measure under Article 107(3) TFEU. Depending on their design and objectives, state aids for PEV infrastructure may also be declared compatible under different instruments. Investments under MEIP or financing through EU funds are excluded from state aid control.

---

[40] Slocock (2002), pp. 23–26.

2.3.1 General Block Exemption Regulation

The vast majority of state aid cases are assessed under the General Block Exemption Regulation (GBER), which does not apply to PEV infrastructure or any other alternative fuels network. Section 7 Article 48 considers aid to energy infrastructure a subtype of aid to environmental protection and deems investment aid for the construction or upgrade of energy infrastructure compatible with the internal market under certain conditions. Article 2(130) defines ‘energy infrastructure’ as any physical equipment or facility located within the EU or linking it to one or more third countries and falling under a category listed by the GBER. Covered electricity infrastructures are limited to transmission, distribution, storage and smart grids.

2.3.2 Environmental and Energy Aid Guidelines

Paragraph 1.3(31) of the Environmental and Energy Aid Guidelines (EEAG) contains the same definition of energy infrastructure as the GBER, thereby also excluding PEV infrastructure. Paragraph 15(b) further clarifies the EEAG do not apply to the financing of environmental protection measures relating to air, road, railway, inland waterway and maritime transport infrastructure.

2.3.3 Important Projects of Common European Interest

Measures in support of PEV infrastructure can declared compatible with the internal market under the Guidelines on Important Projects of Common European Interest (IPCEI), as they contribute towards achieving EU policy goals set i.e., in the Europe 2020 Strategy and the Clean Power for Transport Package. To fall under the IPCEI Guidelines the measure should fulfil certain conditions set out in paragraph 3.2. Notably, the project should be co-financed by more than one Member State plus the beneficiary, and its positive impact should extend beyond the Member States involved to a wide part of the Union.

2.3.4 Services of General Economic Interest

Finally, the development of PEV infrastructure may be entrusted as SGEI. Depending on its design, a measure could fall outside the scope of state aid or amount to compatible aid under the SGEI Decision.[41]

[41]Case C-280/00 Altmark Trans GmbH and Regierungspräsidium Magdeburg v Nahverkehrsgesellschaft Altmark GmbH, Judgment Judgment ECLI:EU:C:2003:415 of 24 July 2003; Commission Decision 2012/21/EU(notified under document C(2011) 9380) of 20 December 2011 on the application of Article 106(2) of the Treaty on the Functioning of the European Union to State aid in the form of public service compensation granted to certain undertakings entrusted with

3 Selected National Experiences

3.1 Estonia

In 2013, Estonia completed the first nationwide network of PEV fast chargers. The network comprises of 165 direct current quick-charging stations, which can deliver a 90% charge to the battery in less than 30 min.[42] Stations are strategically dispersed across the country in an interval of 40–60 km along highways and in every city of more than 5000 inhabitants. Within cities, chargers are located at high-convenience spots such as gas stations, post and bank offices and parking lots.[43] Managed by the public undertaking KredEx, the network operates entirely on renewable electricity and features unified payment and support systems.[44]

The Estonian electro-mobility programme is rooted in the Kyoto Protocol and the global agreement on creating the emissions trading systems (ETS). Specifically, Estonia had an excess amount of around 85 million surplus CO_2 emission permits that was available for trading under the Green Investment Scheme.[45] The sale of surplus CO_2 emission permits to Japan's Mitsubishi Corporation in 2011 financed 100% of the electrical mobility programme, which consisted of three main components: PEV network rollout, acquisition of 500+ PEV by the State and subsidisation of CEV purchases by end-customers.[46]

---

the operation of services of general economic interest; European Commission (2012a, b); Commission Regulation (EU) No 360/2012 of 25 April 2012 on the application of Articles 107 and 108 of the Treaty on the Functioning of the European Union to de minimis aid granted to undertakings providing services of general economic interest.

[42]Estonian World (20 February 2013) Estonia becomes the first in the world to open a nationwide electric vehicle fast-charging network. http://estonianworld.com/technology/estonia-becomes-the-first-in-the-world-to-open-a-nationwide-electric-vehicle-fast-charging-network, accessed 29 May 2017. Reuters (20 February 2013) Estonia goes electric with new car charger network. http://www.reuters.com/article/us-estonia-environment-cars-idUSBRE91J1EM20130220 [accessed 29 May 2017].

[43]Forbes (26 February 2013) Estonia Launches Nationwide Electric Vehicle Fast-Charging Network. http://www.forbes.com/sites/justingerdes/2013/02/26/estonia-launches-nationwide-electric-vehicle-fast-charging-network/#2610e3782610 [accessed 29 May 2017].

[44]Estonian World (20 Febraury 2013) Estonia becomes the first in the world to open a nationwide electric vehicle fast-charging network. http://estonianworld.com/technology/estonia-becomes-the-first-in-the-world-to-open-a-nationwide-electric-vehicle-fast-charging-network [accessed 29 May 2017].

[45]Joller and Varblane (2015), pp. 57–67.

[46]Reuters (20 February 2013) Estonia goes electric with new car charger network. http://www.reuters.com/article/us-estonia-environment-cars-idUSBRE91J1EM20130220 [accessed 29 May 2017]. Grants to acquire PEV, which were available to end-users from 2011 for PEV and 2012 for hybrid CEV until 2014, fell under the *de minimis* threshold and were thus not notified to the Commission. Information on grant period available at http://elmo.ee/about/. Information on the application of de minimis rules obtained through correspondence from 30 September 2016 with Heikki Parve, KredEX Project Manager.

The construction of the network was tendered in 2012 and the programme was fully implemented approximately a year after the winner was announced.[47] The procedure complied with national and EU procurement rules and was overseen by National Competition Authorities.[48] The allocation of funds obtained from the sale of AUU to the electrical mobility programme was legally based on Directive 2003/87/EC, which allows greenhouse gas emission allowance trading.[49] Although this directive does not exempt national measures involving state resources obtained through permit trading from state aid control, the Commission did not open a formal state aid investigation into the Estonian Scheme.[50] Consequently, the compatibility of the national measure financing the CEV charging infrastructure with Article 107 TFEU was not analysed in depth.

By the time the programme was completed, the ratio of plug-in fully electric vehicles to traditional cars was 1/1000 cars, second only to Norway with 4/1000 and followed by the Netherlands with 0.6/1000.[51] With public EV charging infrastructure deployment still in its early days, Estonia's decision to prioritise quick-charging stations can be seen as forward-looking in terms of plug-in technology and may positively impact adoption rates by making recharging fast and easy.

3.2 *The Netherlands*

By 2014 the Netherlands' light-duty PEV fleet was the largest fleet in Europe, the world's fourth largest after the U.S., China and Japan and the second largest per capita after Norway.[52] The ratio of PEV to traditional cars was, as said, second only to Estonia.[53]

---

[47]The Guardian (20 February 2013) Estonia launches national electric car charging network. http://www.theguardian.com/environment/2013/feb/20/estonia-electric-car-charging-network [accessed 29 May 2017].

[48]Correspondence from 14 September 2016 with Heikki Parve, KredEX Project Manager.

[49]Directive 2003/87/EC of the European Parliament and of the Council of 13 October 2003 establishing a scheme for greenhouse gas emission allowance trading within the Community and amending Council Directive 96/61/EC; The programme period of 2011–2014 corresponds to the trade period of AAUs according to the Kyoto Protocol.

[50]Commission response to my application for access to documents—Ref GestDem No 2016/6662, Brussels, 16 December 2016, GROW/C3/NM/mm(2016) 7609437. The letter states that the Estonian scheme was encompassed in the 'Impact Assessment Study Concerning the Charging of Electric Vehicles (Report, May 2013)' from DG MOVE, which remained confidential by the time the response was issued.

[51]Reuters (20 February 2013) Estonia goes electric with new car charger network. http://www.reuters.com/article/us-estonia-environment-cars-idUSBRE91J1EM20130220 [accessed 29 May 2017].

[52]Hybridcars (16 January 2014) Top 6 Plug-In Vehicle Adopting Countries—2013. http://www.hybridcars.com/top-6-plug-in-car-adopting-countries [accessed 12 June 2017].

[53]KredEx (20 February 2013) Estonia becomes the first in the world to open a nationwide electric vehicle fast-charging network. Estonian World in Technology. http://estonianworld.com/technology/

To develop its e-mobility infrastructure, the Netherlands has opted for broad frameworks and fiscal incentives rather than 'launching customer' schemes,[54] i.e., programmes in which a public entity acts as lead customer. For instance, a Dutch framework for the reduction of CO_2 emissions in the transport sector notified in 2000 envisaged aid for the entire transport sector.[55] The Commission would have declared the scheme a general measure falling outside the scope of state aid control, had it not entailed discretional powers for Dutch authorities.[56]

In 2008, the Netherlands developed another state aid scheme to increase sustainability in the transport and water sectors.[57] While covering several transport modes, the measure was more selective than the 2000 framework, as it focused aid on certain markets (e.g. for EEV). The Commission considered that state aid was present even in the absence of discretionary powers and compatible with the internal market.

Additionally, Dutch authorities notified several aid schemes for the acquisition of EEV, as well as charging and supporting infrastructure. For example, in 2013 they sanctioned a measure confined to one mode of transport (i.e., road) and one specific technology (i.e., plug-in) in two markets (i.e., vehicles and infrastructure) and one geographic area (i.e., Amsterdam). Again, the Commission found the aid compatible with the Treaty based on the presence of tenders and incentive effects, and did not oppose the trend towards increasing selectivity of state aid for sustainable mobility.

In 2015, the Commission dealt with the "Green Deal for Publicly Accessible Charging Infrastructure Scheme", the first Dutch State aid measure targeting only charging infrastructure for plug-in EEV on a national basis (the 'Dutch Decision').[58] With a budget of € 33.7 million and a 3-year duration, the scheme sought to contribute to the development of a nationwide plug-in charging network. Envisaging the award of grants and exclusive rights through open, non-discriminatory and transparent selection procedures, the measure was declared compatible directly under Article 107(3)(c) TFEU.

With regards to regulation, it should be noted that the Netherlands has not focused on electricity tariffs that allow for cost recovery. Amsterdam offers free charging in

---

estonia-becomes-the-first-in-the-world-to-open-a-nationwide-electric-vehicle-fast-charging-network [accessed 14 June 2017]. Reuters (20 February 2013) Estonia goes electric with new car charger network. http://www.reuters.com/article/us-estonia-environment-cars-idUSBRE91J1EM20130220 [accessed 29 May 2017].

[54]Netherlands Enterprise Agency (RVO.nl) (2011) Electric Mobility gets up to speed—2011–2015 Action Plan. https://www.rvo.nl/sites/default/files/bijlagen/Action%20Plan%20English.pdf [accessed 29 May 2017].

[55]The decisions analysed here were chosen from a range of aids granted by the Netherlands (i.e., under the de minimis Regulation and the General Block Exemption Regulation) because of their scope and implications (Cf. COM Case SA.34719 2013 NL Page 7).

[56]Commission Decision SG (2001) D/ 289514 of 3 July 2001 on a framework for aid for the reduction of CO2 emissions in the transport sector (The Netherlands).

[57]Commission Decision C(2009) 3289 final of 20 May 2009 on a framework for aid for sustainability in the transport and water sectors (The Netherlands).

[58]Commission Decision C(2015) 5572 final of 11 August 2015 on State Aid SA.38769 (2015/N), The Green Deal for Publicly Accessible Charging Infrastructure Scheme (The Netherlands).

public spaces and, on average, gas costs about five times as much as the electricity needed for a similar journey in the Netherlands.[59]

Moreover, regulation has not yet fully clarified whether DSOs and TSOs are allowed to install charging points. Although unbundling requirements for DSOs are less stringent on EU level that those for TSOs, both are subject to ownership unbundling in the Netherlands. Additionally, the law prescribes that their shareholders must be public entities (e.g. municipalities). Both TSOs and DSOs have legal monopolies in the Netherlands and are not allowed to engage in activities that deviate from their core task. Whether rolling out PEV infrastructure entails a deviation has not yet been clarified. In light of the legal uncertainty, some firms have entered the market for electrical mobility. For example, DSO Enexis and other market players developed a charging point that is 50% cheaper than existing stations.[60] Oversight of the prohibition to stray from core falls to the Dutch Competition Authority (Autoriteit Consument en Markt, ACM), which has taken no steps against DSOs participation in markets for PEV charging infrastructure. The ACM stated in 2015 that network companies increasingly develop more secondary activities and gave a broad interpretation of the prohibition in a decision of May 2016.[61]

3.3 Norway

As of September 2016, sales in the European light-duty plug-in electric segment are led by Norway with over 121,300 units. Norway has thus the fastest growing PEV fleet, the largest per capita fleet and the highest ratio of fully electric PEV to traditional car.[62]

---

[59]The New York Times (9 February 2013) Plugging In, Dutch Put Electric Cars to the Test. http://mobile.nytimes.com/2013/02/10/world/europe/dutch-put-electric-cars-to-the-test.html?_r=0&referer= [accessed 19 June 2017].

[60]Netherlands Enterprise Agency (RVO.nl) (2015) Electromobility in the Netherlands –Highlights 2014. https://www.rvo.nl/sites/default/files/2015/04/Electromobility%20in%20the%20Netherlands%20Highlights%202014.pdf [accessed 19 June 2017].

[61]In this case, the German energy company RWE had requested an investigation into whether the Dutch DSO Alliander had overstepped its core competencies. The reason for this was that three companies under Alliander's wing were developing energy efficiency and flexibility management software, a competitive market in RWE's view. The ACM was of the opinion that Alliander had not overstepped its core competencies. The behind this was twofold. First, the ACM held that the activities under review did not entail the supply or trade in energy but merely an improvement of energy efficiency. Second, the authority believed that the stage for intervention had not yet come; it could not yet decide on the matter conclusively because the software at issue was still under development and it was yet unclear whether the DSO wanted to take on an additional role or not.

[62]Reuters (20 February 2013) Estonia goes electric with new car charger network. http://www.reuters.com/article/us-estonia-environment-cars-idUSBRE91J1EM20130220 [accessed 29 May 2017]; Hybridcars (16 January 2014) Top 6 Plug-In Vehicle Adopting Countries—2013. http://www.hybridcars.com/top-6-plug-in-car-adopting-countries [accessed 19 June 2017].

Electricity utilities, vehicle companies (production and retail) and fuel retail companies have installed a significant portion of the available PEV charging stations.[63] This means that holders of special and exclusive rights in energy markets have entered the PEV infrastructure market, which can be competitive in certain segments. Key industry players have created Electric Mobility Norway (EMN), an industry cluster of Norwegian companies that cooperate and explore business opportunities within the CEV market, including R&D and product commercialisation. In 2012, Electric Mobility Norway became an "Arena project". Arena is a programme designed to foster innovation in business and industry through collaboration between public, private, commercial and academic entities.[64] It is also expected that owners of vehicle fleets and various retail and service companies enter the PEV market in the near future.[65]

Additionally, the Norwegian Government is intervening to accelerate PEV uptake. In addition to para-fiscal incentives, such as opening bus-lines for PEV, intervention encompasses a number of fiscal measures. In 2014, Norway notified a package of fiscal and para-fiscal measures to the EFTA Surveillance Authority (the 'Authority'), which ensures that the participating EFTA States Iceland, Liechtenstein and Norway, respect their obligations under the European Economic Area Agreement (EEAA).[66] The Authority declared the measure did not amount to state aid regarding its direct beneficiaries (i.e., users) and amounted to compatible aid to its indirect beneficiaries (i.e., undertakings active in PEV related markets).The following year, the European Free Trade Association Surveillance Authority (ESA) decided on a package of measures notified by Norway (the 'Norwegian Decision').[67]

The programme envisaged investment aid to be distributed in the form of grants to beneficiaries chosen through open, non-discriminatory and competitive selection procedures. The measure was funded by the Energy Fund, an entity largely financed through a levy on the electricity grid tariff, whose level is determined by the state. The Energy Fund has also received capital from the Norwegian "Green Fund for Climate, Renewable Energy and Energy Efficiency Measures". The Energy Fund is managed by the public undertaking Enova SF, a company fully owned by the Norwegian State via the Ministry of Petroleum and Energy. The undertaking's main purposes are to manage the Energy Fund and administer several Norwegian support programmes aimed at promoting renewable energy and the use of energy-

[63]European Free Trade Association Surveillance Authority, Decision of 16 September 2015 raising no objections to the programme for alternative fuels infrastructure (Norway), 336/1 5/COL.

[64]Mobility Norway website. http://www.electricmobility.no/English [accessed 2 October 2016].

[65]Mobility Norway website. http://www.electricmobility.no/English [accessed 2 October 2016].

[66]European Free Trade Association Surveillance Authority, Decision of 21 April 2015 on State aid measures in favour of electric vehicles (Norway), 150/15/COL.

[67]European Free Trade Association Surveillance Authority, Decision of 16 September 2015 raising no objections to the programme for alternative fuels infrastructure (Norway), 336/1 5/COL.

efficient technologies. The proceeds of the levy are allocated directly to the Energy Fund and allotted to selected projects by Enova SF.

The notified measure supported the development of infrastructure for charging/refuelling with electricity, hydrogen and biofuels for vehicles, and shore-side electricity and liquefied natural gas for ships. This fits into a broader pattern: unlike Estonia and the Netherlands, Norway has made considerable efforts to deploy infrastructure for other types of alternative fuels as well. The government has supported the construction of LNG supply points for ships, while mostly private players are slowly deploying hydrogen infrastructure. By 2015, oil companies had established six hydrogen filling stations. Moreover, an R&D institution and a single purpose hydrogen company installed additional hydrogen filling stations and production facilities.[68]

In its Norwegian Decision,[69] the ESA assessed all measures directly under Article 61(3)(c) of the European Economic Area Agreement, the equivalent to Article 107 (3) TFEU, and concluded that state aid was present and compatible with such agreement. Regarding EEV charging, ESA clarified that "the objective of the aid is to increase the sale and usage of electric vehicles in Norway." For that purpose, it seeks "to ensure the free circulation of electric vehicles with the current technology" (i.e., plug-in). The granting authority "will require a technology for the chargers that will enable as many different vehicles as possible to use the charging stations" (i.e., through AC level 2 and DC chargers). Additionally, it will "monitor the market in order to present requirements that at all times ensure the highest degree of compatibility with the current fleet of electric vehicles."

4 Critical Legal Assessment of the Dutch and Norwegian Decisions

As stated above, the Estonian scheme was left unassessed by the Commission. In the following, the reactions of the competent supranational bodies to the Dutch and Norwegian schemes will be analysed in depth.[70]

---

[68]European Free Trade Association Surveillance Authority, Decision of 16 September 2015 raising no objections to the programme for alternative fuels infrastructure (Norway), 336/1 5/COL.

[69]European Free Trade Association Surveillance Authority, Decision of 16 September 2015 raising no objections to the programme for alternative fuels infrastructure (Norway), 336/1 5/COL.

[70]European Commission, Decision of 11 August 2015 on the Green Deal for Publicly Accessible Charging Infrastructure Scheme (The Netherlands), C(2015) 5572 final; European Free Trade Association Surveillance Authority, Decision of 16 September 2015 raising no objections to the programme for alternative fuels infrastructure (Norway), 336/1 5/COL.

4.1 *Direct and Indirect Aids*

4.1.1 Legal Basis and for the Compatibility of State Aids to CEV Infrastructure

The Commission assessed the measures in support of CEV networks directly under Article 107(3)(c) TFEU. The Authority based its Norwegian Decision on Article 6l (3)(c), the equivalent provision of the EEAA. The methodology to reach this conclusion diverged among the decisions under study.

Dutch authorities submitted that state aid to CEV networks increased environmental protection. Although this argument is in line with EU policies in the CEV sector and the Alternative Fuels Directive, aid to CEV infrastructure is not included in the EEAG. The Commission noted that PEV infrastructure does not meet the definition of eligible energy infrastructures set out in point (31)(a) EEAG. The Commission therefore considered that the assessment of the compatibility of the scheme with the internal market should be based directly on Article 107(3)(c) TFEU.

Norwegian authorities stated that measures in support of CEV networks fall outside the scope of the EEAG, as section 1.2 excludes the financing of environmental protection measures relating to transport infrastructure. The Authority followed this reasoning to conclude that the EEAG did not apply and that the measure must be assessed directly under Article 6l(3)(c) EEAA.

Nevertheless, the Authority noted that "the aid schemes under the alternative fuels programme are intended to promote the development of environmentally-friendly infrastructure, thereby contributing to an increase in environmental protection. The application of maximum aid intensities similar to those in the EEAG is therefore a good proxy in the context of the proportionality assessment." The Commission did not mention a proxy application of the EEAG.

In both decisions, state aid was present and compatible with the applicable Treaty. The presence of tenders and incentive effects played a key role in the reasoning of both oversight bodies.

4.1.2 Direct Aid

The only direct aid beneficiaries identified in the Norwegian Decision are the firms installing infrastructure. Meanwhile, undertakings selling or operating such infrastructure were also listed as direct beneficiaries in the Dutch Decision. The difference regarding infrastructure managers is rooted in the exclusive rights granted by the Dutch (but not the Norwegian) Government to operate the charging poles for a given period of time. Equipment sellers were categorised as direct beneficiaries by the Commission and as indirect beneficiaries by the Authority. The categorisation of equipment sellers as direct or indirect beneficiaries depends on whether installation companies can acquire the machinery from a third party or not. In the affirmative, equipment sellers and manufacturers are indirectly benefitting from the measure's effect on upstream markets.

Unlike the Commission, the Authority looked at infrastructure duplicability when assessing the effects of the measure on the main relevant market. It noted that PEV charging stations may be profitable in some areas and not in others, and Norwegian authorities had already submitted that PEV is being developed commercially in urban areas, while markets a failing in rural areas. Therefore, the granting authority offered to only grant aid in areas where there is no comparable existing or planned infrastructure. The combination of mapping and interoperability requirements or commitments significantly reduces the risk of crowding out previous investments.

In the Dutch Decision, the Commission did not require that the Netherlands conduct a mapping exercise to determine which areas to target. This entails a deviation from Commission criteria applicable in other sectors, such as broadband. The Dutch scheme envisages two modalities: grants only or a combination of exclusive rights and grants to cover funding gaps. The second alternative makes sense only if the local government clusters profitable and unprofitable areas in one tender to finance network rollout in the latter through a mix of direct aid and cross-subsidies from monopolistic rents. Unlike grants, exclusive rights preclude the development of competition on the market for their entire duration, regardless of whether return on investment increases as consumers adopt PEV in urban areas. This makes exclusive rights more distortive than state aids and calls for careful mapping, market forecasts and public consultations.

4.1.3 Indirect Aid to Commercial Users

Once aid is granted to rollout a specific type of CEV network, owners or users of vehicles that refuel in the supported infrastructures profit from increased availability and (potentially) lower prices. Therefore, the Norwegian Decision required that the infrastructure be legally and technologically open to all potential commercial users (i.e., stations were equipped with all PEV available charges). Any residual advantages for commercial users were considered non-selective or, if selective, as having only a very limited impact. The Commission did not address the issue of potential indirect advantages to commercial, likely because the Dutch scheme requires contribution from local business as a pre-condition to subsidise infrastructure in a given area.

Each decision eliminated a different type of selectivity and left another un-tackled. The Norwegian Decision precluded product selectivity through technological neutrality, but did not address geographical advantages derived from the positive local effects of infrastructure development. Dutch authorities saw and countered geographical selectivity through user contributions, but failed to eliminate product discrimination through strict interoperability and upgrade obligations.

4.1.4 Indirect Aid to Equipment, CEV and Fuel Suppliers

The Authority found that the development of CEV infrastructure could boost car sales and manufacturing, but did not address how this would affect other modes of transport.

To minimise technology-based distortions within PEV markets, Norwegian authorities committed to creating a technologically open platform that would support as many different vehicles as possible and be updated based on observable technological development. The Authority was satisfied that the standards were open and could be amended and updated going forward, declaring the measure compatible with the EEAA.

Due to substitution effects and the 'chicken and egg' relationship between CEV uptake and infrastructure rollout, state intervention in favour of one technology (e.g. PEV) favours firms involved in that specific value chain, to the detriment of undertakings selling and manufacturing other types of CEV, fuels and infrastructures. On the other hand, the costs of deploying nation-wide networks for each commercially available alternative fuel are extremely high. Governments need to prioritise technologies, but oversight authorities could inquire into the rationale behind these decisions.

To ensure technological neutrality, Member States must justify preferences for a specific technological solution. For example, a preference for electricity over CGN could be justified by a desire to decrease methane production. However, the Authority did not establish why some fuels were supported and others were not, or inquire into the selectivity of the measure as regards the mode(s) of transport. For instance, an increase of the car fleet will likely reduce the use of collective means of transport as buses, subways and regional trains.

The impact of a measure targeting a specific mode of transport on all others could be assessed when controlling whether the aid is necessary to achieve a common interest objective. For example, according to the Commission Guidelines on state aid to airports and airlines, the need for airport infrastructure depends among other things on the proximity of "another airport or other modes of transport, in particular high-speed train connections." In the field of urban transport, the Commission's Action Plan on Urban Mobility calls for an integrated approach that considers i.e., the interdependence between transport modes.

The Commission neglected to look at potential distortions in markets for CEV and charging equipment altogether. This entails a deviation from previous decisions,[71] including the assessment of a scheme encompassing subsidies to consumers buying CEV and to the installation of charging poles in Amsterdam.[72] Here, the Commission found that indirect aid to charging poles manufacturers could not be

[71]Cf. i.e., Commission Decisions in cases N 142/2005—United Kingdom, N 386/2010– Denmark and SA.30741 (2011/N)—United Kingdom.

[72]Commission Decision SA.34719 (2013/N) of 20 November 2013 on the Netherlands Electric transportation scheme in Amsterdam (The Netherlands).

excluded by competitive selection procedures, and that the measure was liable to favour the car industry through demand stimulation.[73]

4.1.5 Commission Notice on the Notion of State Aid

The Commission Notice on the Notion of State Aid as referred to in Article 107 (1) TFEU ('NOA') gives guidance regarding the classification assessment in infrastructure markets.[74] It limits the scope of state aid control to indirect advantages, excluding effects that are inherent in almost every state aid measure. This creates significant challenges in theory and practice.

From a practitioner's standpoint, it is sometimes difficult to differentiate between indirect advantages and inherent effects. According to the NOA, "An indirect advantage is present if the measure is designed in such a way as to channel its secondary effects towards identifiable undertakings or groups of undertakings." In contrast, the beneficiaries of inherent effects cannot be singled out. In practice, this criterion does not always fit the Commission's conclusions.

This can be seen for instance in a case from the broadcasting market dealing with a direct subsidy granted by Italy to consumers purchasing or renting digital equipment for the reception of TV signals transmitted using digital terrestrial (but not satellite) technology.[75] Here, the Commission found that benefits to terrestrial broadcasters amounted to indirect aid while those to producers of decoders did not. The delimitation was not based on the possibility to pinpoint potential beneficiaries, as 'producers of decoders' are prima facie as identifiable as 'terrestrial broadcasters'. The deciding factor was that any measure in support of digitalisation would inevitably favour suppliers of decoders from digital signals, while the advantage for terrestrial broadcasters could have been avoided by subsidising satellite decoders alongside terrestrial ones.

State intervention measures that do not discriminate between undertakings are considered general and uncontrollable under state aid law. On the opposite end of the spectrum are measures that discriminate beyond what is strictly necessary to achieve the aim in view. In the middle, schemes that discriminate in a manner that is proportionate to reach a common interest objective and amount to compatible aid. Discriminatory effects inextricably linked to the aim in view are considered inherent, while avoidable discrimination amounts to (incompatible) indirect aid. This is why the Commission and the Authority should have assessed the proportionality of the choice of mode of transport, fuel and charging system.

---

[73]Since the funds and number of charging stations were limited, the measure could not distort competition under the de minimis principle.

[74]European Commission (2016a).

[75]Commission Decision 2007/374/EC of 24 January 2007 on State aid implemented by the Italian Republic for the subsidised purchase of digital decoders.

4.2 *Broader Impact of the Aid Measures*

4.2.1 Impact on Electricity Markets

Neither the Commission nor the Authority looked into who is providing the electricity for CEV charging or under what terms. However, where owners of subsidised charging poles influence tariffs, competition in electricity markets may be distorted. In countries where holders of special or exclusive rights such as DSOs and TSOs can enter competitive markets or bid to develop PEV infrastructure, distortions may be higher as they can result in a de facto expansion of monopolistic power. Even in the absence of exclusive rights, an overcompensated operator can charge prices below market levels to force competitors out of the market.

While antitrust and state aid law allow an ex-post control, regulation has a key role to play in avoiding these risks before they materialise. Both the Commission and the Authority can make positive decisions contingent upon the fulfilment of certain obligations. For example, in Ireland, unbundling obligations have been imposed used to keep the revenue from electric vehicle-charging tariffs in a company that is a separate legal entity from the holder of special or exclusive rights.[76] Transparency obligations and price regulation in line with Article 4(10) of the Alternative Fuels Directive can also help minimise cross-subsidisation and dumping.

Under the scheme declared compatible in the Dutch Decision, contracts with holders of exclusive rights set maximum tariffs. Beneficiaries of direct grants had to include tariffs in their application, thereby making prices an integral part of their bid. In both cases, operators would be precluded from overcharging but not from sinking prices below market levels. The framework assessed in the Norwegian Decision is legally based i.e., on Norwegian Regulation No 1377 of 10 December 2001 concerning the levy on the electricity distribution tariff. This national law stipulates a homogenous electricity retail tariff and mandates the establishment of separate accounting and balance sheet accounts that clarify billing of and payments from end-customers.[77]

The Commission and the Authority could also impose access obligations for retailers. Such obligations are not generally applicable in the largely unregulated market of CEV infrastructure but have played a key role in the development of broadband and electricity markets.

4.2.2 Impact on the Environment and the Energy Mix

Article 2(6) of the Alternative Fuels Directive provides that all measures must be in line with EU environmental and climate-protection legislation in force. "The

[76]Meeus and Hadush (2016), pp. 1–6.

[77]Norwegian Regulation No 1377 of 10 December 2001 concerning the levy on the electricity distribution tariff, Section 2 and 3.

Commission will (...) evaluate whether the promotion of electric vehicles leads to the additional provision of low-carbon electricity generation via the promotion of low carbon energy sources to ensure that the electricity consumed by electric vehicles does not go to the detriment of low carbon electricity already expected from meeting the requirements of the Renewable Energy Directive", in accordance with Section 4 Action 2 of the CEV Strategy.[78] In the same vein, the Opinion of the European Economic and Social Committee on proposed Alternative Fuels Directive "underscores the need to ensure a smooth and viable transition to a modified energy mix, and the importance of bearing in mind the potential of improving the environmental record of fossil fuels."[79]

Additionally, the Authority dealt with a complaint stating "that electric cars are not more environmentally friendly than conventional cars since an important part of the electricity used in Norway is generated in German coal-fired plants."[80] The complaint objected to a wide range of measures, including fiscal and para-fiscal incentives for PEV, as well as free charging at public charging stations (i.e., a subsidy to electricity for PEV). Despite this, the Authority did not address the specific issue of the source of the electricity used for charging. It merely stated that the reduction of CO_2 emissions from vehicles remains one of the objectives of the EEAG and that the aid was in line the White Paper on Norwegian climate policy of 2001 (St. Meld nr. 54 (2000–20014)99).

Similarly, the Commission found that

> Even when the electricity is not fully produced from renewable energy sources, most of the benefits remain as the emissions stemming from generation are located far from the Air Quality hotspots and the emission sources – power plants – are more amenable to pollution control.[81]

While it is true that CO_2 emissions are reduced by all PEV, other aspects may significantly impact the overall effect of a measure on environmental protection. Coal production has an extremely high environmental and social impact, damaging the soil and often resulting in the relocation of entire communities. Additionally, increasing electricity production from non-sustainable sources is counterproductive to other key EU goals, as the energy transition.

Nevertheless, neither the Commission nor the Authority looked in depth at the impact of measures in support on CEV on electricity markets, and more specifically on production from non-renewable sources. They did not demand that granting authorities carry out an in-depth assessment of the environmental impact of traditional vehicle fuels versus PEV powered through electricity from so-called 'black' sources, or require proof that the measure would not negatively impact the transition

---

[78]European Commission (2010b).

[79]European Economic and Social Committee (2013a).

[80]EFTA Surveillance Authority Decision No 77595 of 16 September 2015 raising no objections to the programme for alternative fuels infrastructure (Norway).

[81]Commission Decision C(2015) 5572 final of 11 August 2015 on State Aid SA.38769 (2015/N), The Green Deal for Publicly Accessible Charging Infrastructure Scheme (The Netherlands).

to a greener energy mix. This is inconsistent with the CEV Strategy or the Opinion of the European Economic and Social Committee on proposed Alternative Fuels Directive.

4.2.3 Impact on Technological Development

A technology lock-in can be roughly defined as a situation where the technological option securing an initial lead in adoption goes on to dominate the market.[82] Measures creating a lock-in may confine society into an inferior design, thereby causing markets to fail, and distort the development of competition by creating barriers to market entry.[83] Particularities of network infrastructure markets, such as economies of scale, extremely high investment costs and interoperability issues significantly increase lock-in risks.

In the PEV sector, the risk of locking into wired technologies is not negligible. The Committee on Transport and Tourism expressly noted that this "Directive should not prevent the development and introduction of other recharging technologies, such as wireless charging."[84] Similarly, the Opinion of the European Economic and Social Committee draws attention to the danger of blocking the development of new and more viable technical solutions for different modes and user groups.[85]

Decisions in the field of state aid law should be interpreted in light of the dangers of technological lock-ins and of the requirement to facilitate innovation and ensure technological neutrality set out in the Alternative Fuels Directive. In the Norwegian Decision, the Authority required that the subsidised PEV network be fully interoperable, encompassing all existing chargers. Additionally, the granting authority committed to monitoring market evolution and ensuring "the highest degree of compatibility with the current fleet of electric vehicles." This last requirement seems to call for an infrastructure upgrade once the vehicle fleet has already evolved. However, it is unclear whether consumers would buy cars whose circulation is not yet ensured.

The existence of a given infrastructure incentivises the purchase of vehicles compatible with it. Therefore, to further reduce lock-in risks, subsidised infrastructures should be upgraded as soon as new technologies become commercially available, regardless of the adoption rate. It is important to make modification requirements mandatory and consider them in the economic analysis of the aid measure, as they can be associated with high costs. Upgrades to include new PEV charging standards are less expensive than investments to ensure interoperability with an entirely different system such as wireless charging. Adding a plug for the

[82]David (1985), pp. 332–337; Arthur (1989), pp. 116–131; and Perkins (2003).

[83]EFTA Surveillance Authority Decision No 77595 of 16 September 2015 raising no objections to the programme for alternative fuels infrastructure (Norway).

[84]Committee on Transport and Tourism (2013), amendment 70 (Article 4—para. 3—subpara. 2a).

[85]European Economic and Social Committee (2013a).

upcoming SAE J3068 standard to an existing plug-in charging pole is evidently less costly than embedding inductive charging elements i.e., in roads and parking lots.

4.2.4 Impact on Other EU Infrastructure Targets

Wireless charging enables flexibility for the underlying smart grid if a communication function is embedded into the system. This smart feature allows putting battery power stored in parked cars back into the grid and at times of high demand. The energy sold back as flexibility can be marked as a credit on the customer's bill, ensuring that drivers only pay for the electricity they actually use.[86]

Once wireless CEV charging systems become commercially available, Member States might prefer them over plug-in networks if they significantly decrease investments in smart grids through flexibility. The economic assessment would thus encompass EU policy goals in the fields of electricity and sustainable mobility, and look at the overall investment costs.

In this scenario, the Commission and the Courts must decide whether selectivity aimed at reaping synergies is compatible with the Treaty. This could be supported by a positive approach taken by EU institutions to the use of synergies in infrastructure markets in general and to CEV networks and smart grids in particular. For example, Paragraph 16 of the Alternative Fuels Directive highlights that extra funding is available under the Connecting Europe Facility for actions exploiting synergies between at least two of the sectors covered by it (i.e., transport, energy and telecommunications).[87]

4.2.5 Impact on Global Competitiveness

From a competition perspective, state aid effects considered inherent under the NOA may be highly distortive and used as an industrial policy vehicle. For example, even technologically neutral frameworks in support of CEV favour undertakings active in CEV-related markets, including the sale and manufacture of CEV and charging systems. These markets are key for EU global competitiveness.

In 2010, the Commission issued the CEV Strategy based on two main considerations: environmental protection (i.e., meet environmental protection targets and reduce hazardous emissions of particulate matter, NOx, HC and CO_2) and global competitiveness. Here, the Commission expressly acknowledged that the European

[86]The Engineer (2010) Unplugged: inductive charging on the road. http://www.theengineer.co.uk/unplugged-inductive-charging-on-the-road [accessed 6 April 2016].

[87]Directive 2014/94/EU of the European Parliament and of the Council of 22 October 2014 on the Deployment of Alternative Fuels Infrastructure; Regulation (EU) No 1316/2013 of the European Parliament and of the Council of 11 December 2013 establishing the Connecting Europe Facility, amending Regulation (EU) No 913/2010 and repealing Regulations (EC) No 680/2007 and (EC) No 67/2010.

automotive industry is a world leader in the development of clean and energy efficient technologies and supports a wide range of related sectors. It also stated that

> the EU's global competitors on both the American and Asian continents are also investing in research in low-carbon technologies and launching targeted programmes to shift to low-carbon road transport. They are taking steps to rapidly develop standards for alternative technologies. In order to permit its industry to stay competitive and ensure its position in green technologies, the EU must create the right framework for advanced products that will be needed worldwide.

The Opinion of the Committee of the Regions on 'Clean Power for Transport' "highlights the Commission's view that strong action by the EU to pioneer innovative solutions for alternative fuels will open up new market opportunities for European industry".[88] It is therefore clear that EU institutions (including the Commission) purposely targeted CEV markets (like CEV infrastructure) as a means to enhance European competitiveness in certain global markets.

In addition to favouring the PEV industry, the programmes reviewed positively impacted players in the electricity markets by increasing the demand for both electricity and flexibility services. This will, in turn, call for more active network and data management, favouring firms active in markets related to smart electricity systems (SES) active in that jurisdiction.

Unlike World Trade Organization (WTO) rules, which govern global trade, State aid rules are only meant to minimise competition distortions within the internal market. From an EU State aid law perspective, there seems to be nothing wrong with boosting the global competitiveness of certain EU industries as long as such support does not uneven the playing field within the Union.[89] However, undertakings active on certain markets, such as those for environmentally friendly technologies and state-of-the-art infrastructure, may be located in some Member States only. In the Netherlands, key stakeholders noted that

> The arena is constantly changing and we must continue to convince the manufacturers of electric vehicles in the coming years that the Netherlands is an attractive option, competition-wise, otherwise the vehicles, which are still scarce, will be supplied to other countries first and we will fail to achieve our objective of a becoming a large-scale, international test bed. Concerted government action involving electric mobility, a rapid rollout of infrastructure and an innovative business sector, supported by knowledge institutes and government, remain essential to prevent failure.[90]

Therefore, EU agenda setting in the state aids sector is a centralisation of industrial policy decisions that impacts GDP distribution within the EU.

---

[88]Committee of the Regions (2013), p. 68 [8].

[89]Such measures can be declared illegal under WTO law.

[90]Netherlands Enterprise Agency (RVO.nl) (2011) Electric Mobility gets up to speed—2011–2015 Action Plan. https://www.rvo.nl/sites/default/files/bijlagen/Action%20Plan%20English.pdf [accessed 14 Jun 2016].

5 Summary and Conclusions

5.1 Funding Strategies for CEV Infrastructure

Market failure regarding the development of recharging infrastructure represents a fundamental barrier to the development of alternative fuels in the transport sector.[91] Intrinsic economic risks (more acute regarding unprofitable areas and innovative technologies) result in a so-called chicken and egg problem, by which lack of infrastructure hinders CEV uptake vice versa.

The Alternative Fuels Directive acknowledges the need for a coordinated EU approach and that national support measures are necessary. The impossibility to finance the rollout with commercial tariffs persists in jurisdictions where CEV purchases are highly incentivised, such as the Netherlands and Norway.[92] State aids are thus an adequate policy instrument to either partially or totally remedy the lack of refueling infrastructure.

Dutch measures have become more focused on PEV over time, and Estonia has also developed a PEV-centred programme. While Norway strongly supports PEV, its current approach is more neutral in terms of alternative fuels, CEV and modes of transport.

Financing strategies present similarities. All three countries granted state aids through competitive selection procedures to stimulate the development of PEV charging stations. Sometimes schemes encompassed subsidies for the purchase of fully electric PEV (often in combination with tax rebates).

State resources covered the entire expense; they were not combined with EU funds. Such resources were obtained through different means. Estonia sold excess ETS permits while Norway imposed a levy on energy tariffs. The Netherlands financed the rollout through a mix of users' contributions and funds from the central and local governments.

In addition to granting investment aid, the Netherlands allowed local governments to award exclusive rights to install and operate charging stations for a period of 10 years, after with ownership would revert to them. In these areas, networks built by the beneficiaries cannot be duplicated even if this would become economically feasible. It is likely that this is the case in densely populated areas once PEV are more widely adopted. Considering the population and urbanisation rate, more duplication could have been expected in the Netherlands than in Norway and Estonia (in that order), thereby increasing distortive effects.

Tariffs have not been used to partially finance the networks. To the contrary, all Member States under study subsidise electricity on a more general basis for PEV charging.[93] This raises the issue of sustainability, as subsidising PEV charging may

---

[91]European Commission (2013c).

[92]EFTA Surveillance Authority Decision No 77595 of 16 September 2015 raising no objections to the programme for alternative fuels infrastructure (Norway).

[93]In Estonia subsidies paid to the renewable energy producers are financed by electricity consumers through the renewable energy charge, paid by every end user in Estonia in accordance to their

not be feasible on the long run. Member States will be confronted with the choice of (gradually) introducing commercial tariffs or not. As these tariffs may undermine PEV uptake, Member States could consider moving in the direction of a network tax, either as a separate tax (e.g. for PEV owners) or as part of the ordinary tax system. Financing of charging networks would thereby be similar to the system used for other types of infrastructure, such as roads, railroads and water supply.

As regards regulatory barriers to market entry, it should be noted that in the Netherlands, holders of special and exclusive rights participated in the rollout of charging infrastructure despite stringent regulation. In Estonia and Norway, monopoly holders face no barriers for participation in CEV infrastructure markets.

5.2 *State Aid Decisions on PEV Infrastructures*

Both the Commission and the Authority assessed the measures in support of CEV networks directly under Article 107(3)(c) TFEU and the equivalent provision of the European Economic Area Agreement (EEAA), Article 6l(3)(c). [115].

The Authority believed CEV charging networks pertained to transport, while the Commission checked whether it met existing legal definitions of energy infrastructure. This shows that current instruments are too narrow to accurately account for state-of-the-art infrastructures. The convergence of ICT, energy and transport infrastructures in intelligent, clean and efficient transport systems challenges sectoral rules. Additionally, as pilot projects build a bridge between R&D and commercialisation, blurring the lines between R&D and investment aid as conceptualised in horizontal instruments.

In the Dutch and Norwegian decisions, state aid was present and compatible with the applicable Treaty. Both oversight bodies largely correctly identified primary beneficiaries. The Authority imposed safeguards to avoid crowding out of private investments in the main relevant market. The Commission should have taken similar steps, especially considering that the Netherlands envisaged awarding exclusive rights that could hinder the development of competition in areas where infrastructure duplicability becomes feasible.

Regarding indirect aid to users, Dutch authorities required contributions from both users but did not ensure full interoperability of the subsidised platform. Norway committed to keep the infrastructure fully compatible with the evolving PEV fleet, but did not require users to share the financing burden. To minimise distortions, contributions should be required and compatibility insured.

The authority identified sellers and manufacturers of vehicles and infrastructure elements eligible for state aid as indirect beneficiaries and found it compatible with

---

network service capacity (Estonian Wind Power Association 2015). For the Netherlands and Norway, see Commission Decision State Aid SA.38769 (2015/N)—The Netherlands and EFTA Surveillance Authority, Decision No 76339—Norway, respectively.

the common market. The Commission did not even assess advantages to PEV charging equipment manufacturers, which constitutes a deviation from a previous decision making criteria.

The Authority's analysis seems deeper than that of the Commission regarding CEV sellers and manufacturers too. It classified these undertakings as indirect beneficiaries and imposed safeguards to minimise technology-based distortions within PEV markets. Again, the Commission departed from previous criteria and did not discuss the positive effect of the measure on car manufacturing and sales.

The Commission and the Authority should have assessed in depth the proportionality of the choices of fuels and transport modes with the objective of increasing environmental protection in the transport sector to ensure technological neutrality in accordance with Recital 22 of the Alternative Fuels Directive. Specifically, they should have asked whether schemes must ensure that the electricity supplied through the subsidised infrastructure should come exclusively from renewable sources. This issue pertains directly to the adequacy of the measure to increase environmental protection and is highlighted in the CEV Strategy, the proposed Alternative Fuels Directive and the Opinion of the European Economic and Social Committee on such a proposal.

References

Arthur B (1989) Competing technologies, increasing returns, and lock-in by historical events. Econ J 99:116–131

Committee of the Regions (2013) Opinion of the committee of the regions on 'Clean Power for Transport'. OJ C 280, 27 September 2013. 66–74

Committee on Transport and Tourism (2013) Report A7-0444/2013 on Amendments 001-119 to the Proposal for a directive on alternative fuels infrastructure. COM(2013)0018 – C7-0022/2013 – 2013/0012(COD)

Daintith T (1987) Law as an instrument of economic policy: comparative and critical approaches. Walter De Gruyter, Berlin

David PA (1985) Clio and the economics of QWERTY. Am Econ Rev 75:332–337

European Commission (2010a) Commission communication, Europe 2020 – A strategy for smart, sustainable and inclusive growth. COM(2010) 2020 final. Brussels

European Commission (2010b) Commission communication to the European Parliament, the Council and the European Economic and Social Committee, A European strategy on clean and energy efficient vehicles. COM(2010) 186 final. Brussels

European Commission (2011) Commission white paper, roadmap to a single European transport area — towards a competitive and resource efficient transport system. COM(2011) 144 final. Brussels

European Commission (2012a) Communication from the Commission on the application of the European Union State aid rules to compensation granted for the provision of services of general economic interest. OJ C 8, 11 January 2012. 4–14. Brussels

European Commission (2012b) Communication from the Commission, European Union framework for State aid in the form of public service compensation (2011). OJ C 8, 11 January 2012. 15–22. Brussels

European Commission (2013a) Commission Proposal for a Directive on the deployment of alternative fuels infrastructure. COM(2013) 18 final. Brussels

European Commission (2013b) Commission Staff Working Document, Actions towards a comprehensive EU framework on LNG for shipping, accompanying the Communication from the Commission on Clean Power for Transport: A European alternative fuels strategy. SWD/2013/04 final. Brussels
European Commission (2013c) Commission Staff Working Document on impact assessment accompanying the document "Proposal for a Directive on the deployment of alternative fuels infrastructure". SWD/2013/05 final. Brussels
European Commission (2016a) Commission Notice on the notion of State aid as referred to in Article 107(1) of the Treaty on the Functioning of the European Union C/2016/2946. OJ C 262. 1–50. Brussels
European Commission (2016b) Commission Communication, "A European strategy on Cooperative Intelligent Transport Systems, a milestone towards cooperative, connected and automated mobility. COM(2016) 766 final. Brussels
European Commission (2016c) Commission Proposal for a Directive of the European Parliament and of the Council on the promotion of the use of energy from renewable sources (recast). COM (2016) 767 final. 2016/0382 (COD). Brussels
European Commission (2017) Commission communication of 20 July 2017, A European strategy for low-emission mobility. SWD(2016) 244. Brussels
European Economic and Social Committee (2013a) European economic and social committee, opinion on the communication from the commission to the European Parliament, the Council, the European economic and social committee and the committee of the regions – clean power for transport: a European alternative fuels strategy, COM(2013) 17 final
European Economic and Social Committee (2013b) Opinion of the European Economic and Social Committee on the Communication from the Commission to the European Parliament, the Council, the European Economic and Social Committee and the Committee of the Regions "Clean Power for Transport: A European alternative fuels strategy" COM(2013) 17 final and the "Proposal for a Directive of the European Parliament and the Council on the deployment of alternative fuels infrastructure", COM(2013) 18 final – 2013/12 (COD). OJ C 271, 19.9.2013. 111–115
European Parliament (2013) Position of the European Parliament adopted at first reading on 15 April 2014 with a view to the adoption of Directive 2014/.../EU of the European Parliament and of the Council on the deployment of alternative fuels infrastructure. (EP-PE_TC1-COD (2013)0012
European Parliament (2014) Position adopted at first reading on 15 April 2014 with a view to the adoption of Directive 2014/.../EU of the European Parliament and of the Council on the deployment of alternative fuels infrastructure. (EP-PE_TC1-COD(2013)0012
Hancher L (2016) Greening transport up to 2020 and beyond. Florence School of Regulation. http://fsr.eui.eu/greening-transport-2020-beyond
Joller L, Varblane U (2015) Learning from an electromobility living lab: experiences from the Estonian ELMO programme. Case studies on transport policy. Elsevier, Tartu
Meeus L, Hadush S (2016) The emerging regulatory practice for new businesses related to distribution grids. Florence School of Regulation; policy briefs; 2016/02. European University Institute, Florence
Perkins R (2003) Technological lock-in. International Society for Ecological Economics Internet Encyclopaedia of Ecological Economics. http://isecoeco.org/pdf/techlkin.pdf
Slocock B (2002) The market economy investor principle. European Commission Competition Policy Newsletter 2

Ana Trías Tilburg. Master of European Studies, Master of European Regulation of Network Industries (LL.M.) and Senior Fellow of the Center for European Integration Studies (ZEI) of the University of Bonn; External Researcher at the Tilburg Law and Economics Center (TILEC) of Tilburg University. ana.m.trias@gmail.com. Fields of Interest: EU Law, Competition Law, Technology Law, Economic Analysis of Law, Compared Law.

Index

K. Mathis, B. R. Huber (eds.), *Energy Law and Economics*, Economic Analysis of Law in European Legal Scholarship 5, https://doi.org/10.1007/978-3-319-74636-4

The manufacturer's authorised representative in the EU is Springer Nature Customer Service Centre GmbH, Europaplatz 3, 69115 Heidelberg, Germany. If you have any concerns regarding our products, please contact ProductSafety@springernature.com

Printed and bound by CPI Group (UK) Ltd, Croydon, CR0 4YY
01/10/2026
02225851-0014